From the same publisher

The Smithsonian Collection of Classic Jazz
selected and annotated by Martin Williams,
Smithsonian Institution

JAZZ: A HISTORY

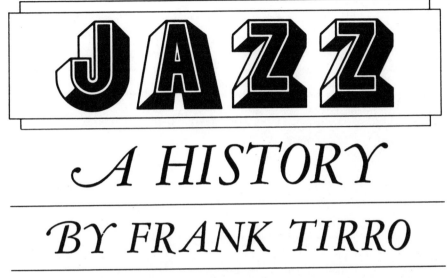

JAZZ

A HISTORY

BY FRANK TIRRO

YALE UNIVERSITY

W · W · NORTON & COMPANY · NEW YORK · LONDON

W. W. Norton & Company, Inc., 500 Fifth Avenue, New York, N.Y. 10110
W. W. Norton & Company Ltd., 37 Great Russell Street, London WC1B 3NU

Library of Congress Cataloging in Publication Data

Tirro, Frank.
  Jazz.

  Bibliography: p.
  Discography: p.
  Includes index.
  1. Jazz music.
ML3561.J3T5   781.5'7'09   77–22623
ISBN 0-393-09078-7

FRONTISPIECE BY RUS ANDERSON
BOOK AND BINDING DESIGN BY ANTONINA KRASS

5 6 7 8 9 0

TO THE MEMORY OF

FRANK TIRRO, SR.

He played his way to America,
gigged with a ragtime band, and
gave me my first clarinet lesson.

CONTENTS

CONTENTS

12
LOOSE ENDS AND PERIPHERAL EVENTS · 319

Loose Ends. Vocalists. Other Instrumentalists. Classical Musicians. Peripheral Events. The Beat Poets. Jazz Educators. Jazz and the Church. Modern-Day Blues.

13
FREE JAZZ AND ITS PRICE · 341

Free Jazz—Ornette Coleman. Musical Reactions. A Central Figure—John Coltrane. Miles Davis. The New Groups. The Third World. Progress Report.

TRANSCRIPTIONS · 365

Armstrong, *S.O.L. Blues*. Armstrong, *Struttin' With Some Barbecue*. Armstrong, *West End Blues*. Hawkins, *Body and Soul*. Young, *Lester Leaps In*. Gillespie, *I Can't Get Started*. Parker, *Embraceable You*. Parker, *Little Benny*. Parker, *Parker's Mood*. Coltrane, *Giant Steps*.

SYNOPTIC TABLE · 387

ANNOTATED BIBLIOGRAPHY · 403

GENERAL BIBLIOGRAPHY · 403

Dictionaries and Encyclopedias. Histories and Chronologies. Bibliographies. Discographies. Indices and Bibliographies of Music. Periodicals. Indices to Periodical Literature. Jazz Archives. Pedagogy. Miscellaneous—Literature, Philosophy, Interviews, etc.

CHAPTER BIBLIOGRAPHIES · 415

SELECTED DISCOGRAPHY · 427

GLOSSARY · 431

COPYRIGHT ACKNOWLEDGMENTS · 435

INDEX · 440

LIST OF
ILLUSTRATIONS

PREFACE

As I SET down these words, I am comforted by the happy thought that jazz is alive and well and thriving in the metropolitan centers of America and Europe. A few short years ago, during the '60s, I doubted whether this music could survive much longer as a living, evolving organism. Now, the clubs in Chicago, New York, and elsewhere are featuring live music again; the record shops are selling new jazz and "golden oldies" in real competition with rock, country, and classical music; bands are beginning to tour again; and colleges are starting to revive the once-defunct prom. Things are looking up.

The history of jazz is a fascinating subject, and a variety of writers—musicians, scholars, enthusiasts, journalists—have treated it with love and respect. Of all the works presently available, however, no single volume offers the reader an analysis and interpretation of jazz, both historical and musical, which incorporates recent research from allied fields—sociology, cultural anthropology, and American history—as well as from music history and theory. Obviously, no single volume could totally embrace so broad a subject, and this one does not pretend to be the definitive, final word. It is designed as an introduction to the principal movements, schools, performers, and peripheral aspects of American jazz from its origins to the present. It is a historical survey, and one will quickly note that some movements are passed over and many significant names are not mentioned. Historians try to be objective, but this writer was ultimately forced to include and emphasize those aspects of the historical development which seemed to him to be the most important, most representative, and most germane to present-day readers.

Since the history of music is primarily the history of musical styles, and since an understanding of musical style is meaningless without first-hand knowledge of the music itself, the reader is urged to become a listener as well. Not only is this text mere verbiage without the living sounds of jazz, but a critical evaluation of my opinions must certainly stand or fall upon the evidence: the sound recordings which document the history of jazz. It was particularly fortunate for me to have Martin Williams's superb anthology of jazz recordings, *The Smithsonian Collection of Classic Jazz,* available as an accompanying set of examples. When it was necessary to go beyond this collection, I made every attempt to select works that were easily accessible. Further, I documented all my references so that the reader should have the opportunity to test my statements, weigh my evidence, and render an independent and enlightened judgment.

It has not been my aim in writing this book to display erudition or pronounce lasting decisions, but rather to lead the interested layman to the varied aspects of the subject and help him proceed in areas that hitherto might have been new or unknown. Toward this end, the chapters deal with many subjects outside the scope of jazz, and the bibliography is organized as a guide to individual inquiry. As the reader becomes more informed and more involved, he should grow in historical understanding, aesthetic sensitivity, and philosophical awareness. The prehistory of jazz is stressed, for one cannot understand the culture in which one lives without a firm grasp of the circumstances leading to it. The concepts of evolution, change, and history itself are questioned not so much to prove one idea wrong or another superior, but to bring the entire study into focus and perspective. American jazz has not yet acquired universal recognition as a major artistic creation; still, some would say that it is America's *only* native art form. Others claim it is not American at all, but African or Afro-American, and the reader must determine the truth for himself. Most important, of course, is the hope that these pages will help the reader enjoy more fully what he hears and derive more lasting satisfaction from every kind of jazz that strikes his ear. I have written what follows with the assumption that greater interest in and awareness of jazz will develop inevitably from understanding specific monuments of the art, and much more space is devoted to the analyses of important solos and recognized works than to an encyclopedic listing of names, dates, works, and places. An abundance of facts is presented here, it is true, but one should not expect to find the name of the second trumpet player in the 1936 Benny Goodman band without going through the bibliography to outside references.

This volume, therefore, unlike many general histories, is not simply a compilation of secondary sources, for many lacunae exist and many fallacious arguments are published, reprinted, plagiarized, and published anew. Still, my debt to other scholars is enormous, and I hope I have given credit where it is due throughout the book. The writings of Leonard Feather, Gunther Schuller, Marshall Stearns, Martin Williams, André Hodeir, Samuel Charters, Joachim Berendt, William Austin, and many others are the seminal studies upon which this modest volume is constructed. Still, the essence of my writing is the verbal distillation of what I have actually heard live or on record, what I have rea-

soned from the factual evidence that is now available, and what I have con-
strued after studying the opinions of the authors who have treated the same
subjects I consider. The resultant picture illustrates, I hope, that jazz is a major
component of a rich and complex culture, one of the proudest creations of the
American people.

I have received assistance from several quarters, and am especially grateful to
the Duke University Research Council for financial support to visit archives,
collect material, and acquire some editorial assistance. Particular thanks are
due my friends Richard Wright at the University of Kansas and Richard Wang
at the University of Illinois–Chicago Circle. Dick Wright made his enormous
collection of recordings available to me and taped many examples I needed for
my course work, as well as for this book. Richard Wang has the understanding
only a jazz performer–music scholar can possess, and his advice, encourage-
ment, and criticism have always been helpful and enlightening. Christopher
White, talented bassman and former Director of the Rutgers Institute of Jazz
Studies in Newark, New Jersey, generously opened the doors of the Institute
and the drawers of the files. Many libraries and librarians were always ready to
provide one more document, and a few that were particularly helpful were
those of the University of Chicago, New York Public Library, Library of Congress, Duke University Libraries, Chicago Public Library, New Orleans Jazz
Museum, Kansas City Public Library, Newberry Library, University of Kansas
Libraries, Tulane University Library, and University of North Carolina Libraries. Mr. Gary M. Shivers, Programming Director of Station WUNC(FM)
at the University of North Carolina–Chapel Hill, has read the entire manu-
script and cleansed it of many errors. Those that remain are mine, not his.
Mr. J. Samuel Hammond, music librarian at Duke University, has provided invaluable assistance in preparing the index and checking the bibliography.
These tasks, so important and yet so thankless, could never have been accomplished without his help and expertise. Claire Brook, music editor of W. W.
Norton, has been most understanding, and her knowledge, impartiality, and
patience have contributed in important measure to the completion of this
volume.

My largest debt, however, I owe my wife, Charlene. She has steadfastly
believed in the project and my ability to complete it from the moment of inception to the present. Both her support and her thoughtful criticism have
improved every page of this work.

Drum on your drums, batter on your banjos,
sob on the long cool winding saxophones.
Go to it, O jazzmen.

CARL SANDBURG, from *Smoke and Steel* (1920)

JAZZ: A HISTORY

THE STATE OF MUSIC IN
THE U. S. IN THE LATE
NINETEENTH CENTURY

NATIONAL ENVIRONMENTS MAY change with rapidity and drama; America during the late nineteenth century was very different from the America we know today. High culture, in the European sense, and renowned institutions of learning existed only in the major cities of the Eastern seaboard and in a few isolated metropolitan areas. New Orleans, St. Louis, and San Francisco had their opera houses and Philadelphia had its public library, but most of America was an agrarian society which moved from place to place on horseback and on foot. Although a railroad eventually spanned the continent from east to west and riverboats plied the north-south Mississippi waterway, the latest art music of Europe—Wagner, Verdi, Liszt, and the other great Romantics—meant little to the Carolina cotton picker, the Chicago merchant, or the majority of post– Civil War Americans. A "cultivated tradition" was not absent in America from 1865 to the First World War, but it developed primarily in the Eastern metropolitan centers plus Chicago, St. Louis, New Orleans, and San Francisco, and its emergence can be traced through the rise of music conservatories and concert halls.[1]

These isolated pockets of art music represented only one aspect of the vibrant musical activity taking place in every corner of the nation. America was a religious nation, and a multitude of local music traditions developed in quasi isolation. First-generation Americans who had recently emigrated from Europe tended to live and work together, and their worship music was that which they knew and loved from their homeland. This was true from the time of the

[1] H. Wiley Hitchcock, *Music in the United States: A Historical Introduction*, p. 127 ff.

Pilgrim fathers, with but one major exception: the worship music of the black slaves from Africa. Legislation prevented the black population from cultivating their tribal ceremonies, and in most of the United States their culture was squeezed, as much as possible, into a white Protestant mold. The results of this process had a profound influence on a new music which was to develop in America, a music later called jazz.

American church music did not totally account for the musical environment of the times. The average American worked hard, for the Protestant ethic praised the virtues of industry, and a need for recreation was as real then as it is now. Music played an important role in filling this need. Since records, television, and radio had not yet come into existence, the live performance of music, by both professionals and amateurs, achieved a remarkable importance. The sheet-music publishing industry of America grew exponentially during this century, and its chief product was songs simple and tuneful enough to become popular among amateurs. Because of the wide dissemination of the solo song, this genre also played a significant part in the development of jazz.

Somewhat similar to popular music in its appeal and general audience, folk music was sung and played wherever men and women gathered to pass the time of day. No single tradition of American folk music predominated, however, for the styles of the Western cowboys, the New York canal workers, the Appalachian Mountain dwellers, and the black field workers were considerably different. A unifying force among the heterogeneous popular styles of America was the concert band, for these bands transmitted a rich repertoire in a standard format to a broad spectrum of Americans. Many of them acquired regional and national renown.[2] Most were directed by Europeans or Europe-trained conductors, and their repertoire was a mixture of band arrangements of orchestral "light classics," American-style marches, orchestrated popular music, and ephemeral virtuosic instrumental solos. In addition to the European traditions of melody, harmony, and rhythm which these concerts spread, they also served to introduce band instruments to a rural population. These instruments, both solo and in ensemble, were also key ingredients in the amalgam of musical sounds which finally solidified to produce the new music.

The post–Civil War American black obviously was the most important element in the creation of jazz, that new music with a distinctive sound which emerged in the southern United States at turn of the twentieth century. Amiri Baraka (LeRoi Jones) explains the phenomenon this way: "[Blues] is a native American music, the product of the black man in this country: or to put it more exactly . . . blues could not exist if the African captives had not become American captives."[3] Blues, a parent of jazz, developed during the latter part of

[2] H. W. Schwartz, *Bands of America.*
[3] LeRoi Jones, *Blues People: Negro Music in White America*, p. 17.

the nineteenth century. Jazz does not owe its existence totally to any one culture or race, but unquestionably the Southern black population played the dominant role in the early years. Since the cultural traditions of West Africa, Europe, and America all contributed to this embryonic music, we must investigate each to see what it is we actually hear when we listen to the music called jazz.

Art Music

The Civil War ended in 1865, Lincoln had been assassinated, and the South lay in ruins. There was no art music in America equal to that being produced in Europe. Stephen Collins Foster (1826–64) was the preeminent American composer working primarily before the Civil War, and by 1852 he was well-known as a writer of both household songs and minstrel-show tunes. His music and other sentimental ballads of the same genre continued to receive public approbation during the second half of his century. Foster's craft should not be compared to the best European art-song composers, for the richness of harmony and the expressiveness of melodic detail in the music of Schubert and Schumann far exceed the capabilities of Foster. Still,

> [Foster's] songs are no mechanical repetitions of a type, but individual handcrafted products. The narrow limits and the slight, unpredictable variations within the limits help to place Foster's work in its historical context; they help us imagine him at work, a "nice young man" in a changing world that he is very little acquainted with.[4]

His best-known composition, *Old Folks at Home*,[5] contains many of the characteristics commonly found in American music of the period. The work consists of a catchy, easily sung tune; it maintains a simple, tonal key relationship; the words are sentimental and somewhat naive; the harmonies are regular and uncluttered; and the rhythm is simple, repetitious, and, like everything else, easily remembered.

Foster's understanding and sympathy for the situation and ways of blacks in

---

[4] William W. Austin, *"Susanna," "Jeanie," and "The Old Folks at Home": The Songs of Stephen C. Foster from His Time to Ours*, p. 82 f.

[5] Originally published, for financial reasons, as a composition of E. P. Christy, the leader of Christy's Minstrels.

FIFTIETH EDITION.

Old Folks at Home,

ETHIOPIAN MELODY,

AS SUNG BY

CHRISTY'S MINSTRELS.

WRITTEN AND COMPOSED BY

E. P. CHRISTY.

25 c. Nett.

GUITAR.   *PIANO.*

NEW-YORK :
PUBLISHED BY **FIRTH, POND & CO.,** No. 1 FRANKLIN SQUARE.
PITTSBURGH, H. **KLEBER.**

Entered according to Act of Congress, A. D. 1851, by Firth, Pond & Co., in the Clerk's Office of the District Court of the Southern District of New-York

OLD FOLKS AT HOME.

Words and Music by E. P. Christy.

Way down upon de Swa - nee rib - ber, Far, far a-way,

Dere's wha my heart is turn - ing eb - ber, Dere's wha de old folks stay.

Stephen Collins Foster (1826–64)

America is open to question, for the popular account by the family servant, Olivia Pise, taking young Stephen to church is now considered a conjecture by Foster's brother, Morrison.[6] Still, Stephen Foster expressed a sentiment that was beginning to gain currency among whites sympathetic to the human feelings of blacks in servitude who had been carried away from their families.

> All de world am sad and dreary,
> Ebry where I roam,
> Oh! darkeys how my heart grows weary,
> Far from de old folks at home.

The charm and beauty of *Old Folks at Home* lies in its simplicity, but in concept it stands diametrically opposed to the most advanced musical thinking prevalent in Europe at the time. When *Old Folks at Home* was being published in America, Richard Wagner's essay *Opera and Drama* was appearing in Germany. In it, he explained his concept of the total stage production which unifies and integrates the arts of music, drama, dance, and design. A few years later, Wagner completed his opera *Tristan und Isolde,* an exemplary work of the composer's mature style. Unified through a system of leitmotifs,[7] the opera's

[6] Austin, "*Susanna,*" p. xvi.

[7] Recurrent musical motifs or melodic ideas which denote or represent extramusical ideas, characters, and situations in operas by Wagner and his followers.

musical progress takes place by means of extremely chromatic functional harmonies. *Tristan und Isolde* employs melodies that are progressive rather than repetitious, nontonal rather than key-centered, and expansive in range, phrasing, and dynamics rather than simple and restricted.[8] There is a world of contrast between *Old Folks at Home* and *Tristan und Isolde*. Obviously, aesthetic norms for art music in the mid-nineteenth century spanned an immense range of musical ideas.

Following the Civil War, several gifted men wrote in a musical tradition that was a logical extension of that in which Stephen Foster worked. The most significant of these were the European-trained composers George Chadwick (1854–1931), Horatio Parker (1863–1919), and Edward MacDowell (1861–1908). All created works more musically complex than Foster's, but all still wrote in an idiom characterized by rhythmic, melodic, and harmonic rigidity. However, taken as a whole, they developed a Classical-Romantic art-music tradition which flourished and influenced all forms of musical life in America. One admirer writes:

> [T]hey belonged to that wing of Romanticism that maintained a belief in the viability of the abstract instrumental forms. Like Brahms, and like Beethoven, Schubert, Schumann, and Mendelssohn before him, they wrote symphonies, sonatas, and chamber music; like Brahms, and like Handel, Bach, Mozart, and Beethoven before him, they wrote fugues and contrapuntal choruses. To the late nineteenth century such composers as Paine, Chadwick, and Parker might have seemed "classicists"; our perspective should let us rather see them in context as a group of Romantics of a particular persuasion.[9]

Some of the music of the last part of the nineteenth century was complex and employed involved and complicated musical techniques.[10] But for the most part it did not, and the familiar American music consisted of marches, waltzes, hymn tunes, jigs, sentimental ballads, and the like. In many of these works elements similar to those found in jazz can be discerned and they certainly were part of the great catalytic processes fermenting at this time. The prevailing harmonies, both tonal and modal, were to be borrowed by jazz from the great stock of Western art music. Certainly some of the song and dance forms— marches, ballads, etc.—while firmly rooted in the European tradition were at

---

[8] A miniature score of the Prelude to *Tristan und Isolde* which is particularly suitable for student use is available in *The Norton Scores: An Anthology for Listening*, 3rd ed., ed. Roger Kamien (New York: W. W. Norton, 1977), p. 595 ff. of the Standard Edition, and p. 179 ff. of the Expanded Edition, Vol. 2.

[9] Hitchcock, *Music in the United States*, p. 138.

[10] The passage from John Knowles Paine's *Oedipus Tyrannus*, Op. 35, quoted by Hitchcock, ibid., p. 131, is a splendid "Wagnerian" example.

the same time borrowing from vernacular elements such as African themes and rhythms.[11] An American "sound" was in the process of developing by the end of the nineteenth century.

Bands were of great influence on the musical climate of America during this period. Patrick Sarsfield Gilmore (1829–92) was the most influential bandmaster in America from the time of the Civil War until his death. In 1864 he staged an extravaganza comprising a chorus of 5,000 and a band of 500 and added cannons and churchbells for their effect. Four years after the close of the Civil War, he staged the National Peace Jubilee in Boston and this time used 10,000 voices, 1,000 instrumentalists, two batteries of cannons, more bells, and 100 anvils played by members of the Boston Fire Department. It is difficult to consider this kind of production or the normal band concert as art music, but even symphony orchestras of the period offered potpourri concerts. On June 25, 1839, three years before the founding of the New York Philharmonic, a memorial concert for the distinguished pianist Daniel Schlesinger was given in New York City featuring the following pieces:

Grand Overture	Schlesinger
Kyrie Eleison	Concordia
Aria "Was Sag Ich"	Weber
Violin solo (Variations from *Norma*)	Bellini
Bass aria (from *Il Flauto Magico*)	by an amateur
The Spirit Song	Haydn
Elegie	Panaika
etc.	

The first concert by the Boston Symphony, conducted by Georg Henschel on October 22, 1881, offered only *six* works: orchestral numbers by Beethoven, Gluck, Haydn, Schubert, Bruch, and Weber; but as late as 1908, the St. Louis Symphony, in its twenty-ninth season, under the direction of Max Zach, was programming a strange mixture:

Processional March (from "Queen of Sheba")	Gounod
Overture to "Mignon"	Thomas
Aria (from "Queen of Sheba")	Gounod
Intermezzo (from "Hoffman's Tales")	Offenbach
Selections from "Mme. Butterfly"	Puccini
Songs "Extase"	Beach
"Du bist wie eine blume"	Chadwick
"Heart's Springtime"	von Wickede
Waltz "Bad'ner Mad'ln"	Komzak

[11] George Chadwick's *Symphony No. 2* (1888) employs folk themes and pentatonicism, and his light opera *Tabasco* (1894) incorporates hymn tunes, waltzes, jigs, marches, and galops.

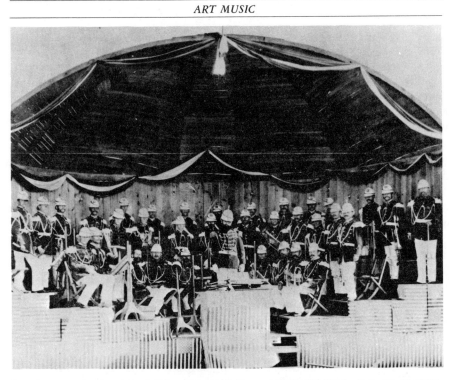

One of the great bandmasters of all time, John Philip Sousa, with the U.S. Marine Corps Band in 1891.

This is the music that reached the ears of the American public from the concert stage,[12] and as we shall see, many of the early jazz musicians, both black and white, were familiar with and were trained in this tradition.[13]

[12] John Erskine, *The Philharmonic-Symphony Society of New York*; M. A. DeWolfe Howe, *The Boston Symphony Orchestra 1881–1931*; the St. Louis Symphony Society, program of November 15, 1908 (St. Louis: St. Louis Symphony Society, 1908).

[13] For students unfamiliar with American art music of this period, a recorded sample might prove useful. Currently-available recordings of works by three leading American composers are listed here.

> *The Sea*, by Edward MacDowell (*The Art Song in America*, Duke University Press Recording, 1965).
> *Sonata Tragica*, Op. 45, by Edward MacDowell (Spa Records, Spa-63).
> *Oh, Let Night Speak of Me*, by George Chadwick (*The Art Song in America*, Duke University Press Recording, 1965).
> *Theme, Variations, and Fugue*, by George Chadwick (Nonesuch Records, H-71200).
> *Variations on "Austria"* by John Knowles Paine (ibid.).
> *Recorded Anthology of American Music*, 30 vols. to date (New World Records, available only in music libraries of educational institutions).

The instrumentation of the typical nineteenth-century orchestra was similar to that with which we are familiar today: pairs of winds and brass, four horns, two or three percussion instruments, and strings. Toward the end of the century there was an expansion to accommodate the new orchestral demands of composers like Richard Strauss and Gustav Mahler. The instrumentation of bands, however, was never standardized and was frequently quite different from what we know today. The Allentown, Pennsylvania, Band had five cornets, two trombones, four clarinets, and about a dozen "over-the-shoulder" valve brasses in 1872. The Brass Band of Glenville, New York, had only ten players in 1876: two E^b cornets, two B^b cornets, one B^b valve trombone, two E^b alto horns, one B^b tenor horn, one B^b baritone horn, and one E^b tuba. The most famous band of the late nineteenth century was Gilmore's, and this world-renowned organization had sixty-six players in 1878: twenty-seven brass, four percussion, and thirty-five reeds. His instrumentation was similar to that of a modern band, and among the reeds we find all four of the saxophone family—soprano, alto, tenor, and baritone.

Popular Music

If American art music differed widely from that of Europe, popular music was even more dissimilar to its European counterpart. Although much of the lyric theater and the minstrel show could be traced back to the Opéra comique of Paris, the Opera buffa of Italy, and the Beggar's Opera of Britain, the "Ethiopian Opera" of the New World had developed, by the mid-nineteenth century, into a distinct American entertainment. Early in that century, white American composers began treating the black man as a comic figure. Blackface minstrelsy, a form of entertainment where white men blackened their faces and went on stage to dance and sing "Negro songs," impersonate slaves, and tell jokes based on slave life in a thick dialect, became immensely popular during the 1860s and '70s.[14] Stephen Foster intentionally incorporated tunes and harmonies of American blacks into his music, and his best-known minstrel songs—*Camptown Races, Old Black Joe, Old Folks at Home,* etc.—were a blend of black and white traditions. As this music was carried from coast to coast by live performance and sheet music, an American musical sound developed in which black and white taste blended together:

> Here was a curious kind of interaction. The minstrel songs, originally inspired by genuine slave songs, were altered and adapted by white minstrels to the taste of

[14] Eileen Southern, *The Music of Black Americans*, p. 100 ff.

white America in the nineteenth century, and then were taken back again by black folk for further adaptation to Negro musical taste. Thus the songs passed back into the folk tradition from which they had come. [15]

But one crucial aspect of this music is not represented in the notation of the copyrighted printed music—performance practice. The white singer, whether schooled by a European singing master or emulating by ear the concert style of European singing, probably did not perform this music in a manner identical to that of the newly freed blacks. Oral tradition suggests, since sound recordings are not available from this period, that black singing had inflections, rhythmic subtleties, distinct pitch, vibrato, and timbrel elements that are closely akin to the vocal and instrumental sounds in the early days of jazz—sound qualities that differ substantially from those same elements as they appear in the European tradition. Throughout this period, black music was absorbing European harmonies, rhythms, melodies, and phraseology while maintaining its own distinct parameters. The product that was to emerge shortly as jazz was an American mixture of African, European, and American ingredients.

Another category of American popular music of the late nineteenth century was the melodramatic song, a favorite of both white and black America. The subject matter ranged from mother and home to death, the war, and prohibition. Although we are not concerned here with lyrics, songs like *The Old Armchair* (Henry Russell, 1840), *All Quiet along the Potomac Tonight* (John Hill Hewitt, 1861), and *I Dream of Jeanie with the Light Brown Hair* (Stephen Foster, 1854) had a great deal in common: a declamatory melodic style, 4/4 rhythms, regular phrasing, occasional chromaticism, and an inevitable harmonic progression of I–IV–I. The prevalence of these same elements in early jazz is more than coincidental. They are the sounds that permeated the musical atmosphere of America, the sounds played and sung by black and white alike, the sounds that comprised the musical vernacular. Throughout America there were various groups with common ethnic and social backgrounds, each with its own popular music; but minstrel music and sentimental ballads were popular everywhere. The simplicity, the conformity to melodic types, the basic harmonic patterns which were deeply rooted in age-old folk traditions developed in Europe and transplanted to America were all assimilated into early jazz. Although many elements of nineteenth-century American art and popular music were essential in the mix, we must look further, for these types alone do not, and could not, account for the emergence of a new style—jazz.

[15] Ibid., p. 104.

Folk Music

The white rural folk tradition may or may not have had anything to do with jazz, but it was present as a living force in the musical scene of the nineteenth century. Gilbert Chase, in his exciting journey through *America's Music from the Pilgrims to the Present*, [16] describes the preaching, praying, and singing characteristic of the Protestant circuit rider as he traveled up and down the countryside on horseback. American camp meetings began in Kentucky around 1800 and quickly spread throughout the United States. Both blacks and whites attended the same camp meetings and sang the same songs, once again sharing the same musical heritage. The dancing, jerking, and swooning which often accompanied the sounds of the revivalists are aspects of a physical participation in music not unlike those associated with African and Afro-American rituals, as well as most jazz.

Revival music frequently required a leader who would draw upon a large reserve of standard material, usually in the form of rhymed couplets, to carry the verse between each refrain of this popular verse-refrain pattern. This was extremely effective for mass participation, since the short melodic and textual phrases set to catchy tunes and rhythms had a tremendous popular appeal. Major, minor, modal, and pentatonic materials all went into this repertory, and these new revival songs were sung along with the old hymn tunes transplanted from Europe. Also, one new aspect of white American music not previously mentioned was refined in this campground tradition—improvisation:

> [T]here is one aspect of revival singing that cannot be reconstructed from the printed music and can be but inadequately described with words. That is the practice of taking familiar, conventional hymns and ornamenting the melodies with what Mr. Asbury [Samuel E. Asbury, a descendant of the Rev. Francis Asbury who was America's pioneer circuit rider] calls "numberless little slurs and melodic variations." He mentions "Jesus, Lover of my Soul" and "How Firm a Foundation" as hymns that were sung in this manner. [17]

Secular white folk music was primarily rooted in an Anglo-Saxon tradition brought over from Britain in the seventeenth through the nineteenth centuries. Although this music retained its most distinctive traits in the isolated regions of the Appalachian Mountains, the tradition spread west to Missouri, Mississippi, and even Texas. The two types of secular Anglo-Saxon folk music may be neatly summarized thus:

[16] P. 207 ff.
[17] *America's Music*, p. 224.

No. 94. There is Glory in My Soul.

Mrs. Grace Weiser Davis. CHAS. H. GABRIEL.

1. Since I lost my sins, and I found my Saviour, There is
2. Since He cleansed my heart, gave me sight for blindness, There is
3. Since with God I've walked, having sweet communion, There is
4. Since I en-tered Canaan on my way to heav-en, There is

glo-ry in my soul! Since by faith I sought and obtained God's favor,
glo-ry in my soul! Since He touched and healed me in loving kindness,
glo-ry in my soul! Brighter grows each day in this heav'nly union,
glo-ry in my soul! Since the day my life to the Lord was given,

CHORUS.

glo-ry, glo-ry,
glory, glo-ry,

There is glory in my soul. Yes, there's glory, glory, there is glory in my soul

Ev-'ry day brighter grows, And I conquer all my foes; There is

glory, glory, yes, there's glory in my soul, There is glory in my soul!

glory in my soul!

Copyright, 1894, by C. H. Gabriel. E. O. Excell, owner.

No. 198. JESUS SAVES ME.

G. R. STUART. ZOLLIE STUART.

1. Je - sus, my all, to heav'n is gone, Glory hal- lelujah, Jesus saves me;
2. This is the way I long have sought, Glory hal- lelujah, Jesus saves me;
3. The King's highway of ho-li- ness, Glory hal- lelujah, Jesus saves me;
4. My grief a burden long has been, Glory hal- lelujah, Jesus saves me;
5. Lo! glad I come; and Thou, blest Lamb, Glory hal- lelujah, Jesus saves me;
6. Noth-ing but sin have I to give, Glory hal- lelujah, Jesus saves me;
7. Then will I tell to sinners 'round, Glory hal- lelujah, Jesus saves me;

He whom I fix my hopes up-on; Glory hal- lelujah, Jesus saves me.
And mourned because I found it not; Glory hal- lelujah, Jesus saves me.
I'll go, for all His paths are peace, Glory hal- lelujah, Jesus saves me.
Be - cause I was not saved from sin, Glory hal- lelujah, Jesus saves me.
Shalt take me to Thee, as I am; Glory hal- lelujah, Jesus saves me.
Noth-ing but love shall I re-ceive, Glory hal- lelujah, Jesus saves me.
What a dear Saviour I have found, Glory hal- lelujah, Jesus saves me.

CHORUS.

He saves me, He saves me, Glory hallelujah, Jesus saves me.
Hallelujah, Hallelujah,

Copyright, 1896, by Charlie D. Tillman.

From The Revival No. 3, by Charles D. Tillman (c. 1899).

No. 207. HOW FIRM A FOUNDATION. 11s.

GEO. KEITH.

*M. H. B. H. P. H.
546. 502. 325.

Arr. by R. M. McINTOSH.

1. How firm a founda - tion, ye saints of the Lord, Is laid for your
2. In ev - 'ry con - di - tion—in sickness, in health, In pov - er - ty's
3. Fear not: I am with you: O be not dismayed: I, I am your
4. E'en down to old age all my peo - ple shall prove My sov'reign, e -
5. The soul that on Je - sus still leans for re - pose, I will not, I

faith in His ex - cel - lent word! What more can He say than to
vale or a - bounding in wealth, At home and a - broad, on the
God, and will still give you aid; I'll strengthen you, help you, and
ter - nal, unchange - a - ble love; And when hoar - y hairs shall their
can - not de - sert to his foes; That soul, tho' all hell should en -

you He hath said, You who un - to Je - sus for ref - uge have fled?
land, on the sea— As your days may demand, so your succor shall be.
cause you to stand, Up - held by my righteous, om - nip - o - tent hand.
tem- ples a - dore, Like lambs they shall still in my bo - som be borne.
deav - or to shake, I'll nev - er, no, nev - er, no, nev - er for - sake.

No. 212. JESUS, LOVER OF MY SOUL.

CHARLES WESLEY.

*M. H. B. H. P. H.
354. 499. 305.

S. B. MARSH.

FINE.

1. { Je - sus, lov - er of my soul, Let me to Thy bo - som fly, }
   { While the nearer wa - ters roll, While the tem-pest still is high; }

D.C.—Safe in - to the ha-ven gnide, O re-ceive my soul at last.

D.C.

Hide me, O my Sav-iour, hide, Till the storm of life is past;

From *The Revival No. 3*, by Charles D. Tillman (c. 1899).

1. Narrative songs—often tragic, dramatic, and sorrowful—dealing with traditional, historical, and sometimes imaginary people and events. These strophic ballads were originally sung by a single unaccompanied voice and were passed down in oral tradition. Neither words nor music were written down.

2. Dance music, jigs, and other fast dances played on the violin—or, more accurately, the fiddle. These too were passed on as an oral tradition, with each performer trying to retain the tune in a clearly recognizable form, yet also trying to vary it according to his own technique and taste so that his version was distinctive. [18]

Obviously, the ideals of folk music were akin to those of jazz. One of these ideals was to create a version of the music distinctive to a particular performer without destroying the image of the original in the ears of the audience.

In addition, folk singers developed a performing tradition that differed from the classical, trained style of white performers. Folk singing in the rural South tends to have a nasal timbre that is sometimes described as thin and high. Some claim this is merely the sound of the untrained voice, but more likely it is the timbre of the tradition, a characteristic sound quality passed on from master to apprentice. Instrumental performance of folk music tends to vary from classical norms as well. The country fiddler may rest his violin on his arm rather than place it under his chin; he normally stops the string without creating vibrato; and he often bows or plucks the strings in a manner foreign to the classical tradition. Recognition of the individuality of the performer as part of the understanding and appreciation of this music is just as important as a sympathy for the social setting, the moral and religious attitudes, and the language of the people for a real understanding of this musical phenomenon. Also, in the nineteenth century, instruments, especially the guitar, came to play an important part in the performance of what were once solo vocal pieces. The concept of chordal accompaniment to a free-floating tune is also related to the music we call jazz.

The elements of jazz were present in both white and black society during the nineteenth century, but it seems that the catalyst for the creation of a new music was the particular social condition of American blacks. The case for an Afro-American ancestry for jazz is clearly the strongest, and the music of the black American seems to have generated the new and distinctive sounds of jazz.

[18] Charles Hamm, "The Acculturation of Musical Styles: Popular Music, U.S.A.," in *Contemporary Music and Music Cultures*, ed. Charles Hamm, Bruno Nettl, and Ronald Byrnside, p. 136.

Black Art Music

If music in nineteenth-century America can be divided into art, popular, and folk, then black music during the same period may also be seen in the same three categories. Art music, in the European sense, played a minor role among American blacks after the Civil War, but black musicians were not totally absent from the concert stage. Coloratura soprano Marie Selika (b. 1849) toured the United States and Europe during the 1880s to critical acclaim.

Madame Marie Selika (1849–?).

Soprano Nellie Brown sang professionally in New York, Baltimore, Washington, and Boston. Blacks began to receive diplomas from the New England Conservatory in Boston during this period, and two graduates, Rachel Washington and Samuel Jamieson, followed professional music careers. Walter Craig was a skillful violin recitalist during the 1870s and '80s, and was favorably received by the critics for his playing in New York.

Not many black Americans were afforded the opportunity of studying music in the European tradition, and when they did they often found their careers handicapped by racial prejudice. Still, black America was interested in European art music, and during the 1870s black musical societies were organized in several of the nation's cities. The Colored American Opera Company was founded in Washington, D.C., in 1872, and several others emerged shortly thereafter. Although black symphony orchestras seem to have been nonexistent, black brass bands flourished, undoubtedly as a result of the war. Army bands trained black men as instrumentalists along with white, and after the Civil War several black bands established solid musical reputations throughout the country.

Black touring choirs came into great prominence at this time. The best-known and most influential of these was made up of students from Fisk University in Nashville, Tennessee, an institution that opened its doors immediately after the Civil War. In 1871, under the direction of George L. White, the Jubilee Singers toured to raise money to help with the building program at Fisk University. They sang a standard concert repertoire that included a new item for the concert stage—arranged spirituals. These harmonized versions of plantation slave songs are but one example of the magical transformations that took place in the post-war years.

Black society was every bit as complex as white, and the old stereotypes of the late nineteenth-century black American no longer suffice in depicting the

The Original Fisk Jubilee Singers, London, 1873.

environment from which jazz sprang. Alain Locke, pioneer scholar of *The Negro and His Music,* evaluates the spirituals as

> . . . the most characteristic product of Negro genius to date. They are its great folk-gift, and rank among the classic folk expressions in the whole world because of their moving simplicity, their characteristic originality, and their universal appeal. [19]

However, when the Civil War ended slavery, the spirituals almost disappeared, and Locke credits their transformation into "Jubilees" for their preservation.

One of the leading classical musicians of the nineteenth century was a creole, Louis Moreau Gottschalk. He electrified musical Europe with his extraordinary skill at the piano, and included among his many compositions works remembered from his childhood in New Orleans—*Bamboula, Negro Dance, The Banjo,* and others.

Black Americans were aware of and participated in the European art-music tradition. [20] To deny this aspect of black American society in the nineteenth century in order to emphasize the African origins of jazz would do disservice to both the historical facts and the splendid talents of the black Americans who achieved a great deal in the realm of European art music.

Black Popular Music

Minstrelsy, vaudeville, the sentimental ballad, and band music appear to have been the genres reaching the greatest musical public, both white and black. Black minstrel companies, as well as white "blackface" groups, were organized after the war and together represented America's main form of stage entertainment. One company, Lew Dockstader's, even employed both white and black entertainers, but the performances were not integrated—with the possible exception of the finale. Usually the first half of the show was played by whites and the second half by blacks.

The songs of three black writers, James Bland, Gussie Davis, and Samuel Lucas, were popular with the black companies and audiences. In particular,

[19] Washington, D.C.: The Associates in Negro Folk Education, 1936, p. 18.

[20] The best single source of information about black concert artists and ensembles for the period immediately following the Civil War is James M. Trotter, *Music and Some Highly Musical People* (1881), reprinted in The Basic Afro-American Reprint Library (New York: Johnson Reprint Corp., 1968).

the music of James Bland achieved enormous popularity. Bland (1854–1911) was advertised as "the world's greatest minstrel man," and although he was born in New York and raised and educated in Washington, D.C., he is best remembered for his sentimental ballad *Carry Me Back to Old Virginny* (1878). He also composed *In the Evening by the Moonlight* and *Oh, Dem Golden Slippers*.

We have already noted that certain elements in American popular music were the norm: simple harmonic patterns, melodic stereotypes, standard rhythmic models, etc. Since the same approximate repertoire was popular among black Americans, we should take note of another element in American popular music that showed up prominently in jazz as it developed toward the turn of the century. Most popular songs and most marches adhered to stereotypes.

James Bland (1854–1911).

Bland's *Carry Me Back to Old Virginny* is a typical example of a piece in "popular-song form"— **AABA** (A musical idea is stated twice, followed by a contrasting phrase and concluding with a restatement of the original theme).

We shall see later that jazz improvisation and ornamentation are superimposed over certain fixed elements of precomposed music. In a great many cases the formal structure (**AABA**) and the simple harmonic vocabulary of previously composed popular music supply the basis over which jazz improvisation operates. This pattern, **AABA,** was part of the common musical vocabulary of the popular song of the late nineteenth century and remained in vogue through the first half of the twentieth century.

TWO PLANTATION MELODIES!   STANDARD AND POPULAR!

CARRY ME BACK TO OLD VIRGINNY.

Song and Chorus.   Words and Music by James A. Bland.   40.

THERE'S A HAPPY LITTLE HOME.

Song and Chorus.   Words and Music by Harry Woodson.   40.

BOSTON:
OLIVER DITSON & CO.,

New York: C. H. DITSON & CO.   Chicago: LYON & HEALY.   Philadelphia: J. E. DITSON & CO.

Sherman, Clay & Co., San Francisco.   Ludden & Bates, Savannah.   Otto Sutro, Baltimore.   L. Grunewald, New Orleans.
Thos. Goggan & Bro., Galveston.   Geo. D. Newhall & Co., Cincinnati.   J. L. Peters, St. Louis.

CARRY ME BACK TO OLD VIRGINNY.

SONG AND CHORUS.

Words and Music by

JAMES BLAND.

Author of "The Old Homestead," "In the morning by the bright light," &c., &c.

1. Car - ry me back to old Vir - gin - ny, There's where the cot - ton and the

2. Car - ry me back to old Vir - gin - ny, There let me live 'till I

corn and ta - toes grow, There's where the birds war - ble sweet in the spring-time,

with - er and de - cay, Long by the old Dis - mal Swamp have I wandered,

There's where the old dar - ke'ys heart am long'd to go,   There's where I labored so
There's where this old dar - ke'ys life will pass a - way.   Mas - sa and mis - sis have

hard   for old mas - sa,   Day   af - ter day   in   the   field of yel - low corn,
long   gone   before me,   Soon   we will meet   on   that   bright and gold - en shore,

No   place on earth do I love more sin-cere -ly   Than   old Vir-gin - ny, the   state where I   was born.
There we'll be hap - py and free from all sorrow,   There's where we'll meet and we'll   nev - er part no more.

ritard.

ritard.

1,402—3.   Carry me back to old Virginny.

By same Author—THE OLD PLANTATION'S LONELY.   Price 35 cents.

CHORUS.

Car-ry me back to old Vir-gin-ny, There's where the cotton and the corn and tatoes grow,

Car-ry me back to old Vir-gin-ny, There's where the cotton and the corn and tatoes grow,

ritard. Repeat pp last time.

There's where the birds warble sweet in the spring-time, There's where this old darkey's heart am long'd to go.

ritard.

There's where the birds warble sweet in the spring-time, There's where this old darkey's heart am long'd to go.

ritard.

Carry me back to old Virginny. 1,403—3.

MY DEAR SAVANNAH HOME. by Danks. Price, 40 cents. **Very Popular.**

Page 5.

March music brought a stricter structural scheme to the popular music audience that was taken up by many ragtime composers.

> *Maple Leaf Rag,* from the formal standpoint, might almost be a Sousa march: first strain (16 measures, repeated); second strain (16, repeated); first strain again; "Trio," so named and consisting of a third strain (16, repeated) in the subdominant and a fourth strain (16, repeated) back in the tonic.[21]

The "interplay of black and white derivations and the intricate racial cross-currents of the minstrel shows"[22] were part and parcel of the creation of ragtime. Again we can see that a common musical language was prevalent for the majority of Americans during the last half of the nineteenth century in both its art and popular music. Black folk music, which had more direct links with its African origins, however, introduced certain new elements into the American culture that were definitely the property of the black race.

Black Folk Music

Before tracing the black folk tradition back to Africa and offering an explanation of how this tradition produced the jazz explosion, we ought first examine the status of black folk music in America after four million Americans achieved freedom in the year 1865. There was a tremendous influx of blacks into the metropolitan centers as thousands fled the despised plantations. Most accounts of the history of jazz concur that the blues were indigenous to black folk music and offer something like the following as explanation:

> Though extensive scholarship documents the existence of the blues in the 20th century, there is almost no mention of the form previous to 1900. Since statements by blues performers such as W. C. Handy and Big Bill Broonzy indicate that the blues were sung before 1900, we can only speculate about their origin. It seems probable, however, that the blues tradition developed after the Civil War when blacks were no longer forced to live and work on the property of their white masters.[23]

It is possible that elements of the blues go back much further, and we will try to trace them back to African music in the next chapter. Let it suffice for now to

---

[21] Hitchcock, *Music in the United States,* p. 123.

[22] Ibid., p. 123.

[23] William Ferris, Jr., *Blues from the Delta* (London: Studio Vista, 1970), p. 28.

assume that the blues, in some recognizable form, developed and stabilized in the period under consideration.

Two other forms of black folk music were carried from slavery into this era, the work song and the spiritual, and both underwent a transformation during these years. Eileen Southern explains that the antebellum repertoire of American blacks was quite large because the songs, following the tradition of their African forebears, were related to the complex social and political organization of their society.[24] Even though this music is insufficiently documented, Southern describes many types: work songs, dance songs, play songs, story songs, satirical songs, field and street cries, and spirituals. What we may assume about pre–Civil War black folk music is primarily derived from information dating from after the war through modern times.

Since accurate conclusions about the prewar music are not possible in light of the scanty evidence available, our description of the transformation which probably took place after the war is a little tenuous. However, certain elements deriving from this body of music are seen as being important in the formation of jazz, such as: melodies in major in which the seventh tone of the scale is flatted;

Roll, Jordon, Roll (Traditional)

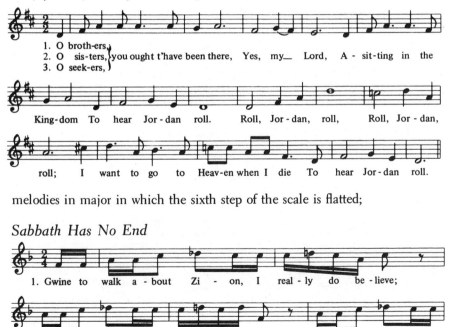

melodies in major in which the sixth step of the scale is flatted;

Sabbath Has No End

---

[24] Southern, *Music of Black Americans*, p. 175.

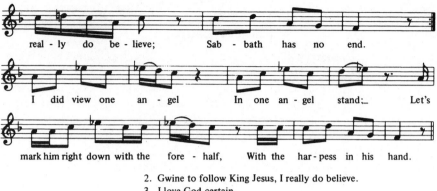

real - ly do be - lieve; Sab - bath has no end.

I did view one an - gel In one an - gel stand;_ Let's

mark him right down with the fore - half, With the har - pess in his hand.

2. Gwine to follow King Jesus, I really do believe.
3. I love God certain.
4. My sister's got religion.
5. Set down in the kingdom.
6. Religion is a fortune.

and in which the third step of the scale is flatted;

The Day of Judgment

And de moon will turn to blood, And de moon will turn to

blood, And de moon will turn to blood in dat day. O

joy, my soul! And de moon will turn to blood in dat day.

melodies which use tonal organizations other than our major and minor melodic systems with chromatic alteration (modal, pentatonic);[25]

Jesus on de Water-Side

Heaven bell a-ring, I know de road, Heaven bell a - ring, I know de road;

Heaven bell a - ring, I know de road, Je - sus sit - tin' on de wa - ter - side.

[25] All transcriptions in standard modern notation of vocal music in the folk idiom are inaccurate, to a degree, because microtonal divisions of the scale cannot be readily accommodated in the notational system.

Do come a-long, do let us go,   Do come a-long, do let us go,

Do come a-long, do let us go,   Je-sus sit-tin' on de wa-ter-side.

The hexatonic scale of *Jesus on De Water-Side*

M3   M3
      m3

syncopated melodies against an understood, regularly recurring beat; call-and-response patterns; a rhythmic accompaniment of foot tapping, hand clapping, or percussion instruments; a tendency to improvise in subsequent verses; and a freer, less inhibited melodic style of singing that included glissandos, falsetto, and other musical sounds not normally found in a trained singer's vocabulary.

The blues tradition seems to have developed among individual singers rather than groups; work songs and hymns, although possible in solo performance, were generally a form of social singing. The lyrics of postwar work songs often dealt with the railroad or prison, but some still told of farm life and others touched on all the occupations in which the newly freed blacks engaged—lumbering, mining, boating, and shopkeeping. All the folk music of the black American, including the newly arranged spirituals of the Jubilee Singers, seems to retain certain melodic, harmonic, and rhythmic elements that form a common body of sound. The similarity of this sound to that of early jazz, along with the preponderance of black musicians among the early jazz performers and the emergence of jazz from the American South and Southwest, are important points testifying to the blacks' central position in the development of this new style.

In conclusion, the state of music in America in the late nineteenth century was such that a large number of people representing many cultures contributed to the musical and social elements found in jazz and necessary for its production. However, it was the American black, the Afro-American musician, who first seized the pieces and put them all together. David A. Cayer points out a significant paradox in the new music:

> Jazz derives neither from a dominant elite enjoying educational and cultural advantages nor from the masses of a numerically dominant majority. Most "high art" has historically come from the former, most "folk art" from the latter. But jazz . . . sprang instead from an enslaved minority, under conditions far less conducive to creativity than those faced by most other oppressed minorities. . . . [This] minority produced a major art form and powerfully shaped the majority's culture.[26]

Jazz, an American art form, developed from the environment just described.

[26] "Black and Blue and Black Again: Three Stages of Racial Imagery in Jazz Lyrics," *Journal of Jazz Studies*, 1 (1974), p. 39.

It was not created in Africa, nor was it shaped in Europe, but it is truly an American product forged from native American genius. It has influenced the music of America and the world in a profound way and stands as a distinct body of music with its own vocabulary, grammar, syntax, and history. We do not know, and in all probability we shall never know, the complete history of its origins, but a better understanding of African music and black music in British and French America might serve us well in our search for enlightenment.

AFRICAN MUSIC

Music in Africa

Although black slaves were brought to America from many regions of Africa, most were torn from clans and tribes which populated the west coast of Africa south of the Sahara. This region has been called the Ivory Coast, the Gold Coast, and the Slave Coast and includes such tribes as the Yoruba, Ibo, Fanti, Ashanti, Susu, Ewe, and others. Since they are nonliterate societies, documentary evidence of the cultures themselves does not exist from as far back as the sixteenth, seventeenth, and early eighteenth centuries. However, the current research of anthropologists, ethnomusicologists, and African historians has provided a wealth of information about most of those societies we wish to study. Also, contemporary documentation of African music and society does exist in the accounts of many voyagers who traveled, observed, and recorded those items that caught their attention.[1]

African tribes, unlike many other nonliterate societies, award a place of honor in the social structure of the tribe to professional musicians who make a living from their music. The entire tribe participates in musical activities, but the call-and-response pattern of West African music, an important link between the blues of jazz and the music of Africa, was a result of the division between the individual singer, the soloist or professional musician, and the rest of the group. The professional musician created and manipulated verses to which

[1] Bruno Nettl, *Folk and Traditional Music of the Western Continents*, Chapter 7 and bibliography.

the working group would respond with a refrain. The trained specialist would also perform on one or more of the many instruments used in African tribal music, and it seems that instrumentalists had a higher status than singers. A wide variety of instruments and types of song may be found in the music of each of these different groups, and, in each, different attitudes toward the music, the activities, and the instruments themselves prevailed.

African music, to be understood, must be examined in context, for the attitudes about the music held by the musicians determined their behavior. This, in turn, affected the musical product, which, in its turn, influenced the musicians in performance and altered their concept, which, to come full circle, determined their behavior and therefore the performance. In contrast to the traditional approach of Western music, in which the finished composition is studied, performed, reperformed in exactly the same way, and admired as an entity in itself, African music is so integrated into the actual performance and lives of the participants that its description must include all of these elements.

In Africa, music often expresses what could never be expressed in everyday life; the concept of talking drums and a private language reserved for a subculture are elements that seem to have continued unchanged right through slavery and into jazz. In pre–Civil War America, and to a certain extent after the War as well, blacks were not permitted freedom of expression, but the messages of the "grapevine telegraph"—the underground railway—were sent from station to station in codes, some of them musical, that only initiates could understand. This system of closed-circle communication was carried into the practices of black jazz musicians, too. For example, when J. Frederick MacDonald interviewed Bud Freeman, a white jazz musician of the Bix Beiderbecke era, and questioned him about the black jazz musician's behavior in the twenties, Freeman replied:

> When I say the black man's language, you have to understand that the black man of that day [1920s], who was not educated, had to find a way to make it in the white world. He had to "yes" the white man; there were underground phrases that he had to use that the white man didn't understand. [2]

Eileen Southern shows how songs played a significant role in the activities of the Underground Railroad, for some songs would alert slaves to danger, others would call them for the trip with their "conductor," and some, like *Follow the Drinkin' Gourd* (the North Star of the Big Dipper), served as maps to guide the slaves on their passage to freedom. [3]

[2] J. Frederick MacDonald, ed., "An Interview with Bud Freeman (May 29, 1974)," *Popular Music and Society*, 3 (1974) p. 332.
[3] Eileen Southern, *Music of Black Americans*, p. 129 ff.

An African *griot* (praise singer) collects passersby as an American bluesman might on payday.

Dancing African drummers.

The Yoruba tribe has at least ten kinds of drums, and these are used within a general culture of tonal languages (talking drums). In their part of Africa, voice inflection can change the meaning of words, and these subtleties in the music and language are, in a sense, privileged and reserved for the members of that subculture. Because of this tonal language, any instrument can be made to talk. A much closer association between musical sounds and extramusical ideas is present in this music than is usual in Western art music. A basically percussive attitude toward music persists in West Africa, and it seems that percussion and rhythm are even more important than melody. If words can be transmitted through the drums, they can also be transmitted through the body, for with an equation of music and dance or drums and dance, body motions can be specifically expressive.

African dancers creating their own rhythmic accompaniment with gourd rattles strapped to their legs.

In the night ceremony of the Efe/Gelede rituals of the Yoruba, leg rattles (*iku*) provide rhythmic punctuation for songs, but they also "speak" to frighten away spiritual forces seeking to destroy the dancer. When the dancer sharply inclines his torso and stamps slowly and methodically, he is expressing reverence to spiritual powers. Satiric Gelede imagery is sometimes used to ridicule the whites and their influence—crossed legs indicate prudery, hands joined above the head mimic the praying posture of Christians, and squinting eyes and jutting chin ridicule the visage of a "typical" European.[4]

No definitive studies on African tuning exist, probably because this is an impossible task, for tuning is not precise in most instances, as it is in the West. This imprecision casts a new light on the common expression "close enough for jazz," for what may be out of tune to a Western symphonic musician is actually part of the melodic tradition of jazz.

Relative pitch and talking drums—specifically, how are these used in Africa? Here is one example:

> Thus in Jabo, a language spoken in Liberia, there are four "tones"; that is, four different relative pitch levels of speech are distinguished for purposes of meaning, . . . [and] the word *ba* may mean four different things, depending on the pitch . . . in signalling, the pitches of the words—or rather their internal relationship, for of course the language tones are not fixed pitches but can be understood only in terms of the pitch of the surrounding syllables and of their place within the speaker's voice range—are transferred to the drum. Jabo signalling is done with two drums, one large, the other smaller, made of hollowed logs with slits. . . . Only a few men are qualified to signal, and only certain things should be said in signal language. Understanding must come from knowledge of the kinds of things likely to be signalled, and evidently the Jabo restrict themselves to expressing thoughts such as "our neighbors are on the warpath," or, more appropriately in this period of acculturation, "Hide! the tax collector approaches!"[5]

When considering African music, it is useful to categorize at least seven different events of performance in order to make useful comparisons: community context, musical performers, instruments (including voice), rhythm, melodic material, form, and texture. All African music is occasional music, that is, it functions as an accompaniment or an ingredient of a social activity. Religious and social music exists, as do work songs, story songs, hunting songs, and music specific to all the activities of the tribe. One question we need to ask ourselves as we view the transition from Africa to America is, "What happens to

[4] See Henry John Drewal, "Efe/Gelede: The Educative Role of the Arts in Traditional Yoruba Culture" (Unpublished Ph.D. dissertation, Columbia University, 1973), and listen to *Anthology of Music of Black Africa* (Everest 3254/3), Record 3.

[5] Nettl, *Folk and Traditional Music*, p. 122.

tribal music when the conditions of life are rapidly and radically changed through geographical displacement, enslavement, and the infusion of non-tribal, Western musical and cultural elements?" If music "is a primary vehicle for man's communication with the supernatural, [and] it symbolizes a person's identity with a group, and it reflects and reinforces the dominant character-istics, values, and directions of a culture,"[6] then what happens to the music when a society is moved, changed, and not allowed to pursue its old religion?

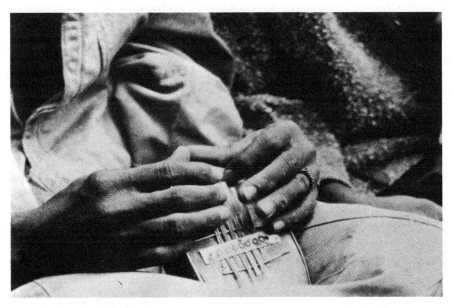

The African *sansa* or *kalimba* (thumb piano) in performance.

One can see that rural African work songs might be used, unchanged as rural Afro-American slave work songs, but music used to praise the hunter or cele-brate a great African victory must undergo severe transformation in a slave soci-ety.

The music makers of Africa, the performers, include both men and women, both soloist and ensemble. A complete piece of music may be played by an in-strumental soloist such as the Senegalese griot performer of the twenty-one string kora,[7] or a soloist in an instrumental ensemble such as the Dan player of

[6] Nettl, "The Role of Music in Culture: Iran," in Charles Hamm, Bruno Nettl, and Ronald Byrnside, *Contemporary Music and Music Cultures*, p. 99.
[7] *La Musique des Griots* (Ocora Records, OCR 15-a), band 1.

the sansa (thumb piano).[8] The soloist may be the leader in a call-and-response ceremonial song,[9] and may be either a woman or a man. African women sing and dance, but only African men play the instruments. Instruments are used singly and in combination, and a wide variety of types is present: tuned and untuned percussion instruments, bowed and plucked strings, and wind instruments of all types—flutes, reeds, and lip-vibrated winds. The intimate relationship between language and musical sound in the performance of all these instruments is an essential feature of African instrumental music. Absolute music, in the Western sense, has little place in African society.

Perhaps the most highly developed feature of African music is its rhythm, and no one seems to question its complexity. A metrical structure with regular beats is characteristic of most tribal music. According to one authority,

> Consistent use of isometric patterns (those without change in meter during the course of the music) occurs only in African Negro music, not in the music of preliterate cultures in any other area of comparable size. This phenomenon suggests some relationship between African Negro and Western music. . . . a great deal of isometric material may have assumed this form because of repeated rhythmic patterns in a percussive accompaniment.[10]

Having thus established a beat, the African musician, or musicians in ensemble, proceed inevitably to the creation of syncopation. Another feature of West African drumming also seems to be universal and to have been carried into the new world: steady tempo for long periods of time. This monotonous, propulsive, metronomic effect gives a cohesiveness to the music and affects the listener with a force bordering on the physical. The rigid, unchanging, steady beat is termed "hot" not only in early jazz, but also in West African terminology.[11]

Rhythmic polyphony is often present in West African drumming, not only in ensemble but in solo playing as well, and its most complex form displays the superimposition of many varying meters over the basic pulse pattern. The unusual rhythmic complexity of native African folk music has led many observers to raise this issue as a *sine qua non* to demonstrate that jazz must have come directly from African origins. Some interested commentators observe:

> One of the common misconceptions in discussing the origins of jazz is that jazz rhythms came from Africa. Actually, it is only the emphasis on rhythm that we can

[8] UNESCO collection, *An Anthology of African Music* (Bärenreiter Musicaphon, BM 30 L 2301), band 7.

[9] Ibid., Music for the Mask Race, band 11.

[10] Bruno Nettl, *Music in Primitive Culture*, p. 64.

[11] Richard A. Waterman, "'Hot' Rhythm in Negro Music," p. 25 ff.

truly designate as African, not the direct influence of particular peculiar rhythmic patterns. At the time when the chief exponents of jazz were generically closest to their African ancestry, the rhythms utilized by these jazz performers were of a very simple nature, far removed from the complex pattern combinations actually used by the natives in Africa.[12]

This is a most fascinating conjecture, and it is one the reader might keep in mind while studying early jazz. Perhaps the answer is to be found in the rhythmic complexity of the polyphonic ensemble and not specifically in the music of the drummer or rhythm section. If the quoted observation is indeed correct, then it points up a strange incongruity in the smooth transformational pattern of African music, slave music, black American music, and jazz.

With regard to melody, one trained observer has concluded that "African music, on the whole, fits more or less into the diatonic scheme that is also the basis of most Western art and folk music."[13] He explains that despite repeated attempts to identify a truly "African" scale, scholars have been unable to uncover any single system. Some of the systems in use are the diatonic, ditonic, tritonic, pentatonic, pentachordal, heptatonic, and occasionally chromatic. He notes exceptions, and also points out the tendency in heptatonic songs to use minor-third and minor-seventh intervals above the tonic. He stresses that "the interest in this feature stems from our desire to explain certain phenomena of jazz (the lowered seventh is a 'blue note'), but it seems doubtful that these intervals constitute a special feature common to all African music."[14]

We have already touched on responsorial forms, and later we will see how these may be equated to blues patterns. Another fundamental characteristic of African music is the striking tendency to use short phrases or short motives to build larger patterns. The additive nature of the melodies in combination with the additive nature of the rhythms are two of the key ingredients that set African tribal music apart as a unique and distinct body of music. We might conclude by saying that true West African folk music is, and was, socially oriented music performed as solos and in ensemble. The professional musician played a major role in performing this music, and instruments as well as voice, both alone and in combination, were used to produce pieces with characteristic rhythms, forms, and melodies. The close association between rhythm and tone with language and body movement is an essential feature of this repertoire, and this music was the heritage of the black Africans who were enslaved and brought to America.

[12] Paul O. Tanner and Maurice Gerow, A Study of Jazz (Dubuque, Iowa: Wm. C. Brown, 1964; rev. 1972), p. 7. It is interesting to note that in their second edition of the same book (1973), they softened their view by eliminating the last sentence of this quotation (p. 15).

[13] Nettl, Folk and Traditional Music, p. 127 f.

[14] Ibid., p. 128.

African Music in the Americas

North America was not the only country to import Africans as slaves. Africans were captured and taken to South and Central America as well as the islands of the West Indies, and one might rightfully wonder why jazz did not develop there instead of here. The slaves brought their music with them as they were transported across the sea, and there was a partial continuation of their African traditions in each of the areas into which they were thrust. Scholars have systematically combed archive after archive in an attempt to flesh out the skeleton of black music in America during the colonial period, and have finally admitted that "despite the real contribution of such men as Gilbert Chase and Marshall Stearns, documentation is sketchy."[15] Still, much has been done to give us a healthy and balanced view of the state of black American music before the Civil War. Possibly the most cogent questions for this study are posed and partially answered thus:

> What kind of music did the Africans bring with them when they first arrived on the North American mainland? How long did that music persist in its new environment, and how was it transformed into something we now call Afro-American?[16]

These studies, which are models of carefully documented, painstakingly objective scholarly investigation, show that the African musical heritage was brought over more or less intact, but that it met least opposition in the islands of the West Indies. Consequently, it maintained itself there with less change for a longer period of time. Whether the islands were British or French seems to have made no difference initially, for the slave culture was basically African in all locations.

From 1619 through 1788, the laws prohibiting African music and customs became increasingly stringent. An attempt to suppress African dancing was made on the island of Martinique in 1654, but the records show that these measures seem to have met with little effect. African instruments abounded, the dances continued, and music in the characteristic manner persisted. Perhaps the laws were more strictly enforced on the mainland, but drumming and African singing continued unabated in the West Indies.

A similar situation persisted for a while on mainland North America as well. Although Sunday dancing by blacks inflamed the ire of parish priests, documents indicate that African dancing was prevalent in Virginia and South Carolina at least in the early eighteenth century. Mid- to late-eighteenth-century ac-

---

[15] Dena J. Epstein, "Slave Music in the United States Before 1860: A Survey of Sources," p. 195.

[16] Dena J. Epstein, "African Music in British and French America," p. 61.

counts indicate that African singing, dancing, and piping still took place in many areas of the South, and during this period, of course, the arrival of fresh slaves reinforced the African attitudes of the older ones.

> The acculturative process was complex, involuntary to all parties, and unavoidable. Of all the aspects of African music in the New World, the most difficult to document has been acculturation—its transition from being purely or almost purely African to a form recognizable as something different—Afro-American, Jamaican, Creole, or whatever the term might be. . . . The descriptions of African and European music and dancing coexisting side by side give incontrovertible evidence of the process by which acculturation proceeded.[17]

A number of available historical accounts seems to confirm a consistent picture of African and European music and dancing coexisting, side by side. In the Georgetown district of South Carolina in 1805, black violinists fiddling for dancing was later followed by native Africans dancing to hand clapping. In New Orleans, in 1808, two groups danced side by side, one dancing a bamboula and the other a European contredanse. European instruments gradually began to appear in the hands of Negro musicians, but the impact was not one-sided. African dances and performance practices affected white music as perceptibly as white music gradually transformed that of the blacks. Dena J. Epstein's description of the transitional years would seem to conflict with the more popular views expressed by other scholars, such as Marshall Stearns[18] and Ernest Borneman,[19] for she documents an acculturation process that took place simultaneously in the British and French colonies of North America as well as on the islands and in South America. The resulting music was different, but different only in the sense of being a local variety. The standard view, as explained in the works of the latter two authors, contends that British slavery was different from Spanish, French, and Portuguese slavery. For this reason, the significant changes that ultimately led to jazz occurred in the music of African slaves under British rule, but no such changes took place in the music of African slaves under continental European rule. New Orleans remains problematic, however, for this important early jazz center was strongly influenced by French Catholicism.

Ernest Borneman explains a dichotomy in the transformational process of African music in the New World in these terms: Greek and Roman concepts of slavery survived on the European continent because slavery survived on the Iberian Peninsula down to the fifteenth century. On the other hand, the British islands had no slavery at this time, nor did they understand the Greek or

---

[17] Ibid., p. 83.
[18] Marshall W. Stearns, *The Story of Jazz* (London: Oxford University Press, 1970), pp. 3–66.
[19] Ernest Borneman, "Black Light and White Shadow," p. 48 ff.

Roman concepts of slavery. In the sixteenth century, they were totally unfamiliar with Africans and African patterns of culture, whereas the Mediterranean people had maintained trade links with Africa over the years.

The Mediterranean people had a place in their society for slavery; the British did not. Thus, the Spanish and Portuguese slaveowners assumed slavery to affect only the body of the slave, not his mind. Slavery was a misfortune rather than a human element. The British, on the other hand, found slavery to be morally indefensible, and consequently assumed that all slaves were morally tainted. Therefore, the slave had to be considered inferior in order to be wholly owned, body and soul. The Spanish master was considered the owner of the slave's labor, not of the slave, and cruelty, although not absent, was against the law. The British owner could do what he would with his slave, and theoretically the slave could never buy his own freedom because he was an inferior being, outside the normal order of things.

The Catholic Church, the church of the Mediterranean countries, took an interest in the souls of slaves and required slaveowners to provide religious instruction. The Protestant Church, the church of England, had no interest in the slaves, and allowed the slaveowners to do as they saw fit. Within the Catholic Church, marriage was a sacrament which, when applied to a slave couple, kept the family together. Under British rule, enslaved couples could be separated at the owner's will. Under British rule, slavery was a closed system which tended to undermine all the personal and social values of the blacks. Borneman argues that under Spanish slavery, black society would tend to undergo less drastic changes than it would under British slavemasters. Therefore, jazz, if it was indeed truly a new music, resulted from an environment where change inevitably had to take place. Jazz, by this logic, could not have developed on the islands or in South America because there was no inner need for something new.

Marshall Stearns views New Orleans as a cauldron that melted French and British influence in a post–Civil War society, and sees the Catholic-Protestant, French-British, white-black polarities as being key ingredients at the proper moment.

> New Orleans has a special place in the story of jazz. A Latin-Catholic possession for eighty-two years, it became part of a predominantly British-Protestant country after the Louisiana Purchase. At times, the patterns of music in New Orleans resembled those of different islands in the West Indies. The combination and the timing in the blend of West African music with European was unique, however, and led to the birth of a new music. For the New Orleans environment was decidedly different from that of the rest of the United States.[20]

[20] Stearns, *Story of Jazz*, p. 33.

There may be some truth to this view, for certainly New Orleans was an important center in the early days of jazz, but more recent scholarship tends to support a belief in origins throughout the southern portion of the United States. If this is the case, then how are we to account for these careful, logical arguments that demonstrate why jazz could not have been created elsewhere? At any rate, we have glimpsed African music and seen how it was carried to America during the colonial period. We have traced some lines of transition for this music and examined some explanations for this change. Earlier, we examined both black and white music in America after the Civil War, and now we will briefly survey the black American music which was the immediate predecessor of post–Civil War American music—the music of the black American slaves.

Black American Music during the Colonial Period

After 1800, regular organized missions to the slaves began. The gospel singing of blacks is described by a contemporary white observer:

> [M]y ears were assailed by the voice of singing. . . . I saw a group of about thirty Negroes, of different ages and sizes, following a rough-looking white man . . . as they came nearer, I saw some of them loaded with chains to prevent their escape; while others had hold of each other's hands . . . they came along singing a little wild hymn of sweet and mournful melody; flying by a divine instinct of the heart, to the consolation of religion. . . . "It's nothing at all but a parcel of Negroes sold to Carolina, and that man is their driver, who has bought them." . . . the truth is, they feel, and exquisitely too. . . . Even in the land of their banishment, it is said, they . . . have several little wild songs which they sing with tears, recalling the images of past felicity, their cabins, and their cornfields. [21]

Whether these blacks were singing spirituals as we know them cannot be deduced from this account, but one may assume that they sang music of the black-spiritual type. However, little hard evidence remains from these early days, and we cannot be certain of the precise type of music or the specific mode of performance comprising a spiritual before the Civil War. We can fairly certainly guess that some were led by a soloist, often improvising, with others answering in refrain; we can imagine the melodies are made up of fairly short fragments with frequent blue notes; we can assume that the voices in song

---

[21] *Letters from Virginia, translated from the French* (Baltimore: F. Lucas, Jr., 1816), pp. 29–34, quoted by Dena J. Epstein, "Slave Music in the United States," p. 203.

have a distinctive quality different from the trained white tradition of singing; and we know that some of this monophonic music was accompanied by foot stomping, hand clapping, and dancing.

Chromatic Alterations (Blue Notes) in *Ol' Hannah,* a Folk Melody

Many problems arise in attempting to depict fairly the black slave community and its musical culture. Eyewitness accounts by whites are of limited value, because they generally represent only what blacks wanted whites to hear. Double entendre, words with at least two disparate meanings, has long been a part of the African musical heritage. It has been demonstrated time after time how black musicians have masked their feelings of social protest in their songs by using this device to avoid complications, first with their masters, later with the dominant white society, and more recently with the demands of the recording companies.[22] Also, white observers were sometimes offended by what they saw and heard, and thus their accounts represent a censored historical record. When these observers were unfamiliar with the African languages and were untrained in black musical traditions, they were often likely to misinterpret the slave songs.

A well-documented study specifying the degree and quality of African survivals in black American music has not yet been accomplished, and the dangers of attempting to attribute all musical elements of jazz to African music are as real as the dangers inherent in supporting the opposite view. When studies of this type have been made, they have usually sought analogies in the two repertories, to form a musical bridge on which the distinctive elements of each can be seen to cross over.[23] Any suggestion that the black slave was

[22] Paul Oliver, *Aspects of the Blues Tradition* (New York: Oak Publications, 1970), p. 216 ff. and *passim.*

[23] See Paul Oliver, *Savannah Syncopators: African Retentions in the Blues* (New York: Stein and Day, 1970), and Gunther Schuller, "The Origins," *Early Jazz: Its Roots and Musical Development,* pp. 3–63.

willingly accepting elements of the white culture and integrating them into his own music are certainly not acceptable for first-generation slaves. Although not carefully documented, it is possible, and more likely probable, that the slave in America desired to maintain his African musical heritage and was motivated by a need to preserve his African identity and avoid incorporation into the hated white society. The intensity of these feelings is recorded in the words of a slave song, *Sound the Jubilee!*

> See the poor souls from Africa
> Transported to America;
> We are stolen, and sold in Georgia,
> Will you go along with me?
> We are stolen, and sold in Georgia,
> Come sound the Jubilee!
>
> See wives and husbands sold apart,
> Their children's screams will break my heart;
> There's a better day a comin',
> Will you go along with me?
> There's a better day a comin',
> Go sound the Jubilee!

Nevertheless, a process of transformation and acculturation took place, willingly, intentionally, or otherwise.

In a study of the slave community, it is argued that the slave quarters provided a largely private environment in which blacks could develop self and group conceptions contrary to those expected by the masters.[24] We are told by some that black slaves were prevented from maintaining their African heritages through legislation and enforcement by their white slavemasters, but if this thesis is correct, African norms could be perpetuated in the all-black slave quarters.

Black American Work Song, *Julianna Johnson*

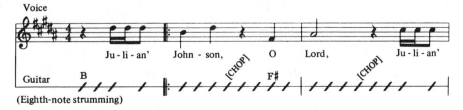

[24] John W. Blassingame, *The Slave Community: Plantation Life in the Antebellum South.*

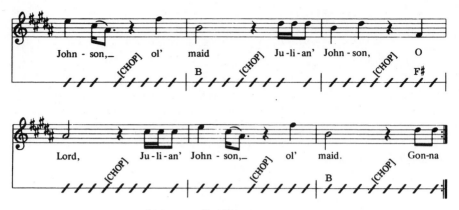

John-son,— ol' maid [CHOP] Ju-li-an' John-son, [CHOP] O [F#]

Lord, Ju-li-an' John-son,— [CHOP] ol' maid. Gon-na [CHOP]

Leave you, ol' maid,
gonna leave you, ol' maid.

Look out Ju-li', ol' maid,
look out Ju-li', ol' maid.

What's a matter with Ju-li'. ol' maid,
what's a matter with Ju-li', ...

A portion of the slave's leisure time was spent dancing, but European reels, minuets, and schottisches held little appeal for him. The slave's dance was often a test of physical endurance, a way of earning respect, and a channel through which he could express his inner feelings. In this manner, the slave sought relief from the tensions of plantation life. Often, the physical labor of picking cotton, digging ditches, hammering railroad spikes, or chopping wood was alleviated by singing a musical accompaniment. He refreshed his spirit while retaining a vestige of his mother culture and a sense of his African identity. Songs were sung at the dances, and these tunes were noted more for their rhythmic qualities than for their lyrics. When no instruments were available, slaves accompanied themselves by "patting juba," a syncopated, polyrhythmic method of clapping one's hands and tapping one's feet.

The more somber songs from the slave culture often expressed the reality of the slave's oppression and sometimes celebrated the proud defiance of runaways, the courage of black rebels, the stupidity of white patrollers, and the heartlessness of the slavetraders. The kindness or cruelty of the masters was not overlooked. These songs often accompanied their work in the fields and were frequently in the African call-and-response pattern. By masking the true meaning of these songs from their white overseers, by carefully selecting words that were seemingly innocent but in reality held subversive meanings for the initiates, the black was able to repress his anger and project his aggressions in a way that safeguarded his mental health, involved little physical threat to himself and his family, and provided some form of recreation. It would seem that black antebellum music in America was distinctly African in its quality. If this is so, it appears that a fairly rapid transformation of this music took place during the first few decades after the Civil War, for as we have seen in Chapter I, black

American music just before the jazz period had incorporated many European musical elements.

In most areas of the South, specific legislation outlawed drumming, but the blacks substituted hand clapping and foot stomping in their own private gatherings. Thus, the African rhythms could be practiced and perpetuated without offending their white masters. One important exception to this situation was the Place Congo, a square in New Orleans where, until the Civil War, slaves were allowed to gather to dance, sing, and play percussion instruments.[25] Detailed

The slave's dance was often a test of physical endurance. From an engraving, c. 1800, artist unknown.

accounts of the activities in Place Congo certify that many instruments were used, including several types of drums, pebble-filled gourds, jew's harps, jawbones, thumb pianos (African sansa), and the four-string banjo.

The most significant aspect of African music in America, as it might be applied to our considerations of jazz origins, is its rhythm. In this regard, Erich von Hornbostel posits a theory of tension and relaxation in African drumming which he uses to explain the importance of syncopation as a dominant element in the rhythm of black African music.[26] He contends that the upbeat motion

[25] Dena Epstein, "African Music," pp. 73, 86, 87, and 90.
[26] See John Blacking, "Some Notes on a Theory of African Rhythm Advanced by Erich von Hornbostel."

Dancing the *bamboula* in Place Congo.

receives the stress or tension and the downbeat motion the relaxation; consequently, the sound is more positive on the offbeats than on the beat. Combining this with a continuous metronomic pulse, typical, as we have seen, of West African music, results in a highly syncopated music. In African dance drumming, the complex polyrhythmic structure is made possible and at the same time generates excitement through various tone contrasts that are repeated throughout the dance.[27] The most complex and varied rhythm is usually played by the male, or master, drum; a lesser drum establishes the underlying pulse and maintains a steady ground, which is used as a point of reference. Intermediary drums act as accompanying instruments and are important, as they add their own rhythms and interact with the rhythms of the master drum. Bells and rattles may be used along with the accompanying drums, and one can see that dance drumming is a most complex and intricate musical art of overlapping and interweaving rhythmic lines.

One last observation may be useful in understanding the techniques of African drumming. There appear to be four distinct drum techniques used:

1. the hand technique, in which different parts and shapes of the hand are used to beat the drumhead;

2. the stick-and-hand technique, in which one hand uses a stick to beat the drum while the other acts to mute or muffle the beat, or provides a second beat;

[27] Schuller, *Early Jazz*, Chapter 1.

3. the stick-and-armpit-control technique, in which the drum is held in the armpit and is hit with a stick, pitch variations being determined by changes in pressure of the armpit;

4. the stick technique (the most common), using two sticks to play the drum.

The variety of drums and of percussion techniques, the central importance of drumming to African dance music, and the metronomic time-keeping aspect of drumming in conjunction with overlapping layers of syncopated rhythms are all features that would seem to be distinctly African in origin, features which seem to have been brought to jazz by no other route than through the African musical heritage.

Black American Music from 1800 to the Civil War

No introductory gloss can do justice either to the vast musical tradition of Africa or to the smaller, but in some ways less well known, repertoire of black music in America. It is our intent here to introduce the major subject areas only and indicate possible paths for further exploration. Although folk-song scholarship before 1900 deals only with religious material, it is easy to see that the verses of religious songs were often used as work songs as well. Not only was there an interchange between religious and secular functions, but a specific song was frequently reworked to become appropriate for another occasion. A song used for "shuckin' ob de corn" could be slowed down for use as a rowing song,[28] and the secret of this amazing flexibility was the improvisational nature of the genre. Although religious songs tended to be rhymed, secular songs frequently were not.

One final element of black American music during this period remains to be touched upon, that is, anonymous or communal authorship. As in most other folk musics, individual composers were not identified. The music was thought of as belonging to the whole people, and master musicians, group leaders, or master drummers contributed to an anonymous repertoire that belonged to and represented an entire people. The criteria for inclusion were performance and function, and in this regard the music was directly akin to its African sources. Performance was highly personal, and involved the performer totally. A creative intermediary, a composer, was not necessary in order to communicate with an individual's deity, animals, or associates. The repertoire changed, but

[28] Epstein, "Slave Music," p. 212.

essentially it was unchanging, for it was based on age-old patterns of sound and rhythm, which needed only day-to-day modifications in order to make them appropriate for the occasion or the individual. This creative performance tradition also finds an easy parallel in the aesthetic of jazz performance.

In the first six decades of the nineteenth century, black music in America included voodoo dancing and ritual accompanied by drumming forbidden anywhere other than in the Place Congo of New Orleans. Black American music included ring-shout, ceremonial dancing, and singing; music on the banjo, drums, fifes, fiddles, and other instruments; dancing to the patting of juba, singing for work songs; and a vast repertoire of spirituals. Certain elements were common to many of these activities; others were not. Certain elements transferred to the black music of the post–Civil War period; others did not. Some aspects incorporated Western music readily within themselves and proceeded with a rapid transformation, while others lingered on in an unchanging, basically African mode. The drummers of Place Congo were not jazz drummers, and the singers of the cotton fields were not jazz singers. Still, their heritage profoundly influenced music in America at the turn of the twentieth century, and jazz did emerge. We have surveyed these black elements not so much to prove a point, but to underline the importance of this generally little-known body of music to that new style which was to become a dominant force in the musical culture of the twentieth century.

Without question African music came to the New World with the first Africans to arrive here. This music persisted, not without change, but in a clearly recognizable African form for over one hundred fifty years in the West Indies and for a shorter time on the mainland. Where black slaves were forced to convert their cultures to that of the dominant society, their African tribal patterns either declined or went underground. But however it was preserved in America, enough essential, distinctive elements remained to help infuse new lifeblood into the old West European music and to create a new child of the new society, jazz.

JAZZ BEFORE THE
NAME "JAZZ" EMERGED

1917 WAS A LANDMARK for jazz because it marks the date of the first recording by any musical group in which the word "jazz" is used as a descriptive qualifier,[1] and it is the year in which the word "jazz" first begins to appear regularly in print. The first occurrence thus far uncovered was in the March 6, 1913 issue of the San Francisco *Bulletin*, where it is written:

> The team which speeded into town this morning comes pretty close to representing the pick of the army. Its members have trained on ragtime and 'jazz.'[2]

Damon Runyon, in his regular column, "Th' Mornin's Mornin'," which appeared in all the Hearst papers, wrote on January 21, 1917:

The Old Jaz Band

> New York. Jan. 20.—A Broad way cafe announces, as something new to the big Bright Aisle, the importation from the West of a syncopated riot known as a Jaz Band.[3]

Walter Kingsley, writing for the *New York Sun* on August 5, 1917, offered his readers a little musical history following the headline, "Whence comes jass? Facts from the great authority on the subject":

[1] The Original Dixieland Jazz Band made a New York recording in January of 1917.
[2] San Francisco Bulletin, March 6, 1913, p. 16. The 'team' referred to is a baseball team.
[3] I am indebted to J. R. Taylor, who called this article to my attention.

Variously spelled Jas, Jass, Jaz, Jasz, and Jascz. The word is African in origin. It is common on the Gold Coast of Africa and in the hinterland of Cape Coast Castle . . . Jazz is based on the savage musician's wonderful gift for progressive retarding and acceleration guided by his sense of 'swing.'

Unquestionably, the new music did not actually begin at this date, and one discovers, for example that *Baby Seals Blues* had been published in St. Louis on August 3, 1912. How widespread the genre had become by that time is documented by two other publications in the same year: one in Oklahoma City on September 6, 1912, of the *Dallas Blues*, and the other in Memphis, Tennessee, on September 23, 1912, of W. C. Handy's *Memphis Blues*. This much publishing activity over so large a geographical area suggests the possibility of a well-established market, a mature tradition, and a number of musicians associated with the field.

If we count ragtime as jazz, and there seems to be no stylistic reason for not doing so, then we can find an even older publishing history. Chicago takes the honors for the first ragtime publication, for in 1897 bandleader William H. Krell saw his *Mississippi Rag* come off the press. Later that same year, Tom Turpin's *Harlem Rag* was published in St. Louis, Missouri, thus becoming the first rag by a black composer to achieve publication. In 1899, the great Scott Joplin's *Original Rags* appeared from Kansas City, Missouri, and was followed later that year by his first major ragtime success, the *Maple Leaf Rag*, published in Sedalia, Missouri, in March of 1899.

The syncopated rhythm of the cakewalk was part of every American minstrel show, which carried this popular dance from hamlet to city in its travels across the country. By the end of the century, contests for cakewalking and ragtime piano playing were the rage, and pianists were given an allotted amount of time in which to demonstrate their improvisational ability in ragtime style. "Coon songs" in the new syncopated style became popular in the 1880s, and J. S. Putnam's *New Coon in Town*, published in 1883, became a popular addition to the new ragtime school. As Samuel B. Charters and Leonard Kunstadt point out in their history of jazz in New York: "in a 1903 minstrel recording, 'The Cakewalk in Coontown,' the 'dancing' is accompanied by a five-piece band— two clarinets, cornet, trombone, and piano, playing an unmistakably jazz style."[4] That minstrelsy and syncopated coon songs were popular as far west as San Francisco is attested to by the characteristic ragtime rhythms of *There's No Coon That's One Half So Warm.*[5] With blues and rag publications in Missouri, Oklahoma, Tennessee, Illinois; with ragtime "combo" recordings in

[4] *Jazz: A History of the New York Scene*, p. 14.

[5] *A San Francisco Songster 1849–1939*, ed. Cornel Lengyel. History of Music in San Francisco, 2 (San Francisco: W.P.A., 1939), p. 106 f.

New York; and with "Ethiopian Minstrelsy" traveling from coast to coast, it is clear that the story of jazz begins neither with the origin of the word nor with the magic of a single creative genius in a specific, isolated locale.

Jazz developed in America during the last decades of the nineteenth century with a kind of spontaneous combustion that singed both coasts. Two distinct varieties, ragtime and blues, seemed to develop side by side, with many variant forms within each category. Coon songs, ragtime vocal solos, piano rags, and ragtime bands developed the "hot" rhythms and angular melodic styles; and the blues, which came from spirituals, field hollers, and work songs, were sung solo, accompanied by a guitar or other simple folk instrument, and were eventually played by instruments alone.

The word "blues" had currency as early as 1853, when a Boston newspaper recommended light reading "to all who are afflicted with the blues, or ennui,"[6] and an even earlier use of the word as an abbreviation for "blue devils," a phrase meaning despondency or depression of spirits can be found in Washington Irving's colorful observations of America, *Salmagundi* (1807). No definite association between the word "blues" and the music known as "the blues" can be established before the 1910s, but the performance of this distinctive musical type must certainly date back to the beginning of the century. Jazz, or its immediate antecedent, was actively being performed across the country in the years before 1917. The name seems to have come into common usage in the years 1913–15, according to jazz musicians of that period, and the exact derivation of the word "jazz" is totally unclear. It may have been used originally as a minstrel or vaudeville term, but it may also have had African or Arabic origins. That it was possibly associated with the sex act, for which the word is used in slang as a synonym, has been suggested by a number of writers; and a particularly intriguing possibility, because of the French culture of New Orleans, is a derivation from the French verb *jaser*, which may be translated "to chatter or have an animated conversation among diverse people." All the suggestions and viewpoints advanced in the literature from 1917 through 1958 have been systematically examined.[7] The study, although fascinating, settles nothing and leaves the reader stranded with: ". . . the need for linguistic and philological research although we are not at all sure that the origin of jazz, the word, can ever be found."[8]

Ragtime and blues as performed before 1917 had certain musical characteristics in common, such as melodic improvisation to a harmonic scheme, special timbres, scales, and intonations, syncopated rhythms applied to a basic unwavering pulse, and other features peculiar to jazz. Their diffusion and

[6] Samuel B. Charters, *The Country Blues* (New York: Rinehart, 1959), p. 34.
[7] Alan P. Merriam and Fradley H. Garner, "Jazz—The Word."
[8] Ibid., p. 396.

more-or-less simultaneous emergence across the country are phenomena worth viewing, and before we undertake the actual study of the music itself, we will survey briefly some of this activity in several different locales.

A major problem of jazz historiography is the lack of agreement on a working definition—a musical, stylistic definition—of jazz. Rudi Blesh, a leading historian of ragtime and author of an important text, separates jazz from ragtime and blues, counting the latter, along with work songs, spirituals, the music of the marching bands, the French dances, and the rhythms and tunes of Spanish America and the Caribbean, as being elements all outside the sphere of jazz. He also excludes the new jazz of the 1930s, swing:

> The dilution and deformation of jazz took place from 1920 on because of the influences of commercialism, white playing, and sophistication of the Negroes themselves. . . . Swing, which is not jazz, is a type of European music with transplanted Negroid characteristics. [9]

This point of view, while conveniently limiting the subject to an easily circumscribed area, does not meet the demands of musical or historical criteria. Blesh and others who hold this view would limit jazz to the improvisational instrumental music typical of the New Orleans jazz bands from circa 1900 to 1920. All groups with a rhythm section and a front line of three instruments— clarinet, cornet, and trombone—employing black personnel and playing in a group improvisational manner are easily categorized as exponents of "classic jazz," sometimes referred to as "traditional jazz" ("trad jazz"), or New Orleans Dixieland jazz. Musically, this approach runs aground on the sandbars of stylistic analysis. Jelly Roll Morton's Red Hot Peppers was a ragtime band; at least, Jelly Roll Morton was a ragtime pianist. If a ragtime band plays the same music in the same style as a classic New Orleans jazz band, such as King Oliver's Creole Jazz Band, and if the music of one is jazz, then the music of the other must be too. Likewise, if the blues singing of Bertha "Chippie" Hill and Mamie Smith is included in the corpus of jazz, then where does one draw the line separating blues folk singing from blues jazz singing?

From a purely historical, nonmusical point of view, the historian is obliged to look back at the music considered jazz by its performers and its audience and accept their decision as final. The incongruities fostered by the purists who maintain that classic jazz is the only jazz become apparent when we observe that for most of the history of that music the word "jazz" was never uttered. In contrast, the music of the swing era was called jazz, and it was common knowledge in America that organizations like the Duke Ellington Orchestra, the Count Basie Band, and the Charlie Parker Quintet, as well as the New Orleans–style ensembles led by men such as Louis Armstrong, were jazz bands.

The exact time when country blues made the musical transition to jazz has

[9] *Shining Trumpets: A History of Jazz*, pp. 3, 6.

not been isolated, nor has the stylistic cleavage been charted between those ragtime compositions and performances that are clearly jazz and those that do not qualify. Therefore, a broad definition which includes all those musics popularly categorized as jazz will be considered in this study. The more exclusive reader may eliminate any portion he chooses, but all those musics that have survived in the repertoire or significantly influenced its development will at least be touched upon and given a place in this history. As a working definition, we will consider jazz to be that music which came into being in the southern part of the United States during the late nineteenth century and first blossomed in the vicinity of New Orleans at the turn of the twentieth century. This music has undergone many stylistic changes, and may be considered to include ragtime, blues, classic or Dixieland jazz, Chicago-style jazz, swing, boogie-woogie, Kansas City–style jazz, bebop, progressive jazz, and free jazz, as well as others. Certain musical elements are common to all, and the musical sound produced in combination is usually recognizable as jazz even by the untrained listener. These elements may be present in varying proportions, depending upon the style, the performers, and sometimes accidental circumstances, but the common features usually are:

1. improvisation, both group and solo;
2. rhythm sections in ensembles (usually drums, bass, and chordal instrument such as piano, banjo, or guitar);
3. metronomical underlying pulse to which syncopated melodies and rhythmic figures are added (in this regard, additive rhythm[10] is frequently employed);

[10] Additive rhythm and divisive rhythm are terms used to explain, in contrasting ways, the organization of beats or pulses into regular groupings. The former organizes quick beats into larger units, and the latter subdivides slow pulses and large groupings into smaller units. For example, a measure in 4/4 meter may be notated as follows to indicate a basic "rhumba" beat:

The traditional method for drummers schooled in the African-derived genres to play this pattern is to organize the lowest common denominator, the eighth note ($\flat$), into two groups of threes and one group of twos:

This method of thinking, organizing smaller units of the hierarchy into larger units, is called additive rhythm. The traditional method for drummers schooled in the European tradition to play this pattern is to subdivide larger beats, the quarter notes ($\downarrow$), in half, and accent the offbeat of beat two as well as the onbeat of beat four, a normally unaccented beat, thereby producing an equivalent rhythmic pattern.

The difference, in this instance, is subtle—a succession of irregularly spaced downbeats as opposed to suppressed downbeats and accented afterbeats, but one method, additive rhythm, provides the means by which African drummers and jazz musicians create complex, polyrhythmic ensembles.

4. reliance on popular song form and blues form in most performances;

5. tonal harmonic organization with frequent use of the blues scale for melodic material;

6. timbrel features, both vocal and instrumental, as well as other performance-practice techniques which are characteristic of particular jazz substyles, such as vibratos, glissandi, articulations, etc.;

7. performer or performer-composer aesthetic rather than a composer-centered orientation.

In any particular jazz performance, one or more of these elements may be absent. For example, some big-band arrangements of the swing era allowed for no improvisation, and others limited improvised solos to one or two short instrumental breaks. Duke Ellington and his music represent a jazz composer's world much more than that of the jazz performer. Buddy DeFranco's clarinet sound is closely akin to symphonic clarinet timbre, while Johnny Dodd's sound has a roughness, imperfection, and charm typical of classic jazz. Likewise, it is important to note that these features are not exclusive to jazz. Improvisation is not limited entirely to jazz musicians, and we may see it in the work of European organists and many avant-garde ensembles today. Furthermore, it was a major practice in music of the Baroque, the Renaissance, and other great periods of Western classical music. A metronomic pulse can be observed in marches and classical symphonies, and additive rhythms may be observed in French secular music of the late fourteenth century as well as in African drumming. It is the employment of several of these features in combination which is unique to jazz and which characterizes its distinctive sound and spiritual essence.

The East

The "gay nineties" and the first decade of the twentieth century in America saw young people dancing to a new kind of syncopated music. American minstrelsy had disseminated the coon song and cakewalk, and ragtime piano playing had became popular. The latter proliferated from the saloons, whorehouses, and riverboats to a larger audience, and composers were taking the new syncopated sounds seriously. Ragtime gained world-wide distribution as keyboard music and in orchestral transcription, and its impact on American music was felt through classic jazz, popular music, and vaudeville. In 1881, when Tony Pastor moved his Music Hall to East 14th Street, he advertised his new house as "the first specialty vaudeville theater of America, catering to polite tastes, aiming to amuse, and fully up to current times and topics."[11] Vaudeville acts spread out in ever-widening circles and carried their songs and dances on a circuit that touched every major American city and many smaller ones. They spurred public interest in the purchase of sheet music and made the latest musical sounds familiar. Some of the places where performances were held had only a piano, others used a small ensemble, and only a few employed full-sized orchestras. Ragtime, like other popular music, was adaptable to the circumstances, and improvisation was the cheapest and most practical way of filling out an arrangement with the forces available.

If New York City was the center for vaudeville, it was also a center for syncopated dance music in the East. As Eileen Southern points out, the center of

[11] David Ewen, *The Life and Death of Tin Pan Alley*, p. 27.

An Orpheum Circuit vaudeville tour, scheduled for 1914, that never materialized, brought together in rehearsal: (standing, left to right) Clarence Williams, John Lindsay, Jimmie Noone, Bebé Ridgley; (seated, left to right) Oscar Celestin, Tom Benton, Johnny St. Cyr. The snare drummer (left front) is Ernest Trepagnier; the violinist (center front) is Armand J. Piron

fashionable black life in New York was "Black Bohemia," on the west side of Manhattan.[12] One of the most successful and influential musicians and band directors was Will Dixon, who led a group called the Nashville Students (not one from Nashville or a student) that was comprised of banjos, mandolins, guitars, saxophones, drums, a violin, a couple of brasses, and a bass. They played at a vaudeville theater, Hammerstein's Victoria, and on the Roof Garden for dancing at night. Probably the most influential black musician in New York was James Reese Europe, who organized a black musician's union called the Clef Club in 1910, and developed an orchestra of mandolins, banjos, guitars, saxophones, and drums. For an exceptional concert at Carnegie Hall in May, 1912, Europe directed an orchestra of 145, including mandolins, bandoras, harp-guitars, banjos, violins, saxophone, tuba, cellos, clarinets, baritones, trombones, cornets, tympani, drums, basses, and ten pianos. They played and sang in syncopated style, and although professional criticism was mixed, they seem to have had a dynamic impact upon their audiences.

Dixon and Europe were not the only men propagating jazz sounds in New York before 1917. Ragtime pianists abounded there: Jess Pickett, Sam Gordon, "Jack the Bear," William Turk, Eubie Blake, "One-Leg" Willie Joseph, and James P. Johnson are almost legendary names of the stride piano school (see p. 90). They improvised, syncopated, and occasionally published. Eubie Blake was one of the first Eastern black ragtimers to get his instrumental pieces published, but he was not the only one.

A fascinating African tradition persisted in New York at least until 1950, when it was claimed that the ringshout "is still danced in some of the churches of Harlem, the most sophisticated of all American Negro communities."[13] The ringshout is an African dance that features a group of singers circling counterclockwise around the leader of the religious chant. Ragtime pianist Willie "The Lion" Smith relates New York–style ragtime directly to the ringshout.

> [S]houts are stride piano—when James P. [Johnson] and Fats [Waller] and I would get a romp-down shout going, that was playing rocky, just like the Baptist people sing. You don't just play a chord to that—you got to move it and the piano-players do the same thing in the churches, and there's ragtime in the preaching.[14]

The blues were also in New York, first, perhaps, as a part of the ragtime, popular-piano style repertoire. Jess Pickett's *The Dream* (also called *Lady's Dream, Bowdigger's Dream,* and *Digah's Dream*) was performed "first fast and

[12] Eileen Southern, *The Music of Black Americans*, p. 344.
[13] Rudi Blesh and Harriet Janis, *They All Played Ragtime*, 4th ed. (New York: Oak Publications, 1971), p. 187.
[14] Ibid., p. 188.

James Reese Europe conducting the Hellfighters Band at an army hospital in Paris during World War I.

W. C. Handy and the band of the Teachers' Agricultural and Mechanical College, Huntsville, Alabama, 1900.

then slow-drag with blues."[15] W. C. Handy's blues circulated freely in New York, and "so many blues were being written on Twenty-eighth Street and its environs that by 1917 one of the songs to come out of the Alley was called 'Everybody's Crazy 'bout the Blues!'"[16]

Handy, being the first to write a blues composition, did, in effect, initiate a genre we have come to call the city blues, a standardized twelve-measure form sung to an instrumental accompaniment. However, his real fame lies in having popularized a portion of American folk music that had been around much longer in the rural areas of America, especially the South: the country blues. Handy did not begin his career in New York, but when he got there in 1917, there was a large group of black songwriters there already writing blues hits: Perry Bradford, Joe Jordon, Clarence Williams, Noble Sissle, and two ragtime pianists we have already mentioned, James P. Johnson and Eubie Blake. Two white New Yorkers, Irene and Vernon Castle, became the first successful dance

[15] Ibid., p. 191.
[16] Ewen, *The Life and Death of Tin Pan Alley*, p. 192 f.

team to anticipate the moods and attitudes of the jazz age. They joined Jim Europe's orchestra and, in a sense, became patrons of New York's early jazz style. Black syncopated music became fashionable in New York. White musicians there took a serious interest in learning the new styles, and two of the more successful songwriters composing blues were Irving Berlin and Gus Kahn. But the real leaders and innovators were the blacks. They felt they were playing their own music, and indeed they were. Eubie Blake had been playing professionally since around 1899 and in New York soon after the turn of the century.

> I picked up ragtime by ear. I first heard it when I was about eleven or twelve. It had no name. It just swung and made me feel good. It was my baby. Goodbye, Beethoven. . . . I didn't hear ragtime until a little later [after starting piano lessons around the age of six], but I heard syncopation in the Negro bands coming back from the funerals and, of course, in the shouting in the church. That was all right, it seems, but not at home. I'm in there ragging hell out of *Traumerei* on the organ and my mother opened the door and laid down the law, 'Take that ragtime out of my house.' That was the first time I ever heard the word.[17]

[17] Rudi Blesh, *Combo U.S.A.: Eight Lives in Jazz*, pp. 188, 190.

Vernon and Irene Castle were the first dance team to adopt the moods and attitudes of the Jazz Age.

The Midwest

When did the raggedy sounds hit Chicago? In 1893, for the World's Fair. The Chicago midway hosted the World's Columbian Exposition at that time, and the catchy, new raggedy music was present even if the name "ragtime" was not. This exposition, like the others that followed, brought Americans from every corner of the nation to view and hear the latest. The Chicago Exposition was followed by the Trans-Mississippi Exposition at Omaha, Nebraska, in 1899; the Pan-American Exposition at Buffalo, New York, in 1901; and the Louisiana Purchase Exposition at St. Louis, Missouri, in 1904. In 1897, the name appeared on the first published rags, but before then ragtime piano was called "jig piano," and the syncopated bands were called "jig bands." Jig piano, syncopated coon songs, and the stage entertainment of vaudeville and minstrel shows were current in the Midwest before the turn of the century.

The cover of Metronome Magazine in September, 1904, featured Weil's Band, playing at the St. Louis Exposition.

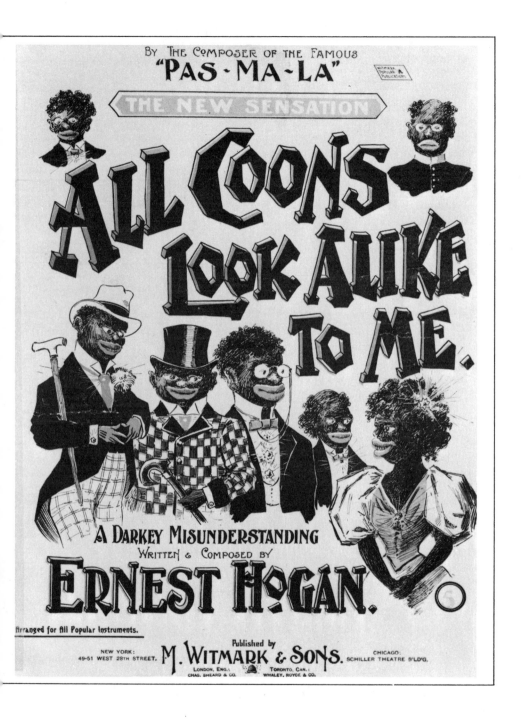

All Coons Look Alike To Me.

Words and Music by ERNEST HOGAN.

1. Talk a-bout a coon a hav-ing trou-ble, I
2. Nev-er said a word to hurt her feel-ings, I

think I have e-nough of ma own, Its all a-bout ma Lu-cy Jane-y Stubbles, And
always bou't her presents by the score, And now my brain with sorrow am a reel-ing, Cause

she has caused my heart to mourn, Thar's an-oth-er coon bar-ber from Vir-gin-ia, In so-
she won't accept them any more, If I treat-ed her wrong she may have loved me, Like

ci-'ty he's the leader of the day, And now ma hon-ey gal is gwine to quit me, Yes she's
all the rest she's gone and let me down, If I'm luck-y I'm a gwine to catch my pol-i-cy, And

Recite.

gone and drove this coon a-way, . . She'd no ex-cuse, . . To turn me loose, I've been a-
win my sweet thing way from town, For I'm wor-ried, . . Yes, I'm des-p'rate, I've been Jo-

-bused, . . I'm all con-fused, . . Cause these words she did say. . . .
-nahed, . . And I'll get dang'rous, If these words she says to me. . . .

All coons look alike to me. 4—3. M. W. & Sons.

"Two Little Piccaninies sitting on a stile."

"HONEY YOU'SE MY LADY LOVE."
BY NAT. D. MANN.
An Entirely New Style of Coon Ballad.—Dreamy and Magnetic.
TRY IT AT YOUR DEALERS.

CHORUS.

All coons look a - like to me, I've got an-oth-er beau, you see,

And he's just as good to me as you, nig! ev - er tried to be,

He spends his mon - ey free, I know we cant a-gree, So

I don't like you no how, All coons look a-like to me. me.

All coons look alike to me. 4.—4.

Without doubt the Best Pathetic Descriptive Published.

"I LOVE YOU IN THE SAME OLD WAY"

BY FORD & BRATTON.

Sung by all Leading Balladists, including R. J. Jose, the Famous Contra-Tenor.

LOOK IT OVER.

In Toledo, Ohio, the Tuxedo Club Minstrels were organized in 1897, and in their early performances their repertoire included the new ragtime hit *All Coons Look Alike to Me.* [18] This song and its brethren helped foster bigoted attitudes in America, and one puzzles over the motivations of the black songwriter, Ernest Hogan, who exploited the clichés and superstitions of white America seemingly for the sake of financial profit and fame.

> The chorus expounds what is clearly a white attitude (all black people look alike and therefore are alike, all inferior, lacking individuality or distinctive human souls); but it puts the sentiment in the mouth of a black persona. The song, then, is doubly damning, for it makes "black" people say exactly what a white racist would want them to admit:
>
> > All Coons look alike to me,
> > I've got another beau, you see,
> > And he's just as good to me
> > As you, nig! ever tried to be.
> >
> > He spends his money free,
> > I know we can't agree,
> > So I don't like you no how,
> > All Coons look alike to me.
>
> The black woman purportedly singing this satisfies complex demands of the devious racist mind. She is promiscuous, going from one "beau" to another; she is stupid (only a stupid person could not identify members of her own race); she is avaricious, looking only for a free-spender; and she says precisely what all racists want to hear, that there really are no differences between black individuals, that they lack the nobility and intelligence of real human beings. [19]

The psychology and sociology of the text of this song offer areas of investigation for longer serious studies, but for our purposes, it is representative of a large number of pieces of music in the coon song fad of the day: it is a syncopated ragtime piece that had currency in the heartland of America.

If ragtime traveled north to Chicago, Toledo, and Omaha, it certainly was well known in Missouri, the home of Scott Joplin and the seat of the early rag-

---

[18] Marion S. Revett, *A Minstrel Town* (New York: Pageant Press, 1955), p. 74. The cover of the sheet music of *All Coons Look Alike to Me,* as well as many other coon song covers, can be found in William J. Schafer and Johannes Riedel, *The Art of Ragtime* (Baton Rouge: Louisiana State University Press, 1974), pp. 170–75. Also, music excerpts from *All Coons Look Alike to Me* by Ernest Hogan are given in Southern, *Music of Black Americans,* p. 315.

[19] Schafer and Riedel, *The Art of Ragtime,* p. 26.

time publications. If ragtime, minstrel shows, gospel songs, and American band music were well known in Missouri at this time, so were the country blues. Missouri had a large black population, and George Morrison, black violinist and bandleader, reports of his early days in Fayette, Missouri:

> My father was a musician. In fact, as far back as you can trace the Morrison family, the men were all fiddlers—in those days instead of violinists they called them fiddlers. . . . they couldn't read a note—never knew what a note looked like—played everything by ear. . . . I first heard the word jazz way back around 1911. Yes, when I married, that word was coming in then.[20]

Sedalia, Missouri, the town that figured so prominently in the early history of ragtime, was a railroad center in the middle of Missouri that attracted large numbers of blacks to work in the shops and yards after the Civil War. Newly emancipated blacks were also attracted to St. Louis by the jobs provided by the riverboat trade. The levees of St. Louis and the farmland around Sedalia were populated by rural blacks, who carried their blues tradition with them.

The Southwest

Some of the men who settled in Sedalia had traveled a long way. One was the ragtime pianist Scott Joplin, who arrived in 1896 after a long, roundabout trip from his home town of Texarkana, Texas. Texas was a slave state before the war, and the work-song and blues tradition in Texas is well documented as being continuous from slave days through the 1930s. At that time, two great scholars of black music in America, John and Alan Lomax, recording in the prison camps along the Brazos River, found that the prisoners still sang the slow rhymed choral songs that had almost disappeared everywhere else in the South. Perhaps the most exciting blues singer of all was Blind Lemon Jefferson, born in a small farmhouse near Wortham, Texas, in 1897. His success eventually carried him to Chicago, where he died at the age of thirty-three. He recorded for only four years, but of the eighty-one blues left for posterity, we learn:

> It was a beautifully moving and sensitive group of blues. Many of them were direct reworkings of old field cries and work songs. He shouted the melody in a long, free rhythmic pattern, and the guitar sang behind the voice in a subtle counterpoint. Many of the songs were from the Texas prisons.[21]

[20] Gunther Schuller, *Early Jazz*, pp. 359, 362.
[21] Charters, *The Country Blues*, p. 67.

The blues tradition was strong in Texas, and Blind Lemon passed it on to Sam "Lightnin' " Hopkins, a man who has been called "perhaps the last of the great blues singers."[22] The rural country blues was present everywhere in the twenty or so years that preceded jazz recording, and if we single out Lemon Jefferson and Lightnin' Hopkins as two of the representatives from the Southwest, we must realize that these men were not isolated phenomena. The thousands of players who never left their farms, their small towns, their black "suburbs," were the main force in this style, a style that depended less on the great and famous players than on its thorough permeation and saturation of the society.

The country blues was a spontaneous music expressing a wide range of thought and mood as well as a great diversity of subject matter. Where the city or urban blues tended to concentrate on love and sex, the country blues continued to reflect the work songs, the religious pieces, and the general life and environment of the rural black. No expensive instruments or formal training was required of the country blues singer, and consequently, wherever large numbers of blacks congregated, an abundance of country blues was present in the early years of the twentieth century. In Texas and Sedalia they farmed; in New Orleans and St. Louis they worked on the levees; and the texts and the music were fluid and highly personal.

If blues was to be found in Texas, so was ragtime, for the greatest composer of all, Scott Joplin, stemmed from there. He was born in 1868 in the northeast corner of the Lone Star State, and he wandered all over Texas, Louisiana, the Mississippi Valley, and as far north as Chicago in 1893 for the World's Columbian Exposition before he returned to St. Louis and its Tenderloin district. The itinerant nature of the black musicians of this period was more typical than exceptional, and as they traveled and worked, listened and played, they created and spread a blues and ragtime culture that was omnipresent in American society.

The leading question that can be seen emerging from this introductory discussion is: "At what point in the history of American music did an identifiable sound emerge which can be classified as the new American jazz?" What portion, if any, of ragtime and blues was actually jazz, or merely its predecessor? The older histories would have us believe that jazz was laid at the doorstep of New Orleans in the form of a fully developed infant with a loud voice and keen rhythm.

The same confusion exists among students of ragtime. Scholars have identified at least three types of pianists who play ragtime: pseudo-ragtime (honky-tonk) pianists, jazz stylists, and classic ragtime pianists.[23] The distinction between ragtime and its earlier and later styles would seem to be more than aca-

---

[22] Ibid., p. 254.
[23] Schafer and Riedel, *The Art of Ragtime*, p. 176.

demic; it would seem to border on the pedantic, for the evidence in hand clearly shows that the composers, the performers, and the knowledgeable listeners of the day clearly identified all of this music as ragtime. If minstrelsy and jazz can be seen as a part of the total repertoire known as ragtime, then just as plainly it can be seen that ragtime and the blues were a part of the total repertoire we now know as jazz.

In the years before 1917 and the first jazz recording, one can see a living, dynamic music taking hold in all of the United States. Here we indeed sense the phenomenon that was the birth of jazz. It was not an isolated event that took place at a particular time in the city of New Orleans, but a widespread cultural development that was taking place over a number of years throughout the land. The strongest concentrations of improvising ensembles appear to have collected in the Delta; the major heartbeats of ragtime and jazz piano playing seem to have been felt in the metropolitan areas and entertainment centers of the East Coast, the Mississippi River, and the Great Lakes; and the blues seems to have emerged from every field and back alley where black Americans lived and worked.

The South

Most of the musical considerations that permeate the historical discussions of jazz music before 1917 are close to pure speculation, for what most people now call jazz was unrecorded in any form that can be accurately brought back to life. The best musical record of that period is the piano-roll archives, and even here we can see that the great classic ragtime composers and players, like Scott Joplin, added embellishment and did not play their music literally from the published scores, as our conservatory-trained pianists of today would do. Still, using the best evidence available, we think we can reconstruct a fairly accurate musical picture of the improvising New Orleans ensemble in the years before the Original Dixieland Jazz Band. Gunther Schuller underscores the difficulty of determining the real sound of early jazz by pointing out the many contradictions that writers and musicians face when they discuss early jazz, ragtime, novelty, minstrel, and blues. He wisely states:

> In those years of vast changes, as several musical styles coalesced into the one that finally came to be known as jazz, the only tributary source of jazz that seemed to remain constant was the blues. It is unlikely that the blues changed basically between the 1880's and the early 1920's. And one can be sure that when Bunk Johnson says that as a kid he "used to play nothin' but the blues" in New Orleans barrelhouses, he was playing essentially the same instrumental blues that spread like

wildfire in the 1920's race recordings, or—going back in time—that he had heard Buddy Bolden play in the 1890's.[24]

Who was Buddy Bolden? According to *The New Edition of the Encyclopedia of Jazz*,[25] he is the almost legendary cornet player and bandleader who is said to have been one of the first, if not the first, New Orleans musicians to play in the style subsequently called jazz. Charles "Buddy" Bolden was born in New Orleans in 1868, and died there in 1931. He was a barber by trade and sup-

[24] Schuller, *Early Jazz*, p. 64 f.
[25] Leonard Feather, p. 139.

Probably the only known picture of the legendary Buddy Bolden (standing, second from left), taken sometime before 1895. Two other members of his band are recognizable in this photograph: trombonist Willie Cornish (at Bolden's left) and clarinetist Frank Lewis (seated).

posedly led several early jazz bands. Bunk Johnson, who claims to have played with him from 1895 to 1899, is one of the chief witnesses to the existence of this musician and his music. Ostensibly, Bolden was one of the world's loudest cornet players, and the legends stretch the carrying power of his sound from one to five miles. There seems to be a certain amount of truth in this claim. Apparently, at the turn of the century, there were two amusement parks in New Orleans, Johnson and Lincoln parks. Legend has it that Buddy Bolden, when playing in Johnson Park, would stick his horn through a hole in the park fence and play a call that the people would recognize as a signal to leave Lincoln Park for Johnson Park and the entertainment of the Buddy Bolden Band.

William J. Schafer attempts to separate fact from fiction and concludes, "We have been asking 'Who was the man who first played jazz?' when we should ask 'Who were the *people* who first played jazz?' The second question can be answered in elaborate detail."[26] The members of the Bolden bands were men like Willie Warner, clarinet; Frank Lewis, clarinet; Frank Keely, valve trombone; Willie Cornish, trombone; Willie "Bunk" Johnson, cornet; Bob Lyons, bass; Albert Glenny, bass; Bebe Mitchell, bass; and Frankie Dusen, the trombone player who finally took over the band. Bolden played all over New Orleans, and, with extra musicians, he marched on the street. For funerals the band would improvise Baptist hymns like *What a Friend We Have in Jesus* and lead the people away from the cemetery to the traditional *Oh Didn't He Ramble*. They marched for Mardi Gras and for whatever occasion a little festive music was appropriate, and they marched through the red-light district so frequently that the "working girls," according to the legend, would recognize the band by their theme song, the second strain of *Sensation Rag*.[27] Heavy drinking and syphilis led to symptoms of insanity beginning around 1906, and the last job Buddy Bolden was known to have played was as a cornetist in the Allen Brass Band in the spring of 1907. He was committed to a state institution in June of 1907 and died there in 1931.

New Orleans

Two types of orchestras were at work in New Orleans at this time, "sit down" orchestras from downtown and improvising bands from uptown. This was so because New Orleans was in reality two cities in the nineteenth century:

[26] "Thoughts on Jazz Historiography: 'Buddy Bolden's Blues' versus 'Buddy Bottley's Balloon,' " p. 13.

[27] Note that rags were a part of the repertoire of an acknowledged early jazz band.

an American city west of Canal Street (uptown), and a French city east of Canal Street (downtown). The east side contained the French Opera, chamber ensembles, polished dance orchestras, and all the paraphernalia that accompanies the social and cultural values of the upper class. French New Orleans was peopled with whites, black servants, and Creoles of Color—families of mixed blood which, while not accepted socially, were successful in business and became prominent in the cultural and economic life of the section.

Uptown presented an enormous contrast, for it was populated by newly freed blacks who were poor, uneducated, and lacking in all the cultural and economic advantages available to the Creoles of Color. The musical standards of the downtown orchestras were very high, for most of these musicians were conservatory trained and played at the Opera House, and prided themselves on their ability, knowledge, propriety, and general refinement. A well-known orchestra leader, John Robichaux, hired the best musicians and took over most of the city's best jobs. In contrast, very few of the uptown musicians could read music, and until 1894 they frequently studied with their opposite numbers from across Canal Street. Then, in 1894, a restrictive racial segregation code was enacted throughout the city, which included the Creoles among those segregated. The Creoles found themselves forced to live on the other side of the tracks, and there began a very passionate struggle to maintain status in a hostile atmosphere. Where there was a tendency for black music on both sides of Canal Street to be moving toward a common polished goal before this date, there was no such attempt made after the odious law was passed. The uptown musicians reacted by playing as loudly as possible, because the Creoles prided themselves on their soft, delicate tone. Even the uptown musicians who could read music, and it was reported that Buddy Bolden had been trained in the solfeggio method of sight reading, reacted by placing emphasis on the attributes of being musically illiterate. Memorization and nascent improvisation were characteristics of the uptown bands; sight reading and correct performance were characteristic of the Creole bands.

A few years later, in 1897, the city council passed another ordinance which would have a profound effect on music in New Orleans. The city fathers legislated to move all the prostitutes from the city brothels into a thirty-eight-block area which became known as Storyville, the Crescent City's legendary red-light district. From Basin Street to Robertson Street, from Perdido Street to Gravier Street, the lines were drawn. Lewd women were not permitted to occupy any house, room, or closet outside of Storyville. At the height of its activity, there were probably between 1,500 and 2,200 registered prostitutes in Storyville, and the sporting houses employed everything from string trios to ragtime pianists and brass bands. Storyville brought black and tan musicians together, and one of the local activities was the brass bands' uptown-downtown

The main thoroughfare in New Orleans, ca. 1910.

cutting (carving) contests in the streets and at picnics. The atmosphere has been described as follows:

> The 1890's had been an especially tough period for middle class and poor people in the Crescent City. The younger Creoles of Color, whose parents had struggled for almost two generations, reached out for economic stability wherever they could find it. Storyville was there. For most, the pay was small, but anything was a gain. Young Creoles like Sidney Bechet often worked the District without their proud relatives' knowledge, because, for many Creoles of Color, playing in Storyville meant a loss of status within their own community. Jelly Roll Morton's grandmother kicked him out of the house when he was 15 for playing in Storyville. She loved music, but said people who played in such places were bums, and she didn't want him to be a bad influence on his sisters. Many of the "dark" Negroes, though, "didn't give a damn" if it was a whorehouse they were playing in. They had an opportunity to play the music the loved and get paid for doing it. [28]

Among the early bandleaders working the district, in addition to Buddy Bolden and his follower Frankie Dusen, were Joe "King" Oliver, Freddie Keppard,

[28] Jack V. Buerkle and Danny Barker, *Bourbon Street Black*, p. 20.

and, somewhat later, Manuel Perez, Pops Foster, George Baquet, and Sidney Bechet. What these musicians played and how well they played it is almost entirely speculation based on the friendly recollections of interested parties. The repertoire included polite social dances by string orchestras, instrumental blues, ragtime on the piano and in combination, and every variety of entertainment music appropriate for the patrons of a red-light district.

The influence of Storyville on New Orleans jazzmen, especially black musicians, was profound, but one should not forget that similar music was also played in the cabarets and dance halls surrounding the district, at the resort areas around Lake Ponchartrain, on the riverboats, in the French Quarter, and in the cafes and hotels scattered all over town.

At least one music historian of the period would argue that no jazz was being played anywhere before 1916,[29] but what can anyone say with certainty about an improvised music that was never recorded? The weight of the evidence leans heavily the other way, and even if Buddy Bolden was not playing jazz around 1895, some other black musician in the New Orleans area probably was.

It is less likely that the New Orleans Creole groups were playing jazz in the early days, but one technical innovation was introduced by John Robichaux in 1894 or 1895 that profoundly influenced its development. Robichaux's drummer, Dee Dee Chandler, built a crude wooden pedal for a bass drum so that he might play the bass drum with his foot and a trap drum with sticks in his hands. His invention was a sensation and was widely imitated. Chandler helped establish Robichaux's reputation as "the first man to add traps to the orchestra."

The Jazz Combo

One of the key elements in the emerging jazz ensemble was the rhythm section, a group of musicians within the larger ensemble who had a nonmelodic function in the band. Eventually, the rhythm section became standardized with three players: piano, bass, and trap drums. All of these performers had to develop the ensemble style of playing characteristic of a well-functioning rhythm section; even the piano player had to adapt the ragtime piano style to the jazz-ensemble piano style. Where the ragtime pianist is basically a self-contained unit, performing all the melodic, harmonic, and rhythmic elements of the piece, the jazz-ensemble pianist specializes in but two of these three functions: the harmonic framework and the motor-pulse rhythm. By using two

[29] H. O. Brunn, *The Story of the Original Dixieland Jazz Band* (n.p.: Louisiana State University Press, 1960), p. v.

hands to play what the ragtime pianist normally plays with his left hand alone, the ensemble pianist carries the harmonies of the piece (roots on the strong beat in the left hand and complete triads in the right hand) and the steady eighth-note pulse at the same time.[30] The steady pulse of the African rhythm ensembles to which additive rhythmic figures are superimposed by other percussion instruments has its parallel in the jazz rhythm section. The steady eighth-note pulse of the piano player supplies the common denominator for additive groupings as well as presenting a basis for syncopations by others and the strong beat–weak beat grouping of Western meters. When Dee Dee Chandler added the foot-activated bass-drum pedal and attached a trap drum to the larger bass drum, he developed a purely percussive instrument operable by one man, capable of synchronizing with the motor-pulse of the piano player (the foot pedal would strike simultaneously with the left hand of the piano) as well as adding a grouping of smaller-value rhythmic figures, some in conjunction with and some syncopated against the rhythm of the piano, through the employment of sticks operated by two hands. The speed and dexterity of sticks on a trap drum gave life, excitement, and syncopation to the early ensembles.

The bass of these early ensembles often was a brass, for the groups frequently derived from brass bands. Functionally, the bass added nothing to the music beyond what was played by the left hand of the piano, but it was louder, had a more compatible envelope of sound, and was portable. Also, early rhythm sections were not standard, and frequently a banjo or a guitar might sound in place of the piano.[31] When this happened, the left-hand function of the piano was missing totally, for although these plucked string instruments were capable of carrying the offbeat chords which the piano might have played in the right hand, they were not capable of laying down the harmonic root with power on the strong beats. Consequently, bass, banjo, and drums; or piano and drums; or bass, piano, and drums; or bass and piano; or some other similar combination was considered necessary to provide a satisfactory harmonic and rhythmic framework for the music called jazz.

The other members of the early jazz ensembles were grouped in what is familiarly called the "front line." The melodic instruments of the classic jazz band, frequently clarinet, cornet, and trombone, would often stand in front of the rhythm section, and their musical functions, different from those of the rhythm section, comprised the portion of the improvising jazz ensemble that was primarily melodic and syncopated. The function of the Dixieland trom-

[30] Quarter-note pulse in 4/4 or eighth-note pulse in 2/4. Rags were notated most frequently in 2/4.

[31] The original Superior Orchestra (c. 1908–13) with Bunk Johnson on cornet used violin, clarinet, cornet, trombone, guitar, string bass, and drums. The only photograph extant of the Bolden band reveals two clarinets, cornet, valve trombone, bass, and guitar.

bonist, however, was not as clear-cut as that of the two higher melody instruments. Frequently he was the bass of the rhythm section, and, except for an occasional rhythmic break, solo, or characteristic rhythmic trombone figure, he resembled the bass of the rhythm section. Consequently, many early jazz ensembles had trombone or bass, but not necessarily both. When both were present, the opportunity for the trombonist to be freed from his normal bass function presented itself, but the new role as harmonic filler and secondary melodic instrument took years to develop.

The trumpet or cornet was the key melodic instrument of the ensemble, and basically he played melodies in ragtime style; that is, he ragged or syncopated the tune. The clarinet was responsible for adding a high-speed, high-pitched obbligato to whatever else was going on in the ensemble. Occasionally, he would play parallel harmonies with the trumpet or cornet, but his chief function during the group-improvisation passages was to add another layer of fast-moving melodic and rhythmic groupings.

Group improvisation was facilitated by the tacit understanding among the musicians that each had a specific musical role to perform as determined by his instrument. The trumpet played "lead," the clarinet created the obbligato, and the trombone customarily played what has come to be described as the "tailgate trombone" part,[32] a melodic-harmonic line deriving from the harmonic structure of the piece but acting as a countermelody to the trumpet. The Dixieland piano reinforced the harmonic structure by playing triads on the offbeats with the right hand, while the left hand, the brass bass, and the foot of the bass drum established the two-beat ragtime rhythm by emphasizing the strong beats in 2/4 time. The hands of the drummer were free to use sticks on a variety of percussion instruments in a free and ornamental manner. The Dixieland band's repertoire was heterogeneous, for anything could be molded into its style by the improvising musicians.

Early Jazzmen and Their Music

Among the early great musicians who played authentic jazz before the 1920s were King Oliver, Freddie Keppard, Louis Armstrong, Jelly Roll Morton, Sidney Bechet, and, of course, Buddy Bolden. Also, some groups that did

[32] "Tailgate trombone," or New Orleans–style trombone playing, is said to derive its name from the customary location of the trombonist on a horse-drawn parade cart. Because of the freedom of movement necessary to operate a trombone slide, the open tailgate was the favored seat of most trombonists.

not use a leader's name for identification were probably playing the new improvised music at an early date. The Excelsior Brass Band, a group of ten to twelve pieces organized before 1885 and active until 1931; the Onward Brass Band, a group of the same size, organized before 1889 and active until about 1925; the Alliance Brass Band; the Big Four String Band; the Excelsior String Band; and many other novelty groups and orchestras were active at this time.

An important trumpet player who seemed to function as the transition between Buddy Bolden and Louis Armstrong was Joseph "King" Oliver. Born in 1885, he was but a young man when he first played in the Melrose Brass Band in 1907. Oliver worked with several brass bands before leaving New Orleans, among them the Olympia Band under A. J. Piron, the Eagle Brass Band, the Onward Brass Band, and the Magnolia Brass Band. He also played with trombonist Kid Ory's group and, in 1915, led his own band with Sidney Bechet on clarinet as a sideman. Exactly what and how these musicians played at that time is anyone's guess, but as Martin Williams points out:

> There seems greater emotional range and depth in [Dixieland] jazz [than in normal Ragtime] (an infusion of the feeling of the blues is the answer here). It also seems different, more varied, rhythmically. It *is*—and that is why the layman had to get a new name for it. *Jazz* became that name.[33]

When King Oliver recorded with his Creole Jazz Band in Chicago in the 1920s, he brought New Orleans musicians with him. Perhaps the music played then was considerably different from what went before, but the most likely possibility seems to be that his recordings closely approximate original Dixieland jazz, and are, therefore, the most authentic classic jazz recordings we have available to us today.

What are the characteristics of King Oliver's *Dippermouth Blues*, which he recorded in Chicago in June, 1923, with Louis Armstrong as second cornet, Johnny Dodds on clarinet, Honoré Dutrey on trombone, Lil Hardin (later to become Mrs. Louis Armstrong) on piano, Bud Scott on banjo, and Baby Dodds (the brother of Johnny Dodds) on drums (*SCCJ*, I/6)? What is there about this recording that is most likely to convey a real sense of New Orleans Dixieland music? Before we analyze this piece, let's examine some of the problems that stand in the way of a totally accurate reconstruction.

When ethnomusicologists make field records of non-Western music, they assume the music they are hearing is historically correct if the tradition was passed down from master to apprentice and if other musical influences do not

---

[33] Liner notes to *The Smithsonian Collection of Classic Jazz*, selected and annotated by Martin Williams (Washington, D.C.: The Smithsonian Institute, 1973), p. 5 f. Henceforth, the abbreviation *SCCJ* will be used to designate this work. In references to side and band numbers, side 1, band 6, for example, will be abbreviated I/6.

Joseph "King" Oliver's Dixie Syncopators, Plantation Cafe, Chicago, 1925. (Front row, left to right) Bud Scott, banjo; Darnell Howard, Albert Nicholas, and Barney Bigard, reeds. (Back row, left to right) Bert Cobbs, bass; Paul Barbarin, drums; King Oliver, cornet; George Field, trombone; Bob Schoffner, trumpet; Luis Russell, piano.

seem to have affected the culture. In other words, a recent recording of an unchanged musical tradition probably represents, fairly well, what might have been recorded years earlier had such recording equipment been available. In early jazz, the only valid comparison is the guild-system method of training musicians. If the master Buddy Bolden passed his skills on to apprentice Joe Oliver, and if Joe "King" Oliver passed his skills on to apprentice Louis Armstrong, then supposedly what the mature Louis Armstrong played would represent, with a fair degree of accuracy, the music Buddy Bolden played, in an unchanging tradition.

The guild system was present, but the tradition was not. Jazz was not only evolving at this time, it was changing rapidly. Indeed, it had no history. Edmond Souchon, M.D., acts as an interested and educated informant with regard to this question. Born in New Orleans, Souchon first heard Joe Oliver play around 1901–02, when the future doctor was four or five, and the musician was sixteen or seventeen. From approximately 1907 through 1917, Dr. Souchon listened to Joe Oliver play fairly regularly. He picked up on him again in 1924 in Chicago, when Joe had acquired the title "King" and was leading the Creole Jazz Band. At this time, Souchon reports, "He was now 'King,' the most important personage in the jazz world, surrounded by his own hand-picked galaxy of sidemen." Souchon claims that even before Oliver left for Chicago "he had acquired a technique that was much more smooth, and that his band was adapting itself to the white dances more and more." Souchon continues, "By the time Oliver had reached Chicago and the peak of his popularity, his sound was not the same. It was a different band, a different and more polished Oliver, an Oliver who had completely lost his New Orleans sound."[34] We have no way of measuring the accuracy of Dr. Souchon's statements, but he was an interested participant, a member of the jazz community of both New Orleans and Chicago.

If Souchon's observations are correct, and Oliver's sound in Chicago was a distortion of the New Orleans jazz-ensemble sound, then see how much further the evidence is distorted by the poor recording techniques of the early 1920s. Larry Gushee, when reviewing a recent remastering of the April 1923, recordings of the Creole Jazz Band (Riverside, RLP 12-122), comments on the uncertainty of determining the real sound of the band, explaining that some of the reissue sides must have been "cut in marshmallow—with Johnny Dodds crouched inside the recording horn." To his ear, good reproduction shows that the "clarinet is toned down, cornets are strong, with the second part actually being heard, the piano chording does not run together in an amorphous droning, and the bass line is generally clearer."[35]

[34] Edmond Souchon, "King Oliver: A Very Personal Memoir," pp. 27, 28, 29.
[35] Larry Gushee, "King Oliver," *Jazz Panorama*, ed. Martin Williams (New York: Collier, 1964) p. 40.

If the original recording distorted an already changed sound, then our newly mastered track of the June, 1923, recording of the same piece piles insult upon abuse. The original performance in 1923 was played in the key of B♭ ; our new 33⅓ rpm disc reproduces the piece in the key of B♮. How significant is this change? The same reviewer makes the following observation about tempo in New Orleans style:

> Whether the tempos, so often felicitous, were Joe Oliver's independent choice, or determined by prevailing dance style, I cannot know. The fact remains that the Creole Band (and the New Orleans Rhythm Kings) played a good deal slower than bands like the Wolverines and the Bucktown 5, which recorded only a year later. The tempos they chose never exceeded their technical limitations, while, for instance, the Wolverines and, especially, the later Chicagoans often played too fast for comfort (theirs and ours). I am sure that this accounts for much of the superb swing of the Creole Band.[36]

John Mehegan stresses the critical nature of tempo in the total mixture of jazz: "[T]empo in jazz has always been a primary consideration for the performer in choosing the pulsation best suited for 'swing' and urgency."[37] He then goes on to chart tempo differences between New Orleans groups and Chicago groups, saying that the former work with a quarter-note span of 104–248 per minute, the average being 166.7; Chicago groups span 108–264 per minute, for an average pulse of 179. This seemingly innocent mistake at the rerecording level has completely transformed one of the most important stylistic elements of New Orleans jazz, tempo. The original performance in B♭ moved at 186 beats per minute; fast enough! The "new" performance travels at 200 beats per minute!

To a certain extent, the relative tempos of New Orleans and Chicago groups is based on intuition, for all the recorded music of the early New Orleans groups was made in Chicago while the musicians worked regularly for a Chicago audience. We have no accurate way of proving that Chicago jazz was indeed faster than New Orleans jazz; the observation is logical and probable, but not conclusive. The purpose of these introductory remarks is not to prove one case or the other, but to show how little we know with certainty about classic New Orleans jazz.

The next step in our "scientific" investigation will be to see how much we can actually discover about the music preserved for us on the 1923 recordings. Using the modern master (*SCCJ*, I/6) as our original source, what can we actually hear the individual musicians doing? If we slow the recording down to a key of B♭ with a 440A (it is probable that the A of the 1920s was closer to 435

[36] Ibid., p. 41.
[37] *Jazz Improvisation*, vol. 2 (New York: Watson-Guptill, 1962), p. 22 ff.

vibrations per second), we can listen to the work of Baby Dodds on drums. He is virtually inaudible except for the stoptime chorus, when the tone of a wood block cuts through the timbre of the percussive chords. At times, one can imagine that he is playing the trap drum on beats 2, 3, and 4, or beats 2 and 4, but this sound blends so well with the attack of the banjo and piano that the ear cannot be certain whether this is, in fact, what Baby Dodds was playing. The sound of the bass drum is not heard. The fact of the matter is that Baby Dodds

Warren "Baby" Dodds (1892–1940).

was probably not playing any instrument except wood blocks at this recording session. The powerful sounds of a trap drummer could not be accommodated by the recording instruments of the time. W. C. Handy describes his first recording session in 1917 as follows:

> Our clarinetist sat in the corner on a six-foot stool and played into a megaphone near the ceiling. There were stools of varying heights for the other players. The three violinists stood directly in front of the recording apparatus and played into megaphones there. The saxophonists were seated on the side and played into their own megaphones. Cornet and trombone played into one in the rear. The cellist oc-

cupied another corner and another megaphone. But the poor drummer was a dead goose where the record was concerned. While they played as hard as ever in life, the drums and basses could not be recorded in those days. All megaphones emptied into one recording horn. . . .

To my way of thinking the records were not up to scratch.[38]

In live performance, Baby Dodds played differently from the way he did in the studio, for the trap drummer is almost omnipresent in a jazz group.

Little definition exists between the sounds of piano and banjo. Lil Hardin's left hand makes little impression, and the four-beat strumming of banjo melts with the right-hand chording of the piano. Likewise, Louis Armstrong's second cornet playing in ensemble can be identified only by the connoisseur-specialist. What remains of the earliest recordings of a genuine New Orleans black jazz ensemble are the melodies of the principal three of the front line: clarinet, cornet, and trombone. We have already been told by a great connoisseur of King Oliver, Edmond Souchon, that the Chicago sound of King Oliver had already changed from the New Orleans sound he heard as a young man, and our simple observations of this one recording help confirm his conclusion that "those records even miss conveying the way that Oliver was playing in Chicago when I heard him."[39]

So what was jazz like in New Orleans in the years before the first jazz recordings? We simply don't know. The best we can do is recall the names, look at the photographs, interview the old-timers, and make an educated guess. As one thoughtful commentator has observed:

Because jazz lacks a supreme master and written masterpieces, the study of jazz differs from the study of concert music. The chief documents of its history are the performances on phonograph records, which were very rare before 1923, and nonexistent before 1917. How the style arose and what it was really like before many examples of it were recorded we can never know as surely and thoroughly as we might wish. Hence, legends are rife, and opinions differ. Opinions and even legends based on personal recollections are invaluable, although of course they need to be critically compared with each other and with all other evidence.[40]

The characteristics of jazz before the name "jazz" emerged that seem to inspire general agreement are these: Jazz was the music played by people like Louis Armstrong, Lil Hardin, King Oliver, Buddy Bolden, Nick LaRocca, Jelly Roll Morton, Kid Ory, Honoré Dutrey, Johnny Dodds, Baby Dodds, and Jimmy Noone, and sung by women like Ma Rainey and Bessie Smith. It is possible that the music played by pianists such as Scott Joplin and Eubie Blake

---

[38] W. C. Handy, *Father of the Blues: An Autobiography*, p. 173 f.
[39] Souchon, "King Oliver," p. 30.
[40] William Austin, *Music in the 20 Century*, p. 182.

should also be included, as well as the music of thousands of others who played or sang ragtime, blues, novelty, jazz, and so on. The most common instrumental groups had a front line of clarinet, cornet, and trombone and a back line of rhythm section which included piano, drums, bass, and banjo, all together or in any combination.

The rhythm of the New Orleans group, like that of most jazz styles to follow, operated on three levels of time: the quarter-note pulse, the half-note harmonic unit, and the eighth-note melodic or ornamental unit. New Orleans tempos were probably slower than those commonly used by the groups recording in Chicago and New York in the later years, and it would seem that the volume level of New Orleans groups was far in excess of that used elsewhere. The improvised polyphony of the front line consisted of ornamentation, obbligato playing, and countermelody invention. The lead cornet would rag an identifiable melody, and would superimpose a rhythmic configuration upon the basic structure laid down by the rhythm section of quarter notes syncopated by the addition of eighth-note values. The clarinet obbligato moved primarily at eighth-note speeds or faster, and the trombone moved at the slow half-note or whole-note harmonic-rhythm speed. However, when the trombone played countermelodies, it moved at approximately the same speed as the lead cornet. When the lead cornet broke the melody at the end of a phrase to take a breath, the trombone or clarinet picked up the slack with an improvised "fill," and this is a procedure that most writers on early jazz like to compare with the call-and-response patterns of African tribal music. The bass drum and piano would usually play a nondifferentiated 4/4 pulse, while the piano and snare drum, sometimes aided by a bass instrument such as the tuba, would tend to superimpose a 2/4 structure over the continuous 4/4 pulse. Blues form, ragtime forms, and popular-song form were all employed, and we will investigate these as we analyze other specific pieces of music.

New Orleans jazz was very closely tied to social functions in that it provided music for funerals, weddings, dances, and as background in the whorehouses. As we shall observe in subsequent recorded examples, classic jazz employed the diatonic system of harmony, and kept triadic extensions limited to the minor seventh. Some claim that dominant preparation in the New Orleans style was restricted to a secondary dominant constructed by altering the natural triad built on the second scale step. Without any music surviving from the period, this seems to be a bit presumptive. It is possible that New Orleans jazz limited the trombone to a purely harmonic role, and it is thought by some that the evolution to a melodic-harmonic function took place during the Chicago period. In addition to the regular use of the instruments, the New Orleans jazz musicians employed mutes of various kinds for the brass, and they altered the attacks, vibratos, and regular pitches by lipping, half-holing, and sliding.

Kansas City Stomp (1928)

Stoptime and the New Orleans stomp are two common rhythmic character-istics. They differ in that stoptime produces homophony, while stomp patterns are polyphonic. These are characteristics the classic-jazz buff looks for in the New Orleans jazz performances. Stomping, the process of taking a rhythmic figure, placing it into a melodic line, and repeating it in an ostinato or riff pat-tern, leads to a polyphonic accentuation that produces strong rhythmic momentum within the improvising polyphony. Rudi Blesh explains the process thus:

> The stomp pattern, which forces the melody into a rhythmic design, derives indirectly from the polyrhythmic drum patterns of West Africa; these were transmitted through the functional figures of the work-songs and play patterns of the children's songs, then revived in guitar and banjo strumming. . . .
>
> In stomping [by a jazz band], the regular beat or pulse is maintained by the full rhythm section. The lead, one or two cornets or trumpets, plays the melody fitted into the stomp pattern. The clarinet plays a free melody of many notes around the lead, placing the accents to correspond with the stomp pattern.[41]

The early jazz of New Orleans and elsewhere was probably primitive in the sense that virtuoso solo playing had not been developed. Here, however, there are conflicting reports, and one cannot tell whether the big names of New Orleans were great soloists in the early days or not. At any rate, New Orleans mothered the infant music until 1917. Then, the Navy stepped in and closed Storyville:

> Early in August [1917], Secretary of War Newton D. Baker issued an order forbidding open prostitution within five miles of an army cantonment, and a similar ruling was made by Josephus Daniels, Secretary of the Navy, respecting naval establishments . . . on September 24, and again on October 1, [1917] he [Mayor Martin Behrman] was notified by Secretary Daniels that unless the red-light district was closed by the city it would be closed by the Army and the Navy. . . . after midnight of November 12, 1917, it would be unlawful to operate a brothel or assignation house anywhere in New Orleans.
>
> The exodus from Storyville had begun two weeks before November 12. . . . As late as midnight of the 12th, there was a stream of harlots and their servants, laden with property, leaving the segregated area. . . . The next day [November 15] many leading churchwomen, and members of the Louisiana Federation of Women's Clubs, held a meeting and appointed a committee to help the prostitutes. But none applied for succor. Few, in fact, needed it. They had simply moved from Storyville into various business and residential sections of New Orleans and were doing very well.[42]

The great patron of jazz in New Orleans went out of business, and as a result, black musicians began to look for work elsewhere. Some went to New York, some went to Chicago, and some stayed home. But jazz would have

---

[41] Blesh, *Shining Trumpets*, p. 188 f.

[42] Herbert Asbury, *The French Quarter* (New York, 1936), quoted in Blesh, *Shining Trumpets*, p. 202 f.

spread like wildfire whether Storyville closed or not. Nick LaRocca's Original Dixieland Jazz Band, which had been playing in New Orleans under various names from 1908 on, was about to record in New York. Subsequently, Victor released a sales catalog of new recordings on March 17, 1917, and on the front cover it advertised the world's first jazz phonograph record:

The Original Dixieland Jass Band

Spell it Jass, Jas, Jaz, or Jazz—nothing can spoil a jass band. Some say the jass band originated in Chicago. Chicago says it comes from San Francisco—San Francisco being a way off across the continent. Anyway, a jass band is the newest thing in the cabarets, adding greatly to the hilarity thereof.

They say the first instrument of the first jass band was an empty lard can, by humming into which, sounds were produced resembling those of saxophone with the croup. Since then the jass band has grown in size and ferocity.[43]

[43] Brunn, *Story of the Original Dixieland Jazz Band,* fourth unnumbered illustration after p. 92.

RAGTIME

RAGTIME WAS THE first black music ever to achieve widespread popularity and commercial distribution. It not only profoundly affected American music, but it had a world-wide influence on classical composers even while it was still in its own infancy. Charles Ives composed a ragtime dance and thirteen ragtime pieces for theater orchestra between 1902 and 1904; Claude Debussy composed *Golliwog's Cakewalk* as part of his *Children's Corner Suite* during the years 1906 to 1908; and the list of major composers who listened to ragtime and composed music either in the style or incorporating elements of the style include Erik Satie, Igor Stravinsky, Darius Milhaud, Arthur Honegger, and Paul Hindemith.

During the years 1895–1915, ragtime was available to the public in published piano scores, on piano rolls, and in live performance by resident and itinerant ragtime pianists. Also, classic ragtime—"which may be defined very simply as the piano rags of Scott Joplin, James Scott, Joseph Lamb, and their immediate collaborators, students, and followers"[1]—was adapted for use by instrumental ensembles, minstrel companies, and vaudeville groups, and the names of Tom Turpin and Scott Joplin, as well as many others, became household words in America.

The piano was the principal performing instrument of ragtime, but the style, since it was also suitable for other combinations, was frequently adopted by brass bands, solo banjo, and vocal solo with accompaniment. The chief stylistic characteristics of this music are its duple meter (2/4 or 4/4, but almost invari-

[1] William J. Schafer and Johannes Riedel, *The Art of Ragtime*, p. 49.

ably written in the former); functional diatonic harmony stressing tonic, dominant, subdominant, and applied dominants in a major tonality; compounded
song-form structures with 16- or 32-measure periods and shorter introductions,
vamps,[2] and codas; a syncopated treble melody which operates in opposition to
a harmonic and nonsyncopated bass line; and a bass line that moves approximately at half the speed of the melody. The chief ragtime syncopations occur
on the second and fourth eighth notes in a 4/4 measure (second and fourth sixteenth notes in a 2/4 measure), while accented melody notes often, but not
always, reinforce beats three and four (fifth and seventh eighth notes in a 4/4
measure).

Ragtime Characteristics

a. **Meter**   [occasionally]   [very rarely]

b. **Harmony: Common Progressions**

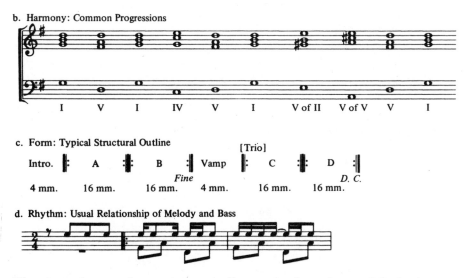

Thus it can be seen that ragtime typically contained two layers of rhythmic activity, a fast-moving treble melody which strongly cross-accents the regularly
accented progression of the bass.

Ragtime, when played by solo piano, would normally call for the pianist's

---

[2] A short, connecting passage, usually four or eight measures long, connecting two sections of
music which lie at different harmonic levels by modulating (changing key). Sometimes no modulation takes place and a simple chord pattern is repeated as a "filler" between sections.

left hand to "stride" up and down; that is, he would use the left hand in a downbeat-upbeat manner (an oom-pah, oom-pah rhythm) in which beats one and three (in 4/4) were heavily accented single notes, octaves, or tenths, and beats two and four were unaccented triads. The characteristic syncopated melodies of the right hand would have rhythmic figures like the following:

Rhythms of Melodic Motives

a. Charles Hunter, *Tickled to Death Ragtime March* (1899), mm. 17-18

b. Scott Joplin, *Maple Leaf Rag* (1899), mm. 1-2

c. James Scott, *Frog Legs Rag* (1906), mm. 1-2

d. Joseph F. Lamb, *American Beauty Rag* (1913), mm. 1-4

The ragtime pianist's touch was percussive, and it seems that the pedal was used very sparingly, even for legato effects.[3] Occasionally, the feet (or foot) would be called upon to add a rhythmic effect to the performance of the work. Scott Joplin, in the introduction to his *Stoptime Rag* (1910), advises the performer that "to get the desired effect of 'Stoptime' the pianist should stamp the heel of one foot heavily upon the floor, wherever the word 'Stamp' appears in the music."[4] Strangely enough, the indication is to stamp twice in each measure, once on each beat of the piece in 2/4 time. Although the foot-stomp instruction is rare in the works of this composer,[5] many of his rags begin with the warning "Do not play this piece fast. It is never right to play 'Ragtime' fast."

[3] In most published ragtime compositions there are no pedal indications, but in a few by Joplin, such as *Eugenia*, he does indicate pedaling. However, its employment in this piece is sparse, and there are passages with a legato indication notated in which the pedal is not used.

[4] Scott Joplin, *The Collected Works of Scott Joplin*, ed. Vera Brodsky Lawrence, I, p. 215 ff.

[5] In the composition *The Ragtime Dance* (1905), which has the subtitle *A Stoptime Two-Step*, he gives a stamp instruction as before, but adds to it, "Do not raise the toe from the floor while stamping." And here there is one variation from stamping only on the beat, and it comes in the third measure of the trio.

While syncopation is the chief characteristic of ragtime melodies, these syncopes were usually placed in simple proportion to the beat (usually a ratio of 2 : 1). Rhythms of more complex proportions, although they do occur, are exceptional. These configurations tend to appear in the music of the later ragtime performers, such as Jelly Roll Morton and James P. Johnson, whom some would view as transitional figures from ragtime to jazz. However, it has been pointed out that first-hand experience with the performances of ragtime pianists of recent vintage—e.g. Willie "The Lion" Smith (1897–1973)—"suggests that, as with most dance music of any era, the rags in print tend to be a simplified form of the music as performed."[6]

The first composition entitled "rag" was not published until January 27, 1897, when there was a publisher's race to copyright ragtime pieces.[7] William H. Krell, a successful Chicago bandleader who toured through the Mississippi area, won the honor of being the very first composer to publish a ragtime composition, *The Mississippi Rag*. It was followed three days later by Warren Beebe's *Ragtime March*, and the next month by R. J. Hamilton's *Ragtime Patrol*. Others followed throughout the year, and on December 17, 1897, the first rag by a black composer was copyrighted: Tom Turpin's *Harlem Rag*.

The word "rag" seems to have come from black clog dancing, which they called "ragging." The division of the melody into syncopated patterns is traceable to patting juba, a procedure which produces dance music by clapping hands, stamping feet, and slapping thighs. Fred Stone published a song called *Ma Ragtime Baby* in 1893, and, interestingly enough, *Turkey in the Straw* (1896) was subtitled *Ragtime Fantasie*. However, most critics would term these compositions primitive ragtime, because they lack the characteristic syncopations in the melody. It becomes quite clear that ragtime must have been widespread in the early 1890s, for if in a single year so many white composers could have published composed music in ragtime style, the music, by whatever name it was called, had to be present in abundance.

Piano Rags

The big three of the classic ragtime world are Scott Joplin (1868–1917) and his two disciples, James Scott (1886–1938) and Joseph Lamb (1887–1960), the latter a white ragtime composer who most closely approximates the clas-

---

[6] H. Wiley Hitchcock, *Music in the United States: A Historical Introduction*, p. 123.

[7] Rudi Blesh and Harriet Janis, *They All Played Ragtime*, p. 100.

sicism of Scott Joplin. During the heyday of ragtime, many lesser names composed and published excellent rags, among them the black composers Tom Turpin, Louis Chauvin (1883–1908), Arthur Marshall (1881–1956), and Scott Hayden (1882–1915); and the white composers Charles Hunter (1878–1907) and Charles Johnson (1876–1950).

Thomas Million Turpin (c. 1873–1922) was born in Savannah, Georgia, and raised in St. Louis, Missouri, where he worked in his father's saloon as a boy. Turpin was a big man, over six feet tall, and, in his later years, about 300 pounds in weight. He was a self-taught pianist, and after an excursion to the Nevada gold mines around 1890, he eventually returned to St. Louis where, with his brother, he opened his own saloon, The Rosebud, at 2220 Market Street, in the Tenderloin. His saloon became a ragtime center, and it was at The Rosebud that he wrote his music. His *Harlem Rag*, the first published black rag, had a catchy tune, characteristic syncopations, and a relative simplicity that made it performable by less than professional talent.

Harlem Rag (1897; arr. by D. S. DeLisle)

Turpin's first work follows an **ABA** song form where the sixteen-measure **A** section in the key of C is comprised of an eight-measure antecedent-consequent phrase, repeated. The **B** section is divided in three, each subsection being thirty-two measures long. Consequently the bulk of the piece, in the key of G, seems to be framed by two shorter sections in the key of C. In each of the three subsections of the middle, Turpin composes but one eight-measure theme for each. Then he invariably uses the same developmental pattern: the theme is repeated, and after, that entire sixteen-measure section undergoes a written repeat where the melody is ragged with more syncopation and is thickened by a fuller chording in the right hand. In the last of these middle sections, Turpin slows the rhythm of the right hand to equal that of the left. The characteristic layer effect of ragtime is absent here. However, this passage effectively closes off the section in G and sets up the return to the key of C. He employs no introductions or vamps, but each section begins smoothly from the last.[8]

---

[8] The music of Tom Turpin and others is available in *Classic Piano Rags*, selected by Rudi Blesh.

His published music displays many characteristics one might expect in the work of a self-trained musician: simple forms, simple keys, regular phrase structure, and uncomplicated harmonies. This is certainly true of *Bowery Buck* (1899), *Rag-Time Nightmare* (1900), and *St. Louis Rag* (1903). All three are in the key of C, the first having an **ABC** structure with thirty-two measures in each section, and each section formed from an eight-measure phrase, repeated. *Rag-Time Nightmare* is a little different, for it has a four-measure introduction with an **ABCB** form and employs four-measure phrases in the **C** section. But still, simplicity can be seen as the chief hallmark. All of Turpin's works have a naive charm which emanates both from the characteristic rags and an innate melodic skill. The *St. Louis Rag* is slightly more complex, for the piece, whose form may be outlined as Intro-**ABA,** moves to the subdominant key, F, in the **B** section. But this is no great musical surprise.

However, in Turpin's last published rag, *Buffalo Rag* (1904), a new harmonic activity is displayed. It is generally acknowledged that the profusion of new ideas that appear in this later rag was partially the result of Turpin's association with Scott Joplin in St. Louis. In the introduction, we can see a rapid modulation of barbershop harmonies and the employment of a diminished chord in the first full measure, a vertical structure common in this piece but unusual in his earlier efforts.

The cover of Tom Turpin's *Harlem Rag.*

Buffalo Rag

In the introduction we can see a harmonic progression which changes chords on every beat: F $G^{\sharp\ \text{dim}}$ F_4^6 $D^7 G^7 C^7$ F; in the first eight-measure phrase there is a similar rapid progression, and in the fourth measure of the first phrase, a particularly rich vertical sound, the superimposition of a $G^{\sharp\ \text{dim7}}$ over a D-minor triad on the second beat. The rattle of $G^{\sharp}$ –A–B was not at all unusual for symphonic composers of this period, but for Turpin this piece marks a high point of harmonic sophistication. Tom Turpin, his music, and his St. Louis establishment provided both an influence and an impetus for all Midwestern ragtime composers.

Scott Joplin was born on November 24, 1868, in Texarkana, Texas, and was raised in a musical atmosphere. His father, an ex-slave, played the violin; his mother sang and played the banjo; his brothers played the guitar, sang, and composed. Joplin's first instruments were the guitar and bugle, and when an eight-year-old, he became fascinated with a neighbor's piano. He was improvising well enough by the age of eleven to impress the local music teacher, and he received free lessons in piano, sight reading, and harmony. When his mother died (Joplin was fourteen at the time), his father tried to force him to learn a trade, so Joplin left home in 1882. He traveled throughout the Mississippi Valley in these very formative years, and it is generally assumed that the music he came in contact with during his peregrinations served as a source of melodic and rhythmic inspiration. He arrived in the St. Louis–Sedalia area in 1885 and worked with other ragtime pioneers like Tom Turpin, Arthur Marshall, and Louis Chauvin. The first pieces Joplin published were songs, *A Picture of Her Face* and *Please Say You Will*, in 1895, and he published his first ragtime piece, *Original Rags*, in 1899. Earlier, in 1893, Joplin formed a small orchestra and, doubling on piano and cornet, he went to the World's Columbian Ex-

Scott Joplin (1868–1917).

position in Chicago. Pianists from all over the central United States gathered on the midway as well as in the Chicago red-light district, and a comparison of styles and ideas took place both informally and in the many ragtime contests. This was the first time the general public had an opportunity to hear the new ragtime music.

He returned to St. Louis and Sedalia to play and later publish. In the same year that *Original Rags* appeared, 1899, he published his most famous work, *The Maple Leaf Rag*, a composition that sold hundreds of thousands of copies and allowed him to free himself from the duties of a honky-tonk pianist. Between 1895 and 1917, Joplin wrote fifty-three pieces for piano, including six instructional exercises for teaching ragtime, as well as ten songs, a ragtime ballet, and two operas. Joplin was not interested in haphazard ragtime improvisation. His dream was to develop a classic ragtime that would compare with serious European music and would be used in the larger, traditional forms such as operas and symphonies. In 1902 he composed a twenty-minute work, the *Ragtime Dance*, a ballet based on black social dances of the time with added narration. In it there are a clean-up dance, jennie cooler dance, slow drag, World's Fair, buckstep prance, dude's walk, Sedalia walk, town talk, and stop-time dance. Partly because of its length, this composition did not sell well and was a major disappointment to the composer. John Stark was Joplin's publisher, and although the success of *Maple Leaf Rag* set him up in the printing business, he could not afford to publish compositions that did not sell. Consequently, after the financial disaster of *Ragtime Dance*, Stark refused to publish Joplin's first opera, *A Guest of Honor*, when it was finished in 1903. It was performed once in St. Louis, and although a card dated February 18, 1903, is on file in the copyright office in Washington, no copy can be found.

Joplin's rags used many meters: 2/4, 4/4, 6/8, and 3/4. Although there is much variety in his works, most rags have four themes of sixteen measures, each repeated, with an introduction and a modulatory passage before the third theme. Sometimes the first theme is repeated before the third, and this form is the same as that standardized by the march composers of the time. Except for the fact that it lacks an introduction, *The Maple Leaf Rag* exactly parallels march form: first strain (16 measures, repeated), second strain (16 measures, repeated), first strain again, trio or third strain (16 measures, repeated) in the subdominant, and a fourth strain (16 measures, repeated) in the tonic. Joplin's trios are usually in the subdominant, although he sometimes uses a contrasting minor theme or a more remote key.

In 1906 Joplin moved from St. Louis to Chicago and then to New York, where his publisher, John Stark, had relocated. In 1907 he went on a series of vaudeville tours, and in 1909 he settled in New York to devote himself to teaching and composition. He began writing his opera, *Treemonisha*, at this time. The socially oriented plot tells the story of Treemonisha, a black baby, who was found under a tree by a childless couple. They raised her and provided an education. Treemonisha is made to fight superstition, black conjurers, voodoo magic, and a murder plot. She becomes a leader of her people and begins to show them the way to freedom and equality through education. Joplin spent more than ten years of his life on this work and began seeking a publisher as early as 1908. John Stark refused the opera, and Joplin finally financed publication himself in 1911. The three-act opera was written for eleven voices and piano accompaniment; it contains twenty-seven complete musical numbers, including an overture and a prelude to Act III. He could find no sponsors for a performance and finally undertook the project himself, rehearsing the cast and playing the piano. There was one performance in 1915 without scenery, and the middle-class black audience, which resented the reminder of their not-too-distant past, was less than receptive. Joplin became depressed, and it was not long before he began to lose his physical coordination as well as his mental faculties. In 1916, gravely ill with "dementia paralytica cerebral" caused by syphilis, he was committed to the Manhattan State Hospital on Ward's Island, where he died on April 1, 1917.[9] Scott Joplin is generally acknowledged as the consummate genius of ragtime. "He was the central figure and prime creative spirit of ragtime, a composer from whom a large segment of twentieth-century American music derived its shape and spirit."[10]

[9] Rudi Blesh, "Scott Joplin: Black-American Classicist," in *The Collected Works of Scott Joplin*, I, p. xxxix.
[10] Ibid., p. xiii.

The rags of Scott Joplin are meant to be reproduced from the score with accuracy and metrical precision. A significant factor in his life and philosophy was his musical training. Unlike the pioneers of the country blues and many of his contemporary honky-tonk piano players, Joplin had a thorough musical education, at least as thorough as was available for black musicians at that time in American history. His first formal instruction in Texarkana, Texas, was with a German music teacher who included harmony, in the traditional European sense, as part of Joplin's piano instruction. He also, apparently, spoke about opera and other traditional large forms and impressed the youthful Joplin with the significance of concepts like tradition, composition, masterpieces, and large-scale works. When Joplin moved to Sedalia, he attended George Smith College for Negroes and took advanced courses in harmony and composition, which provided the necessary technical facility to allow him eventually to notate the syncopations that seemingly had proved to be elusive to others interested in scoring the new music. Certainly his education was a decisive factor in establishing a framework for classic ragtime, a composed music to be played under exacting performance standards.

Joplin's preoccupation with classical music is most clearly seen in his systematic attention to matters of balanced form employing closely related keys, for example:

Maple Leaf Rag	**AA BB A CC DD**	with A, B, and D in the tonic, and C in the subdominant
Original Rags	**I AA BB CC V A DD EE***	with A, B, and E in the tonic, C in the subdominant, and D in the dominant
The Easy Winners	**I AA BB A V CC DD**	with A and B in the tonic, and C and D in the subdominant
Peacherine Rag	**I AA BB A CC DD**	with A in the tonic, B in the dominant, and C and D in the subdominant
The Chrysanthemum	**I AA BB A CC DD C**	with A in the tonic, B in the dominant, and C and D in the subdominant
Reflection Rag	**I AA BB CC DD EE**	with A, B, and C in the tonic, and D and E in the subdominant

---

* In formal schemes, **I** represents an introduction and **V** a vamp.

Joplin displays great talent in his melodic invention, for beneath the broken, arpeggiated, and ragged sounds, a catchy tune resides. In graceful patterns up and down, Joplin's melodies tend to follow the classic antecedent-consequent phrase pattern in which an eight-measure melody is broken into two related halves. The first is similar to the second but leaves the listener at a point where, musically, the melody cannot end; the second half takes up the material from the former but closes out the phrase comfortably. If Joplin's classic rag has typically four "tunes," the opening phrase of each is played at least four times, providing a musical experience that is easily remembered by the most unsophisticated listener.

Although it is Scott Joplin's classic rags that earned him lasting popularity, they have a significant shortcoming that would have prevented him from achieving the kind of stature as a composer to which he aspired: an absence of developmental passages. Within the confines of eight-measure phrases and sixteen-measure sections, there was no room for creative expansion. In spite of their perfection within the norms of the style, the predictable regularity of the form, phrase length, and harmonic patterns are limiting factors. Still, each rag is a gem.

Joplin had grander ambitions, and, to a certain degree, he was able to achieve his goals in two other kinds of composition: an occasional experimental rag, like *Euphonic Sounds*, and his large-scale work *Treemonisha*, an opera in three acts. In *Euphonic Sounds*, Joplin explores harmonic relationships not at all common in popular music of the period.

Euphonic Sounds

In the second strain of *Euphonic Sounds*, Joplin moves without modulation from the key of B♭ to F♯ to B minor, climaxing with a diminished-seventh

chord on which he pivots back to the original key. On the third strain, he abandons the regular oom-pah ragtime left hand and employs harmonic devices that may have been commonplace with Continental composers, but were quite striking within the context of an American popular piece.

Treemonisha is much more an opera than ragtime composition, even though the syncopated features characteristic of rag permeate the music. Arias, such as *The Sacred Tree* (No. 6), in triple meter, are spun-out sentimental ballads. And yet, if the naiveté is one of its major faults, it is also one of its strongest features. Just as a Grandma Moses painting is able to capture the essence of simple country life, so do the language, melodies, harmonies and rhythms of this Joplin opera bring to life the characters and emotions of the simple people portrayed in the drama. A thoroughly modern device is Joplin's employment of *Sprechstimme*, a kind of stylized declamation wherein the vocalist neither sings nor sustains a steady pitch, but creates a speech-melody to heighten the dramatic action. The device was not unique to Joplin, for Charles Ives used it in his *Soliloquy, or A Study in Sevenths and Other Things* (composed in 1907 but unpublished until 1933), and it appears in Schoenberg's *Pierrot Lunaire* of 1912, two works which Joplin could not possibly have heard before he completed *Treemonisha* in 1911.

Two other facets of Joplin must receive comment before we move on— Joplin the piano player, and Joplin the collaborator. Although there is not general agreement about the quality of Joplin's piano technique, it must have been prodigious. Legend has it that he always fared exceedingly well in formal or informal competition, and the technique necessary for the correct performance of his own music is sufficient to mark him as an accomplished professional pianist. However, we have no direct evidence about his playing, for although at least thirty-three piano-roll recordings bear his name, recent research has ascertained that only piano rolls made in late 1915 or early 1916 can be positively

A scene from the Houston Grand Opera's 1975 production of Scott Joplin's *Treemonisha*.

attributed to Joplin's fingers. As one authority points out, "made in the culminating period of his illness, they are more evidence of his fading powers than of his playing style at its earlier best."[11]

Not all of Scott Joplin's works bear the name of a single composer. Although some of his songs indicate that Joplin wrote both words and music, Henry Jackson, Louis Armstrong Bristol, Sidney Brown, and others frequently supplied his lyrics. At least seven rags were collaborations: *Swipesy* and *Lilly Queen* with Arthur Marshall; *Sunflower Slow Drag, Something Doing, Felicity Rag,* and *Kismet Rag* with Scott Hayden; and *Heliotrope Bouquet* with Louis Chauvin. Also, one work, *Sensation,* was written by Joseph F. Lamb but arranged by Scott Joplin. It was not uncommon for ragtime composers to collaborate, and the same Arthur Marshall is responsible for completing the last known rag composition by Tom Turpin, *Pan-Am Rag,* registered in 1914 but not published until its inclusion in *They All Played Ragtime.*[12]

[11] Blesh and Janis, *They All Played Ragtime,* first unnumbered page before page 1.
[12] Following p. 209.

The music of James Scott (1886–1938) is considered closest to that of Scott Joplin and of enough consequence to entitle him to a position of prominence in the history of ragtime. Born in Neosho, Missouri, Scott moved to Ottawa, Kansas, at the age of thirteen or fourteen. He was basically self-taught in music, although an older black pianist in Neosho, John Coleman, gave the boy lessons in piano and sightreading. He moved to Carthage, Kansas, in 1900, and at the age of seventeen published his first composition, A *Summer Breeze*. He continued working at Dumars Music Store in Carthage until around 1914, when he moved to St. Louis. There, on an earlier visit, he had met Scott Joplin. Probably through Joplin's good offices, he had made contact with John Stark, who eventually published many of his ragtime compositions. In St. Louis, Scott supported himself at first by giving piano lessons, house to house, and later by working for the Panama Theater as organist and musical arranger. He moved again in 1919 to Kansas City and continued publishing until 1922, when his *Broadway Rag* appeared, although by this time ragtime had been eclipsed by the newer form called jazz. He continued teaching until well into the 1930s. He also led an eight-piece dance band during that period, and, after his wife died, he moved across the river to Kansas City, Kansas, to live with a

James Scott (1886–1938).

cousin. He remained active in composition until shortly before his death in 1938.

The rags of James Scott are consistent to a flaw. He was not an experimental composer, but a craftsman who turned out remarkably regular works in standard form. *Frog Legs Rag,* although one of his earliest (1906), is one of his best, for the balance between stride left hand and melodic right hand gives it a rhythmic suppleness sometimes lacking in his other works. Scott was satisfied to work within the restrictions of standard rag form, both in melodic design and harmonic scheme. Invariably, the harmonic level moved up to the subdominant in the second half. Occasionally he would begin his rags with a minor theme—for example, the opening theme of his *Rag Sentimental* (1918)—but he quickly moved back to the major on the appearance of the second theme. Parallel thirds appear to be one of Scott's favorite sounds, and they appear at the opening of *Evergreen Rag* (1915)

Evergreen Rag

and in the second strain of *Kansas City Rag* (1907).

Kansas City Rag

A favorite melodic device Scott employed is a rocking pattern in the right hand that produces both syncopation and alternation of chords with single notes.

Hilarity Rag (1910)

Ragtime Oreole (1911)

Paramount Rag (1917)

Rag Sentimental (1918)

Experts have seen in the music of James Scott "an impression of charm and directness closer to folk style than to a finished art form" and point out that "Scott shared with Joplin a belief in the dignity and value of his music, the idea that this music labeled 'ragtime' was an art music developing under a wholly new aesthetic. Since Scott worked with Joplin, studied his compositions, and delved into the same regional folk background, it is not remarkable that their rags should be so similar. Yet while Scott has existed in Joplin's shadow, he is clearly a composer of great genius, with a talent as large as Joplin's"[13]

The last of the ragtime giants is Joseph F. Lamb, a white man born in Montclair, New Jersey, in 1887. Until his meeting with Scott Joplin in 1907, he was totally unfamiliar with blacks, black culture, and black-American music, except what he may have been able to learn from ragtime sheet-music publications. Without being deliberately derivative, Lamb was able to write rags that connoisseurs describe as characteristic of the black-American style, substantiating the contention that classical ragtime had become an American, not an ethnic, music. Lamb attended college in Berlin (Kitchener), Canada, and later passed his entrance examinations in engineering for Stevens Institute. However, after he found a job in New York he decided not to matriculate. Although two of his sisters were classically trained pianists, he took no lessons and was self-taught both as a composer and pianist. He had already composed several rags before meeting Joplin in 1907, and the well-known composer took an interest in the younger musician and helped him both with his composition and with publication. Although Lamb's first ragtime publication with John Stark, *Sensation Rag*, (1908) bears the name of Joplin as arranger, Lamb recalled that Joplin had agreed to add his name to help sell the rag and not because he had in fact arranged any of the music.

Joseph Lamb disappeared from public notice when the ragtime vogue passed after the First World War. Most ragtime followers assumed that Lamb was black, until Blesh and Janis discovered him living modestly in Brooklyn, New York, and working in the import business, thirty years later. The quality of his rags had given rise to the theory that Joseph F. Lamb was but a Scott Joplin pseudonym! Lamb continued to publish rags with Stark until 1919, and although another publisher, Mills, accepted a few works after that date, they were never issued. He stopped composing until his rediscovery, and in the years before his death he completed several unpublished rags and made some recordings. He published twelve rags between 1908 and 1919, and when he died in 1960 another two dozen were found, unpublished. In addition, he composed songs, four of which were published between 1908 and 1913; an additional fifty-one are known but unpublished.

In his ragtime compositions, Lamb would borrow and transform material

---

[13] Schafer and Riedel, *The Art of Ragtime*, p. 79 f.

Joseph F. Lamb (1887–1960).

from other compositions as well as invent completely new material. For example, his *Sensation Rag, American Beauty Rag,* and *Patricia Rag* all have motives that derive from Scott Joplin's *Maple Leaf Rag. Patricia Rag* also borrows from Joplin's *Gladeolus Rag,* and three of his compositions, *Cleopatra Rag, Champagne Rag,* and *Reindeer Rag,* share motivic material.[14] Lamb's rags display a harmonic sure-footedness which does not exclude chromaticism or key signatures with many flats. *Excelsior Rag* (1909) begins in D♭ and has a trio in G♭. Occasional double flats grace the pages as accidentals. Likewise, his *Ethiopia Rag* (1909) shares these characteristics. The fact that these works were

Ethiopia Rag

[14] Ibid., p. 80 ff.

Ragtime Nightingale

bought in large numbers points out that the average American household before the First World War, with its square piano, was fairly proficient in home music making. Lamb's rags tend not to be as consistently syncopated as those of Joplin and Turpin. The Trio of Lamb's *Ethiopia Rag* has only two syncopations in the first four measures. The opening section of his *Ragtime Nightingale* (1915), with the title and tempo indication deleted, could easily be mistaken for a Romantic character piece so popular among the classical piano students of that generation.

Lamb, like Turpin, Joplin, Marshall, and the other composers of classic ragtime pieces, was locked into the formulas of the style in that all of his pieces are divisible in half, each half being separated by key and divisible into sections, usually two, of sixteen measures each. However, he had a tendency to interpret these formal restrictions loosely, and to insert a little developmental material within the confines of the structure. His *Champagne Rag* (1910) is an excellent example of the integrated and developmental nature of his compositional thinking. In its form, **I AA BB' A—CC' DA' DA'**, the introduction borrows material from the first **A** phrase. The second **B** is not a direct repeat but a version written at the octave so that it has at least some developmental characteristics. The same is true of the two **C**s; and the last strain, which has two themes, the second of which is a transposition and variation of the opening theme, rounds out the form of the rag and marks this as an unusually integrated work, within the style.

Champagne Rag: March and Two-Step

Form:

Trio

I ‖ :A:‖ B │ B' │ A ‖ C │ C' ‖ :DA': ‖
4   16   16   16   16   16   16   32

Thematic redundancy: each pattern is 8 measures long, except the first (introduction), which is 4 measures long.

[A] A A A A B B B' B' A A C C C' C' D D A' A' D D A' A'

Themes:

A

Scott Hayden (1882–1915), Louis Chauvin (1883–1908), and Arthur Marshall (1881–1956) are three of the important early pioneers of ragtime who traveled in the same circles as Scott Joplin. But piano players were legion during the heyday of ragtime. Alfred Wilson and Charlie Warfield won the ragtime contest at the Louisiana Purchase Exposition in 1904; Tony Jackson, Plunk Henry, Ed Hardin, "Old Man" Sam Moore, Robert Hampton, Charles Hunter, Artie Matthews, and Percy Wenrich are all names known to the connoisseur of this music.

To the classic ragtime buff, the name of Ferdinand "Jelly Roll" Morton (1885–1941) denotes not a ragtime player but a jazz pianist and composer. His career and music will be discussed below in Chapter VI, but now might be an appropriate time to compare the two versions of *Maple Leaf Rag* recorded in the *Smithsonian Collection* (*SCCJ*, I/1–2) to observe the significant differences that appear in these two performances of the same work. Scott Joplin recorded his *Maple Leaf Rag* but a year before his death and only a few months before his commitment to the Manhattan State Hospital on Ward's Island in the East River, and it is truly remarkable that it was played as well as it was. Clearly the variations from the score, such as the left-hand flourishes which occur on the last half beat of measures 2, 8, 12, 16, and elsewhere, were intentional. Occasionally Joplin would embellish the first beat of a measure, as in the second ending of the trio. In one instance, measure 14 of the trio, he rewrites the left hand by playing the octave on the first beat, inserting rests in the middle of the bar, and playing a crush of four thirty-second notes and an eighth note on the second half of the second beat. Perhaps Joplin was playing from memory, perhaps he was reading from a score at a time when his vision was impaired; but, no matter, the changes are but minor decorations of a written composition. In the treble part, he occasionally misses octaves. Often the performance lacks the precision and cleanliness we might hope for, but for a critically ill man this is a remarkable testament to his pianistic prowess. His performance shows us that, essentially, ragtime rhythms are played exactly as written, that is, time is measured in ratios of two to one. Four sixteenth notes in a row are all equal in length, quarter notes are twice as long as eighth notes, and dotted figures balance three-fourths of the whole with one-fourth.

Ragtime Jazz

Jelly Roll Morton's performance of Scott Joplin's piece is instructive about jazz performance in general. The time relationships of the harmonies remain fixed regardless of all other rhythmic and melodic variation. However, the time relationships of individual notes are no longer limited to the two-to-one ratio, but include three-to-one as the most commonly recurring element in the rhythmic patterns. In ragtime, a brace of two equal eighth notes is performed with each note receiving equal time; in jazz, at mid-range tempos, two notated eighth notes are performed as a triplet figure: a quarter note followed by an eighth, all squeezed into the time allotted for one beat. This smooths off the ragged edges of the ragtime syncopation, and this must have been what James Scott had in mind when he named his ragtime composition of 1921 *Don't Jazz Me Rag—I'm Music*. The jazz age was under way, and the neat metrical divisions scored by composers such as Scott were being ignored by the jazz players, who played their pieces in the new style. Morton's performance of Joplin's *Maple Leaf Rag* is not ragtime at all, but jazz. The notes Joplin composed for the right hand are heard only in Morton's imagination, if at all. All that remains of Joplin's piece is the harmonic progression, the form (although

Maple Leaf Rag
a. Notated

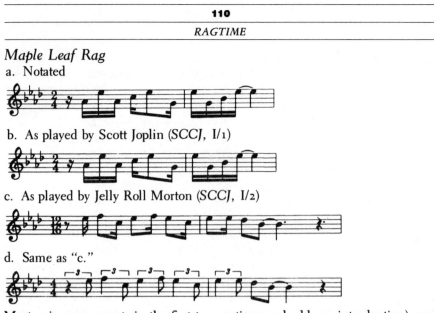

b. As played by Scott Joplin (*SCCJ*, I/1)

c. As played by Jelly Roll Morton (*SCCJ*, I/2)

d. Same as "c."

Morton ignores repeats in the first two sections and adds an introduction), and the references to the essential elements of the melody that Morton chooses to throw in from time to time.

Melodic Rhythm (Moderate tempo)

A common rhythmic cliché that Morton employs with relative frequency in this performance is the following:

It should be noted that duplets are inserted into the pattern to provide the ragtime syncopations at the end of beat three of the first measure and beat two of the second measure. This is one of the elements jazz borowed from ragtime. Morton offers the listener a very subtle harmonic shift at the end of his eight-measure introduction. The meter of the first five measures of the introduction is very clear, for Morton begins with three pickups and then strongly accents the first beat of each measure. The sixth measure begins as expected, but the downbeat of measure 7 does not get the expected stress, and Morton inserts the rhythmic cliché illustrated above on the second beat of the measure, forcing a new accent where none is expected. The normal reaction of the untrained listener is to hear this pattern as a mistake, where a beat is either lost or gained. But, in fact, Morton changed measure 6 to a five-beat measure, kept measure 7 as a four-beat measure beginning where the old second beat was, and shortened the eighth measure to a three-beat measure. One can see the rhythm of the notes in the last two measures of *Maple Leaf Rag* as played by Jelly Roll Morton:

As Martin Williams points out, "Morton's music also reflects the changes that had taken place in New Orleans, and at this point these changes are perhaps best understood as rhythmic changes. To go back for a moment . . . [ragtime] melodies had more syncopations than were heard in the cakewalk. In New Orleans, when the form of ragtime came together with the soul of the blues, even more rhythmic variety and complexity were introduced."[15]

The New York School

Four Eastern ragtime pianists achieved significance both for their playing and for their published compositions: James Hubert "Eubie" (or "Hubie") Blake (1883–); Charles Luckeyeth "Luckey" Roberts (1895–1965); James Price Johnson (1894–1955); and Thomas "Fats" Waller (1904–43). Eubie Blake was playing in the red-light district of Baltimore as a ragtime pianist at the age of fifteen, and was one of the first Eastern black ragtime composers to see his works in print—*Chevy Chase* and *Fizz Water* (both 1914). He joined forces with Noble Sissle in 1915, and the Sissle and Blake composing-and-writing team began turning out successful Broadway musicals in 1921 (*Shuffle Along*).

[15] *SCCJ* liner notes, p. 6.

More renowned as a composer of popular songs than of ragtime compositions, Eubie Blake is best known for his tunes *I'm Just Wild About Harry* (1921) and *Memories of You* (1930).

Luckey Roberts, a giant of a man, was born a Quaker in Philadelphia. His huge hands were comfortable playing tenths and twelfths in the ragtime basses. His first publication, *Junk Man Rag* (1913), was immediately successful, and he published another the same year, *Pork and Beans,* and two more the next, *Music Box Rag* and *Palm Beach.* He maintained a successful career as a bandleader and pianist in New York, gave a well-received concert in Carnegie Hall in 1931 and another at Town Hall in 1941. He was a friend of, and influence on, many Harlem pianists, including Duke Ellington and James P. Johnson.

James P. Johnson, like Scott Joplin, entertained the same dream of concert ragtime in larger forms. Born in New Brunswick, New Jersey, he moved to San Juan Hill in New York City as a child, where he received a solid musical education from an Italian music teacher, a Professor Giannini. His lessons included harmony, counterpoint, and opera, as well as classical piano. His first rag was published in 1914 (*Caprice Rag*), and he continued writing in this style for most of his life. In addition, a larger work, *Rhythm Drums,* is scored for flutes, oboes, English horns, bassoons, French horns, trumpets, trombones, etc., and his *Jazzmen* (*Jazz-o-Mine*) *Concerto* is for piano and full orchestra. His *Harlem Symphony* (1932) has has been played at Carnegie Hall, the Brooklyn Academy of Music, and elsewhere. He composed the music for a musical comedy, *Sugar Hill,* in 1948, but in spite of favorable reviews it ran for only three months in Hollywood, where it opened.

Fats Waller was born in New York and died in Kansas City at the height of his fame. Son of a middle-class black family, he received excellent instruction in classical keyboard performance, and was only twenty years old when he recorded his first solos on the Okeh label in 1924. When he died nineteen years later, he had recorded almost five hunded pieces, as well as a large number of player-piano rolls. He copyrighted over four hundred musical compositions! A nimble ragtime pianist, an influential jazz performer, Waller composed many popular songs which have become standards in the jazz repertoire—*Ain't Misbehavin, Honeysuckle Rose,* and *I've Got a Feeling I'm Falling* (all in 1929). He was a well-known public figure, and even made a number of movie shorts.

Piano ragtime virtually came to an end with the close of the First World War, but New Orleans ragtime bands developed into the jazz bands of the twenties, and Harlem ragtime was partly responsible for the development of swing in the thirties. The stride pianists of New York in the twenties trained both Fletcher Henderson and Duke Ellington, and the young Count Basie was at home playing stride left hand. Their groups were to become the leaders in the evolution of the big bands. Whether ragtime is jazz, whether it is peripherally related to jazz, or whether it is a totally isolated, independent form are moot questions whose resolution leaves little profit for the debater. The music is interesting of and by itself, its derivation from American and black American music is plain, and its influence upon American and black American music, as well as popular and classical music in Europe, is undeniable.

Remarkably enough, ragtime, like classic jazz, has undergone a revival, and today young composers like Max Morath, Robert R. Darch, Donald Ashwander, Thomas W. Shea, and others are composing new music in the old style. Hundreds of new recordings of ragtime have been issued since the 1950s; books, periodicals, and reprinted sheet music are pouring forth in a steady stream. The old music has found a new audience, both popular and scholarly. In the words of Treemonisha and Lucy:

> Marching onward, Marching onward,
> Marching to that lovely tune;
> Marching onward, Marching onward,
> Happy as a bird in June.
> Sliding onward, sliding onward,
> Listen to that rag.
> Hop and skip, now do that slow,
> Do that slow drag. [16]

[16]*The Collected Works of Scott Joplin*, II, pp. 221–34.

THE BLUES

Rats in my kitchen. Got so many in my kitchen—
Order me a Model T cat.
The way they stolen my groceries,
  You know it's tough like that.
That's blues.

—SLEEPY JOHN ESTES, FROM AN INTERVIEW
BY GLENN D. HINSON AND BRUCE S. BABSKI, NOVEMBER 1973

THE BLUES IS A personal statement made in musical terms which is nevertheless valid for all members of a society. There are many instances in literature, as well as folklore, of the word's use to describe a disconsolate or depressed emotional state. In a letter to Peter Garrick, written on the 11th of July, 1741, the British tragedian David Garrick wrote:

> The Town is exceeding hot & Sultry & I am far from being quite well, tho not troubled wth ye Blews as I have been.[1]

At the very beginning of the nineteenth century, Washington Irving wrote:

> My friend Launcelot concluded his harangue with a sigh, and as I saw he was still under the influence of a whole legion of the blues, and just on the point of sinking into one of his whimsical, and unreasonable fits of melancholy abstraction, I proposed a walk . . .[2]

The blues can differ in mood, theme, approach, or style of delivery. Blues are not intrinsically pessimistic even though they often tell of defeat and

[1] David Garrick, *Letters*, ed. David M. Little and George M. Kahr, I (Cambridge, Mass.: Harvard University Press, 1963), p. 26.

[2] Washington Irving, *Salmagundi*, No. 15 (New York: David Longworth, 1807), p. 310.

downheartedness, for in expressing the problems of poverty, migration, family disputes, and oppression, the blues provides a catharsis which enables the participants to return to their environment with resignation, if not optimism. There is an expressive sensuality in the blues that is almost exultant in its affirmation of life, and the music eases the pain, providing an outlet for the frustration, hurt, and anger the blues singer and his audience feel. In his natural setting, whether rural or urban, the blues singer maintains a feeling of kinship with his audience. His statements are a description of his state of mind, but they are generalized by his audience when they recall the same or similar experiences.

The advent of recording was not necessary to sustain the blues, for country blues have thrived in rural America as a living tradition within a society often so impoverished that recordings were not available to them. But recordings preserved a poverty-stricken folk art and spread the genre first throughout the nation and later throughout the world. Down home, in the ghetto or on the farm, the blues has a social importance which disappears in the popularized, reperformed versions. Personal feelings are verbalized and serve to call community attention to one's predicament and misfortune. The expression of criticism and complaint, the verbalization of these plights, provides the needed catharsis—an antidote to the problem. Within the black community, the words are usually direct, sometimes laced with disguised meaning, but always full of real-life experience.

Innuendo and double meanings are important aspects of blues lyrics, and racial protest as well as sexual feelings are often hidden in humor or metaphor. Victoria Spivey's *Handyman*, for example:

> He shakes my ashes, freezes my griddle,
> Churns my butter, stokes my pillow
> my man is such a handyman.
>
> He threads my needle, gleans my wheat,
> Heats my heater, chops my meat,
> my man is such a handyman.[3]

and Lonnie Johnson's *Hard Times Ain't Gone Nowhere:*

> People is raisin' 'bout hard times,
>   Tell me what it's all about,
> People is hollerin' 'bout hard times,
>   Tell me what it's all about,
> Hard times don't worry me,
>   I was broke when it first started out.

[3] Paul Oliver, *Aspects of the Blues Tradition*, p. 209.

"Red Willie" Smith in York, Alabama.

Friends, it could be worser,
  You don't seem to understand,
Friends, it could be worser,
  You don't seem to understand,
Some is cryin' with a sack of gold under each arm
  And a loaf of bread in each hand.

People ravin' 'bout hard times,
  I don't know why they should,
People ravin' 'bout hard times,
  I don't know why they should,
If some people was like me,
  They didn't have no money when times was good.[4]

Although metaphors, puns, and other methods of expressing double meaning have been traditionally a part of the blues, the most blatant expressions of sexual imagery and racial protest were reserved solely for the ears of the black community. The record companies acted as censors, although not always rigorous enforcers, in order to make recorded blues inoffensive to the sensibilities of the white customer. But vocal blues are essentially racial, and the language employed is shot through with words particular to the subculture. It has been pointed out that:

> The existence of a strong tradition of black music which has continued to the present is in part due to the isolation of blacks from the mainstream of American life. Though Gellert [author of *Negro Songs of Protest*] accurately stressed the presence of protest in black music, it is also separated from white ears by factors such as style and the language used in verses. Few whites would be familiar with voodoo terms such as "black cat bone" and "John the Conqueror root" which are found in many blues tunes. In effect, the language of blues is a cultural code, in the sense that few whites would grasp its sexual and racial levels of meaning. Terms such as "jazz" and more recently "nitty gritty" have been assimilated by popular white culture, but scholars suggest their meanings are considerably altered from their original usage.[5]

Had it not been for the phonograph, the blues artists of the 1920s and '30s would be virtually unknown to us today, and until 1920 no recordings were made of this folk art. Beginning in the 1930s and '40s, field recordings were made of prisoners on work gangs in prison farms and penitentiaries and of Southern rural laborers, chiefly through the pioneering efforts of Alan Lomax. Although these recordings are useful in ascertaining the musical antecedents of

---

[4] Paul Oliver, *The Meaning of the Blues* (New York: Collier Books, 1963), pp. 58 f.
[5] William Ferris, Jr., *Blues from the Delta*, p. 100.

the blues, it is important to note that they were made relatively late. Also, Paul Oliver points out that we have no way of determining whether recorded blues give an accurate picture of the genre, for there is almost a total absence of contemporaneous research and notated blues music.[6] Using a convenient, tripartite division of the blues—country blues, classic or city blues, and urban blues—we might examine each category briefly to observe those characteristics salient to our study of jazz.

The country blues, sometimes called Southern blues or folk blues, is a rural folk expression usually performed by a male singer. If it is accompanied, the singer usually plays the accompaniment himself on a simple folk instrument, like the fiddle, banjo, or guitar. Taking the repertoire of country blues preserved and recorded by our older bluesmen and extrapolating backward, we believe that blues form was originally variable and stretched from eight to sixteen measures in length, but that a predominant form emerged: the twelve-measure stanza of three lines, each accompanied by simple chordal harmony of tonic, subdominant, and dominant. By the time blues were taken over by improvising instrumental jazz ensembles, the twelve-measure blues form had become standard.

In country blues, with vocal lines approximately two measures long, the singer was able to play instrumental "breaks" between each phrase, and this pattern is commonly cited as the tie between American blues and African call-and-response singing. Bruno Nettl has pointed out that

> African and Western music are by their nature compatible; that is, important elements of each are structurally capable of being accommodated by the other. . . . the way the voice is used and the kinds of sound produced by the singer . . . is one of the ways in which the musics of the world differ most obviously and consistently. A musical culture may change its songs, scales, and rhythms, but it will tend to keep its singing style unchanged even over many centuries; it appears to be the musical element most resistant to change.[7]

The country blues gave jazz not only one of its most important forms, but also a mode of performance with all its concomitant sounds and attitudes.

Classic blues, often sung by women, bridged the gap between folk music and the entertainment world. Developed in minstrel shows and black theaters, the city blues gave voice to the more callous aspects of ghetto life and attitudes. The fine distinctions between classic, city, and urban blues as performed by the

---

[6] Oliver, *Meaning of the Blues*, p. 29.

[7] Bruno Nettl, "The Western Impact on World Music: Africa and the American Indians," in *Contemporary Music and Music Cultures*, by Charles Hamm, Bruno Nettl, and Ronald Byrnside, pp. 112, 119.

female singers within the jazz repertoire serves no useful purpose here, so performers like Ma Rainey and Bessie Smith, who joined forces with jazz musicians in New Orleans, Chicago, and New York, will not be discussed here. Rhythm and blues, a post–World War II phenomenon, will also be described in a later chapter.

"Blues" refers to a style of music, a type of performance, a musical form, and a state of mind. Structurally, its chief characteristic is a repeated harmonic pattern of twelve measures' duration in 4/4 time. This twelve-measure period is divided equally into three four-measure phrases, the first in the tonic, the second in the subdominant and tonic, and the last in the dominant and tonic (frequently, the dominant slips back to the subdominant before resolving to the tonic in this final phrase).

A.

measure	1	2	3	4	5	6	7	8	9	10	11	12
harmony	I————————				IV————		I————		V————		I———	
									(IV)			

B.

measure	1	2	3	4	5	6	7	8	9	10	11	12
harmony	I	V⁷	I	I♭⁷	IV	II	III♯	VI	II⁷	V⁷	I———	

C.

measure	1	2	3	4	5	6	7	8	9	10 11		12
harmony	B♭ F♯m⁷ B M⁷	Em⁷ A⁷	Dm⁷ B m⁷E⁷		E♭⁷	B♭ºA⁷B♭Cm⁷	Dm⁷G⁷		Cm⁷	F⁷ B♭ G⁷		Cm⁷F⁷
	(I)				(IV)		(I)		(II⁷)	(V⁷)(I)		

Example A represents the simplest harmonic plan, whereas B and C show embellished and more harmonically complicated schemata. Vocal blues most often overlaid an **AAB** text and melody on an **ABC** harmonic structure. That is, the singer's first phrase was repeated, but the harmonies continued to move on. In the classic blues phase, instruments would play background music for the first two measures while the singer would carry the text and tune. The melody instruments would then fill in with a break during the following two measures. This call-and-response pattern between singer and instrumental soloist can be seen graphically as follows:

Typical Blues Pattern

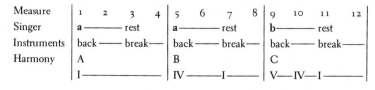

Measure	1	2	3	4	5	6	7	8	9	10	11	12
Singer	a———— rest				a———— rest				b———— rest			
Instruments	back—— break—				back—— break—				back—— break—			
Harmony	A				B				C			
	I————————				IV———I————				V—IV—I————			

Blues harmony, although appearing to be a major-mode phenomenon upon first inspection, is actually neither major nor minor, for the characteristic blues sound results from the simultaneous use of major and minor tonalities and nontempered scale intervals. The blues scale, in the key of C, often admitted A♭ as well as E♭ and B♭ . These are the minor thirds of the major I, IV, and V harmonies. Although any chromatic note could be admitted, the flatted fifth, G♭ , was also commonly stressed. In performance, all of these notes were unstable in intonation and function, and this quality was an important characteristic of the blues. Also, since blues stems from a vocal, rather than an instrumental, tradition, portamentos, "falloffs," nonstandard vibratos, and nontempered tuning were all part of the melodic style.

The Blues Scale

a. In the key of C

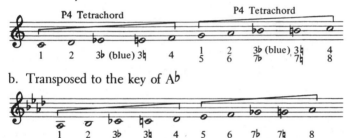

b. Transposed to the key of A♭

c. A blues in A♭ (*Chi Chi*, by Charlie Parker) with flat and sharp thirds and sevenths (to an A♭ harmony [tonic chord]) marked with asterisks.

Chi Chi: take 1

[The asterisks, in order - 3♮ , 7♮ , 7♭ , 3♭]

The lowered third and seventh scale steps are commonly called "blue notes," a phenomenon which has been variously described by writers on jazz. One describes the blues scale as two disjunct tetrachords with a variable third, and labels the result a purely negroid scale.[8] Another expert accepts this reconstructed jazz scale, but explains the blue notes as "neutral thirds," pitches that sound flat to a classical musician expecting a major third.[9] He, too, ties these sounds to an African tradition and explains that a noted British Africanist, A. M. Jones, says he has never heard an African sing the exact third or seventh of our tempered scale. A third authority, reviewing the work of the first, correctly observes, "[He] could not have found the full blues scale in African recordings, since indeed it does not exist in that form in Africa, but developed out of melodic-harmonic practices peculiar to African music only, as we have shown, upon contact with European harmony."[10] Supporting this view, a fourth writes:

> A frequently mentioned characteristic of U.S. Negro songs is the so-called "blue note," the flatted or slightly lowered third and seventh degrees in a major scale. The origin of this phenomenon is not known, but it probably cannot be traced to Africa. Here is a musical trait which may, possibly, have come into folk music from the practices of American Negro popular and jazz musicians.[11]

Referring to the paired tetrachords mentioned above, another commentator states, "This, in fact, is the blues scale. It is, as we said, a scale that constitutes the common denominator of all American Negro folk music; but while all other American Negro idioms may occasionally take recourse to it, the blues is the only one that makes exclusive use of it."[12] Taken from a different context, but aptly applying to our situation, are the following words:

> It cannot be repeated too often that the blues are one of the sources of jazz, but they are not jazz. The Negro-American minstrels' art is divorced in a number of ways from the jazzmen's. It is true that the blues are a constant element of the jazz repertory, but they are not the only one.[13]

In sum, there are African scales that contain an untempered third and seventh degree, but the blues scale is a composite sound which developed in the United States when the African melodic idiom was tempered by European har-

---

[8] Winthrop Sargeant, *Jazz, Hot and Hybrid*, pp. 132–144.

[9] Marshall Stearns, *The Story of Jazz*, pp. 276–280.

[10] Gunther Schuller, *Early Jazz*, p. 47.

[11] Bruno Nettl, *Folk and Traditional Music of the Western Continents* (Englewood Cliffs, N.J.: Prentice-Hall, 1973), p. 185.

[12] Ernest Borneman, "Black Light and White Shadow," *Jazzforschung*, 2 (1970), p. 57.

[13] André Hodeir, *Jazz: Its Evolution and Essence*, trans. David Noakes, p. 156, n. 8.

mony. The question of whether or not the blues scale is part of the essence of jazz is moot and need not be settled here. The most commonly held view is that the blues' melodic material is part and parcel of jazz. The blues approach to jazz allows for constant embellishment and variation, in addition to encouraging individualized performances, a kaleidoscope which multiplies the lights of auditory delight.

Rhythmically, blues offer an interesting contrast to ragtime. Whereas the regular rhythmic line of ragtime, the standard against which a melody might syncopate, was an alternation of strong and weak pulses, the regular rhythmic line of blues was a steady stream of strong pulses. Whether the text falls into an iambic pentameter scheme or any other, stretching syllables improvisatorily for musical, as well as textual, reasons makes blues performances unpredictable with regard to beat placement. Whereas the ragtime performer syncopated by accenting midway between beats or on weaker beats, the blues performer often syncopated by missing, rather than hitting, a particular accent. This improvisatory rhythmic style allows for great flexibility.

The unpredictable nature of rhythmic performance in country blues is no-

Robert Johnson (1898–1937) is represented in this drawing in a makeshift recording studio set up in a San Antonio hotel room in November, 1936.

where better illustrated than in Robert Johnson's *Hellhound on My Trail* (*SCCJ*, I/3). Johnson's performance involves four stanzas of blues lyrics. In a standardized version by a blues composer such as W. C. Handy, we would expect to find each stanza twelve measures long in 4/4 time. The introduction would be two, four, or eight measures long. Johnson's performance only approximates this concept, especially in the placement of the blues harmonies at the structural points of each verse. But careful inspection of this performance will show that the introduction has only fourteen beats; a regular four-measure introduction would have sixteen. In the first stanza there are three phrases consisting of 22 beats, 20 beats, and 24 beats; or, 5½ measures, 5 measures, and 6 measures of four beats each. Subsequent verses are of slightly different proportions: 20, 16, 21; 17, 18, 20; 22, 18, 21.

The general characteristics of the blues are ever present: the I–IV–I–V–I harmonies in each stanza, the repeated first line answered by a second and different line; a melodic statement that takes approximately half of the first phrase and is answered by an instrumental statement in the second half; and so on. However, the 253 beats of this particular piece are irregularly divided according to Robert Johnson's own personal style. The performer's freedom to insert words or melismas[14] into the melodic line at whim can be seen, for example, in the second line of the third stanza.

Hellhound on My Trail

You sprinkled hot-foot pow-der   all 'round my door,   all a-round my door,

You sprinkled hot-foot pow-der   all 'round your dad-dy's door,   mm mm mmm,

It keeps me with a ram-blin' mind, Rid-er,   ev-'ry ol' place I go,   ev-'ry ol' place I go.

Only three relative time values were used in the example to approximate free-flowing speech rhythm (short equals eighth note, middle equals quarter note, and long equals half note), but even with this lack of precision, one can readily perceive how Johnson creates irregular groupings in his melodic line. In some blues and jazz performances, the combination of five or seven notes in one part overlapping two or three beats in another part with no points of coincidence for that brief duration is not exceptional. It is just part of the style, part of the rhythmic freedom introduced to jazz through the blues.

[14] A melisma is an ornamentation slipped into a melodic line. The word was originally used to describe a method of singing in which several different pitches are used for a single syllable of text.

Country Blues

Country blues has no history[15] to speak of, at least it has no significant chronology. It most assuredly existed before jazz but its origins are lost in the past, before the days of sound recordings. However, it persists to the present day, and it would seem that country blues is still performed in a manner virtually unchanged from that preserved in the earliest recordings. A few rural blues singers have achieved some degree of national prominence, but to a certain degree this would seem to be the result more of chance than of artistic achievement. The colorful and folksy nicknames taken by Huddie Ledbetter ("Leadbelly"), Son House, Blind Lemon Jefferson, and "Sleepy" John Estes have an earthy quality that seems to signal that the music is an expression of a society, not necessarily the achievement of art and artifice. By definition, folk music is that body of ethnic or traditional music which stems from a particular part of the world where there is also a development of urban, professionalized, and cultivated classical music.[16]

Country blues is such a folk music, for it is perpetuated by oral tradition. Songs are passed on by word of mouth, and performance tradition is learned by watching and hearing. It is a functional aspect of the culture of the people from which it stems, and it reflects their vision and their values. When the people change, so must the music; and if country blues have remained essentially stable over the last fifty or so years, it is because one can still find areas in rural America where farm life and culture for black Americans have changed little since the turn of the century. If we cannot investigate the history of country blues, we can at least survey some of the well-known figures and their music.

In July, 1924, Paramount Records of Chicago produced the first country blues record, *Papa's Lawdy Lawdy Blues*, by "Papa" Charlie Jackson. Born around 1890 in New Orleans, he made his way to Chicago via a couple of minstrel shows. Between his first record in 1924 and his last in April, 1935, Papa Charlie cut seventy-seven works. In 1928 he recorded two duets with Ma Rainey, *Ma and Pa Poorhouse Blues* and *Big Feeling Blues*. During his career, he worked with Ida Cox and Big Bill Broonzy as well as Ma Rainey. In 1925, singing to a fast banjo accompaniment, Papa Charlie recorded *Shave 'em Dry*. (The suggestive title has more than one layer of meaning; as a sexual reference, it connotes intercourse without preliminary lovemaking.) The bawdy song, in folk tradition, celebrates physical love and smiles at the triangle situation.

---

[15] We use "History" in the sense of a written account of what happened. Blues were not notated in the nineteenth century; recordings document later incarnations of the music; recollections are often vague and contradictory; therefore, it lacks a known past.

[16] Nettl, *Folk and Traditional Music*, p. 1.

> Why don't you run here mama, lay back in my arms,
> If your man catches you I don't mean no harm,
> Mama let me holler, daddy let me shave 'em dry. [17]

This work preserves the archaic eight-bar blues form, as well as the original harmonic and poetic structure. Jackson was not the first to record *Shave 'em Dry*; Ma Rainey sang this blues for the same company in August of 1924, [18] so it is possible he either learned the song from her or taught it to her. Jackson's records sold well, and he continued to record for Paramount for the next four years. He was unable to read or write, and during recording sessions someone would sit behind him whispering the words into his ear.

Papa Charlie continued to work the vaudeville circuit, and his early recording *Salty Dog Blues*, [19] the second he did for Paramount, was always associated with him. He rerecorded the number with Freddie Keppard's Jazz Cardinals in 1926.

> Funniest thing I ever saw in my life
> Uncle Bud came home and caught me kissin' his wife.
> Salty Dog, oh, yes, you Salty Dog.

Perhaps the best-known rural blues singer of the 1920s was Blind Lemon Jefferson. Born blind in Couchman, Texas, in 1897, he began singing for money in Wortham, Texas, in 1911 or 1912. He went to Dallas around 1917, and was fairly successful working the red-light district. There he met Leadbelly (Huddie Ledbetter), another important country blues singer, who was in prison most of the time that Blind Lemon was working in Dallas. Jefferson seems to have traveled as far east as Mississippi and Alabama, and some of the older bluesmen tell stories of him in towns like Jackson, Mississippi, and Memphis, Tennessee. Blind Lemon traveled to Chicago in 1925 and began recording there in 1926. He cut his last disc in 1929 and died in Chicago in 1930. One song associated particularly with Blind Lemon was *The Black Snake Moan*. When it was recorded originally by Victoria Spivey in 1926, the *Black Snake Blues* may have had no sexual overtones. It may have simply described a rustic scene where a young girl came upon a black snake in her cabin. But Lemon transformed it into a sexual lament in 1927, recording a second version the same year and a third black snake piece in 1929. In the second version, recorded for Paramount around 1927, he sings

[17] Paramount 12264, recorded February, 1925.
[18] Paramount 12222.
[19] Paramount 12236.

I aint got no mama now,
I aint got no mama now,
She told me late last night you don't need no mama nohow.

Black snake crawlin' in my room,
Black snake crawlin' in my room,
And some pretty mama had better come in and get this black snake soon.

. . . Well, I wonder where this black snake's gone?
Well, I wonder where this black snake's gone?
Lord, that black snake, mama, done run my darlin' home. [20]

This recording, available in a modern reissue, is particularly interesting from a musical standpoint. It retains all the typical characteristics of the blues except that which is usually considered of foremost importance, the harmony. It has an **AAB** melodic structure and an **AAB** text structure; it has a call-and-response pattern dividing each phrase between voice and guitar; and, in spite of the rubato tempo, it maintains a twelve-measure structure. However, although the first four measures are in the tonic, as is traditional, the second four measures do not change to subdominant, but remain at the tonic level. The third phrase, which traditionally moves directly to the dominant, places the harmonic emphasis instead on the submediant (VI) and only implies the dominant harmony when you imagine it as the fifth above the root in the tonic chord.

The flexibility and unpredictability of the country blues is one of its most enduring charms and most important features. A soloist singing to his own accompaniment may wax eloquent and rhapsodize over an interesting word or a catchy melodic figure. Until recently, sex as a topic for song lyrics was held in low esteem by middle-class white America, but it has been argued that there was a social and psychological need for obscenity in black American singing. The unrelenting hard work and oppression which were their lot created the need for a "safety valve of ribald laughter [rather] than a neurotic stimulant and breaker of Puritan inhibitions."[21] Since the early blues were primarily "race" songs, they could flourish without the imposition of white middle-class morals. Still, Victoria Spivey resented the fact that Blind Lemon changed her *Black Snake Blues* to a sex song.

When Blind Lemon recorded *Shuckin' Sugar Blues* in 1926,[22] the standard blues harmonies were more apparent, but liberties were taken with the length of the final line of each stanza. When Jefferson recorded *Risin' High Water Blues* in 1927,[23] he was accompanied by George Perkins on piano. Here the

[20] Paramount 12407, reissued Folkways FP 55.
[21] Alain Locke, *The Negro and His Music*, p. 88.
[22] Paramount 12454, reissued Riverside SDP II.
[23] Paramount 12487, reissued Riverside SDP II.

traditional twelve-measure form was played in its standardized version. The topic of these lyrics is one of the typical rural subjects commonly found in country blues. Events that affect the lives of poor black country folk recur as persistent phenomena: *When the Levee Breaks, The Flood Blues, The Mississippi Flood Blues, Mississippi Heavy Water Blues*, and many others. Spoiled crops, ruined homes, death, and separation are all subjects for the story-telling country-blues singer.

Leadbelly (Huddie Ledbetter) acknowledges the influence of Blind Lemon Jefferson upon his development and recalls hearing him as early as 1917 in the bordellos of Dallas, Texas. Ledbetter, born in Morringsport, Louisiana, in 1885, grew up in Texas, where as a boy he learned work songs as well as blues and other folks songs. He received long jail sentences from several Texas and Louisiana prisons for violent crimes. It was at the Angola Prison Farm, Louisiana, that he was "discovered" by John and Alan Lomax and first recorded the prison songs for their collection, now preserved in the archives of the Music

Huddie "Leadbelly" Ledbetter (1888–1949).

Division of the Library of Congress. Leadbelly led the life of a farmhand, both inside and out of prison, and as a participant in work gangs he frequently acted as lead singer in the work songs. He made a living as a professional folk singer, accompanying himself on the guitar in almost 300 recordings. Although he was cocomposer with John Lomax of a popular song, *Good Night, Irene,* he died in 1949 before the tune was transformed into a commercial hit with orchestral accompaniment and cover singers. During his last years he received recognition as a folk singer; he gave concerts and entertained in clubs on the West Coast.

Juliana Johnson and *John Henry,* [24] two work songs recorded by Leadbelly, are ballads from the preblues tradition, the former setting a rhythm for ax cutting and the latter for hammering with a sledge. One of the characteristics that distinguishes these songs from the blues is the importance of the verse sequence in the total composition. These work songs exist as an entity, are committed to memory, and are passed on orally as a unit. They may change through errors in the process of transmission, but essentially they retain their identity. Since the blues are all based on the same simple structure, the individuality of any particular blues results from the remodeling of the same basic material by the individual singer according to his talents and personal needs. Improvisation is an essential element of the blues, where it is only incidental in the transmission of folk ballads.

Typical blues performances by Leadbelly can be heard on the recordings he made for the Library of Congress in 1938: *The Bourgeois Blues* and *De Kalb Woman.* [25] His style of guitar playing differs from that of Blind Lemon Jefferson in that his four-beat strumming submits to a variety of rhythmic fills. In *Bourgeois Blues* he often strums bass strings as a drone to create a pedal point beneath the changing blues harmonies. Blind Lemon Jefferson, in a sound more akin to country-western guitar playing, accompanies his singing with a boom-chuck or oom-pah bass, one similar to the left-hand pattern of ragtime piano. Also, Blind Lemon's enunciation is clear and fairly understandable to whites unaccustomed to a black dialect, whereas the lyrics of Leadbelly are thrown out in the thick drawl of the black rural South.

Lines of demarcation of country-blues singers, classic-blues singers, popular singers, and jazz singers are not easily drawn, and we can see in the workings of Papa Charlie Jackson and Leadbelly several areas of overlap. If Ma Rainey is a classic-blues singer, then is Papa Charlie Jackson one as well when he sings *Ma and Pa Poorhouse Blues* with her? If Freddie Keppard and Johnny Dodds are jazz-ensemble musicians, is Papa Charlie a jazz singer when he sings a blues to the accompaniment of Freddie Keppard's group? At what point in the history of *Good Night, Irene* does it make a transition from folk music to popular music?

[24] Folkways FP 53.
[25] Electra EKL 301-2, reissued Sine Qua Non, SQN 103.

When Mike Leadbitter and Neil Slavin published their blues discography, they footnoted the entry of Leadbelly as follows: "As this artist has mainly recorded in the true folk vein, only sessions thought to be of interest to blues collectors are listed."[26] Still, they list *Good Night, Irene* in more than one take, and here we have a work that is clearly not blues and only peripherally of folk derivation.

The Mississippi Delta has produced many country-blues singers of note—Charlie Patton, Son House, Skip James, Robert Johnson, and Booker T. Washington "Bukka" White. The Delta is a rich alluvial plain extending from Vicksburg, Mississippi, to Memphis, Tennessee, defined by the Mississippi River on the west and the Yazoo River on the east. It is an agricultural region and contains the densest black population of the state, blacks outnumbering whites by more than a two-to-one ratio. Racial pride is still felt by Delta blacks toward blues singers, who have become the musical spokesmen for the black communities. Although the oral tradition is strong, the area has not proved impregnable to outside musical interests, and white country music with fiddle and banjo have also become a part of the culture. Robert Johnson has been called "King of the Delta Blues," and although little is definitely known of his life, it is generally believed that he was born around 1914 in Robinsville, Mississippi. He was raised near Clarksdale, Mississippi, traveled throughout the country with other blues singers like Son House and Johnny Shines during the late '20s and early '30s, and was either poisoned by a woman or stabbed by her jealous husband in 1938 or 1939, dying in his early thirties. A portion of his blues repertoire suggests that he had a premonition of a violent, sinful, love-related death. His lyrics deal with three recurring themes: the impermanence of human relationships, incessant wandering, and irrational terrors. His blues are shot through with dark foreboding, saying there is no home for him anywhere, not even a place for his body after death. His *Me and the Devil Blues*, recorded in Dallas in 1937, is an example:

> Early this morning when you knocked upon my door,
> Early this morning when you knocked upon my door,
> And I said, "Hello Satan, I believe it's time to go."

> Me and the devil was walking side by side,
> Me and the devil was walking side by side,
> And I'm going to beat my woman until I get satisfied.

> You may bury my body down by the highwayside, I don't
>   care where you bury my body when I'm dead and gone,
> You may bury my body down by the highwayside,
> So my old evil spirit can get a Greyhound bus and ride.[27]

[26] Mike Leadbitter and Neil Slaven, *Blues Records, 1943–1966*, p. 189.
[27] Vocalion 0418.

In *Stones in My Pathway,* Johnson sings again of trouble, death, and travel:

> I got stones in my pathway and my road seems dark at night,
> I got stones in my pathway and my road seems dark at night,
> I have pains in my heart, they have taken my appetite.
>
> . . . Now you's tryin' to take my life, and all my loving too,
> Now you's tryin' to take my life, and all my loving too,
> You made a pathway for me, now what are you tryin' to do?[28]

His insistent, droning bottleneck slide guitar complements his slightly nasal, intense, and passionate voice. His rhythm is always nervous; the irregularities of phrase structure are sometimes matched by an irregularity in beat. But together, the accompaniment and the lyrics provide a powerful musical force capable of expressing an apocalyptic vision. Johnson's *Hellhound on My Trail* (SCCJ, I, 3) has been evaluated as:

> One of the most personal and expressive moments in blues poetry. . . . All of the images, the blues falling down like rain on him, the leaves on the trees over his head shaking with the wind, intensified the desperation he felt at the thought of the hell hound trailing through the day . . . the feeling of the immediate in the first verse, however, still hung over the song like a low line of clouds over the levees along the Yazoo River, and it was one of his most effective performances.[29]

The names of other country-blues singers are as colorful as they are numerous: Peg Leg Howell, Sleepy John Estes, Blind Willie Johnson, Washboard Sam, Big Bill, "Ragtime Texas" Henry Thomas, and more. They created and preserved one of the richest repertories of native American music. The blues tradition continued to change. Just as the country blues was preceded by other folk types, it was followed, although not superseded, by classic blues, urban blues, rhythm and blues, and the more contemporary sounds of Motown and soul music. To the listener raised on the concert-hall or recording-studio sounds, country blues may seem coarse and perhaps even unimaginative at first hearing. To the connoisseur trained to detect the subtle nuance of double entendre and to accept the unexpurgated feelings of an agrarian people sympathetically, country blues offers a musical art form consonant with earthy values.

[28] Columbia CL 1654.
[29] Samuel Charters, *The Bluesmen,* p. 91 f.

The Classic Blues

Gertrude "Ma" Rainey was one of the first black female vocalists who performed classic blues to the accompaniment of jazz band or piano. Born in Columbus, Georgia, in 1886, she was married at fourteen and toured with her husband, Will Rainey, in The Rabbit Foot Minstrels. Her performances brought a degree of professionalism, of polished and consistent artistry, to the genre, and her work is preserved in recordings which span the years 1923 to 1929. She was not the first blues singer to record, and the ones she made (when she was nearly forty) show us the formally standardized, instrumentally accompanied form of city blues.

Ma Rainey was one of the most influential blues singers of the age. She earned the title "Mother of the Blues" both as a leading early figure and as the mentor of the "Empress of the Blues," Bessie Smith. Her earliest recordings of

"Ma" Rainey with her Georgia Jazz Band, 1925.

1923, *Bo Weevil Blues* and *Southern Blues*, depict situations from black American life closely allied to country blues. In *Southern Blues*, she sings of typical black-American homes:

> If your house catches on fire and there aint
>   no water around,
> If your house catches on fire and there aint
>   no water around,
> Throw your trunk out the window and let that
>   shack burn down.[30]

She was backed by Lovie Austin's Blue Serenaders, a group which, on this occasion, consisted of cornet, clarinet, piano, and violin. By the time she had finished recording in 1929, she had cut almost one hundred sides in her simple, direct blues style. She was the first to record *Shave 'em Dry*, and, as was mentioned earlier, she and Papa Charlie Jackson both recorded this number for Paramount within a year of each other. This work, incidentally, is most archaic in its structure, for it is not twelve measures long but eight.

It becomes apparent that in the mid-1920s "the blues" meant not only a standardized instrumental piece twelve measures long, but a style of singing and a type of subject matter. When Ma Rainey recorded *Titanic Man Blues* in 1926,[31] she departed from the standardized blues form with a sixteen-measure strophic piece divided in half into two similar phrases. The first ends with an open cadence, II⁷–V, and the second finishes with a closed cadence, V⁷–I. In other words, each strophe, or stanza, of the song consists of antecedent and consequent phrases. Further, each phrase is divided in three, as though it were a blues piece eight measures long. The last portion of each half carries the characteristic refrain "Fare thee well," but were the word "blues" not part of the title, we would certainly doubt its authenticity today.

Titanic Man Blues

---

[30] Paramount 12083.
[31] Paramount 12374, reissued Riverside RLP 12-113.

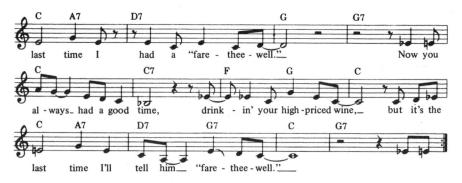

last time I had a "fare - thee - well." Now you

al - ways_ had a good time, drink - in' your high -priced wine,_ but it's the

last time I'll tell him_ "fare - thee - well."_

The four-measure introduction serves as a coda at the end, and its harmonic pattern follows a circle of fifths (I–VI–II–V–I) derived from the last four measures of the sixteen-measure phrase. The accompaniment is played by the Georgia Jazz Band, with Joe Smith (trumpet), Charlie Green (trombone), and Buster Bailey (clarinet) in the front line; and Fletcher Henderson (piano), and Charlie Dixon (banjo), and Coleman Hawkins (bass saxophone) for a rhythm section. Although the front-line instruments perform polyphonically, the trumpet frequently interacts heterophonically with the voice.

Before her recording career ended in 1929, Ma Rainey performed with many notables of the jazz world: Don Redman, Louis Armstrong, Kid Ory, and others already mentioned. Her popularity dwindled after 1930, and she retired from music in 1933. She was virtually unknown when she died in 1939, but her strong voice and straightforward style of projecting the words made her one of the most influential singers of the period.

The distribution of recorded performances of the blues helped standardize the form, but published music also played a significant role. A man largely responsible for the spread and popularity of the blues as we know it today was William Christopher Handy, a black composer, cornetist, and bandleader, who designated himself the "Father of the Blues." Born in Florence, Alabama, in 1873, he traveled throughout the United States, Canada, Mexico, and Cuba as bandmaster of the Mahara Minstrels. He not only composed music, but he collected traditional black-American themes which he incorporated in his own music. The first blues tune ever to be published was one of Handy's own compositions, *The Memphis Blues*. It was originally written as a campaign song in the 1909 election for a Memphis mayor. Handy's band was hired to help promote Edward H. Crump, who was running on a strict reform platform. Since Boss Crump wanted to attract votes from the Beale Street area, which was full of dancehalls and barrelhouses, he needed a gimmick to please the sporting crowd. The result was an extremely popular song entitled *Mr. Crump*, and it was later published, in 1912, as *The Memphis Blues*.

Handy's most famous composition was the *St. Louis Blues*, written in 1914 and given a classic performance in 1925 by the "Empress of the Blues," Bessie Smith, and the great jazz cornet and trumpet player, Louis Armstrong (*SCCJ*,

I/4). Born in Chattanooga in 1894,[32] Bessie Smith went on the road as an entertainer while still in her teens. For years she worked in traveling tent shows, honky-tonks, and carnivals, and she was discovered by Frank Walker, recording director for Columbia Records, singing in a club in Selma, Alabama, in 1917. Everything about Bessie Smith was big: her imposing person, her moving voice, and the quantities of alcohol she consumed. As a full-grown adult, she stood five feet, nine inches tall and weighed in at 210 pounds; the volume of her voice was extraordinary, and it is perhaps for this reason that she was able to record so successfully on the primitive recording apparatus of the early '20s.

As a singer, Bessie Smith displayed a remarkable sense of rhythm, an extremely sensitive feeling for pitch, and a crisp diction which allowed her to convey the meaning of the words to a large audience. Her articulation of words and notes, delivered with a variety of tonal and rhythmic attacks, gave her interpretations a sense of poise as well as an improvisatory feeling. Bessie's first recording, *Downhearted Blues*,[33] made in New York in February of 1923, has great historical significance because of its early date, but is not considered one of her most musical achievements. She was obviously nervous; she was not singing one of her standard songs; and she had had no previous experience in a recording studio.

The key element in blues singing that determines whether a performance has moved into the domain of jazz or remained outside in the world of pop and folk is the extent to which the vocal line is freed, melodically and rhythmically, from the substructure. In other words, when the singer is able to stretch the melody into an improvised line, which blends appropriately with the accompaniment and projects the sense of the text, the music is jazz. The embellishment should add meaning, not smother it. The melodic line should move smoothly from phrase to phrase and connect sensibly with the instrumental breaks that bind the phrases together.

Bessie began to reach this degree of sophistication as early as *Jailhouse Blues*,[34] which she recorded in September of 1923. In a sense, this marks the beginning of the classic-blues style, a method of performance which differs significantly from the previous traditional blues performances. By 1925, Bessie Smith had achieved the maturity of style that marked her as the major recording artist of the era in this genre.

Her performance of *St. Louis Blues* (SCCJ, I/4) is the epitome of the classic-blues performance, and the equality of the vocal and cornet solo work is extraordinary. The similarity of inflection, phrasing, and accent contribute the essential characteristics of tension and release which Bessie and Louis inject

[32] John Chilton gives 1895 and Paul Oliver 1898 as birth years.
[33] Columbia A3844, reissued Columbia GP 33.
[34] Reissued Columbia CL-855.

Bessie Smith (1894–1937).

into this performance and which mark this recording as one of the landmark performances of both blues and jazz. When Bessie recorded the work again a few years later with James P. Johnson at the piano, the Hall Johnson Choir, and members of the Fletcher Henderson Orchestra for a soundtrack of a movie short,[35] the powerful singing and professional certainty of a well-known vocalist are present, but the sensitive interworking of two jazz giants is not.

Throughout the '20s and well into the '30s, the twelve-bar blues as a standard form became more entrenched, but did not totally eclipse the many blues variants, even among performances by classic-blues singers. Bessie's *St. Louis Blues* is an excellent example of a piece constructed with a twelve-bar blues at the beginning, a bridge in between, and a second twelve-bar blues at the end. Her recording of *Blue Blue* for Columbia in 1931[36] begins with a twelve-measure phrase that is blueslike, for it has three four-measure sections. But the pattern is **ABB** rather than **AAB**. It is followed by a sixteen-measure bridge which repeats the same four-measure phrase—**CCCC**. Then Bessie sings a regular twelve-measure blues, once, and this is followed by two instrumental performances of the same twelve-measure phrase. The piece closes with a repeat of the initial **ABB** pattern, and when the overall structure of the entire piece is gathered together, we have **ABCA**, where **C** indicates three repetitions of a regular twelve-bar blues. Her recording of *Shipwreck Blues*[37] at the same session is a regular twelve-bar blues, but she inserts no words into the third phrase of the first two patterns, where one would normally find the refrain.

Bessie Smith's recording of *Lost Your Head Blues* (*SCCJ*, I/5) exemplifies the blues in its most elemental and most comprehensible form (see examples on pages 119–120). It is interesting to note in this recording that Fletcher Henderson's piano playing is in the so-called boogie-woogie style, the left hand performing an eight-notes-to-the-measure ostinato (that is, repeating the short bass riff again and again throughout the number).

Bessie Smith's singing, which combined the flexibility and sophistication of jazz with the elemental appeal of country blues, made her a special favorite with the black public of the 1920s. Her records sold well; she made a short movie in 1929, *St. Louis Blues*; and she was a headline vaudeville star. Unfortunately, she became an alcoholic and began to disintegrate both professionally and personally during the latter part of the 1920s. She continued to record until 1933, but her last recording was more an affectionate token from John Hammond than a professional session made for profit. She made her last public appearance while touring the Memphis area in 1937 and died in September of 1937 in an automobile accident. She worked and recorded with the

[35] Riverside RLP 12-113.
[36] Columbia 14611, reissued Columbia GP 33.
[37] Columbia 14663, reissued Columbia GP 33.

most important musical figures of the day: Sidney Bechet, Fletcher Henderson, Coleman Hawkins, Don Redman, Louis Armstrong, Jack Teagarden, Benny Goodman, and many others. Her influence was felt by all contemporary blues singers, and the vocal tradition she established is still with us today. Gunther Schuller sees her as

> . . . one of the great tragic figures, not only of jazz, but of her period, and she more than any other expressed the hopes and sorrows of her generation of jazz musicians. If that were all, we would have reason enough to eulogize her. But Bessie Smith was a supreme artist, and as such her art transcends the particulars of life that informed that art.[38]

A leading contemporary of Bessie's was Ida Cox, born in Knoxville, Tennessee, in 1889. She too toured with her own tent show in the South. She was one of the most successful blues recording artists, and she began recording for Paramount in 1923. In 1925 she made *Rambling Blues*[39] with her husband, Jesse Crump, at the piano and a New Orleans–born cornetist, Tommy Ladnier. In many ways this is an archetypal blues, for it not only presents the stan-

[38] Schuller, *Early Jazz*, p. 241.
[39] Paramount 12318.

A rare photograph of Ida Cox (1889–1967).

dard blues form and offers the text in the simplest pattern, but it deals with the state of mind most commonly accepted as that of the blues.

> Early this morning the blues came walkin' in my room,
> Early this morning the blues came walkin' in my room,
> I said, "Blues, please tell me what you're doin'
> > makin' me feel so blue."

Another side, probably recorded at the same time, *Coffin Blues*,[40] is a lament to a dead lover.

> Daddy, oh Daddy, won't you answer me please?
> Daddy, oh Daddy, won't you answer me please?
> All day I stood by your coffin tryin' to give my
> > poor heart ease.

Like other singers of the day, not everything Ida Cox recorded with the word "blues" in the title was in fact a blues. Her recording of *I've Got the Blues for Rampart Street*[41] is not a blues at all but a piece in the ragtime-Dixieland style. Eight-measure phrases with chromatic harmonies moving around the circle of fifths form the basis of this piece in contrast to the four-measure phrases and slower-moving harmonies of the blues.

Ida Cox was rediscovered in 1939 by John Hammond and brought to New York for a "From Spirituals to Swing" concert. She recorded *Hard Time Blues*, *Take Him Off My Mind*, and *Last Mill Blues* at this time. She continued to work regularly until she suffered a stroke in Buffalo, New York, in 1945, and eventually retired to her home in Knoxville in 1949. She came out of retirement to record once more, in 1961, before she died in 1967. In some ways, Ida Cox was more truly representative of the singers of the 1920s than Bessie Smith, for where Bessie's artistry towered over the rest, making her performances individual and unique, Ida Cox represents a legion of singers whose work meets high professional standards but is uninspired. She had a good voice, a professional demeanor, and accurate rhythm and pitch, but her recordings are more regular and predictable than subtle and emotional.

Bertha "Chippie" Hill, on the other hand, was a talent equal to that of Bessie Smith, but who, for one reason or another, has not been accorded the fame she deserves. Born in Charleston, South Carolina, in 1905, she, like Bessie Smith, toured with Ma Rainey's show, first as a dancer and later as a singer. Also like Bessie, she went through a period of obscurity which lasted from

---

[40] Ibid.
[41] Paramount 12063, reissued Riverside RLP 12–113.

about 1930 to the mid-1940s, and again like Bessie, died in an auto accident. At her best, Chippie Hill was the equal of any blues singer, past or present. The melodramatic and comic solution of *Trouble in Mind*[42] blues was to lay her head on a railroad track, and this song, composed by Richard M. Jones and recorded by Chippie in 1926, was to become the best-known of all her blues performances. When she was rediscovered, working in a bakery in 1946, by Rudi Blesh, she began recording once again. Her musical powers had not diminished, and her comeback was an exciting historical event. Her recording of *Around the Clock Blues*[43] was made with an authentic group of early New Orleans jazz musicians: Lovie Austin, piano; John Lindsay, bass; and Baby Dodds, drums. It is interesting to note that at so late a date, 1946, a sixteen-bar blues was still being recorded. In form, it resembles a popular song—**AABA**—but the phrases are only four measures long; the second **A** repeats the text of the first; and the short sixteen-measure piece is strophic. *Around the Clock Blues* is a variant of *My Daddy Rocks Me*, recorded by May Alix with Jimmy Noone and his Orchestra in 1929.[44] The forty-six-year-old Chippie belts out the celebration of physical love in the best blues style of the 1920s:

> Now my baby rocks me with one steady roll,
> Now my baby rocks me with words untol',
> Now I look at the clock, the clock struck one,
>   me and my baby havin' such fun,
> I say keep on rockin' me baby with your good old
>   steady roll.

> Now my baby rocks me with one steady roll,
> Now there's no lovin' until he takes hol',
> Now I looked at the clock, and the clock struck two,
>   let's see what he intends to do
> Before rubbin' me, baby, with that good old steady
>   roll.

A name almost forgotten today because her records have disappeared from general circulation is Mamie Smith, "First Lady of the Blues." On August 10, 1920, she recorded Perry Bradford's *Crazy Blues*,[45] the first vocal recording with choruses based on a twelve-measure structure. A few months earlier, she had cut the first disc to be made by a black singer, and because of its success, she was called back to the studios for what was the beginning of the history of

---

[42] Okeh 8273, reissued Folkways FP 59.
[43] Circle J1013, reissued Riverside RLP 12-113.
[44] Vocalion 2779.
[45] Okeh 4169, reissued Columbia C3L-33.

recorded blues. According to the composer, 800,000 copies of Mamie Smith's performance of *Crazy Blues* were eventually sold. Her recording career lasted from 1920 through 1931, but whereas the entire Bessie Smith oeuvre has been reissued on long-playing records, not a single long-playing record of Mamie Smith's works has been issued on a major American label. Her only modern recorded appearances are in two anthologies, *Women of the Blues* and *The Sounds of Harlem*.[46] A fair evaluation of her singing style is not really possible from this sample.

Mamie Smith (1890–1946).

The song that brought black vocalists to the recording studios was Perry Bradford's *That Thing Called Love*,[47] which was backed by the Rega Orchestra, a group of five men playing trumpet, trombone, clarinet, violin, and piano. Although it is not a blues, the text is in the blues tradition.

> I'm worried in my mind,
> I'm worried all the time,
> My friend he told me today,

[46] Victor LPV-539 and Columbia C3L-33.
[47] Okeh 4113.

> That he was going away to stay,
> Now I love him deep down in my heart,
> But the best of friends must part . . . .[48]

A common fallacy held by many jazz buffs is that classic blues were sung only by women; but even as early as the 1920s, men were recording the same repertoire. A list of leading blues singers of the 1920s always includes Ma Rainey, Bessie Smith, Ida Cox, Chippie Hill, and others like Sarah Martin, Clara Smith, Victoria Spivey, Mamie Smith, Sippie Wallace, and Trixie Smith, but it hardly ever lists Louis Armstrong, Big Joe Williams, Jimmy Rushing, and Jack Teagarden, who all sang the classic blues. It is true that Louis Armstrong did not specialize in blues singing as did most of the women singers, but his performance of *Gully Low Blues*,[49] recorded in May, 1927, is a classic blues in form, delivery, and text.

> Now mama, why do you treat me so?
> Oh mama, why do you treat me so?
> I know why you treat me so bad, you treat me mean,
>   baby, just because I'm gully low.
>
> Now if you listen baby, I'll tell you somethin' you
>   don't know.
> If you just listen to me honey, I'll tell you
>   somethin' you don't know.
> If you just give me a break and take me back,
>   I won't be gully no more.

The preceding day, Louis recorded the same blues but used a different verse in his vocal chorus. As a result, it received a different title, *S.O.L. Blues*.[50]

> Now I'm with you sweet mama as long as you have the
>   bucks (I mean money, mama).
> I'm with you sweet mama as long as you have
>   bucks.
> When the bucks run out, sweet mama, I mean you
>   are out of luck.

Two years earlier, Louis recorded *I'm Not Rough*,[51] and although this version lacks successive verses and fails to pair the first two lines, he still sings the sophisticated classic blues.

[48] Quoted by Paul Oliver, *The Meaning of the Blues*, p. 21.
[49] Columbia CL-852.
[50] Columbis CL-851.
[51] Ibid.

Now I aint rough, and I don't bite,
    but the woman that gets me gots to treat me right.
Cause I'm crazy 'bout my lovin',
    and I must have it all the time.
It takes a brown skinned woman to satisfy my mind.

Perhaps the most poignant vocal performance by Louis Armstrong is his 1929 recording of *What Did I Do to Be So Black and Blue?*[52] Although this song is in thirty-two-measure, pop-song form (**AABA**), both its lyrics and style of performance place it among the monuments of classic blues. At the peak of commercial success, and at the height of his mature solo style, Louis let slip for a moment the smiling mask of the black stage personality and revealed a bit of the desolation that crowded his inner being.

Old empty bed, springs hard as lead,
    feel like "Ol Ned," wish I were dead.
All my life through I been so Black and blue.

Even a mouse, ran from my house,
    they laugh at you, and scorn you too.
What did I do to be so Black and blue?

Oh, I'm white inside, but that don't help my case,
'Cause I can't hide what is on my face.

How will it end, aint got a friend,
    my only sin is in my skin.
What did I do to be so Black and blue?

Although Ethel Waters (born in Chester, Pennsylvania, in 1900) lacked the musical virtuosity with which Louis imbued his performance, she laid out the text even more melodramatically in her recorded version of the same song.

(Intro)   Out in the street, shufflin' feet, couples
        passing two by two.
    And here am I, left high and dry, Black,
        and cause I'm Black, I'm blue.
    All the race fellows crave "high yellow,"
        gentlemen prefer them light.
    I'm just another spade who can't make the grade,
    Looks like there's nothin' but dark days in sight.

---

[52] Columbia CL-854. *Black and Blue* was composed for the 1929 stage show *Hot Chocolates*, by Andy Razaf, Thomas "Fats" Waller, and Harry Brooks.

(Verse one) With a cold empty bed, springs hard as lead,
     pains in my head and I feel like "Ol Ned,"
    What did I do to be so Black and blue?

    No joys for me, no company
     even the mouse, ran from my house,
    All my life through I been so Black and blue.

    I'm white, but it's inside,
     so that don't help my case,
    Cause I can't hide just what is on my face.

    Oh, sad and forlorn, life's just a thorn,
     my heart is torn, oh why was I born?
    What did I do to be so Black and blue?

(Verse two) Just cause you're Black, boys think you lack,
     they laugh at you and scorn you, too.
    What did I do to be so Black and blue?

    When I draw near, they laugh and sneer,
     I'm set aside, always denied.
    All my life through I been so Black and blue.

    How sad I am, and each day
     the situation gets worse.
    My mark of Ham seems to be a curse.

    Oh, how will it end, can't get a boyfriend,
     yet my only sin lies in my skin.
    What did I do to be so Black and blue?[53]

In Waters's performance, we can clearly see how this thirty-two-measure piece relates to the blues tradition. It is strophic not only in having two verses, but in matching each phrase against the next as a constant embellishment of the blues' theme, "What did I do to be so Black and blue?" Each eight-measure phrase, except that of the bridge, pairs two lines of commentary as preparation for the refrain answer. In its musical structure, *Black and Blue* lacks both the twelve-measure pattern and the characteristic harmonic sequence, but as we have seen in recorded examples of other classic-blues singers, the notion that their repertoire consisted only of standardized twelve-measure blues pieces is not substantiated in fact.

James Andrew Rushing, born in Oklahoma in 1903, is best known as a blues singer in the Kansas City style of Count Basie, for he went to New York City with

[53] Columbia Archive Series, C3L-35.

Basie's band in 1936 and worked as a blues singer with Basie until 1950. He began working in California in 1923 or 1924 at the Jump Steady Club, where he was occasionally accompanied by Jelly Roll Morton. In 1927–28, he was singing with Walter Page's Blue Devils, and in 1929 he was the vocalist for Benny Moten's band. There are no recordings by Jimmy Rushing from this period, but if his singing style resembled what he recorded later, he was singing the classic blues in the 1920s.

Blues singing and jazz singing have been continuous from the earliest appearance of the genre until the present day, and a connected line of development can be traced from Mamie Smith and Ma Rainey to Bessie Smith and Chippie Hill and on to Billie Holiday, Ella Fitzgerald, and Janis Joplin. Once recording and radio made the music of star vocalists available to the country at large, it was no longer necessary to have a direct apprentice-master relationship. Similarly, connecting a historical line from early jazz and blues singers like Louis Armstrong and Jimmy Rushing to Nat King Cole, Billy Eckstine, and Frank Sinatra is made possible for the same reason. The interchange of musicians between bands, the path-crossing on the vaudeville, club, and concert circuits, and the personal meetings which naturally brought musicians in contact with each other in the large metropolitan areas provided an artistic exchange which had an extraordinary effect on the musical activity of America.

Urban Blues

The classic blues was, in a sense, a city version of the country blues, for although standardization of form was taking place, it was never fully achieved. Also, although the stereotype would have the city blues performed with piano or jazz ensemble, some of the major figures, like Ma Rainey, did sing and record the blues with folksy instruments. Her *Traveling Blues*,[54] recorded in 1929, is accompanied by a tub, jug, and washboard band. The city blues, as they continued into the mid and late '30s, have recently been given a new name, "urban blues,"[55] and are characterized by the introduction of big-band riff accompaniments, a greater importance of saxophone as a characteristic sound, and, in its later phases, the introduction of electric guitar and, eventually, totally amplified ensembles. Jimmy Rushing, who began his professional career in the '20s, became one of the leaders of the new style with the Count Basie Band from Kansas City in the late '30s, but by this date blues no longer

[54] Paramount 14011, reissued Folkways FP 59.
[55] Charles Keil, *Urban Blues* (Chicago: University of Chicago Press, 1966).

need consideration separate and distinct from jazz. Instead, blues, except for country blues, have been totally integrated into the jazz repertoire both instrumentally and vocally, and the major events, musicians, and performances of that repertoire will be taken up in chronological order. But one aspect of the blues of the 1920s needs to be investigated further at this time—the music called blues that has no vocal lyrics.

Instrumental Blues

Although the vocalists rejected the idea, the twelve-bar blues did become standard with instrumental ensemble musicians during the 1920s. No further instruction was necessary once an experienced jazz musician was told "Blues in B♭ " or "Blues in three" (three flats, or, key of E♭). Although they were capable of performing blues outside the standardized schema, this structure, with its set harmonic pattern, became the norm. *Dippermouth Blues* (SCCJ, I/6) as played by Joe Oliver and his Creole Jazz Band in 1923 is but one of thousands of similar performances of the B♭ blues. The four-measure introduction and the two-measure ending obviously had been worked out in advance. In its formal outline, it consists of a four-measure introduction, nine improved blues choruses of twelve measures each, and a two-measure tag. The remainder of the performance is improvised, except for the stoptime chords of choruses 3 and 4, which accompany the clarinet solo of Johnny Dodds. It is also typical that two ensemble choruses of the blues begin the piece, for the twelve-

Dippermouth Blues

Intro	I Blues	II Blues	III Blues	IV Blues	V Blues	VI Blues	VII Blues	VIII Blues	IX Blues	Tag
4 mm.	12 mm.	12 mm.	12 mm.	12 mm.	12 mm.	12 mm.	12 mm.	12 mm	12 mm.	2 mm.
Comp.*	Impro.† Ensemb.‡	Impro. Ensemb.	Impro.	Impro.	Impro. Ensemb.	Impro.	Impro.	Impro. Ensemb.	Impro. Ensemb.	Comp.
			Dodds clarinet (stop-time)	Dodds clarinet (stop-time)		Oliver cornet	Oliver cornet		"Oh play that thing"	

* Composed
† Improvised
‡ Ensemble

measure form at a moderate-to-fast tempo is too brief to establish the sound of the particular piece in the listener's ear. The muted solo by King Oliver that begins in the sixth chorus and continues for the seventh is one of the classic trumpet riffs[56] that was imitated by hosts of other trumpet players who admired both the style of the music and the details of this performance.

Dippermouth Blues, Oliver Solo on Choruses 6 and 7

The way Oliver bends his minor third against the major harmonies of the accompaniment (D^b against a B^b-major chord; chorus 6, mm. 1 and 3); the way he inflects notes both upward and downward (chorus 6, m. 10, and chorus 7, mm. 2 and 3); and the tantalizing manner in which he stretches the solo rhythm patterns off the beat in contrast to the regular pulse of the accompaniment (chorus 7, mm. 3 and 4) are some of the elements in this performance which help make it a great jazz solo of the 1920s. Motivically, too, it has great structural integrity, for Oliver plays with the minor and major third intervals $B^b–D^b$ and $B^b–D^{\natural}$. At one point he stretches the sound up to F (the end of chorus 6) and lets it melt back from D to B^b (chorus 7, mm. 3 to 4).

Sound recording in 1923 was not perfected to the point where it could reproduce, distinctly, all the sounds of the instruments in ensemble. Consequently, it is difficult to show exactly what each instrument is playing at any

---

[56] A "riff" usually signifies a short, repeated melodic figure, but here it is used to indicate a blues melody (e.g. Charlie Parker's *Bird Feathers* or *Big Foot* refer to blues melodies known and performed by other jazz men).

one moment. As Martin Williams explains, this is a "sample of the dense polyphonic style of the New Orleans ensemble, performed by one of the great New Orleans groups."[57] At the end of the seventh chorus, as Joe Oliver finishes his solo, Johnny Dodds picks up the lead and the group moves off into a collectively improvised chorus.

* The author has reconstructed an appropriate drum part, since the drums are inaudible in this recorded performance.

Even though only the notes of Dodd's clarinet, Oliver's cornet, and Dutrey's trombone have been transcribed with a fair degree of certainty, the notation for the rest of the instruments can only be a close approximation. Bud Scott strums a straight four on the banjo in simple triads. Baby Dodds, who cannot be heard here on the record, most likely would have balanced the four-beat pattern of the banjo with a two-beat pattern of alternating bass drum and snare. The right hand of Lil Hardin's piano playing cannot be positively ascertained from the congealed sound of banjo and piano, but the left hand moves along in a four-beat walking-bass pattern. The notes of Louis's second cornet are totally ob-

[57] *SCCJ* liner notes, p. 17.

scured when the solo cornet of King Oliver enters, but those sounds that can be heard indicate that he was providing short riffs to fill the gaps in the rhythm of the solo lines. The counterpoint does not have the smooth, balanced quality of classic polyphony, where dissonances are carefully introduced and just as carefully resolved, but the happy, free flow of lines that remain distinct by virtue of their contrasting timbre, difference in range, and diversity of rhythmic values. In this particular example, the speed of notes for the clarinet line does not differ from that of either of the trumpet lines, but this is a small sample. The layerlike separation between the speed of the soprano instruments and trombone is more obvious.

The blues is omnipresent in the repertoire of instrumental jazz, and this sample might serve as a prototype of the typical jazz performance blues pattern of introduction, ensemble, solos, ensemble, and out. Derived from a vocal form that never achieved any real uniformity, even as late as the mid-1930s, the blues pattern in instrumental jazz was a *forme fixe*, a set form, by the time this recording was made.

Gunther Schuller, commenting on "Oliver's own justly famous solo on both *Dippermouth Blues* recordings," sums up the effect of this performance and the significance of that particular year:

> Here the Okeh performance especially has a remarkably dense and well-balanced texture, perfectly captured by the engineers; and its great swing must have had an overwhelming effect in person in 1923.
>
> Since that year jazz has experienced a prodigious development in terms of instrumental virtuosity, dynamic and timbrel variety. It is, therefore, all the more amazing that we can still listen with interest to the Creole Jazz Band, since these features are virtually nonexistent on its recordings.[58]

The blues is many things—the music of people, a style of music, a type of performance, a despondent state of mind, and a musical form. As all these things, the blues has contributed to jazz. Within the formal concept of continuous improvisation over a constantly recurring harmonic framework, the blues has given jazz its most significant element.

---

[58] Schuller, *Early Jazz*, p. 85

THE EARLY YEARS
OF JAZZ, 1900 TO 1917

IT MUST BE remembered that jazz is, first of all, a dance music. Further, it is not defined by what is played, but by how it is played. In other words, jazz is a way of performing that can be applied to many types of music. Third, a good jazz performance maintains the integrity of both the sound-concept of the leader of the group and the basic characteristics of the composition being played. Lastly, harmony, in jazz, is a guide rather than a goal. Within the context of late nineteenth-century and early twentieth-century Western music, this last point is of great significance, for this was the time when the works of Gustav Mahler, Richard Strauss, and Arnold Schoenberg had reached new heights of extravagant harmonic display.

During the first decade and a half of the twentieth century, in the years before sound recording, there were at least twenty-three Creole and black dance orchestras and brass bands working in New Orleans for which sufficient documentation exists to enable us to reconstruct, rather accurately, their organization and their music. Among the better-known groups were the Excelsior Brass Band, The Olympia Orchestra, the Tuxedo Brass Band, the Silver Leaf Orchestra, and the Onward Brass Band. Employment was plentiful for qualified musicians, and many establishments in the red-light district, the river steamers, and the black fraternal organizations provided employment on a regular basis for professional musicians. Thousands of people were employed in the lively port entertaining the travelers and visitors with ready money. In 1897 a resolution proposed by town alderman Sidney Story was passed that allowed legal prostitution to flourish in a thirty-eight block area uptown bordered by Canal and Basin Streets. In newly christened Storyville, bars, sporting houses, dance

The Onward Brass Band in 1905. (Left to right) Manuel Perez, Andrew Kimball, Peter Bocage, Lorenzo Tio, Jr., Adolphe Alexander, Sr., Bebé Matthews, Dandy Lewis, Isidore Barbarin, Buddy Johnson, Vic Gaspard, Eddie Atkins, and Eddie Jackson.

halls, and other nighttime establishments flourished, and it quickly became the principal tourist attraction in New Orleans. Tom Anderson, a bar owner in the area, published the *Blue Book—An Illustrated Directory and Gentleman's Guide to the Sporting District*. Elegantly bound in pale blue, with harps and flowers on the cover, it enumerated the various Storyville houses in detail, to the extent of describing the beautiful girls within.

Ragtime Jazz Bands

If a pleasure palace did not support an entire orchestra, it maintained, at the least, a piano player from evening to dawn. An entry in the New Orleans *Daily Picayune* of March 25, 1913, informs us that

> The Tuxedo, a model of the dance halls which make up a good part of the Tenderloin, occupies a berth on North Franklin. . . . Here a Negro band holds forth and from about 8 o'clock at night until 4 o'clock in the morning plays varied rags, conspicuous for being the latest in popular music, interspersed with compositions

ιe musicians themselves. The band has a leader who grotesquely prompts the
ιs pieces, which generally constitute several brass pieces, a violin, guitar,
ιlo, and a piano.[1]

ι without sound recordings, we can reconstruct the music of these rag-
ιands with a fair degree of accuracy, for ragtime orchestrations are extant
ι this period. Also, photographs of some of the early bands show us the
ιise instrumentation of the performing ensembles. A photograph of the Su-
ιⲣⲁrior Orchestra, a dance ensemble active from 1910 to 1913, reveals cornet,
clarinet, trombone, violin, guitar, string bass, and drums (one player for snare
and bass).[2] A photograph of the Imperial Band from the same period shows exactly the same instrumentation.[3] The Onward Brass Band, pictured about
1913, has twelve members: clarinet, three cornets, two horns, baritone, two
trombones, bass, snare drum, and bass drum.[4] All of these groups had only
black or Creole musicians, but white musicians did play in the area at the same
time. The all-white Reliance Brass Band, photographed in 1910 before the
"Big Show" tent of Laine's Greater Majestic Minstrels, which was pitched
behind a car barn at Canal and White Streets, is pictured with a group of seven
musicians: clarinet, cornet, trombone, baritone, bass, snare drum, and bass
drum and cymbal.[5] The pictures, written reports, and notated music all help
prove that ragtime is an early form of hot jazz. For example, *Knock Out Drops
Rag*, by F. Henri Klickmann, arranged by the famous bandmaster Harry L. Alford, could have been purchased and adapted to the various musical combinations present in New Orleans and elsewhere at that time. A typical four-strain
rag with introduction, it assigned the ragged melody to the solo cornet most of
the time, worked a counter melody into the baritone part, as was common in
many marches, and left the oom-pah of the ragtime pianist's left hand to the
bass and horns. The performance direction for the second strain of the trio is
"Noisy," as was New Orleans jazz, and these rags were the newest, most modern thing at that time.

Many of the musicians who later acquired fame as recording jazz stars
belonged to these ensembles: Jimmy Noone, John Lindsay, and Johnny St. Cyr
played in Oscar "Papa" Celestin's Tuxedo Band; Willie "Bunk" Johnson played
for the original Superior Orchestra; and Alcide "Yellow" Nunez, of the Original Dixieland Jazz Band, was a member of the Reliance Brass Band. White

---

[1] Quoted in Samuel B. Charters, *Jazz: New Orleans 1885–1963*, p. 17.
[2] Orin Keepnews and Bill Grauer, Jr., *A Pictorial History of Jazz* (New York: Crown Publishers, 1955), p. 7.
[3] Ibid.
[4] Al Rose and Edmond Souchon, *New Orleans Jazz: A Family Album*, p. 193.
[5] Ibid., p. 185.

KNOCK OUT DROPS

Rag
A Trombone Jag

Solo B♭ Cornet.

F HENRI KLICKMANN
Arr. by Harry L. Alford.

Knock Out Drops Rag: Trio, Second Strain

153

musicians were in the minority, but they occupied a significant place in the musical picture of those early days. Jack "Papa" Laine, sometimes described as the "Father of White Jazz," was a disciple of Buddy Bolden and formed successful bands of his own in New Orleans. His Reliance Brass Band was eventually renamed Jack Laine's Ragtime Band.

Another important white musician from New Orleans was Tom Brown, a trombonist who was the first to bring a Dixieland band to Chicago in 1915. A hot jazz group, the Louisiana Five, led by Alcide "Yellow" Nunez, played at Bustanoby's Restaurant in New York in 1915, and although he missed out on the first recording sessions with the Original Dixieland Jazz Band, he was later to become a member of the group.

"Tailgate trombone" is a term which developed in the early days of jazz in New Orleans, for dancehalls would advertise by sending a horse-drawn wagon through the town carrying a loud-blowing jazz ensemble. The trombonist, who needed more room to manipulate his slide, sat on the tailgate of the wagon. The music of this era included many novelty tunes, and not only were non-standard instruments such as jugs and homemade horns used, but new ways of playing the old instruments were developed. Burt Kelly, leader of Frisco's Jazz Band, reported in a newspaper interiew of 1919 that Ray Lopez was the first cornet player to use a derby mute and Tom Brown the first trombonist to use a hat over his bell.

Most of the influential early jazz musicians were black, and they came from a community which has been called "Bourbon Street Black." Within the larger black community there was

> . . . a semi-community in New Orleans of musicians, their relatives, peers, friends, and general supporters whose style of life is built around the fundamental assumption that the production and nurture of music for people, in general, is good.[6]

From 1897 to 1917, members of this community filled the major houses of Storyville with music. In the early 1910s, the Eagle Band was at Globe Hall, Celestin was at the Tuxedo, Perez was at Rice's, King Oliver was at Huntz's. Freddie Keppard, Bunk Johnson, and others worked the remainder of the houses. Outside the district, the musicians played for society dances, parades, and funerals. The Excelsior and Onward were probably the best brass bands in the city, but Papa Celestin's Tuxedo Brass Band, by playing the more up-to-date music, began taking jobs away from the older bands.

[6] J. V. Buerkle and D. Barker, *Bourbon Street Black*, p. 41.

Jazz and Morality

The lifestyle of the New Orleans musician was automatically associated with the music he played, and in spite of its immediate popularity, jazz was met by impassioned opposition from the Victorian, pro-prohibition majority of white America. Just as Storyville had its public, it also had its enemies, and there is no question that the business of prostitution also brought with it drug addiction, alcoholism, venereal disease, gambling, and the syndicate. Jazz became the symbol of crime, feeble-mindedness, insanity, and sex, and was under constant attack by the press from the early 1920s on. It was seen as a symptom of general cultural decay, and Karl Engel, writing in the *Atlantic Monthly*, urged his readers not to become alarmed because "almost every race and every age have known social conditions which result in an unloosing of instincts that nature wisely has taught us to hold well in check, but which, every now and then, from cryptic reasons, are allowed to break the bonds of civilization."[7] *The New York Times* ran an article in April of 1922:

> Musician is Driven to Suicide by Jazz;
> Wouldn't Play It, Couldn't Get Employment

> His fellow-lodgers at 124 East Thirty-first Street said yesterday that jazz was responsible for the death of Melville M. Wilson. . . . Then came jazz. The old man revolted. He wouldn't insult his 'cello, he said, nor the old melodies he had played so long and loved so well. . . . Jazz was everywhere and no one seemed to have any use for Wilson and his cello.[8]

The 1916 election campaign which preceded the closing of Storyville included a major push by the "drys" to secure legislation prohibiting the sale and advertisement of liquor. At that time there were nineteen prohibition states. Jazz, along with ragtime, which seemed to be an accessory of whorehouses and saloons, was spreading across the country at the same time that the Puritan tradition in the form of prohibition was moving toward its moment of triumph. While women were campaigning for prohibition and the vote, jazz was extolling fun, excitement, and the pleasures of youth.

> Beer is bad,
> Whisky's worse;
> We drink water—
> Safety first.

[7] "Jazz: A Musical Discussion," *Atlantic Monthly*, 130 (August, 1922), p. 182.
[8] *New York Times*, April 7, 1922, section 1, page 1.

> We can't vote,
> Neither can Ma.
> If Nebraska goes wet—
> Blame it on Pa.[9]

One commentator has noted:

> The degree to which jazz served as a symbol of culturally defined evil in the United
> States, and in other countries as well, may seem incredible to us today, but it was a
> real fact in the 1920's and 1930's. It is an extremely clear illustration of how music,
> and in this case not individual sounds but an entire body of sound, can be used
> symbolically on the level of affective ascribed cultural meaning.[10]

Jazz was, and is, a powerful cultural force, and it is ironic that we preserve, study, and enjoy a music today that was felt to be insidious and lascivious only yesterday.

Following the successful conclusion of the First World War, girls' skirts moved high above the knees, women were seen smoking and drinking in public, and sex became an acceptable topic for discussion. Those who were incapable of coping with the rapid changes they saw taking place around them turned on dancing and the music that accompanied it, declaring the music not merely a symptom but a cause of moral decay. Another newspaper article ran:

Jazz Ruining Girls, Declares Reformers

> Chicago, Jan. 21—Moral disaster is coming to hundreds of young American girls
> through the pathological, nerve-irritating, sex-exciting music of jazz orchestras, according to the Illinois Vigilance Association.
>
> In Chicago alone the association's representatives have traced the fall of 1,000 girls
> in the last two years to jazz music.
>
> Girls in small towns, as well as the big cities, in poor homes and rich homes, are
> victims of the weird, insidious, neurotic music that accompanies modern dancing.
>
> The degrading music is common not only to disorderly places, but often to high
> school affairs, to expensive hotels and so-called society circles.[11]

The teens and twenties of this century were without question a time of ferment in the United States. The First World War, prohibition, the closing of Storyville, and the invention of sound recording were all elements that had a

[9] *Nebraska Campaign Songs* (Lincoln: Nebraska Dry Federation, 1916), p. 14.

[10] Alan P. Merriam, *The Anthropology of Music* (Evanston: Northwestern University Press, 1964), p. 244.

[11] *New York American*, June 22, 1922.

profound effect on the development of the new music. World War I brought American popular music, including jazz, to Europe. It had lured thousands of young American men away from home and placed them in an environment that made them receptive to jazz and all its implications. When the war and prohibition served as an excuse to close Storyville, the criminal syndicates opened similar establishments elsewhere, most notably, of course, in Chicago. The riverboats had already carried Dixieland jazz to St. Louis and Kansas City, and when New Orleans musicians were left without anyplace to play, they began a further exodus to New York and Chicago.

But even before the first recording, several musicians had achieved prominence as leading jazz performers, and several numbers of what was to become the standard repertoire had already been developed. *Tiger Rag* and *Oh Didn't He Ramble* were played long before the first jazz recording, and the names of Buddy Bolden, Jelly Roll Morton, Bunk Johnson, Papa Celestin, Sidney Bechet, King Oliver, Freddie Keppard, Kid Ory, and Papa Laine were already well known to the jazz community.

Bunk, Papa, and Sidney

Willie Geary "Bunk" Johnson was a leading figure in the days of early Dixieland jazz in New Orleans. His association with Buddy Bolden in the earliest period of New Orleans jazz was the turning point in his musical career. He achieved more recognition among his fellow musicians than he did from the listening public, for his playing did not resemble that of the popular Bolden, Keppard, and Oliver. He was acknowledged for his ability to swing a band in a conservative, restrained manner. Born in 1879, he began playing second cornet in Bolden's band as a teenager. He has recounted this experience:

> Here is the thing that made King Bolden's Band be the first band that played jazz. It was because it did not Read at all. I could fake like 500 myself; so you tell them that Bunk and King Bolden's Band was the first ones that started jazz in the City or any place else. [12]

He played with other bands during this period, including the Excelsior, and traveled to New York City in 1903 with a minstrel show, Holecamp's Georgia Smart Set. He traveled to Dallas and San Francisco, and returned to New Orleans in 1910 to join the Superior Orchestra. Between 1911 and 1914, John-

[12] Quoted by Rex Harris, *Jazz*, p. 82.

William Geary "Bunk" Johnson (1879–1949).

son, with Sidney Bechet, was a member of Frankie Dusen's Eagle Band, playing and marching at the many occasions that called for music. He left New Orleans permanently in 1914 and worked on and off with innumerable vaudeville, minstrel-show, and club bands. He was with Evan Thomas's Black Eagle Band in Crowley, Louisiana, when the leader was murdered on the bandstand and Johnson's horn was destroyed in a fight. Johnson worked less and less as a musician in the ensuing years. When he was rediscovered in 1937, he was hauling sugarcane in the fields. The remainder of his musical life is a part of the New Orleans revival, but his work is mentioned here because of its significance in the years before recording.

Johnson serves as a useful example of both the problems and the blessings that surface when one tries to reconstruct history on the basis of information supplied by "knowledgeable" informants. Although Bunk Johnson, without doubt, was a performing musician in New Orleans during the early years of this century, it seems that much of the information he furnished about early jazz is questionable. For example, it would seem that he, better than anyone else, could settle the question of which of Buddy Bolden's bands he played in. However, we still do not know whether he played in the Olympia Band or in one of the others that Bolden was leading at the same time. Johnson claimed to have been Louis Armstrong's teacher and influence, but Armstrong denied this, saying King Oliver was his only teacher and that although he admired Bunk Johnson's tone, it went no further than that. Just as Jelly Roll Morton once claimed to have "invented" jazz, Bunk also claimed a thing or two which have been contradicted by his contemporaries. As a spokesman for early jazz, Johnson did provide us with some insights into the music from the viewpoint of a Dixieland jazz musician.

He was, without doubt, a fundamental participant in the history of early jazz. His relationships with Buddy Bolden and Frankie Dusen's Eagle Band were intertwined with the roots of Dixieland improvisation. Although he remained unrecognized in the annals of jazz until after the New Orleans revival, around 1942, it was evident, even at such a late stage in life, that he was a jazz musician of high calibre. His style and attitudes toward jazz seem more representative than unique, and he acted as a leading figure in the reconstruction of traditional jazz.

A popular bandleader in New Orleans for forty-four years, Oscar "Papa" Celestin formed the Original Tuxedo Orchestra in 1910 and the Tuxedo Brass Band in 1911. For most of his career, Celestin was one of the most popular musicians in the city, and to a certain degree, his colorful mannerisms rather than any extraordinary musical abilities contributed to his success. He was a strong cornet player and is usually regarded as a pioneer jazz musician. He was not a good reading musician, and often used a second cornet player to handle the hot solos. Born in Napoleonville, Louisiana, in 1884, he moved to New Orleans in 1906. His orchestra opened the Tuxedo Dance Hall in Storyville in 1910, and after a gun fight at the Tuxedo Bar in 1913, where five men were shot to death, he and his orchestra were out of work. In New Orleans, he worked with many of the leading musicians, including Clarence Williams, A. J. Piron, Jimmy Noone, Johnny St. Cyr, Peter Bocage, and Louis Armstrong. He recorded for Okeh in 1925,[13] and unlike the Armstrong recordings from the same period, the performances are noted more for their polish in ensemble than for exciting improvisational flights. His recording group, which he still called Celestin's Original Tuxedo Jazz Orchestra, included one or two trumpets, a trombone, two or three reeds, piano, banjo, bass, and drums. During his last years, Celestin was honored as one of the great men of New Orleans

[13] Okeh 8215, reissued Columbia C3L-30.

music. He died in 1954, and 4,000 people marched in his funeral procession.

Sidney Bechet, the only jazz performer to achieve fame on the soprano saxophone, was active in Paris as a professional almost as many years as Papa Celestin played in New Orleans. Born in New Orleans in 1897, he was introduced to the famous Eagle Band of New Orleans by Bunk Johnson around 1912. He left the Crescent City in 1914, touring with Clarence Williams and Louis Wade, and returned in 1916, when he worked with King Oliver's Olympia Band. In 1917, he traveled to Chicago, and later, in 1919, moved to New York, where he joined Will Marion Cook's Southern Syncopated Orchestra. This organization took him to Europe, where Bechet became the first jazz musician to receive serious consideration by a distinguished classical musician when Ernest Ansermet became interested in Cook's orchestra and Bechet's playing. Bechet remained in Europe, primarily in Paris, until 1921, when he returned to New York City and made his first records with Clarence Williams's Blue Five. It was here that he played sessions with Mamie Smith and other blues singers, and worked briefly, during 1924, with Duke Ellington. For the next fifteen years, he worked in Europe and America with various artists, including Noble Sissle, Tommy Ladnier, and Willie "The Lion" Smith. He returned to jobbing in New York and appeared with Eddie Condon in many Town Hall concerts in the early 1940s. After shuttling back and forth between Europe and America from the late 1940s on, he died in Paris in May of 1959.

Bechet's solo work in *Texas Moaner Blues*,[14] recorded with Clarence Williams and Louis Armstrong in 1924, exhibits most of the characteristics associated with his playing throughout the years: a facile and liquid technique, a melodic line heavily shaded by blue notes and blues intonation, and a large and rapid vibrato. Bechet thought of his instrument as a medium by which he might dramatize and communicate his own personal feelings to sensitive listeners. And, as a result, his recorded solo work is generally considered in extramusical terms as dignified, empathic, and so on. But on a purely musical level, his solos have great structural integrity. Decorated with an occasional virtuosic flight, musical ideas proceed with logic and rational order. His thirty-two-measure solo on *I've Found a New Baby*,[15] recorded in 1932 with Tommy Ladnier, is a classic example of developmental technique in jazz improvisation. The first of the four phrases states a musical idea of a descending melodic motive. Each of the following three phrases amplifies the same idea, with the last phrase stating it most clearly and rounding it off with a melodic turning figure that provides a passageway to the next solo.

Bechet achieved great public success in France, not only for his musical powers, but also for his position as a vaudeville figure, an entertainer, and a

[14] Okeh 8171, reissued Columbia C3L-30.
[15] RCA Victor LPV-535.

personality. Because of his self-imposed expatriation, he had less influence on the course of American jazz than would probably have been the case had he remained in America to pursue his musical career. His style and sound were highly personal and seemed to have inspired few followers. Still, he won the respect of leading jazz musicians and must be counted one of the important personalities of early jazz. Perhaps more than any other single figure, Bechet was responsible for introducing jazz elements into French classical composition of the early twentieth century.

The New Orleans Sound

The musical characteristics of jazz before 1917 will always remain something of a mystery, but descriptions of the early sound based on photographic evidence, verbal recounting, notated music, and the earliest sound recordings have considerable value, even if they are not one-hundred percent correct. Certain features are highly probable. The tempo of early jazz probably ranged between moderate and moderately fast. With the possible exception of early piano players, instrumental virtuosity does not seem to have been highly developed by 1917. Still, liveliness and excitement are the most commonly expressed feelings about the music which are mentioned by people who first encountered jazz.

Whether early New Orleans jazz was two-beat, four-beat, or a mixture is an unsettling question. The New Orleans revival of the 1940s would have one believe that true New Orleans jazz was two-beat, and the four-beat rhythm section was a result of Chicago and swing. Still, the majority of the earliest recordings have an insistent strumming pattern of guitar or banjo. Beneath the four-beat chording of the banjo, the drums most often seem to play four-beat with the sticks and two-beat with the pedal. The same mixed performance occurs with ensemble piano playing. Sometimes left hand and right hand alternate beats, but just as often the left hand plays either a walking-bass pattern or a boogie-woogie configuration. The dances that developed in conjunction with early jazz are not informative, for their performance is equally successful in two-beat and four-beat subdivisions. One interesting point to note is that the instrumental breaks in many of the early pieces corresponded to dancers' trick steps. In general, it seems safe to say that early jazz tended to display democratization of the rhythm-section activity, that is, bringing the weak beats up to the level of the strong beats.

The front line of the various ensembles created a rhythmic layer of syncopa-

The New Orleans Rhythm Masters in 1926. (Front row, left to right) Jack Teagarden, trombone; Red Bolman, trumpet; Sidney Arodin, clarinet; Charlie Cordilla, sax and clarinet; Amos Ayala, drums. (Back row, left to right) Terry Shand, piano; George Shaw, vocals, Jerry Fresno, bass.

tion, polyrhythms, cross rhythms, and call-and-response patterns. The static insistence of the rhythm section was balanced by the flexibility and unpredictability of the front line. Unison playing in early jazz is totally absent. On occasion, when a band accompanies a singer, the cornet weaves a countermelody. But two instruments in unison are unheard of in classic jazz. On some of the early recordings, two or three instruments play in harmony; however, this seems to be a later development resulting from the influence of the society bands of New York and Chicago. Individual responsibility within the front line is the norm in classic jazz.

The repertoire of early jazz consists of a collection of thirty-two-measure, four-phrase, **AABA** popular-song-form tunes; four-strain, two-key, ragtime tunes; and twelve-measure instrumental blues. The harmonic rhythm of the ragtime pieces tends to move more quickly than in the other two categories. The harmonic rhythm of the blues, by definition, moves most slowly; and in compensation, the solo lines of blues pieces tend to have more inflections, variety of attacks, and pitch variation. Of course there are exceptions, and many songs of the early repertoire have the word "blues" in their title when they were clearly in popular-song or some other related form. By and large, the word "blues," as we've already seen, was just as likely to denote an emotional state as a form.

The instrumentation of the early ensembles tends to average eight players. This means that the accepted stereotype of the New Orleans jazz ensemble was in fact usually augmented by two instruments. Sometimes an extra cornet and extra rhythm-section instrument are added; sometimes a violin is used as a lead instrument in the ensemble. The orchestras of Armand J. Piron (1888–1943) and Peter Bocage (b. 1887) were important early jazz groups which featured the violin as a lead instrument.

Another characteristic of early New Orleans jazz, and perhaps its most important, is group improvisation. The members improvise in ensembles, not merely as soloists. The spontaneous give and take of all participants in the ensemble, limited only by a framework of chord progressions, was a new sound instantly recognizable to any listener in the early years of the twentieth century as the music called "jazz." In a sense, this feature was at the heart of all the other musical characteristics attributed to early classic jazz, and one of the most fascinating aspects of this type of performance is that the members of an ensemble are both competing and collaborating, both respecting and ignoring the limits imposed upon them, one and all.

The King, the Kid, and Friends

A bandleader of great significance was Joseph "King" Oliver (1885–1938), cornet player, mentor of Louis Armstrong, and musical director of the Creole Jazz Band, the finest jazz ensemble of its day. His sidemen included the best black jazz musicians in the business: Johnny and Baby Dodds, Jimmy Noone, Lil Hardin, Kid Ory, Barney Bigard, Honoré Dutrey, and Louis Armstrong. In spite of the fame and popularity he achieved during his peak years of 1915 to 1928, Oliver was near starvation just before his death in 1938. Born on a plantation near Abend, Louisiana, in 1885, he was blinded in one eye as a child. He began playing with the Melrose Brass Band in 1907, the Olympia Band in 1912, and formed his own band at the "25" cabaret with Sidney Bechet and Peter Bocage as sidemen. It is reported that Oliver played seated in a chair that leaned against the wall, a derby tilted over one eye to hide a scar. He is also reported to have been the first cornet player to play with mutes, cups, and bottles, and brought to jazz a polished, collectively improvising ensemble. He moved to Chicago in 1918 and sent for Louis Armstrong in 1922. His series of recordings in 1923 represents the state of the art of black jazz to that date.

King Oliver's Creole Jazz Band, (1923). (Left to right) Honoré Dutrey, trombone; Baby Dodds, drums; King Oliver, cornet; Louis Armstrong, slide trumpet; Lil Hardin (later Armstrong), piano; Bill Johnson, banjo; Johnny Dodds, clarinet.

One of Oliver's sidemen was a bandleader in his own right. Kid Ory was the most famous of the New Orleans tailgate trombone men and seems to have been the trombonist who first used the instrument for fills, glissandi, rhythmic effects, and the other jazz devices in a consistent manner. Although King Oliver's Creole Jazz Band was the first black ensemble to record a series of jazz pieces, forty-two numbers in 1923 alone, Kid Ory recorded the first records ever made by a black New Orleans band. The 1922 recordings of Kid Ory's Sunshine Orchestra, although of less musical interest than the series produced by King Oliver's group, is of historical moment, for it marks the beginning of the recorded black jazz tradition.

Edward "Kid" Ory was born in La Place, Louisiana, in 1886[16] and organized his own four-piece skiffle band[17] as a youngster. He brought his own band

---

[16] Rose and Souchon, *New Orleans Jazz*, p. 94, and Leonard Feather, *The New Edition of the Encyclopedia of Jazz*, p. 373, cite 1886 as a birth date. Charters, *Jazz: New Orleans*, p. 43, cites 1889.

[17] A skiffle band is a novelty orchestra that depends largely on showmanship, slapstick, and extramusical effects for audience appeal.

Edward "Kid" Ory's Original Creole Jazz Band, c. 1922, probably in San Francisco or Oakland, California. (Left to right) Baby Dodds, Ory, "Mutt" Carey, Ed Garland, and Wade Whaley.

to New Orleans in 1913 and led one group or another until he left the city permanently in 1919. His sidemen included some of the most notable musicians of New Orleans—Johnny Dodds, Jimmy Noone, King Oliver, and Louis Armstrong. He moved to Los Angeles in 1919, then to Chicago, where he joined King Oliver's Dixie Syncopators in 1924. His recorded performances of 1926–27 with King Oliver display a limited repertoire and technique on his solo improvisations, but as the harmonic and rhythmic instrument of the front line, his playing is the epitome of the New Orleans tailgate-trombone style. He later worked with Louis's Hot Five and returned to Los Angeles in 1929. He retired from music during the thirties, but gradually began working again in the forties when the New Orleans revival resurrected the old music. His own composition, *Muskrat Ramble*, [18] which he originally recorded with Louis Armstrong in 1926, was set to words in 1954 and became very popular. He remained musically active on the West Coast, appearing in movies, at Disneyland, and on television. His second recording career, beginning in the 1940s, grew to sizable proportions in the 1950s.

It is unfortunate that many of the fabulous New Orleans musicians either never recorded at all or did so when they were past their primes. Another legendary cornet player from New Orleans was Freddie Keppard. King or Whalemouth Keppard was born in New Orleans in 1889 and acquired a reputation as a performer of extraordinary power. Power seems to be a recurrent theme in the descriptions of the early New Orleans brass players and jazz ensembles, so we must assume that under normal conditions these groups played very loudly. His reputation stems from the period before the First World War, but, since he was an alcoholic, the recorded evidence of his work from his Chicago days in the mid-twenties suggests, but does not demonstrate, that his playing was aggressive and exciting. He died from alcoholism in Chicago in 1933.

Only six black bands were recorded in New Orleans during the twenties—Davey Jones and Lee Collins's Astoria Hot Eight, Sam Morgan's Jazz Band, Armand Piron's New Orleans Orchestra, Oscar "Papa" Celestin's Original Tuxedo Jazz Orchestra, Fate Marable's Society Syncopators, and Louis Dumaine's Jazzola Eight, but these recordings, of poor quality and late date, probably present a distorted picture of the sound of the earlier days. The other New Orleans bands recorded in other cities where outside influences left their mark on the musicians as soon as they arrived. The reconstructed sound of New Orleans during this crucial period is at best fragmentary, and possibly, at the very worst, a misrepresentation of what actually took place.

[18] Also known as *Muskat Ramble*.

The ODJB

White musicians unquestionably played a role in the development of jazz in New Orleans before the advent of recording, for when Nick La Rocca brought his white New Orleans musicians to New York and recorded in January of 1917, they displayed a fully developed Dixieland style, a Dixieland repertoire, and all the musical characteristics necessary to satisfy the contention that they were the first musicians to record in the idiom. La Rocca's claim to have been the founder of jazz has as much truth in it as Jelly Roll Morton's claim to have been the inventor of jazz, but due honor should attend La Rocca as the primogenitor of jazz recording.

Dominick J. "Nick" La Rocca was a white, left-handed cornet player born in New Orleans in 1889. He first played with Papa Laine and later formed the Original Dixieland Jazz Band, which he took to New York during World War I. The band remained active until 1925, and their early recordings display ensemble work of the highest quality in the Dixieland idiom. The band did not boast outstanding soloists, but La Rocca played a clear, precise lead. Larry Shields, the clarinetist, commanded a smooth technique and liquid sound, and Eddie Edwards, the trombonist, played rhythmically, in tune, and with the ornamental grace of a skilled tailgate trombonist. The repertoire of the Original Dixieland Jazz Band consisted of ragtime and early dance music played in the jazz idiom. Still, their performances were convincing and authentic, and the criticism leveled against their animal-sound performance of *Livery Stable Blues* is unfair, for all the bands, including the black ensembles, employed a variety of squeaks and squawks derived from the skiffle bands and their repertoire. In fact, Freddie Keppard, black trumpet player and bandleader, had a reputation for earning tips by neighing like a horse with his trumpet.

The group's ensemble performance of *At the Darktown Strutters' Ball*,[19] recorded at a single session in January of 1917, is excellent in every way. The rhythm section's steady beat is overlaid with the three lines of the lead instruments. The group swings along nicely as the members fill the spaces according to their individual functions. Had the personnel roster included a great soloist or two, this recording would be a monument on musical as well as historical grounds. Strangely enough, the polish of the Original Dixieland Jazz Band's performances is frequently criticized by the purists, who insist that "the tone quality is considerably more pure—more of a 'white' tone—than vocal in the Negroid way."[20] It would seem that some criticism is based more in a pref-

[19] Columbia 2297, reissued Columbia C3L-30.
[20] Rudi Blesh, *Shining Trumpets*, p. 211.

The Original Dixieland Jazz Band in London, England, c. 1920. (Left to right) Anthony Sbarbaro (Spargo), drums; Emile Christian, trombone; Dominic James "Nick" La Rocca, cornet; Larry Shields, clarinet; and Billy Jones, piano.

erence for black ensembles than from an objective evaluation of the performance itself. The following statement, written by an eminent historian of ragtime and early jazz, is not consistent with the recorded facts:

> While the playing of the Original Dixieland Jazz Band does not equal the fine Negro playing of classic jazz, or even that of the more average bands, like Sam Morgan's Jazz Band, or Louis Dumaine's Jazzola Eight, it must be considered a form of jazz. With all its faults of rhythm, tone, and polyphony, it is fairly well integrated and had much more variety in actual performance than it shows on its records. Only one of these men, Larry Shields, was an outstanding musician. Edwards was a good, but by no means a great player. La Rocca was merely adequate as were the others, although Ragas may have been a good ragtime player.[21]

The group's rhythm, tone, and polyphony are not lacking; only outstanding solo playing is. Their sound was exciting to their contemporaries, it was enthusiastically accepted by America at its first introduction, and it influenced other important jazz musicians, most notably, Bix Beiderbecke.

In 1936 La Rocca reformed the Original Dixieland Jazz Band and rerecorded some of his earlier hits. But he continued in music primarily as an avocation from 1938 until 1958, when he retired from the building business and devoted

[21] Ibid., p. 212.

his time to writing songs. He died in New Orleans in 1961 after donating his memorabilia to the archives of Tulane University. La Rocca never moved into the limelight as a leading jazz musician. Had he not been the first to record jazz, he may have been totally forgotten among the thousands of names which passed unnoted through the history of jazz.

The Jelly Roll

The fame of Jelly Roll Morton is primarily a story of the 1920s, but his participation in and contributions to jazz in the first decades of this century are both large and important. Ferdinand Joseph Le Menthe "Jelly Roll" Morton was the best, if not the first, of the classic-jazz pianists, for in his playing he merged the elements of ragtime, blues, and brass-band music. His style of playing is orchestral in concept, ragtime-centered with regard to form and harmonies, and blues-based in its melodic lines and crush dissonances. Born in 1885, he was a second liner before the turn of the century and digested the sounds of the brass bands as they paraded the streets of New Orleans. He played with Bunk Johnson and Jim Packer at Frankie Spano's during the summer of 1900, and continued as a Storyville "Professor" until he left town permanently in 1907. In spite of the voluminous documentation about his life, the result of hours of interviews recorded by Alan Lomax at the Library of Congress in 1938, an account of his career before 1922, when he settled for a while in Chicago, is difficult to piece together. Bunk Johnson recalls seeing him in Gulfport, Mississippi, around 1903 and 1904; James P. Johnson remembers him in New York in 1911; Reb Spikes, Morton's publisher, met him in Tulsa, Oklahoma, in 1912; he is known to have joined a touring show in Memphis, Tennessee, around 1909; and between that time and 1915, when he went to San Francisco to appear at the Exposition, he worked in St. Louis, Kansas City, and Chicago. He returned to Chicago later that year and played a solo-piano engagement at the Fairfax Hotel in Detroit, Michigan. He came back to California around 1917, and by the time he went to Chicago in 1923, where he recorded with the New Orleans Rhythm Kings, he had already made appearances in Alaska, Wyoming, Colorado, Mexico, and California.

The activities of his life are as varied as his travels, for he was not only a remarkable pianist, but the first great jazz composer, a pool shark, pimp, comedian, and, according to himself, "inventor of jazz." Many of his works have become jazz standards, and the dates of composition of some of his works lend credence to his claim of jazz invention and affirm his significance as a major jazz musician of the early years of the twentieth century. *New Orleans Blues* (1902 or 1903), *King Porter Stomp* (1905), *Jelly Roll Blues* (1905), and *Wolverines* (renamed *Wolverine Blues* by a publisher; 1906)—these compositions bear the design and hallmark of ragtime compositions, but display in performance (recorded as piano solos in 1923–24) jazz feel, blues phrasing, and virtuosic improvisation. His recording of *Maple Leaf Rag* for Alan Lomax in 1938 (*SCCJ*, I/2) transforms another man's ragtime composition into a New Orleans–style jazz performance.

Morton claims credit for transforming a French quadrille that was performed in different meters into *Tiger Rag*, [22] but experts have proven that *Tiger Rag* was worked out by the Jack Carey Band, the group which developed many of the standard tunes that were recorded by the Original Dixieland Jazz Band. [23] The work was known as *Jack Carey* by the black musicians of the city and as *Nigger #2* by the white. It was compiled when Jack's brother Thomas, "Papa Mutt," pulled the first strain from a book of quadrilles. The band evolved the second and third strains in order to show off the clarinetist, George Boyd, and the final strain ("Hold that tiger" section) was worked out by Jack, a trombonist, and the cornet player, Punch Miller.

The circumstances surrounding the composition (or compilation) of *Tiger Rag* and the checkered career and far-flung travels of Jelly Roll Morton serve to exemplify that jazz had widespread currency in the public domain before the proliferation of sound recording. That New Orleans was a hotbed of activity, both musical and otherwise, goes without saying; but it would be foolhardy to suppose that Morton was not playing jazz in New York in 1911 or in California in 1915. Also, the existence of compositions like Morton's *Wolverine Blues* and Kid Ory's *Muskrat Ramble* undermines arguments that jazz is a performer's, and not a composer's, art. Admittedly compositions incorrectly played do not represent any genre accurately, be it jazz or classical. To play ragtime, jazz, Debussy, or Beethoven correctly, one must know the performance tradition and acquire the necessary technical facility. Beyond that, great performances in any style require creativity, ability, dedication, and sincerity.

Thoughts on the History of Jazz

The history of jazz before the years that F. Scott Fitzgerald labeled "The Jazz Age" is a narrative of which no definitive version will ever be written. The primary source material is lacking, and the existing documentation, although

[22] See ibid., p. 191 ff.
[23] Charters, *Jazz: New Orleans*, p. 24.

copious, is spotty and often contradictory. Still, there is no question that Americans living in the years before the First World War heard an exciting new music played by some of the most creative musicians America has ever produced. Although we lack sound recordings, we are beginning to acquire a new wealth of historical information that is just as stimulating, albeit in a different way. The recent interest in music of black Americans has stimulated research and uncovered gold mines of historical evidence that is available, accessible, and, to a large degree, in a language understandable by modern Americans. Some of the jazz pioneers are still alive, and oral evidence concerning most of the important historical events is available from many people who observed and participated in the events themselves. As a result, we know a great deal about what we cannot hear.

Jazz was not the only style to emerge just before World War I, for the music of Schoenberg, Bartók, and Stravinsky was in formative stages too. But jazz was the American music of the early twentieth century, the product of a democracy, the work of a group of talented, predominantly black, obscure American musicians. It was a collective effort, just as collective improvisation was its principal feature.

The chief documents of its history were still to be produced, but the infant recording business was growing in tandem with the infant music. It was not until 1909 that popular songs were recorded. The first of these were made on cylinders, but these proved impractical. Columbia and Edison were the pioneers, and they were joined in 1901 by Victor. The 78-rpm record developed in these early years was used, with some improvements, until about 1950. The significance of the development of sound recording to the history of jazz cannot be emphasized too strongly, for records provided improvising jazz musicians a means by which they could sell their product to a widespread audience. The ragtime composer had access to the printing industry, but the jazz musician, whose only product was the performance itself, could reach only those people with whom he came in personal contact. Records provided not only an avenue to employment, but, more important, a forum for the exchange of musical ideas among professionals.

Radio became available to the general public only on a limited scale in 1922, and the first radios, crystal sets with earphones, allowed only one person to listen at a time. Broadcasting and recording developed hand in hand, and the first electrical records appeared in the mid-twenties, contemporaneously with the earliest radios. Before that date, the acoustical recording process was the only means of preserving sound on cylinder or disc. Until about 1925, the horn of the acoustical recorder collected sound waves which vibrated a diaphragm attached mechanically to the stylus. To achieve any fidelity or volume at all, performers had to shout or produce instrumental sounds loudly and directly into the horn. Even a small, five-piece jazz group of cornet, clarinet,

In 1937, several of the members of the Original Dixieland Jazz Band recreated a 1917 recording session for the March of Time.

trombone, piano, and drums had enormous difficulty fitting into the open end of a horn, and one must take into account these restrictions when evaluating the performances themselves. Documentary recording, that is, recording live in the natural environment of the musicians, was not possible, and the music played for the early records had to be modified from an all-night brothel performance to a three-minute studio session. In turn, the new format began to reshape the music itself, for economics dictated that a good three-minute performance on a best-selling record was "better" than a ten-minute improvisation at a local engagement. Not until the advent of the long-playing record after World War II was it possible to record a typical jazz performance and play it back in one continuous, uninterrupted sitting. The existence of any musical spontaneity at all in the early recordings is remarkable and a credit to the dedication and talent of the musicians.

When black blues singer Mamie Smith recorded *That Thing Called Love* and *You Can't Keep a Good Man Down* in 1920 for the Okeh Record Company,[24] the instantaneous success of this record led other companies to rush

[24] Okeh 4113.

into the market. Pace Phonograph Corporation, later renamed the Black Swan Phonograph Company, was the first black recording company to open its doors in 1921, and before the end of the decade the term "race record" was coined by the industry to designate black music. Advertising and distribution of race records was primarily aimed toward a black market, and although whites had access to these recordings, segregationist practice fostered a perfomance style which was so much in the black tradition that it was virtually unaccessible to large numbers of middle-class white Americans. Thus, it can be seen that both the technology and the commercial interests of the recording industry had an impact upon the music itself, and were important dynamic forces in shaping its destiny.

Another influence made its appearance at about this time, although with much less force than either radio or recording: the infant film industry. In 1925, Columbia and Victor began producing electrical recordings; 1926 saw

Gerry Mulligan (baritone sax), Thelonious Monk (piano), Shadow Wilson (drums), and Wilbur Ware (bass) cutting a side, c. 1957.

NBC Radio, the first nationwide network, enter into the scene; and 1927 marked the production of the first talking picture, *The Jazz Singer*, featuring Al Jolson. The dissemination of jazz before World War I was widespread, for we have seen that blues singers, vaudeville musicians, minstrel shows, ragtime pianists, and jazz musicians circulated freely throughout the United States. The First World War expanded the boundaries to Europe and permitted a musical infiltration of American sounds into the Continental culture at a more intense rate. Sound recordings acted as an additional catalyst, and electrical recordings and radio further stimulated an eager market.

Not until 1947 were there any new technological breakthroughs in the recording industry. The shellac, ten-inch, 78-rpm disc recorded by electrical means was the standard medium for jazz, and from the mid-twenties to the mid-forties this did not change. Consequently there were accepted limits within which the music operated, developed, and flourished. Although live performance between the First and Second World Wars was far more important than broadcast or recorded performance in terms of what actually was happening historically in America, the history of jazz has become largely the history of jazz recording. Again, being primarily a performer's art, recordings became the sole means of preserving the music. Consequently, our historical investigation from this point forward will be almost entirely devoted to the analysis and understanding of those significant and representative recordings which document the progress of the art.

WORLD WAR I AND
AFTER—THE TWENTIES

The Jazz Explosion

Jazz began to achieve widespread popular recognition when the Original Dixieland Jazz Band, ODJB, made its debut in New York City at Reisenweber's Cabaret on the evening of January 26, 1917. They were in the right place at the right time, and their first jazz recordings, issued on Victor's popular lists, sold in the millions. All of the musicians were from New Orleans, but three of the group, Nick La Rocca, Eddie Edwards, and Henry Ragas, were fresh from a visit to Chicago, where they had been playing with Stein's Dixie Jazz Band at Schiller's Café. Their first recording sessions in January and February of 1917 produced *Dixieland Jass Band One-Step/Livery Stable Blues*[1] and *Darktown Strutters' Ball/Indiana*.[2] In the same year, W. C. Handy's Orchestra recorded *That Jazz Dance/Livery Stable Blues*,[3] but the front line of the musical onslaught was held by the men of the Original Dixieland Jazz Band.

The *Dixieland Jass Band One-Step*, zinging along at 252 beats per minute, captivated the public by showing the band off at its best. The three men from Chicago, together with Larry Shields, clarinet, and Tony Sbarbaro, drums, formed a cooperative, profit-sharing organization, designating La Rocca the musical leader. The *Dixieland Jass Band One-Step* (originally called *Mutt and Jeff*) is a work in the ragtime-jazz tradition in which two sixteen-measure themes are repeated before a modulation to a "trio" theme for a close.

[1] Victor 18253.
[2] Columbia A-2297.
[3] Columbia A-2419.

Through the veil of the acoustic recording, one can hear the noodling obbligato of Shields's clarinet floating high above the glissando-filled part of Daddy Edwards's tailgate trombone. The ensemble is tight, and the well-rehearsed group cut a ragged path through the grooves of the original jazz disc.

The Livery Stable Blues, which Nick La Rocca claimed to have composed by himself in 1912,[4] is more a novelty number than a jazz piece. It achieved immediate popularity and even became the subject of copyright litigation when Alcide "Yellow" Nunez, former clarinetist of the Original Dixieland Jazz Band, and Ray Lopez, a cornet player with Burt Kelly's Band, wrote out the music, published it in 1917, and credited themselves on the published copies with being members of the Original Dixieland Jazz Band. Judge Carpenter, on October 12, 1917, found that neither the plaintiff nor the defendant was entitled to a copyright, stating that neither conceived the idea of the melody, and stating further that "no living human being could listen to that result on the phonograph and discover anything musical in it, although there is a wonderful rhythm, something which will carry you along, especially if you are young and a dancer."[5]

As the five men of the Original Dixieland Jazz Band were skyrocketing to success in 1917, Scott Joplin died unnoticed in the same city, for public taste had changed dramatically from ragtime to jazz. Storyville had closed that year, and some of the musicians began seeking work elsewhere. Armand Piron teamed up with Peter Bocage and began working at Tranchina's Restaurant at Spanish Fort on Lake Pontchartrain in 1918. A. J. Piron and His Novelty Orchestra, a Creole ensemble of trumpet, trombone, alto sax, clarinet and tenor sax, piano, banjo, drums, and violin, remained in New Orleans and played at Tranchina's from 1918 to 1928.[6] Jelly Roll Morton had left New Orleans, and although he traveled considerably from 1917 to 1922, he spent most of his time in California. Kid Ory worked actively in Los Angeles between 1919 and 1924. Sidney Bechet had already gone to Europe, and was playing in London in 1919 when Ernest Ansermet first heard him and admired his work. Alcide "Yellow" Nunez, who had played clarinet with members of the Original Dixieland Jazz Band in New Orleans and again in Chicago in 1916, chose to remain in the Windy City. After La Rocca, Edwards, and Ragas left for New York, he teamed up with four other musicians to form the Louisiana Five in 1919 and maintained the continuity of white Dixieland music in Chicago.[7] Although the

---

[4] George Brunies, trombonist, counters, "They were tunes originated by the Negro boys of New Orleans."

[5] H. O. Brunn, *The Story of the Original Dixieland Jazz Band,* p. 85.

[6] In 1923, this group recorded, *Bouncing Around* and *West Indies Blues* (Okeh 40021 and Columbia 14007-D, reissued Columbia C3L-30).

[7] *I Ain't-en Got-en No Time to Have the Blues,* recorded in New York City in June, 1919 (Columbia A-2775, reissued Columbia C3L-30).

One of the bands proliferating in 1917 called itself the Original New Orleans Jazz Band when it played at the Alamo Cafe in New York City. Its members (left to right) were Johnny Stein, Achille Bacquet, Jimmy Durante, Frank Christian, and Frank L'Hotag.

Original Dixieland Jazz Band had stolen the limelight, New York jazz was continuously in session through these years. James P. Johnson was fronting a band at the Clef Club at the end of World War I. After that, he played solo piano engagements and vaudeville shows, and made player-piano rolls for the Aeolian Company. Two years earlier, in 1915, Eubie Blake had joined forces with Noble Sissle to form a vaudeville team that lasted successfully for many years. They wrote musicals, and one of their lasting hits was *I'm Just Wild About Harry.*

Around 1917 in New Orleans, Joe Oliver began billing himself as "King." With the demise of Storyville, he moved to Chicago in 1918, working as a sideman until 1919, when he formed his own band. The year 1922 was the fateful one when Oliver sent for the young Louis Armstrong to play cornet in his band. The resulting Creole Jazz Band, led by King Oliver, was an inspirational force which began to reshape the tradition by blending in the latest Chicago jazz sounds. [8]

Shortly before this, another group of white New Orleans musicians literally traveled the riverboat to Chicago. Tom Brown, a trombonist, was the first

[8] *Aunt Hagar's Blues* by King Oliver's Dixie Syncopators, September 10, 1928 (MCA Records, MCA 2-4061).

white musician to bring New Orleans jazz to Chicago. Stein's Dixie Jass Band with Nick La Rocca followed a year later. The New Orleans Rhythm Kings, NORK, began playing at Friar's Inn as the Friar's Society Orchestra in 1921. Before that, during the summer of 1920, Paul Mares and George Brunies were playing a riverboat on the Mississippi. At Davenport, Iowa, they took on Leon Rappolo, a clarinetist who at that time introduced them to a young local cornet player, Bix Beiderbecke. The group that eventually formed the Friar's Society Orchestra—Paul Mares (cornet) George Brunies (trombone) Leon Rappolo (clarinet) Elmer Schoebel (from Illinois, piano) Louis Black (banjo) Frank Snyder (drums) and Arnold Loyocano (bass)—later renamed themselves the New Orleans Rhythm Kings and worked in the Chicago area.[9] The criminal world took advantage of American naiveté by capitalizing on prohibition, and the clubs of Chicago and New York, especially the former, became entertainment centers to rival the halcyon days of Storyville. Audiences for hot jazz were not in short supply during the postwar boom years, and all the young jazz musicians were able to support themselves rather handsomely during the 1920s. Jelly Roll Morton returned to the Midwest in 1923 to record some solo piano work in Richmond, Indiana.[10] Kid Ory came to Chicago about the same time and worked with many groups.[11] He played with Louis Armstrong's Hot Five only when they recorded, but these sides, made in Chicago in the mid-1920s, are perhaps the most extraordinary monuments of classic jazz to have survived. Their closest rivals, and perhaps equals, are the recordings of Jelly Roll Morton's Red Hot Peppers made in Chicago and New York from 1926 to 1930.

After the initial recordings for Columbia and Victor, the Original Dixieland Jazz Band recorded twelve tunes for the Aeolian Company during the remainder of the year. Only four records from that company were released,[12] but the next year the band was back with Victor and placed five more records on the market during 1918 and 1919. The repertoire of the group contained the standards of New Orleans, such as *Tiger Rag* and *Barnyard Blues*, plus some originals: *Reisenweber Rag* and *Fidgety Feet*. The last, a fast one-step, displays La Rocca at his best, a lead trumpet player who can also whip off a snappy break. In 1919, the Louisiana Five made three recordings for Columbia.[13] Once again, the musicians were white, for the Louisiana Five was the Tom Brown band from Chicago rechristened. By 1919, the ODJB had traveled to

[9] An apocryphal recreation in 1934 of the 1923 version of *Tin Roof Blues* by New Orleans Rhythm Kings is available on MCA 2-4061.

[10] *King Porter Stomp* by Jelly Roll Morton, ibid. (April, 1926).

[11] *Wild Man Blues*, recorded in 1927 by Johnny Dodd's Black Bottom Stompers, ibid.

[12] Aeolian 1205, 1206, 1207, and 1242.

[13] Columbia A-2742, A-2768, and A-2775.

England and recorded there for Columbia until 1920. Some were the old favorites, *Tiger Rag* and *Barnyard Blues*, and some were completely removed
from the jazz vein, e.g., *I'm Forever Blowing Bubbles* and *Alice Blue Gown.* [14]
By this time, Emile Christian had replaced Eddie Edwards on trombone and J.
Russel Robinson and Billy Jones played piano with the group.

By 1921, jazz had stirred up an emotional furor in America that can hardly
be rivaled in either intensity or imbecility. Still, the pejorative press could
hardly slow a tidal wave, and in 1921 and 1922, more and more jazz recordings hit the market. The most noteworthy of these were James P. Johnson's first
recordings for Okeh,[15] Ladd's Black Aces recordings for Gennett,[16] The Original Memphis Five recordings for Banner and Paramount,[17] more from the
Original Dixieland Jazz Band, and the first recordings of Mamie Smith: *Lone-
some Mama Blues, New Orleans, You Can Have Him,* and *Wish That I Could
But I Can't.* [18]

James P.

James P. Johnson's earliest recording was made in New York when he was
thirty years old. *Harlem Strut,* recorded on the Black Swan label, was followed
in the same year by his remarkable recording for Okeh, *Carolina Shout* [19]
(*SCCJ,* II/4). *Carolina Shout,* a remarkable bit of piano playing, demonstrates
New York jazz at its best. Although it retains a few of the basic ragtime characteristics in its formal structure, harmonic speed, sixteen-measure phrases, and
oom-pah left hand, even these features are modified far beyond the norm of
ragtime piano. The basic form, in its simplest terms, is Intro **A B** Coda, but
where the ragtime composition normally divides **A** in half, each half repeated,
and **B** in half, each half also repeated, and **B** is usually in the subdominant
key, *Carolina Shout* is laid out as follows:

‖ Intro ‖		A	‖	B		‖ Coda ‖
‖ Intro ‖: a :‖ b ‖: c :‖ d | e | d ‖ Coda ‖						

| mm. | 4 | 16 | 16 | 16 | 16 | 16 | 16 | 4 |

[14] Columbia 735, 736, 748, 759, 804, 805, 815, 824, and 829.
[15] Okeh 4495 and 4504.
[16] Gennett 4762 and 4794.
[17] Banner 1062, 1082, and Paramount 20161.
[18] Okeh 4630, 4670, 4689.
[19] Okeh 4495. The reverse side, *Keep Off the Grass,* is reissued on Columbia C3L-33.

The entire piece is in the key of G, but in the middle of the second half (section e), a feeling of subdominant is implied with the IV–I progression (in the key of C) which opens the phrase. However, via a series of chromatic modulations, that phrase returns to the key of G as do all the others.

The various phrases are not readily identifiable by considering the melodic lines only. Instead, each has a distinctive opening harmonic progression which sets it apart from all others, and listening for the form is facilitated by a chord chart, rather than a melodic chart. In studying this invariable characteristic, one finds the tap root of jazz, for the blues-based practice of improvisation to a given harmonic scheme carries over to jazz from the ragtime repertoire, the pop-song repertoire, and from all other sources. Another blues-derived feature that is immediately apparent in the introduction is the crushed dissonances played by the right hand, a cluster of two notes a half step apart, which most jazz scholars attribute to the pianist's need for representing the neutral third of the blues scale. By striking both the minor and major third at the same time, a blues cluster is produced. The same effect is used by pianists on the seventh scale step.

Carolina Shout

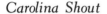

The rhythmic treatment of both hands also differs from the common practice of ragtime piano players. The right hand is syncopated, but mixes eighth-note syncopations with ternary subdivisions of the beat, thus producing a richer collection of rhythmic activity. The two-beat feel of the left hand is constantly interrupted by a walking eighth-note pattern, which totally blends the two-beat and four-beat concepts.

It should be noted that a repeat in jazz is not an invitation to play the same notes. It indicates only that the same harmony is to be used. Listening to James P. Johnson's left hand through the sixteen measures of the first phrase and its repeat, measures 17–32, one can hear the rhythmic variations as well as some harmonic passing chords which were added to the basic harmonic scheme.

The last four measures of the piece reveal a typical cliché of the player-piano style: treble and bass moving in contrary motion just before the final chords. In spite of the rhythmic variety imposed upon the left-hand patterns by the right-hand syncopations and ternary figures, Johnson's metronomic sense of beat is infallible. The layer effect of rhythm section and front line can easily be

a. Intro

equated to left hand and right hand. The rhythmic drive of Johnson's playing with ten fingers constantly filling all available space produces both vitality and swing, those indefinable qualities with which great jazz musicians are able to invest their performances. Gunther Schuller points out that

> *Carolina Shout* also contains in the third strain James P.'s keyboard version of a "shout," in turn the Negroes' extemporized and intensified elaboration of European-American hymn tunes. It is at the same time a call-and-response chorus in the old preacher-to-congregation relationship. In its full-voiced, brass-like chords it is a close relative to the famous last chorus of Morton's *King Porter Stomp*. [20]

Another man to be reckoned with during this period, of course, is William Christopher Handy. In 1917 Handy was already almost forty-five years old, an established composer and bandleader. We can attribute the failure of his first Columbia recordings, intended to compete with the Original Dixieland Jazz Band, to the "pickup" musicians he used to make his recordings in New York. His own band was located in Memphis, Tennessee, and could not make the

[20] Gunther Schuller, *Early Jazz*, p. 219.

Daniel Louis "Satchmo" Armstrong (1900–71).

trip. Many of Handy's compositions were featured by the early bands, and the black bandleader Lieutenant James Reese Europe was successful in Europe during World War I playing Handy's music. But for all his contributions to music in America, especially Afro-American music, W. C. Handy played only a minor role in the history of jazz. After all, he was not an outstanding performer, and jazz has always chosen its leaders from among the virtuoso instrumentalists.

Satchmo

Louis Armstrong was a legend in his own time, and some would even say that he is the single greatest figure in the Jazz Hall of Fame. Born on the Fourth of July, 1900, in the abject poverty of black, uptown New Orleans, Daniel Louis Armstrong was the child of an illiterate turpentine factory worker, Willie Armstrong, and his wife, Mary, later called Mayann. Born in a shack off James Alley in the stifling heat of a Louisiana summer with only the assistance of a midwife, this black baby grew up to earn the international recognition heaped upon him in the decade before his death. When he passed away in 1971, headlines throughout the world announced his death, and front-page obituaries paid tribute and lamented his loss. Everything this landmark musician achieved was earned through fortitude, skill, and devotion. Even during his last years, at the triumphant height of a successful career, he was forced to experience the hardships of prejudice and segregation in the country that so proudly boasted his name as one of its own. His achievements were more than personal and more than musical, for in his striving, he became a symbol of the creativity of the black American. The writers who claim that Louis was born in the right place at the right time, the most wretched ghetto of New Orleans at the turn of the century, are either sadistic or naive, for his early years as a street urchin in the Storyville district are hardly to be recommended as a part of the Great American Dream.

Louis's parents separated when he was five years old, and he lived with his mother at Liberty and Perdido Streets in the Third Ward. He had no musical training until he was arrested at the age of thirteen and sent to the Colored Waifs Home in New Orleans. In the reformatory, he was taught music by two amateur musicians, "Captain" Joseph Jones, director of the Home, and the warden Professor Peter Davis. The latter instructed him in fundamentals, the former in the cornet. He was released after one year and worked at various day jobs selling coal, delivering milk, unloading banana boats, and the like. He made no real progress on his instrument until 1918, when Joe "King" Oliver befriended him, encouraged and tutored him, and eventually recommended that Armstrong replace him during the summer of 1918 or early in 1919 as cornetist in Kid Ory's Band. He played various engagements the next four years, including Streckfus Steamer jobs with Fate Marable. In 1922 he received the call from Joe Oliver in Chicago to join him as second cornetist. His days with Oliver's Creole Jazz Band marked the beginning of Armstrong's most creative and influential period. During the 1920s, Satchmo acquired the technique that allowed him to become the leading jazz virtuoso of the day. His fame among jazz musicians in Chicago is legendary, for the anecdotes describe the local musicians flocking to hear Louis performing in order to learn the secrets of hot jazz. Armstrong's inconspicuous role in the Creole Jazz Band recordings of 1923 (SCCJ, I/6) changed quickly, for by the end of 1924 Louis was known as the most powerful, creative soloist on the jazz recordings promoted by pianist Clarence Williams.

Clarence Williams was a capable early-jazz pianist and combo leader who assumed the musical direction for Okeh race records in 1923 and was responsible for their catalogue through 1928. The list of jazzmen he recorded during that period is impressive, and the recording of *Cakewalking Babies* made in New York in December, 1924, for Gennett with Louis Armstrong and Sidney Bechet is representative of the very latest musical ideas in the pop-jazz field at that time.

From July of 1922 to October of 1924, Louis Armstrong worked in Chicago, first with King Oliver and then with Ollie Powers. It was during this period that he met Lillian Hardin, Oliver's pianist, whom he married in February of 1924. Armstrong was one black New Orleans musician who was impressed by the "sweet" band sounds, especially those of Guy Lombardo and His Royal Canadians. His exposure to Lombardo's music came after he received a call from black bandleader Fletcher Henderson in New York. Louis said,

> Now you dig that *Sweethearts* . . . It reminds you of Lombardo . . . When we were at the Savoy in Chicago in 1928, every Saturday night we'd catch the Owl Club, with Guy Lombardo, and as long as he played we'd sit right there . . . We didn't go nowhere until after Lombardo signed off. That went on for months.[21]

Henderson, who was successful and influential in the East, did not run a New Orleans–style band, but rather one that depended on arrangements and ensemble. Armstrong joined the Henderson band at the Roseland Ballroom in New York on September 29, 1924. There he became impressed with the im-

[21] Quoted in John Chilton and Max Jones, *Louis: The Louis Armstrong Story 1900–1971*, *p.* 111.

portance of sight-reading skills, a facet of his playing that had not concerned him seriously until then. It was also there that he developed his abiding respect for the ensemble playing that emanated from the music of the reading bands. The *Cakewalking Babies* recording displays a blend of elements from the New Orleans tradition and society music, the sweet sound of New York's Fletcher Henderson and Guy Lombardo. (SCCJ, II/2) The instrumentation is New Orleans style, for single instruments rather than sections fulfill the various musical functions. But the ensemble playing, from the beginning through the vocal choruses, is constricted, inhibited, clean, and predictable. Louis plays an accurate but unimaginative lead, and Bechet's arpeggios, on soprano saxophone rather than the New Orleans–style clarinet, are virtuosic but regular. The vocal chorus is typical of the white, pop-jazz style of the day, which became epitomized in the megaphone solos of Rudy Vallee. However, the jazz choruses that follow the vocal performance are in the best polyphonic, jazz-ensemble, Dixieland style. Although Bechet's sound predominates, it is Louis's rhythmic drive that gives the group its forward impetus. Armstrong has no opportunity for solo display here, but this recording shows the stage of development at which Armstrong had arrived during his days with Fletcher Henderson.

His return to Chicago in the summer of 1925, when he joined Lil's Band at the Dreamland Ballroom, marks the beginning of Louis's meteoric rise to the summit of the jazz world. When Louis subsequently organized a recording band for Okeh records with Clarence Williams's approval, the jazz world began to receive recorded music under Louis Armstrong's own name. Time has memorialized these discs as the classic recordings of the period. The series began with *Gut Bucket Blues*,[22] an introductory piece in more than one sense: Louis introduces each of the performers by name, and, secondly, the music is still strongly reminiscent of the sound of the King Oliver ensemble. During the same year, 1925, three other recordings were released by other musicians that show the state of ferment in which jazz found itself. Benny Moten, leader of the Kansas City band that would eventually become the Count Basie Orchestra, recorded *18th Street Blues* and *South Street Blues* for Okeh;[23] Fletcher Henderson released *Money Blues*, *Sugar Foot Stomp*, and *Carolina Stomp*;[24] and a white, twenty-two-year-old star of the Chicago-based Wolverines, Bix Beiderbecke, recorded and issued a hometown lament, *Davenport Blues*.[25]

The year 1925 is a good one to exemplify the jazz activity omnipresent in the United States. In addition to Armstrong, Beiderbecke, Henderson, and Moten,

[22] Okeh 8261, reissued Columbia CL-851.
[23] Okeh 8242 and 8255.
[24] Columbia 383-D, 395-D, and 509-D.
[25] Gennett 5654.

dozens of lesser organizations were recording an extended jazz repertoire: Creath's Jazzomaniacs recorded Morton's *King Porter Stomp;*[26] Sonny Clay, *Bogaloosa Blues;*[27] Jack Gardner, *The Camelwalk;*[28] Halfway House Orchestra, *Maple Leaf Rag;*[29] Original Memphis Five, *Bass Ale Blues;*[30] Original Indiana Five, *Indiana Stomp;*[31] New Orleans Owls, *Stompoff Let's Go;*[32] and Tennessee Tooters, *Milenberg Joys.*[33] Paul Whiteman, whose claim to the title "King of Jazz" does not go undisputed among jazz connoisseurs, had been recording popular music since 1920. That year he issued *Wang Wang Blues,*[34] and before the decade was over his band included sidemen such as Bix Beiderbecke, Frankie Trumbauer, Jimmy Dorsey, Tommy Dorsey, Joe Venuti, and others. The year 1925 also marked the publication of Hoagy Carmichael's *Washboard Blues* (Mitchell Parrish and Fred Callahan, lyricists). All in all, the issuance of the first Hot Five recordings by Louis Armstrong should not be seen as an oasis in a desert, but rather as the tallest trees of a forest. By 1925 live jazz was available everywhere, and leading exponents of both races were cutting recordings with abandon.

The Hot Five was a remarkable group, for all of the front line were the best of the New Orleans–style instrumental soloists. Johnny Dodds was without peer among clarinetists, both in his solo work and ensemble performance. Kid Ory was a well-known bandleader in New Orleans before the closing of Storyville, and Louis had once played in Ory's Brownskin Band. Yet for all their brilliance, Ory and Dodds played second fiddle to Armstrong. When Louis finally broke loose as a soloist in *Cornet Chop Suey,*[35] there was no other jazz soloist on any wind instrument to rival him. His 1926 release of *Heebie Jeebies*[36] marks the introduction of the now-famous Louis Armstrong style of "scat singing," an instrumental solo performed by the voice to vocables, or nonsense syllables. The same year that Okeh issued *Heebie Jeebies* and *Cornet Chop Suey* (1926), they also issued a milestone record, *Big Butter and Egg Man,*[37] one of the most inventive cornet solos ever recorded. The consistency, quality, and quantity of superlative jazz recordings issued by the Hot Five and

[26] Okeh 8210.
[27] Vocalion 15078.
[28] Okeh 40518.
[29] Columbia 476-D.
[30] Victor 19805.
[31] Gennett 3112.
[32] Columbia 489-D.
[33] Vocalion 15068.
[34] Victor 18694.
[35] Okeh 8320.
[36] Okeh 8300.
[37] Okeh 8423.

Hot Seven earned for Louis Armstrong the historic position he enjoys. Where Bix Beiderbecke went generally unnoticed among the public, Louis Armstrong was both a household word with amateurs and a name of significance among professionals. Martin Williams's summation is exactly correct: "Armstrong's story on records between 1923 and 1932 is one of almost continuous sweeping growth—and after that is frequently one of entrenched excellence."[38]

Struttin' With Some Barbecue (SCCJ, II/5) is an interesting combination of sweet-band and hot-jazz sounds. The "cornball" ending lacked only the cymbal sound of a typical Guy Lombardo Mickey ending. The backing chords of the offbeat stoptime choruses, beginning with Kid Ory's solo and continuing through Louis's, are typical of a band arrangement whether or not the notes are actually written out or taught by rote. The rhythm of *Struttin'* is clearly two-beat, and that two-beat/four-beat ambiguity of New Orleans jazz is not present here. The piece, composed by Louis's wife, Lil, has a striking melodic shape at the opening. The ascending octave outlining the major-seventh chord is clearly a modern innovation in jazz pieces of the day. Dodds's and Ory's solos, both excellent in their own ways, are totally eclipsed by the driving, forceful cornet solo, which spans the total compass of the instrument in melodic flights that embellish a germinal idea developed from the initial theme itself. The ragtime grouping of eighth notes into patterns of three, which Louis inserts into the last phrase of his solo (see Transcriptions, beginning on p. 365), plays tricks with the steady rhythm of the accompaniment, which lacks the strong beats. The complete performance embodies both the old and the new, and in the new we find the elements of hot jazz and, in places, some "sweet" sounds from the repertoire of the white popular bands.

S.O.L. Blues[39] is a piece that can be studied in two versions, for *Gully Low Blues* was meant as a rerecording of a partially unsatisfactory first take.[40] Louis's solo on *S.O.L. Blues*, containing five descending phrases, each starting on high C (concert B$\flat$), displays the developmental logic this man was able to incorporate in the best of his solos (see Transcriptions). Each succeeding phrase modifies the initial idea and lays out a pattern that directs the listener's attention inevitably to a musical goal at the end of the blues pattern. The almost extramusical insertion of the Lombardo ending, complete with vibrato chords and cymbal crash, jars the modern listener's sensibilities. But within the musical context of the '20s, it was a cliché which added class and respectability to a music that had suffered considerable abuse.

The *Potato Head Blues (SCCJ,*II/7) is not a twelve-measure blues, in spite of

[38] *SCCJ* liner notes, p. 20.

[39] In the Smithsonian booklet, *Potato Head Blues* precedes *S.O.L. Blues*. The record label, with the reverse order, is correct.

[40] Both versions, complete, are available on Columbia CL-852.

the name, but a thirty-two-measure structure. The chords of Louis's bravura stoptime solo are played, not on the offbeat as in *Struttin' With Some Barbecue*, but on the first beat of every other measure. In other words, seven out of every eight temporal spaces are blank except for the solo line of the cornet. Louis's melodic pattern is, once again, more than virtuosic; it is developmental in a melodic progression that leads to a climax at the *rip* (upward glissando) to the D above high C. The carefully structured nature of the solo is revealed in the rhythmic treatment as well, for the first two measures, which receive regular accentual treatment with respect to meter, are offset rhythmically in the following two measures when Louis shifts his accents to the offbeat. Gunther Schuller points out the strong probability that Hoagy Carmichael was familiar with this solo, for his opening to *Stardust*, written in 1927, is almost a twin to Armstrong's solo line at measure 25. Given the relationship of Carmichael to Bix Beiderbecke, an Armstrong disciple, the similarities between *Potato Head Blues* and *Stardust* are striking. Once again, note the insidious society-band cliché at the ending. Beiderbecke looked to Louis for inspiration, but, strangely, Armstrong looked to Lombardo.

The Louis Armstrong All Stars playing at Symphony Hall in Boston on November 27, 1949. Shown with Louis are Jack Teagarden, trombone; Cozy Cole, drums; Arvell Shaw, bass; and Barney Bigard, clarinet.

Hotter Than That, by Lil Hardin (SCCJ, II/8), is a composition based on a thirty-two-measure harmonic pattern that divides in half, each half receiving a two-measure first or second ending. The thirty-two-measure stanza is repeated three times, is interrupted by an out-of-time vocal and guitar call-and-response duet, and ends with a final thirty-two-measure chorus. A four-measure piano vamp reestablishes the rhythm at the end of the vocal and guitar duet, and an eight-measure introduction precedes the piece. The harmonies for the introduction are derived from the last eight measures of the piece. At the very end, two two-measure cadenzas by trumpet and guitar comprise the closing coda. Every first and second ending is filled by an instrumental break; the vocal scat singing also is being considered instrumental.

Hotter Than That

Introduction	8			
1st chorus	Cornet solo — 8	break — 8	8	break — 8
2nd chorus	Clarinet solo — 8	break — 8	8	break — 8
3rd chorus	Vocal solo — 8	break — 8	8	break — 8
Partial 4th chorus	Guitar & Voice ("Twos") — 16	Vamp — 4		
Last chorus	Trombone solo — 16	break	Ensemble out — 16	
Coda	2			

The overall scheme and the instrumental breaks are not new in concept, but a few features of the piece are extraordinary and herald ideas to be developed by other groups in later years. The last sixteen measures of the final chorus is an ensemble "out" which is accompanied by Louis's trumpet riff on beats four and one, a pattern which was to become a cliché of the swing bands of the thirties.

It is a pattern that transforms the old New Orleans stomp to a brass-ensemble pattern. Also, this work does not close with a typical Mickey ending, but instead, rests on an unresolved diminished chord built on the submediant. This incongruous harmony is but a clue to one of the most important developments in this piece. William Austin sensed the significance of Armstrong's solo work in this performance and offered not only a successful analysis of many of the subtleties that distinguish it from other improvisations, but also a brief justification for analysis itself:

> A study of these few phrases [the last eight measures of the tune in each of its five appearances] can show not only the characteristic details of syncopation and phrasing . . . but also the sweeping progression of melody that gives Armstrong's performance as a whole its cumulative power. The bracketed motif with repeated notes is the outstanding idea of the introduction, where it brings a mild unexpected accent that welds the whole phrase together, as suggested by the metrical signs above the notes; the motif serves at once, slightly varied, to make the cadence. In the first full chorus, Armstrong shifts this motif very subtly, anticipating and consolidating it. In the vocal chorus he simplifies it, and then drastically changes the cadence in order

Armstrong, *Hotter Than That,* variants of last phrase

to dovetail with the interlude, by way of the most expressive blue note in the whole piece. In the final chorus he brings the motif to a real development, starting four measures ahead, rising to the top note of the piece and overriding the caesura that had preceded the motif in each earlier chorus, so that the final, expected appearence of the motif is now late and the cadence is a quick blur of blue notes. A sympathetic listener can enjoy all this intricate melodic thought without benefit of verbal or graphic analysis, just as Armstrong composed it entirely in his imagination of sounds; but analysis can contribute to greater enjoyment, and it can open the way to new enjoyment for some music-lovers who have formerly allowed the melodic intricacy to be overshadowed by the harmonic and rhythmic simplicity of the accompaniment. The accompaniment supports this kind of melody, eggs it on, and gives it freedom. Such melodies seem to be invented only when the accompaniment is giving the right kind of support. Moreover, they probably grow out of the experience of contrapuntal music—Armstrong's single line often seems to be incorporating fragmentary antiphonal answers to its own leading ideas. But the one rich melody is now the proper focus of interest.

The harmonic relation between Armstrong's melody and the band's accompaniment is subtle. Whereas Dodds's melody is composed mainly of broken chords and simple ornaments, Armstrong's is more independent, more long-breathed, bolder in its dissonances—notably in the cross-relations marked by asterisks. [See Example above.] Yet Armstrong's melody does harmonize convincingly, and its drive to the cadence is the Bach-like drive of a melody in counterpoint against a melodic bass. This harmonic subtlety is neglected in most accounts of Armstrong's style. It is what distinguishes him and his best colleagues from their routine imitators. It is also what points ahead most distinctly to the best work of younger men, like Charlie Parker.[41]

West End Blues is another example of the musical excitement generated by Louis Armstrong's extraordinary improvisatory skills (see Transcriptions). Fred Robinson's trombone solo is lifeless, and Zutty Singleton's drum accompaniment to the trombone solo is inept. But we hear in the solo piano a newly developed style that is beginning to lose its ragtime roots. Fatha Hines's solo, the fourth full chorus (*SCCJ*, II/9), employs a right-hand technique that substitutes flowing rapid-note passages for the old-fashioned ragged syncopations. The accompanying left hand, although it begins in oom-pah style, quickly shifts to walking parallels which project a 4/4 meter in undifferentiated quarter notes. Armstrong's ad lib introduction rapidly descends an octave and a third in the first two measures, only to ascend just as rapidly to a climactic high D above high C. It then falls gracefully to a second climactic low note with a facility and instinctive selection of correct notes that leaves the listener breathless. The rhythmic activity of his solo work is no longer regular, for mixtures of duplets, triplets, quadruplets, quintuplets, and other irrational values are incor-

---

[41] William Austin, *Music in the 20th Century*, p. 281 ff.

West End Blues

```
 Intro
| (ad lib)                    |

            9
| Trumpet solo             | Trombone solo                 |
           12                            12

| Vocal solo with clarinet lead | Piano solo               |
           12                            12

| Trumpet solo      piano  | Tag |
         12      (8 plus 4)    2
```

porated in a scheme that is uncanny in its musical logic. The end of his first twelve-measure solo can be found, almost note for note, in the third and fourth measures of the introduction. The descent from his climactic high note in the introduction is carried a step further in his descent from the held opening high note of his last chorus.[42]

Louis Armstrong was not the only hot band leader playing at this time. The three examples of Jelly Roll Morton's ensemble work, *Black Bottom Stomp, Dead Man Blues,* and *Grandpa's Spells,*[43] were all recorded toward the end of 1926. *Black Bottom Stomp* is a superlative tour de force of New Orleans jazz, and one can see that there is a certain overlap of personnel among the groups recording at this time. Kid Ory on trombone and Johnny St. Cyr on banjo were also part of the Armstrong ensembles. Where Morton's group lacked the outstanding trumpet player of the day, it more than compensated by featuring the greatest jazz composer and one of the outstanding piano virtuosos of the period, Ferdinand "Jelly Roll" himself. The clarinetist, Omer Simeon, need take a back seat to no one, for his facility, tonguing, phrasing, tone, and improvisational ingenuity are unmatched by any other clarinetist in jazz at that time. Neither Sidney Bechet nor Johnny Dodds had the technical mastery of the instrument that Simeon displays on this recording. The pure energy of the final chorus, the ensemble close, seems to reach a level of hysteria, and yet one observes that the group remains in control at all times.

[42] A transcription of Armstrong's trumpet solo from *West End Blues* can be found in John Mehegan, *Jazz Improvisation,* Vol. 2 (New York: Watson-Guptill, 1962), pp. 64–65. A similar transcription in a more complex rhythmic notation and the wrong key, B♭ instead of E♭ can be found in Schuller, *Early Jazz,* pp. 116, 118, 119. The Schuller transcription is instructive insofar as it demonstrates the difficulty of notating jazz rhythms accurately, but the incorrect key relationship makes difficult an understanding of the harmonic subtleties of the Armstrong solo.

[43] *SCCJ,* II/1, *SCCJ,* I/8, and *SCCJ,* I/7, respectively. The recordings are listed in chronological order.

Certain features of this performance are typical of Morton, but one is unusual in the recorded jazz at this date. The stoptime phrases, the rhythmetized melodic patterns (stomps), the continuous eighth-note obbligato, and the exciting breaks that gain effectiveness through well-rehearsed ensemble practice are all typical of the Jelly Roll Morton ensembles. The novel feature is John Lindsay's pizzicato string-bass playing. This instrument in the rhythm section became a standard during the swing era, and here we have an early recorded example of the bass used properly to supply the rhythmic life and harmonic ground so essential in the developing idiom.

Where *Black Bottom Stomp* achieves great heights, *Dead Man Blues* (SCCJ, I/8) hardly lifts itself off the floor. The solos of Simeon and Mitchell are sophomoric; the trombone obbligato solo to the rifflike accompaniment of the clarinets is simple-minded; and the continuity of the piece is such that one more or one less chorus would hardly be noticed. Still, to understand a music, one must have some knowledge of the ordinary as well as the failures. Just as a study of the Rocky Mountains would be totally inadequate if one were limited to peaks above 14,000 feet, a survey of jazz of the '20s is misrepresented if one sips only the distilled nectar of the ten best performances. *Dead Man Blues* is typical of the kind of music produced by bands called upon to entertain nightly week after week. The joke of the opening helps enliven a routine night, and the well-worn harmonic patterns of the piece are easily traversed by professional musicians who have been there many times before. But the creative spark cannot ignite four to six hours a day, seven days a week, and this recording shows how competent professionals are able to play a good job without inspiration. Everything is in its place, but nothing exciting happens musically.

On the other hand, when the group cut *Grandpa's Spells* (SCCJ, I/7) in December of 1926, it gave permanence to a classic of New Orleans–style jazz. Morton's cascading right hand is balanced at the bottom by John Lindsay's walking string bass. Johnny St. Cyr's melodic guitar playing (in contrast with the customary chordal harmonic style) is followed by New Orleans polyphony in which Kid Ory, George Mitchell, and Omer Simeon achieve an exemplary contrapuntal balance. It is in their ensemble playing that these musicians are at their best, for the solos, although interesting, are on a plane considerably below those of Louis Armstrong. The solos are inhibited to the degree that this piece is carefully arranged by the composer, for in order to perform all the ensemble requirements of this somewhat complicated work, each player must devote a fair share of his energy to that task. Morton's command of the keyboard is astonishing, but his style of playing was quickly being replaced by the more advanced work of a younger generation of pianists.

Fatha

Earl Kenneth "Fatha" Hines was born and educated in Pittsburgh in 1905, and arrived in Chicago after a tour with Lois B. Deppe's Serenaders in 1923. He played in that area and on the circuit during the early '20s, until the beginning of his association with Louis Armstrong in 1927. In 1928, Hines made a series of recordings with Louis Armstrong that mark a major change in Louis's style and in the role the piano was to take in jazz ensembles. Before this time, the major jazz pianists thought in terms of making full, rich orchestral sounds. Used as a solo instrument, the piano was treated as an inexpensive substitute for a band in establishments requiring live music. The left hand functioned as a rhythm section producing both the rhythm and the harmonic underpinning, and the right hand provided both the melody and the fuller ensemble sound. When used in a jazz ensemble, the piano was still treated in a similar manner, even when the functions were reduced simply to those provided by the left hand. Hines, although obviously capable of playing in the older style, left some of the left-hand work to the drums (and bass) and began to walk that hand around on the harmonies. The major change, however, occurred in his right-hand technique, for he allowed single-note improvisations in melodic-instrument style to predominate. Lastly, in ensemble, he looked upon the role of the pianist as equal to that of any member of the front line. Where the piano's responsibilities in group performance had been almost exclusively accompanimental, Hines developed a style of piano playing that was soloistic within the ensemble. The performance of *Weather Bird* (SCCJ, III/1) by Armstrong and Hines is the product of two major talents competing and cooperating successfully in a musical enterprise. Neither dominates the other, but each spurs his rival on to greater achievement. This 1928 Armstrong-Hines performance represents a slightly altered version of the original recorded by King Oliver in 1923.[44]

Weather Bird

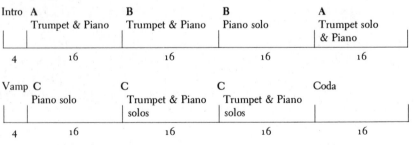

Intro	A	B	B	A
	Trumpet & Piano	Trumpet & Piano	Piano solo	Trumpet solo & Piano
4	16	16	16	16

Vamp	C	C	C	Coda
	Piano solo	Trumpet & Piano solos	Trumpet & Piano solos	
4	16	16	16	16

[44] Gennett 5132.

63   Earl "Fatha" Hines.

The first thirty-six measures of the piece, the introduction and the first statement of **A** and **B**, are played in a straightforward manner, both men refraining from deviations from the original. This procedure establishes, for the listener, the harmonic and melodic structure of the piece, so that the improvisations that follow are more easily perceived within the context of the basic grammar and syntax. The total format is obviously but one of the many typical ragtime patterns, complete with introduction, first and second strain, modulatory vamp, and trio.

Hines's performance during the first statement of the second strain and during the trumpet solo, to the repeat of the first strain, demonstrates perfectly the transformation he had effected in accompanimental piano style. Two-handed, syncopated chords; walking, four-beat progressions; and answering melodic passages decorate a keyboard texture which implies steady rhythm and steady harmony but in fact explicitly provides solo-piano material. Strangely, the first piano solo (the repeat of **B**) reverts to an old-fashioned barrelhouse piano style in which the left hand bounces back and forth and the right hand rolls some chords, syncopates the tune, and provides a ragtime-jazz lead. Hines plays his version of ragtime piano in the first full strain of the trio, but the two succeeding choruses, where trumpet and piano alternate, jostle each other, and romp in playful ecstasy, demonstrate his lead-instrument piano style.

The matching of trumpet and piano, from a harmonic point of view, is not convincing at times, for there is some question of whether their exuberance did not produce a wrong note or two. However, in jazz, there is ample opportunity to make the best of chance sounds, and Hines, in measure 10 of the last full strain of the trio, comes down the keyboard and pounces on a nonharmonic note that complements the sounds that preceded it in the last chorus and a half.

The Jazz Community

Humor in jazz is pervasive, and the ability to laugh at others and one's self is deeply rooted in the blues tradition of black Americans. Louis Armstrong, like Fats Waller, was sometimes criticized as an "Uncle Tom" for guarding his image as an entertainer and his reluctance to engage in political ferment. However, it has been conjectured that black musicians in the twenties wore a smiling mask that was sometimes nudged aside to reveal resentments during "their virtuoso instrumental performances, their mocking renditions of conventional lyrics, and, of course, by creating and singing 'Black and Blue.' "[45] In-

[45] David A. Cayer, "Black and Blue and Black Again: Three Stages of Racial Imagery in Jazz Lyrics," *Journal of Jazz Studies*, 1 (1974), p. 53.

strumental virtuosity was one means of demonstrating superiority in white culture, but even here the black man had to protect his ego with humor. It was never safe to be too good or too outspoken, and special languages, both musical and verbal, reserved for intimates, were necessary for personal and group survival. Bud Freeman, a white saxophonist playing in the Chicago area during the 1920s, who sympathized with the plight of the black musician, explains:

> When I say the Black man's language, you have to understand that the Black man of that day [1920s] who was not educated, had to find a way to make it in the White world. He had to "yes" the White man; there were underground phrases that he had to use that the White man didn't understand.[46]

It has been convincingly demonstrated that a jazz community did in fact exist.[47] This community is not circumscribed by a geographic boundary, but instead by a definition of the people with a given set of values who share an interest in jazz at a high level of intensity and participate, to some extent, in the occupational role and ideology of the jazz musician. The jazz community is different from other occupational groups in that

> . . . not only do the professionals constitute a group, but their public is included in it. This is not to say, of course, that there are not cliques and inner circles of hierarchical nature within this broad social grouping, but rather that the occupational professional people and their public are set off as a relatively closely knit group which shares behaviors and the results of those behaviors in common and in contradistinction to people outside the group.[48]

Many factors contributed to the estrangement of the jazz community from society at large, but it is important to realize that the jazz musicians found acceptance within the culture of black America.

> Jazz musicians, by the middle and late 1920's, were prestigious members of the Black society. Their influence, though not institutionalized, was proportionally greater than their numbers would suggest.[49]

A leading musician in Chicago at this time, a black bandleader and columnist for *The Chicago Defender*, Dave Peyton, served on the board of directors of the black musicians' union, Local 208, and published a weekly column which

---

[46] J. Frederick MacDonald, ed., "An Interview with Bud Freeman (5–29–74)," *Popular Music and Society*, 3 (1974), p. 332.

[47] Alan P. Merriam and Raymond W. Mack, "The Jazz Community," *Social Forces*, 38 (1960), p. 211 ff.

[48] Ibid., p. 211.

[49] John Lax, "Chicago's Black Musicians in the '20s: Portrait of an Era," *Journal of Jazz Studies*, 1 (1974), p. 109.

he claimed was read by 30,000 musicians. Peyton exercised both influence and control within the black Chicago musical establishment, and he championed education, both musical and academic, as a means to higher achievement. It is a misconception to think that the majority of successful black musicians working in Chicago were those men like Louis Armstrong who had emigrated from New Orleans. One observer points out that:

> A *Chicago Defender* directory of local Black groups in August, 1926, included twenty-seven bands. Only six of these could be considered New Orleans-in-Chicago groups. The rest belonged, to some extent, to the establishment. However, it is the New Orleans leaders, King Oliver, Luis Russell, and Louis Armstrong, whose names are recognized in this list. Even the leading establishment figures—Dave Peyton, Erskine Tate, Charles Elgar, Charles "Doc" Cooke, Jimmy Wade, and Sammy Stewart—are little known today.[50]

In Chicago there were four categories of musical employment: 1) cabarets catering basically to a black audience although admitting white patrons; 2) ballrooms for whites only; 3) black-oriented movie and vaudeville theaters; and 4) recording sessions. Of these four types of jobs, the ballrooms and theaters were dominated by the establishment bands, while the New Orleans contingent controlled the cabarets and recording sessions. Similarly, the cabaret audiences were drawn more from the "shady" side of the population, while the theater and ballroom clientele were largely respectable.[51]

In the same way that humor in blues lyrics helps salve the wounds of racial injury, humor in instrumental solos fulfills a therapeutic need for the virtuoso jazzman. He laughs a lot musically, but only a percentage of the humor is good-natured. In the *Weather Bird* repartee of Hines and Armstrong, there is almost a bear-cub playfulness. The instruments roll around, scramble over each other, and do their thing in mutual trust and understanding.

When Louis Armstrong performs *Sweethearts on Parade* (SCCJ, III/2), however, it is difficult to know where the joke begins and ends. Louis's respect for the Lombardo society sound is in full evidence here as his Sebastian New Cotton Club Orchestra performs a composition by Guy Lombardo's brother Carmen, lead saxophonist, composer, and arranger for the Royal Canadians. The sustained, vibrato-laden chordal accompaniment and the "chunk, chunk, chunk" rhythm at the "businessman's bounce" tempo are certainly serious business with Louis. On the other hand, the bugle call that ends the parade is obviously tongue-in-cheek. The juxtaposition of the double-time jazz chorus with sweethearts politely tiptoeing arm in arm may be a joke, but it is probably

---

[50] Thomas J. Hennessey, "The Black Chicago Establishment 1919–1930," *Journal of Jazz Studies*, 2 (1974), p. 16.

[51] Ibid., p. 21.

an uncontrollable jazz impulse bursting forth in a pyrotechnic display. Incidentally, as the years passed, Armstrong achieved even greater technical mastery of his instrument, and here we see him climb to an E above high C (concert D) with complete ease.

Bix

When Louis Armstrong recorded *I Gotta Right to Sing the Blues* (SCCJ, III/3), Bix Beiderbecke had already been dead for a year and a half. Three years younger than Armstrong, he drank so heavily that he returned to his home town in 1929 to dry out. He was back in New York in 1930, but in mid-1931 he collapsed and died at the age of 28 of lobar pneumonia and cerebral edema. This man, who has often been used as a symbol of the Jazz Age, was relatively unknown to the general public and died almost unnoticed except by a small circle of jazz associates and admirers. Leon Bix Beiderbecke was born in Davenport in March of 1903. He began playing the piano before he was five, and took up the cornet, which he played with a self-taught, unconventional fingering at fourteen. During the riverboat days, Davenport was heavily trafficked by boats which came north from Memphis, St. Louis, and New Orleans. During his high school days, 1919–21, he began playing odd jobs and listening to Original Dixieland Jazz Band recordings. He studied the work of Nick La Rocca and was introduced to the playing of Louis Armstrong on one of the riverboats that docked at Davenport. His parents enrolled him in Lake Forest Military Academy, north of Chicago, in 1921, but he was expelled before the academic year was up. During 1921 and 1922, Beiderbecke worked occasionally around Chicago and listened frequently to King Oliver's Band as well as the New Orleans Rhythm Kings. He joined the Wolverines in 1923, and from then until his death in 1931 he developed a solo jazz-cornet style which seemed to have roots in a different musical garden.

Beiderbecke played with the Wolverines, Charlie Straight's commercial orchestra, Frankie Trumbauer's ensemble, several Jean Goldkette units, the Paul Whiteman "King of Jazz" Orchestra, and possibly the Glen Gray and Dorsey brothers' bands. He was not terribly successful as an ensemble musician, for he read music poorly. In fact, he seems to have had a learning disability in this area. Born into an upper middle-class family for whom music was an accepted and fostered art, Beiderbecke's parents hoped that he would develop into a concert pianist. He began his formal study of piano at the age of seven, but the endeavor was futile, for Bix was unable to learn to read music. His teacher discontinued the studies and admitted that "he couldn't teach the boy anything and that the talent was one that lay deep within."[52] Beiderbecke was able, finally, to learn to read as a cornet player when he played in the Paul Whiteman Orchestra in the late 1920s, but he was never expert and maintained a skill level far below the standard required of the other Whiteman musicians. Although his fingers and ears were able to cooperate in expressing his monumental talent, his eyes were almost useless to him in translating musical symbols into audible sounds.

While Bix was in St. Louis in 1925 with Frankie Trumbauer, he began to explore contemporary music outside the domain of jazz. His interest focused on the impressionists, particularly Claude Debussy, and his study and practice of these French impressionistic sounds led him to improvisations which were based on expansions of conventional harmony. He used chord tones and scales that were unusual for jazzmen at that time, sounds foreign to the genre in those early days of its development. He introduced flatted fifths, sixths, ninths, elevenths, thirteenths, whole-tone scales, and augmented-chord harmonies into his improvised melodic lines. Although Beiderbecke took an interest in the works of other contemporary composers—Ravel, Stravinsky, Holst, Griffes, and MacDowell—the influence of Debussy upon his thinking is most easily traced. Beiderbecke's piano composition *In a Mist* is a piece patterned after the short piano sketches of Claude Debussy, but incorporating some of the rhythmic activity of jazz and ragtime. It is interesting to note that this piece was never notated by Beiderbecke, continually reworked in improvisatory sessions, and finally recorded by Bix in 1927.[53]

Given his other frustrations, the inability to work with written music must have played a prominent part in the deteriorating state of his mental health. As was the case with many of the leading ragtime composers, Beiderbecke aspired to write large compositions employing the style he loved. But his discussion of a jazz symphony came to naught, for he was unable to put on paper the ideas he carried in his head. In spite of his problems, and regardless of his limited public recognition, Bix Beiderbecke remains the most important white jazz musician of the 1920s, for his influence upon the playing of other jazz musicians was remarkable. Beiderbecke's legacy may be best summarized thus:

> Bix was known chiefly as a cornetist with an exquisite tone and legato style of improvisation. He was probably the first white musician ever to be admired and imitated by Negro jazzmen. . . . Though often surrounded by musicians of inferior stature and by over-commercialized arrangements, notably in the Whiteman Band, Bix nevertheless left a legacy of performances unmatched in subtlety and finesse blended with a sensitive jazz feeling.[54]

[52] George Hoefer, "Bix Beiderbecke," *The Jazz Makers*, ed. Nat Shapiro and Nat Hentoff, p. 93.
[53] Okeh 40916, reissued Columbia CL 844-7.
[54] Leonard Feather, *The New Edition of the Encyclopedia of Jazz*, p. 132.

Beiderbecke's solo work on the Okeh recording of *Riverboat Shuffle* (SCCJ, III/4)[55] displays the many characteristics for which he was justly famous: legato style, controlled tone, a lilting rhythmic treatment of eighth notes, developmental treatment of motives, and a penchant for dissonances which stressed the upper partials against the simple harmonic substructure:

Riverboat Shuffle

The asterisks mark the harmonic dissonances, and they are:

last note of the 2-measure break	major 9th
m. 1	major 6th (13th)
m. 2 and m. 6	major 7th and 9th
m. 3 and m. 7	minor 3rd against major harmony (blue 3rd)
m. 8	major 9th and minor 13th
m. 9	major 9th

It is particularly instructive to compare this *Riverboat Shuffle* solo with one he recorded at a different date:[56]

---

[55] The SCCJ booklet has bands 4 and 5 reversed.
[56] Taken from Schuller, *Early Jazz*, p. 190, and transposed up a minor third.

Although the solos are different, the stressed harmonic dissonances are the same. They are:

m. 2   major 6th (13th), minor 3rd against a major triad (blue 3rd), major 6th (13th), and augmented 11th

m. 3   minor 3rd against a major triad (blue 3rd)

m. 5   major 6th (13th)

m. 6   augmented 2nd (9th), major 7th, augmented 11th

m. 7   major 9th

m. 9   minor 3rd against a major triad (blue 3rd)

Beiderbecke's soft cornet quality (upper partials are less pronounced than in the characteristic trumpet sound) mutes the subtlety of his intonation, for he places great stress in his solo work on the expressiveness of minutely tempered intonation, a characteristic of hot jazz. Although the sliding harmonies of *Riverboat Shuffle* (introduction, piano break, etc.) seem to coincide with the harmonic framework characteristic of impressionist piano music, this is attributable not to Bix Beiderbecke, but to the composer Hoagy Carmichael. However, it is likely that these patterns were attractive to Beiderbecke and played some role in his selection of this piece for performance and recording.

   Singin' the Blues (SCCJ, III/5) lacks the consistency of *Riverboat Shuffle,* for various flaws are apparent. The polyphony of the ensemble passage following Beiderbecke's solo includes some crude heterophony at the beginning. The Jimmy Dorsey clarinet solo is totally devoid of inventiveness and even has a wrong note in the next-to-last measure. But certain moments in the Beider-

Singin' the Blues

becke solo are exquisite. At the ninth measure, when the harmonic pattern begins a circle-of-fifths progression, Bix plays with a few of his favorite sounds and lets one dissonance melt into the next. The influence of both his harmonic thinking and his "cool" sound on saxophonist Lester Young becomes apparent when we discover that Young, at one time, carried a copy of Trumbauer's *Singin' the Blues* around in his saxophone case. Conceivably, it was Trumbauer's solo that Prez admired, but it is just as likely it was the clean, relaxed, articulate solo work of Bix Beiderbecke.

   In the best of the Beiderbecke solos, just as in the best of the Armstrong solos, one sees a structural integrity that results from reworked motivic patterns and harmonic sounds that are individual to the players themselves. Structural unity and developmental inventiveness are partially accomplished through conscious effort, but they are more likely the result of a subconscious interplay of stored mental images and reflexive lip-and-finger patterns. The working jazzman recycles a finite body of musical phrases to which, from time to time and under the creative urging of the muses and the moment, is added a newly inspired sound, a clever turn of phrase, or an exciting rhythmic idea. The average jazzman is almost totally imitative in his improvisatory technique, for most of his "ideas" are gathered from the plantings of the giants—the Armstrongs, the Beiderbeckes, the Mortons, and the Hineses. The phonograph recording became a teaching aid from its first introduction in 1917, for we know that jazz musicians have traditionally learned their craft not only on the job but through imitation of recorded solos. Bix Beiderbecke had a phonograph as early as 1918 and committed the Nick La Rocca passages to memory. The master jazz musicians are able, however, to move beyond the imitative to the creative, and as they do so, styles fluctuate and change. But for the result to have musical meaning, the notes within any particular jazz solo must be related to each other syntactically. Merely to play scales and arpeggios in the right key with the right harmonies will create little more than an extemporized embellishment. But through a process of reshaping a limited number of musical ideas within the single solo, improvisational composition takes place.

Beiderbecke's musical preoccupation with harmonic dissonances and superimposed blue thirds (see examples on pp. 203–204) is but one instance of the extemporaneous compositional process at work. As saxophonist Bud Freeman explains:

> Everybody plays something over again because you see, there are phrases that you develop . . . they become dear to you. This is the thing the critic doesn't understand. He wants you to play differently all the time. . . . The greatness of Louis was that the phrases he played were dear to him, and yet he didn't play them mechanically. He felt them. [57]

Not every jazz solo is played with the expressive quality of an Armstrong or a Beiderbecke. The first eight measures of Don Murray's clarinet solo on *Riverboat Shuffle* is a good example of a series of correct notes played mechanically. What set Beiderbecke apart was the freshness of his ideas. Even though he reworked familiar material (not only are the two *Riverboat Shuffle* solos related, but one can find strong similarities in solos performed to other compositions, for example, *Sorry*);[58] he also created new music.

[57] MacDonald, ed., "An Interview with Bud Freeman (5–29–74)," p. 336.
[58] Columbia CL-844.

Beiderbecke's solo on *Jazz Me Blues*[59] is one of his best, even though it has a restricted range of note values and pitch. On that same recording one hears the work of another superb musician, Adrian Rollini, a bass saxophonist who is capable of swinging in both ensemble and solo. The consistency of Rollini's solo work in *Jazz Me Blues* marks him as a leading jazzman of the 1920s. But the bass saxophone played badly is a dangerous instrument, and one can hear on *Thou Swell*[60] a grotesque solo by Min Leibrook, a Beiderbecke sideman, and on *Ol' Man River*[61] ensemble work in which Leibrook hits many wrong notes. Beiderbecke stands apart as an important historical figure, in spite of the brevity of his career, for three important reasons: the consistently high level of performance, the innovation of his musical thought within the context of his historical framework, and the influence he had upon other jazz musicians who helped shape the course of the music they played.

Changing Times

Jazz in Chicago during the '20s slowly changed from the classic New Orleans style to a modified Dixieland style usually referred to as "Chicago-style jazz." But a clearly defined line of demarcation cannot be drawn, for the New Orleans bands played both two-beat and four-beat, used clarinet and saxophone, interchanged banjos and guitars, played pieces with introductions, vamps, and codas, worked out arrangements as well as improvised polyphonically, and so on. The real stylistic change did not take place until the development of the big-band concept. In the meantime, however, musicians from widely divergent backgrounds were being attracted to jazz. In the Chicago area, an important group was called the Austin High Gang, because the nucleus of the group was composed of musicians who were once students at Chicago's Austin High School. Jimmy McPartland, Dick McPartland, Frank Teschemacher, Bud Freeman, David Tough, and eventually Floyd O'Brien formed a group which modelled itself after the New Orleans Rhythm Kings. Their ensemble of clarinet, cornet, tenor saxophone (and later trombone), banjo, and drums resulted in a sound usually used to exemplify the Chicago style. These youngsters recorded in a variety of orchestras: the Wolverines, the Jungle Kings, and the Charles Pierce Orchestra, to name but a few.

Some of the musicians of that era were jazzmen of consequence, who can-

[59] Ibid.
[60] Ibid.
[61] Ibid.

not be given fair treatment here for lack of space. Still, Eddie Condon, the remarkable Chicago banjo player; George Wettling, a leading drummer; Wingy Manone, a white, one-armed trumpet player from New Orleans; Pee Wee Russell, one of the most dextrous of all clarinet players; Mezz Mezzrow, a highly controversial clarinetist; Muggsy Spanier, a memorable cornetist and plunger-mute soloist; Bunny Berigan, Gene Krupa, and Benny Goodman, all youngsters who would make their mark in the succeeding decade; all are names of consequence in the musical environment located at the south edge of Lake Michigan. While the white musicians played the north side of Chicago, Johnny Dodds, Freddie Keppard, Lovie Austin, and Jimmy Noone, along with Louis Armstrong and Joe Oliver, worked the south side.

During the '20s, the "national" bands remained close to New York and Chicago, where the majority of the recording studios and radio stations made their headquarters and where large numbers of cabarets and dancehalls provided steady employment. However, this period also spawned hundreds of "territory bands." These groups developed their own sounds, mixing elements

A battered old photograph of the Austin High Gang in 1926. (Left to right) Frank Teschemacher and Bud Freeman, saxophones, with Jim Lanigan, bass, between them; Jimmy McPartland, trumpet; Dave Tough, drums; Floyd O'Brien, trombone; Dave North, piano; and Dick McPartland, banjo.

taken from the national styles with the taste and tradition of the areas in which they worked. Regional styles flourished, and six major territories emerged: East Coast, Southeast, Midwest, Northwest, Southwest, and West Coast.[62] Southwestern bands, such as George E. Lee, Jap Allen, and Walter Page's Blue Devils, toured out of Kansas City and Oklahoma City; Oliver Cobb worked out of St. Louis; Skeets Morgan came from Alabama; and Smiley Billy Stewart traveled north from Florida. Frank "Red" Perkins, Lloyd Hunter, and Ted Adams were all leaders of black bands that toured the hinterlands out of Omaha, Nebraska. An overview of the jazz activities of the late 1920s shows not a draught but a flood. Most of these lesser lights will never receive full investigation, for their passage through history is not marked by a trail of recordings. The cumulative effect of all these musicians, sturdy members of the jazz community, undoubtedly had an impact upon the music. A few area styles did emerge, the most notable of which is from Kansas City, the result of men like Walter Page and Benny Moten.

[62] See Thomas J. Hennessey, "From Jazz to Swing: Black Jazz Musicians and Their Music, 1917–1935," pp. 121–218.

THE BIG-BAND CONCEPT:
PRELUDE TO SWING

WHEN THE MARKET crashed in October, 1929, and fifty leading stocks plummeted almost forty points in one day, jazz in America did not come to an end. The relationship between the music and the economy had always been somewhat loose and informal; nevertheless, in the next six years, many musicians who had been regularly employed in places of entertainment were out of work. America still needed music, perhaps more than ever to lend comfort and solace, but most Americans could not afford to go out as they had in the past. They were no longer in the mood for the lively hot jazz of the carefree and extraordinarily prosperous era which immediately preceded the depression.

Popular songs and crooning prevailed, music of a dreamy, sentimental, fairy-tale nature that soothed the white man's pain as the blues had salved the black man's troubles. For example:

> 1929—*I'm in Seventh Heaven*
> 1930—*Let Me Sing and I'm Happy*
> 1931—*Wrap Your Troubles in Dreams*
> 1932—*How Deep Is the Ocean*
> 1933—*I've Got the World on a String*

Bands with radio contracts and those willing and able to cater to a melancholy general public weathered the financial storm and even prospered. Guy Lombardo established himself at the Roosevelt Hotel, and Paul Whiteman continued to parade an endless supply of popular songsters, semiclassical arrangers and composers, vaudeville tricksters,[1] and name jazz musicians before the public. This entertainment formula earned Whiteman a regal reputation, for he, almost singlehandedly, dominated the popular market. Fletcher Henderson, broadcasting from the Roseland Ballroom in New York City, was a compromise figure in the sense that he led a band of jazz musicians but strayed only rarely from the moderate path of mid-tempo, social-dance music. The leading hot-jazz musicians, like Louis Armstrong, continued to play and record, but their broad base of support was gradually shrinking.

The Emergence of Substyles

Between 1929 and 1935, many of the major jazz organizations crossed the Atlantic to try their luck in Europe. These trips had publicity value on this side of the ocean, and it kept some of the jazzmen employed, for the old world was still eager to receive more hot music from the new. Armstrong ventured across during this period, as did Duke Ellington, and, as if commenting on the general state of big-band music in America, Duke composed, in 1932, *It Don't Mean a Thing If It Ain't Got That Swing.*[2] Although the general public may have been only vaguely aware of the current state of jazz, the years from 1929 to 1935 produced some formidable changes in the music itself. A phenomenon was occurring which could be clearly observed from that time to the present: a multiplicity of substyles emerged and began to coexist. In the early days, ragtime, minstrel, brass band, and blues were fused, so that basically one style of jazz, albeit with individual variants, was played: hot jazz. The jazz of New Orleans, Chicago, the Southwest, and New York was essentially of one style, but gradually, throughout the 1920s, outside influences and ideas started to form new buds on the "old" plant. Where New York stride piano was initially little more than a local variant of ragtime performance, the day had finally arrived when ragtime piano players, like Jelly Roll Morton, would coexist with swing piano players, like Fats Waller, and with a new breed, the boogie-woogie pianists, like Pine Top Smith and Meade Lux Lewis. Before long, the hot combos of the classic Dixieland style would vie for jobs with the newer swing combos, groups that were in their formative stages during these early depression years. Morton's Red Hot Peppers and Nichols' Five Hot Pennies had already mastered their craft of hot jazz, but the young Dorseys, Goodman, and others were learning to play with a new sound.

[1] Whiteman's recording of *Whispering* (Victor 18690), which features a slide whistle as lead instrument, is a classic example.
[2] Brunswick 6265.

The swing bands had few counterparts in the early 1920s, but as some of the smaller ensembles expanded and began playing newly written compositions and special arrangements, the big band emerged toward the end of the decade (see p. 215 ff). In the music of the jazz orchestras, the most significant developments seem to have taken place during the worst of the depression years. The pioneers—Duke Ellington, Fletcher Henderson, and Don Redman—were maturing in the early '30s, while some new names appeared upon the scene—perhaps the most notable of these was Glen Gray and his Casa Loma Orchestra. The musical events of this time are still an aesthetic battlefield. One commentator considers what was happening a cultural tragedy:

> The number of prosperous dance bands at the popular level multiplied, while the jazz content remained slight. At the same time, dancing the Charleston, the Black Bottom, and the Lindy was highly popular and the bands tried to oblige by playing a little hot jazz. . . . None of these large dance bands, however, could swing as a whole. The formula consisted of importing one or two "hot" soloists or "get-off" men, letting them take a chorus once in a while surrounded by acres of uninspired fellow musicians.[3]

Another observer sees things differently and views the situation as fertile and productive:

> Unnoticed at first by the general public, though impressing the musicians and jazz fans as early as 1930, were the brisk, brittle, semi-swinging big band sounds produced by the midwestern Casa Loma Orchestra. . . . Soon, not only musicians were listening to |Glen Gray and the Casa Loma Orchestra| Kids, especially those in the colleges, flocked to hear the handsome-looking band that produced such mellow, musical moods, then stood around in awe as it let loose with an excitingly different-sounding big band barrage. More than any other group, |the Casa Loma Orchestra set the stage for the emergence of the swing bands and eventually the blossoming of the entire big band era.[4]|

Whether jazz during these years was in ascent or decline is a conjectural matter directly related to personal opinion and taste, for just as one man's religion is another man's heresy, jazz might be considered to have been expanding or fragmenting. Historically, however, the issue goes beyond personal judgment. Since most, if not all, of the various schools seem to have maintained a continuous tradition to the present; inasmuch as the musicians themselves considered their own identities to be those of jazz musicians and their own music to be jazz; and because the new music in the big-band style had roots in the past and retained the essential elements of the parent music, it is

[3] Marshall W. Stearns, *The Story of Jazz*, p. 180.
[4] George T. Simon, *The Big Bands*, p. 26 f.

1917		
W. C. Handy	*Livery Stable Blues*	Columbia A-2419
W. C. Handy	*Ole Miss Rag*	Columbia A-2420
ODJB	*Dixieland Jass Band One-Step*	Victor 18253
ODJB	*Darktown Strutters' Ball*	Columbia A-2297
1918		
ODJB	*Ostrich Walk*	Victor 18457
ODJB	*Tiger Rag*	Victor 18472
1919		
Louisiana Five	*Yelping Hound Blues*	Columbia A-2742
1920		
Paul Whiteman	*Whispering*	Victor 18690
1921		
James P. Johnson	*Carolina Shout*	Okeh 4495 (SCCJ, II/4)
1922		
Mamie Smith	*Lonesome Mama Blues*	Okeh 4630
other groups recording jazz or classic blues in 1922:		
Bailey's Lucky Seven		Gennett
Cotton Pickers		Brunswick
Johnny Dunn		Columbia
Friar's Society Orchestra		Gennett
Ladd's Black Aces		Gennett
ODJB		Okeh
Original Memphis Five		Banner & Paramount
Leona Williams and Her Dixie Band		Columbia
Edith Wilson		Columbia
1923		
Fletcher Henderson	*Gulf Coast Blues*	Vocalion 14636
Perry Bradford	*Daybreak Blues*	Paramount 12041
Benny Moten	*Elephant's Wobble*	Okeh 8100
New Orleans Rhythm Kings	*Wolverine Blues*	Gennett 5102
King Oliver's Creole Jazz Band	*Dippermouth Blues*	Gennett 5132 (SCCJ, I/6)

1924

Piron's New Orleans Band	*Ghost of the Blues*	Columbia 99-D
Red Onion Jazz Babies	*Cakewalking Babies*	Gennett 5627 (SCCJ, II/2)
Fats Waller	*Birmingham Blues*	Okeh 4757
The Wolverines	*Riverboat Shuffle*	Gennett 5454

1925

Louis Armstrong	*Gut Bucket Blues*	Okeh 8261
Bix and His Rhythm Jugglers	*Davenport Blues*	Gennett 5654
Duke Ellington	*Trombone Blues*	Perfect 14514
Sonny Clay	*Jambled Blues*	Vocalion 15078
Creath's Jazzo-maniacs	*King Porter Stomp*	Okeh 8210

(plus Henderson, Moten, Bailey, and many others)

1926

Jelly Roll Morton	*Black Bottom Stomp*	Victor 20221 (SCCJ, II/1)
Jelly Roll Morton	*Dead Man Blues*	Victor 20252 (SCCJ, I/8)
Jelly Roll Morton	*Grandpa's Spells*	Victor 20431 (SCCJ, I/7)
Fletcher Henderson	*The Stampede*	Columbia 654-D (SCCJ, III/6)
Papa Celestin	*Station Calls*	Columbia 636-D
Duke Ellington	*You've Got Those "Wanna Go Back Home Again" Blues*	Gennett 3291
Duke Ellington	*East St. Louis Toodle-Oo*	Vocalion 1064 (SCCJ, VI/4)
Freddie Keppard	*Salty Dog*	Paramount 12399
Red Nichols	*Washboard Blues*	Brunswick 3407
Joe Venuti–Eddie Lang	*Stringing the Blues*	Columbia 914-D

(plus Armstrong, Moten, Oliver, Pee Wee Russell, and others)

1927

Bands:

Arkansas Travelers, Louis Armstrong, Bix Beiderbecke, Charleston Chasers, Doc Cooke, Dixie Stompers, Johnny Dodds, Duke Ellington, Jean Goldkette, Goofus Five, Fletcher Henderson, Richard M. Jones, Jelly Roll Morton, Bennie

1927
   Bands:
        Moten, Red Nichols, King Oliver, Red [Nichols] and Miff's [Mole] Stompers,
        Boyd Senter, Jesse Stone, Frankie Trumbauer, Joe Venuti–Eddie Lang, Fats
        Waller, Paul Whiteman, Fess Williams
             Ellington (SCCJ, VI/4)
             Waller (SCCJ, IV/1)
             Trumbauer (SCCJ, III/4–5)
             Armstrong (SCCJ, II/5–8)

1928
   Important additions to 1927 list:
        Dorsey Brothers, Benny Goodman, McKinney's Cotton Pickers, Ben Pollack

---

1929
Important additions to 1928 list:
        Eddie Condon, Earl Hines, George E. Lee, Luis Russell, Pinetop Smith

---

historically imperative to judge this period as one of musical development and
expansion, even though fans of the earliest jazz music condemn it as less creative and exciting. The new music may have been somewhat limited, and it
may have followed some musical paths for commercial rather than purely artistic reasons, but numbered among its accomplishments are the facts that it did
expand the harmonic and timbral vocabularies of jazz and did raise the level of
requisite technical mastery in performance.

Jimmy Noone, Jack Teagarden, Red Nichols, Frankie Trumbauer, Jimmy
McPartland, Miff Mole, Joe Venuti, Eddie Lang, and a host of other musicians were formidable jazzmen who held almost universal respect within the
jazz community during the early 1930s, but they, as well as many others, will
receive brief or no mention in the pages that follow. By this time, the number
of jazzmen had proliferated to such an extent that, in the interest of concision,
we must turn our attention to those masters who most strongly affected the destiny of this American music. Those who steered the course most resolutely at
this time were: for hot jazz—traditionalists Louis Armstrong, King Oliver, and
Jelly Roll Morton; for the establishment orchestras—Guy Lombardo and Paul
Whiteman; and for the new big-band sound—Fletcher Henderson, Don Redman, Jimmy Lunceford, Benny Moten, Glen Gray, and Duke Ellington. It
was the music of the last group that led to the style called swing, and that is
what we shall proceed to analyze here.

The Arranger–Don Redman

Don Redman, alto saxophonist and arranger, joined the Fletcher Henderson band at the Roseland Ballroom in New York in 1923. Two years later, Henderson recorded a Redman arrangement of *Dippermouth Blues, Sugar Foot Stomp.*[5] The instrumentation called for four brass players, three reedmen, and four in the rhythm section, for a total of eleven musicians. At this time, in 1925, the band concept revealed in the Redman arrangements was only a slightly expanded version of King Oliver's New Orleans ensemble. In fact, Louis Armstrong was with the Henderson band at that time to record the hot

[5] Columbia 395-D, reissued Folkways FP 67.

The Fletcher Henderson band in 1925 consisted of (front row, left to right) Kaiser Marshall, drums; Coleman Hawkins, tenor sax; Buster Bailey, clarinet; Don Redman, saxes; Charlie Dixon, banjo; Fletcher Henderson, piano. (Back row, left to right) Charlie Green, trombone; Elmer Chambers, Louis Armstrong, and Howard Scott, trumpets; and Ralph Escudero, tuba.

solos. Where Oliver used two trumpets, Henderson employed three. His three reeds provided a Dixieland clarinetist in Buster Bailey, with the additional saxophones of Redman and Coleman Hawkins expanding the mid-range sonority. The four-piece rhythm section of piano, tuba, drums, and banjo was typical of the Dixieland jazz groups and had already crystallized as a standard grouping for hot jazz. As the years passed, the Dixieland tuba and banjo were replaced by the swing string bass and guitar.

Henderson's 1926 recording of *The Stampede*[6] (*SCCJ*, III/6) uses the same instrumentation as for *Sugar Foot Stomp*, and the following year, his recording band added a second trombone for *Livery Stable Blues*.[7] This work is still strongly related to the New Orleans repertoire and style, being an arrangement of the Dixieland piece introduced on record in 1917 by the Original Dixieland Jazz Band. Redman's arrangement for *The Stampede* "is almost an archetype of the [swing] big band score: written passages that separate the ensemble by sections, antiphonal phrases between the sections, a written variation-on-theme . . . , solo improvisation [at designated points in the music]."[8] The piece,

The Stampede

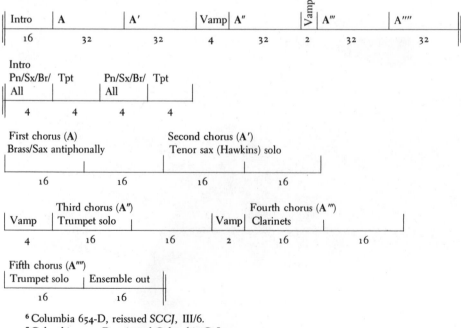

[6] Columbia 654-D, reissued *SCCJ*, III/6.
[7] Columbia 1002-D, reissued Columbia C3L 33.
[8] Martin Williams, liner notes to *SCCJ*, p. 22.

which was arranged by Redman, is thirty-two measures long, divided into two sixteen-measure phrases, the first acting as an antecedent phrase with a feminine (or open) ending (I–V), and the second answering as a consequent phrase with a masculine (or closed) ending (V–I). In his score, Redman repeats the complete piece five times, but orchestrates for the entire band only the first chorus, fourth chorus, introduction, vamps, and last half of the fifth, or final, chorus.

The musical figures played during the first chorus by the brass and saxophone sections are not unlike the riffs developed improvisationally by the Kansas City bands, but in this instance they are the inventions of the composer and arranger. To a certain degree, these riffs probably needed to be written down on paper, because the underlying chord structure of *The Stampede* is neither universally known nor commonly reused by jazzmen, as are the chord patterns of the blues and those popular songs that formed the basis of most of the Kansas City repertoire.

Although the notes of the clarinet chorus (the fourth) are different from those used in the first chorus, they carry the same repetitious rhythmic idea exploited by Redman earlier in the piece. One fascinating aspect of the tenor-saxophone solo by Coleman Hawkins is his improvisatory exploration of some of these same rhythmic ideas. His solo is closely related to this particular piece beyond the mere melodic ornamentation over a given chordal framework. Note too that the trumpet solos are played in mid-range. The emerging swing style calls upon the power of the center range of this instrument, and another swing feature, the jagged and on-the-beat rhythms which are to become a dominating feature of solos in this style, is apparent here too.

Reed solos in swing frequently utilize arpeggiated chordal passages grouped in twos and fours so that accents fall regularly on the beat; brass solos frequently use dotted figures with repeated notes that are rhythmically organized on the beat. Explanations can only be speculative, but it seems likely that the tendency toward increased musical schooling among the musicians and its concomitant technical virtuosity was brought about, and resulted from, woodshedding[9] of scales and arpeggios in the various keys. These practice habits would help account for the former characteristic. The latter, the brass solos, are not really different in kind from the majority of Dixieland-style brass solos (Bix Beiderbecke is almost unique among the brass soloists of this period, and his solos are unlike those being discussed here). The need for great volume to carry a brass solo from the back line of the band over the accompanying reeds and brass may have had something to do with the frequency of mid-range trumpet

---

[9] "Woodshedding" refers to practicing or rehearsing in private in order to gain technical mastery of one's instrument before going into a jam session.

and trombone solos. Rhythmic activity and syncopation are as ever-present in swing as they were in the earlier jazz, but accentuation, in both the solos and the arrangements, falls more frequently on the beat—often on the strong beats—and becomes one of the chief characteristics of the style.

Note too that this style of arrangement is not dependent upon particular personnel. If Coleman Hawkins were not available to play the tenor saxophone solo, Don Redman might just as well have played it on the alto instead. The sidemen of a typical swing band using this archetypal formula arrangement are, in a sense, interchangeable. To some degree, all jazzmen are, but here one can clearly see that Don Redman does not exploit the particular talents of individual instrumentalists, but simply leaves "blank spaces" in his arrangements where available musicians may stand up and "take a ride." His arrangements, although written for the Fletcher Henderson band, could be played by most of the other swing bands with sufficient personnel to cover the parts. When Redman arrangements were played by other bands, they sounded very much like those recorded by the Fletcher Henderson orchestra. The same is not the case with the music of Duke Ellington or the head arrangements of the Benny Moten, later the Count Basie, band.

Don Redman left the Henderson band in 1928, but Henderson continued to employ the same-size group and the same orchestrational concepts for the next six years. In 1928, he recorded *Hop Off*[10] with three trumpets, two trombones, three reeds, piano, tuba, drums, and banjo; and in 1933 he recorded *Queer Notions*[11] with the same forces, except that a bass and guitar had by then replaced the tuba and banjo.

In the meantime, Don Redman had taken charge of the McKinney's Cotton Pickers band, and between 1928 and 1932 he recorded with a group very similar to that of the Fletcher Henderson orchestra. His rhythm section always had piano, drums, and banjo, and the bass part fluctuated back and forth between tuba and string bass. He never went beyond three trumpets and often recorded with four reedmen. Normally, there was only one trombone and it was not until 1932, when he recorded his best-known work, *Chant of the Weed*, that he augmented his trombone section to three. With this particular work, he moved from the domain of the arranger into the realm of the composer, and here, for musical reasons, he found it necessary to use a nonstandard combination.

1923–27   Fletcher Henderson (Roseland Ballroom)
1928–31   McKinney's Cotton Pickers
1932   Harlan Lattimore and Connie's Inn Orchestra
1928   *Cherry* (Victor 21730, reissued Victor LPV-520)
               2 trumpets, 1 trombone, 4 reeds, piano, tuba, drums, banjo

[10] Paramount 12550, reissued Riverside RLP 12-115.
[11] Vocalion 2583, reissued Prestige 7645.

1929   *Gee, Ain't I Good to You?* (Victor 38097, reissued Victor LPV-520)
            3 trumpets, 1 trombone, 4 reeds, piano, bass, drums, banjo
1930   *Rocky Road* (Victor 22932, reissued Victor LPV-520)
            3 trumpets, 1 trombone, 3 reeds, piano, tuba, drums, banjo
1931   *Baby Won't You Please Come Home?* (Victor 22511, reissued Folk-
            ways FP 59)
            2 trumpets, 1 trombone, 3 reeds, piano, tuba, drums, banjo
1932   *Chant of the Weed* (Columbia 2675-D, reissued Columbia C3L 33)
            3 trumpets, 3 trombones, 4 reeds, piano, bass, drums, banjo

The McKinney's Cotton Pickers shown at Jean Goldkette's Greystone Ballroom, Detroit, in the late 1920s.

As was mentioned earlier, with a small improvising ensemble in which the musical functions of the players are clearly defined, it is not difficult to assign roles to the various musicians and expect them to carry out their assignments with alacrity and precision. Adding another front-line instrument, such as Oliver's second trumpet, necessitates a certain amount of increased improvised harmony, but this is not difficult to accomplish by ear, because thirds and sixths are relatively easy to fit with the melody in this style. Therefore, an arrangement for Fletcher Henderson's 1925 band is a fairly uncomplicated matter, for an additional trumpet and two reeds call for a minimum of work for the arranger. When the brass have expanded to six and the reeds to four, the complexity multiplies geometrically, and more careful planning and composer/arranger control are necessary. But the richer harmonic and timbral possibilities compensate for the difficulties encountered. Six-way brass chords stretching from the pedal notes of the trombone (or tuba) to the upper partials of the trumpet produce richer, more resonant sounds and new chordal configurations extending into harmonics beyond the usual root, third, fifth, and seventh.

The Composer—Duke Ellington

The pioneer who scouted these new regions of musical space more than any other jazzman of the time was Edward Kennedy "Duke" Ellington (1899–1974). When he recorded *Rainy Nights* in 1926, he was the leader of a "classic Dixieland combo" of trumpet, trombone, clarinet, piano, drums, and banjo. The following year, his six-piece outfit had expanded to ten, and in *The Creeper*, he employed the typical Fletcher Henderson instrumentation of two trumpets, one trombone, three reeds, piano, bass, drums, and banjo. Tracing his career for the next few years, one can see that he was consistent in his use of string bass after 1927 but it is not until 1933 that he rid himself of the banjo and replaced it with a guitar.

1926 *Rainy Nights* (Blu-Disc 1002, reissued Riverside RLP 12-115)
 1 trumpet, 1 trombone, 1 reed, piano, drums, banjo
1927 *The Creeper* (Vocalion 1077, reissued Folkways FP 67) [Actually December 29, 1926]
 2 trumpets, 1 trombone, 3 reeds, piano, bass, drums, banjo
1928 *The Mooche* (Okeh 8623, reissued Folkways FP 59)
 2 trumpets, 1 trombone, 3 reeds, piano, bass, drums, banjo (guitar)
1929 *Japanese Dream* (Victor 38045)
 3 trumpets, 1 trombone, 3 reeds, piano, bass, drums, banjo
1930 *Maori* (Brunswick 6812 and Brunswick 4776)
 3 trumpets, 2 trombones, 3 reeds, piano, bass, drums, banjo
1931 *Mood Indigo* (Victor 22587)
 3 trumpets, 2 trombones, 3 reeds, piano, bass, drums, banjo
1932 *It Don't Mean a Thing* (Brunswick 6265, reissued Folkways FP 59)
 3 trumpets, 2 trombones, 3 reeds, piano, bass, drums, banjo
1933 *Sophisticated Lady* (Brunswick 6600, reissued Prestige 7645)
 3 trumpets, 3 trombones, 4 reeds, piano, bass, drums, guitar

Edward Kennedy "Duke" Ellington (1899–1974).

Duke Ellington and the Cotton Club Orchestra, 1929.

In his 1928 recording of *The Mooche*, Lonnie Johnson's guitar was added, but this is an unusual effect meant to complement the vocal line of this blues singer. Still, the core of his band consisted of the standard instrumentation of three brass, three reed, and four rhythm instruments. Then, in these early depression years, he began to develop as a composer. One of his most notable accomplishments was the introduction of his personal brand of chromatic harmonic thinking into jazz, undoubtedly the consequence of his piano explorations. Classic jazz had limited itself harmonically to triads and seventh chords, but the Duke developed an expanded chromatic harmonic vocabulary, demonstrated in many of his compositions. The most striking early example of this is *Sophisticated Lady*, a work he recorded in 1933 with an orchestra of fourteen men: three trumpets, three trombones, four reeds, piano, bass, drums, and guitar. This work, along with Redman's *Chant of the Weed*, which the Ellington band also played, stand as landmarks to guide many jazzmen in their subsequent musical thinking.

Duke Ellington composed and arranged scores that were tailored to the special abilities of the musicians in his band, men whose work was intimately familiar to him. His *East St. Louis Toodle-Oo*, recorded in 1927 (*SCCJ*, VI/4), is an early example of an orchestration designed to spotlight the special solo characteristics of specific sidemen.

East St. Louis Toodle-Oo

Introduction	**A**				**B**	
legato, slurred	trumpet (Miley)				baritone sax (Carney)	
intonation, low	mute, growls					
saxes and						
bowed bass						
cymbal on 7						

	8	8	8	8	8	10 (8 + 2)
	a	a	b	a	c	c'
8			32			18

B'		**A'**		**B''**		**A''**
trombone (Nanton)		clarinet (Jackson)		brass section		trumpet
mute, growls		inept				(Miley)
8	10 (8 + 2)	8	8	8	10 (8 + 2)	8
18		16		18		8

In this piece, Ellington collaborated with trumpeter Bubber Miley, and, as is plainly evident, Miley's trumpet growls are not sounds that can be precisely notated and handed on to another trumpeter for accurate reproduction. A chord chart (music in figures which simply indicate harmonies upon which to improvise a solo) would not produce the same effect at all. For Ellington to achieve the compositional sound he envisaged for this piece, it was necessary for him to work with the performing soloists in rehearsal. We know this is a method he subsequently followed throughout his career. Once the recording existed, of course, it was possible for players in the band to imitate and reinterpret the established ideas. Here it is particularly instructive to listen to the two versions of the same piece recorded ten years apart, 1927 (*SCCJ*, VI/4) and 1937 (*SCCJ*, VI/5), and note both the similarities and the differences. To a certain extent, these compositions were created in real time rather than on paper, as is the norm for most classical Western composition, for his creativity would have been hampered by a standard musical notation, to express the variety of compositional ideas in this work. However, it is obvious that these beginning efforts lack the polish and refinement we have come to take for granted in the later pieces by this great master. The baritone-saxophone solo by Harry Carney in the second chorus is strangely out of place in the context of the other orchestrated sounds. The clarinet solo by Rudy Jackson is inept by modern standards, for it hesitates, repeats dull ideas, and is interspersed with occasional wrong notes. Still, as a jazz composition for big band created in 1927, it too stands out as a milestone. The irregularity of the form, the brilliant variety of orchestral timbre, the blend of arrangement and solo, and the total effect of composed music and swinging jazz are the distinctive features which mark the music of Duke Ellington even in its earliest stages.

Throughout the next decade, the pioneer inexorably became the master. *Creole Rhapsody (SCCJ,* VI/6) stands out as Ellington's first piece of absolute music, music without words composed solely for listening, and is an indication

The Duke and 4 Trumpets, Fall, 1959. (Left to right) Willis "Ray" Nance, William Alonzo "Cat" Anderson, John "Willie" Cook, and Eddie "Moon" Mullens.

of the man's growing self-awareness as a composer. In this piece, one notes the striking similarity to Gershwin's *Rhapsody in Blue*[12] and *Concerto in F,*[13] but one is also aware of significant differences: the orchestration, improvisation by the piano soloist, and improvisation by the sidemen.

The expanded instrumentation of these leading dance bands did not come about by a need for a public show, although commercial factors should not be overlooked, but to satisfy the demanding new ideas in timbre and harmony. A new sonority was developing in the ears of the jazz musicians, and just as the brass sounds were stretching from low bass to high soprano, the reed sounds

[12] Recorded by the composer with Paul Whiteman in 1924, Victor 55225.
[13] Recorded by Paul Whiteman in 1928, Columbia 50139-D, 50140-D, and 7172-M.

were reaching from the depths of the baritone saxophone to the upper registers of the soprano saxophone and clarinet. Although these instruments were not foreign to Dixieland combos, their use in homogeneous ensembles, or sections, to use the musicians' parlance, was new.

The impact of Duke Ellington on the world of jazz is not easily measured, for in his long and prolific career he set standards in so many areas: as a composer, harmonic innovator, ensemble leader, recording artist, arranger, patron of aspiring jazz musicians, and spokesman for black Americans and their culture. The very length of his career has resulted in a corpus of Ellington compositions, arrangements, and performances that is unique and, fortunately, almost completely documented. A brief list of the most significant compositions, a very small percentage of his total output, must include:

1926	*East St. Louis Toodle-Oo*	1941	*I Got It Bad* and *Jump for Joy*
1927	*Black and Tan Fantasy* and *Creole Love Song*	1943	*Black, Brown, and Beige*
		1944	*I'm Beginning to See the Light*
1928	*The Mooche* and *Misty Mornin'*	1947	*The Liberian Suite*
1930	*Mood Indigo*	1950	*Harlem*
1931	*Creole Rhapsody*	1953	*Satin Doll*
1932	*It Don't Mean a Thing* and *Sophisticated Lady*	1955	*Night Creature*
		1957	*A Drum Is a Woman*
1934	*Solitude*	1959	*Anatomy of a Murder* (film score)
1935	*In a Sentimental Mood*	1963	*What Color Is Virtue?* (from *My People*)
1936	*Caravan*		
1937	*Diminuendo and Crescendo in Blue*	1965	"First Sacred Concert" (Grace Cathedral, San Francisco)
1938	*I Let a Song Go Out of My Heart* and *Prelude to a Kiss*	1966	*La Plus Belle Africaine*
		1968	"Second Sacred Concert" (St. John the Divine, New York)
1940	*Ko-ko, Cottontail, Harlem Air Shaft*, and *In a Mellotone*		

The list of musicians who found refuge under his sympathetic, but critical and disciplined, gaze includes men who, as his sidemen or on their own, helped shape the history of jazz in positive and creative ways. To mention but a few: the arrangers Don Redman and Billy Strayhorn; trumpeters Bubber Miley, Arthur Whetsol, Cootie Williams, Wardell Jones, Ray Nance, Cat Anderson, and Clark Terry; trombonists Joe Nanton and Juan Tizol; saxophonists Johnny Hodges, Ben Webster, Harry Carney, Barney Bigard, and Paul Gonsalves; drummers Sonny Greer and Louis Bellson; and bassmen Jimmy Blanton and Oscar Pettiford. He and the musicians of his orchestra maintained a symbiotic relationship of mutual interdependence that was exceedingly rare, even in a jazz world, where virtually all the music results from creative artists working collectively.

Early Swing Bands

A remarkable white big band of the late twenties was led by a Frenchman who was reared in Greece and schooled in Russia, named Jean Goldkette. When Goldkette's Victor Recording Orchestra hit the Roseland Ballroom in 1927, the Fletcher Henderson band, which sat on the opposite bandstand, was struck by the imaginative arrangements, the driving rhythm, and the C-melody saxophone of Frankie Trumbauer. In the words of one of Henderson's sidemen, Rex Stewart:

> This proved to be a most humiliating experience for us, since, after all, we were supposed to be the world's greatest dance orchestra. And up pops this Johnny-come-lately white band from out in the sticks, cutting us. . . . The facts were that we simply could not compete with Jean Goldkette's Victor Recording Orchestra.[14]

An offshoot of the Jean Goldkette orchestra was a group known as the Orange Blossoms, led by Henry Biagini. From within this group, a saxman, Glen Gray (Knoblaugh), took over for the opening of a Canadian nightclub completed for the visit of the Prince of Wales to Canada in 1929. The scheduled opening never took place, but the band adopted the name of the nightclub and became the Casa Loma Orchestra; they obtained a booking at the Roseland Ballroom, and proceeded to record six sides for Okeh. Their performance was somewhat stiff, but Gene Gifford's arrangements were flashy, and the band caught the attention of the jazz world and the public. Their somewhat unique contribution to jazz took place in 1931, for the band acquired a trumpet screamer,[15] Sonny Dunham, and his sound soon became a standard part of the American big-band vocabulary. They also acquired a superb jazz clarinet player, Clarence Hutchenrider, and continued to be influential until about 1935. Their recording of *Chinatown*[16] in 1934 displays the rhythmic drive and high brass luster that placed them at the forefront of the hard-swinging jazz big bands.

About this same time, a black big band, which had been organized in Memphis in 1927 and became prominent in Buffalo in the early 1930s, made its first records for Decca. Jimmy Lunceford fronted an ensemble of exactly the same dimensions as Glen Gray's band: six brass, four reed, and four rhythm in-

---

[14] Rex Stewart, *Jazz Masters of the Thirties*, p. 11.

[15] A trumpeter who specializes in high notes, a man with "iron chops." The big-band sound of the swing era called for higher and louder performances from the lead trumpet. Some screamers of distinction—Cat Anderson, Conrad Gozzo, Maynard Ferguson—were also known for their endurance and accuracy.

[16] Decca 199, reissued MCA Records MCA2-4061.

The Jimmy Lunceford big band, 1938

struments. His recording of *Swanee River*[17] in 1935 displays the same precision and showy high brass that was a hallmark of the Casa Loma Orchestra. Lunceford, too, had a talented and able arranger in Sy Oliver, and the disciplined playing characteristic of both Gray's and Lunceford's bands became as much a part of the listeners' expectations as the orchestrations themselves. Power, flash, and precision: the big bands had it, and the public loved it. The *Lunceford Special* (*SCCJ*, V/3)[18] recorded at the end of the decade, shows the band at its best, a prototype of the classic swing band. The driving four-beat rhythm, the up-tempo solos, the power of a final riffing chorus with a stratospheric trumpet piercing the orchestration and leading the band to an attack on the final chord—these are the hallmarks of the swing-era big-band sound.

[17] Decca 668, reissued MC Records MCA2-4061.
[18] Columbia CS 9515, reissued in *SCCJ*.

Kansas City Swing

Gray, Lunceford, Redman, and Henderson tended to move along the same path: big-band jazz versions of popular songs and music in popular-song form. Don Redman, on occasion, straddled the fence, for his interest in original compositions like *Chant of the Weed* brought him closer to the road followed by Duke Ellington and his orchestra, who played not only big-band arrangements of popular tunes but also the original compositions and production numbers for the "African Jungle" of the Cotton Club. Another direction in big-band jazz was being scouted in the Southwest by Benny Moten's Kansas City group. They were exploring the possibilities of creating arrangements for a large ensemble through improvising sections—trumpet, trombone, and saxophone—which used the blues as a base and the riff concept as the functional orchestration device. The distinctive Kansas City sound resulted not only from this type of musical arrangement but also from the creative input of its leaders and arrangers, as well as the improvising idiosyncracies of the individual musicians. This does not imply that sidemen could not be replaced, for they could be and were. But Kansas City trained its own instrumentalists and nourished its own talent. For this reason, particular sidemen had a greater effect on the unique character of these bands than was usually the case with bands using arrangements à la Fletcher Henderson or Don Redman. For one thing, the blues tradition allowed extended solo choruses; the New York swing arrangements normally confined improvisation within narrow compositional boundaries. It should not be forgotten, however, that the big bands, like all other jazz ensembles, needed great musicians to make them come alive and swing with excitement. Regardless of the kind of jazz they made, lesser musicians always had the opposite effect. Still, the musical conception of these three jazz trends—New York, Ellington, and Kansas City—were clearly separate and resulted in music with distinctive sounds easily differentiated by educated and sensitive listeners.

The 1932 recording by Benny Moten's band of *Moten Swing* (SCCJ, III/4) is a good example of a piece that bridges the gap between the Fletcher Henderson and the Kansas City swing styles, for it is based on popular song form, **AABA,** rather than the blues, and it embraces some other stylistic features of the New York bands as well. The chordal framework underlying the piece belongs to a composition by Walter Donaldson, *You're Driving Me Crazy (What Did I Do?)*, which was introduced by Guy Lombardo and His Royal Canadians in 1930.[19] In that same year, it was used in the Broadway musical *Smiles*, sung by

[19] Columbia 2335-D.

Moten Swing
Popular-Song Form, **AABA**, Five Times with Four-Measure Tag

Intro 8 piano (vamp)	A 8 piano	B 8 chordal brass unison sax antiphony	A 8 piano
A sax chorus (written)	A sax chorus (original tune present)	B boogie piano guitar solo	A sax chorus
A brass riff alto-sax solo	A ditto	B piano comp alto-sax solo	A brass riff alto-sax solo
A sax chords tpt solo	A ditto	B piano comp tenor-sax solo	A sax chords tpt solo
A band riff unison rhythm chords	A ditto	B ditto	A ditto
tag 4			

Adele Astaire,[20] Eddie Foy, Jr., and chorus. The pianist on this recording, William "Count" Basie, plays different chords for the first eight measures, an eight-measure vamp, but from that point on, the chordal structure of the piece is identical to that of the popular song. In the **A** section, before the bridge of the second chorus, one can hear the tune of *You're Driving Me Crazy* played by the lead saxophone, but other statements of this melody do not appear in this new version.

The amount of improvisation in this work is totally unlike that found in a typical arrangement by Don Redman, for not only are the complete third and fourth choruses set aside for solo with instrumental backing, but the introduction and **A** sections of the first chorus are piano solo, and the bridge of the second chorus is a piano and guitar duet of solos. The last complete chorus may well have been improvised too, for here we find the typical Kansas City big-band riff: the entire band, minus the rhythm instruments, plays rhythmically in unison a highly syncopated pattern that moves up and down together in what may be called a thickened melodic line.

[20] Sister of dancer Fred Astaire, who also appeared in the musical.

Rhythm of Final-Chorus Band Riff

An interesting feature of this recording is the display of three different piano styles by Count Basie: New York stride piano throughout the first chorus, "boom-chuck" Dixieland-style piano elsewhere, and boogie-woogie–style piano during the bridge of the second chorus. The one hint of the piano style he later developed, which was to become the Count's most distinguishing musical characteristic—a spare, suggestive, simple, and enticing technique—appears at the very end, two measures before the tag. On the first beat, in the middle of a pregnant pause, a single ringing piano chord is struck in the upper register.

The vitality and forward drive of the riff's rhythm for the closing chorus is the critical feature that sets Kansas City style apart from the others. Here we see it translated from blues to popular-song form, and even here it serves to wind up the piece for a final climactic moment. In Kansas City style, we often find a general formal pattern which piles riff upon riff from beginning to end, thus creating a musical pyramid effect of additive forward drive. The surge carries both the soloists and the listeners to a state of near frenzy when properly executed.

The music of these big bands gradually reshaped jazz in America. The swing era had begun, and it would continue to thrive well past the years of World War II. A British observer, Brian Rust, one of the most astute and knowledgeable historians of jazz, has this to say:

> One of the first records by the Basie band [Basie assumed leadership of the Moten band after Moten's death in 1935] was typical not only of the group but of the style of some of the purely instrumental numbers that were popular at that time. It was *Doggin' Around*, [SCCJ, V/7] and it demonstrated the "riff," a phrase of just a few notes repeated in different tones by different sections of the band, sometimes as a background to a soloist or vocalist (which could be very effective), all too frequently as foreground material, which made a very monotonous effect unless used very judiciously. The amateur instrumentalists that haunted the Rhythm Clubs of those days . . . took this simple strain to their hearts and their instruments, and the programme at a Rhythm Club in the days before and in the early part of the war

could hardly be complete without its performance of several dozen choruses of *Doggin' Around* by the resident band. . . . The resulting cacophony had to be heard to be believed. It was perhaps the forerunner of the present-day conception of artistic licence expressed in the inelegant phrase "doing your own thing."[21]

[21] Brian Rust, *The Dance Bands*, p. 132.

THE SWING ERA

THE MYTHICAL "KINGDOM OF SWING" was ruled by a monarch, Benny Good-man; invested with nobility, Count Basie and Duke Ellington; and peopled with subjects who blew, danced, and listened. BG, the "King of Swing," did not invent the style—Redman, Ellington, Moten, Henderson, and their musicians did that—but he convinced the audience, set the standards for performance, became the spokesman for the new music, and in every way was the most important and successful popular, dance, and jazz musician in America from the mid-depression years to the end of World War II.

The coup had taken place in the late '20s, and Goodman only later acceded to the throne. It was no mean achievement. As one jazz scholar perceived the situation:

> Why, after so many years of being relegated to the fringes of social acceptance, jazz should have achieved the wide popularity it did is not easy to say. New York, Kansas City, Chicago, and other jazz centers, like the rest of the country, were in the midst of a great depression. Banking and finance had sunk to a new low level, industry was being bolstered by government intercession, and breadlines were a common sight in the big cities. The year before Goodman made his NBC debut, Prohibition was repealed. . . . Furthermore, musicians came cheap. . . . Working almost as if by plan, the national broadcasters piped hotel music to hundreds of thousands of people who would then flock to dance halls and theaters to hear these same bands on tour. . . . The end result was an endless multiplication of big bands. [1]

[1] Leroy Ostransky, *The Anatomy of Jazz*, p. 224 f.

The King of Swing—Benny Goodman

The most polished, and perhaps the best, of all the big bands of the swing era, a group blessed with a leader who could improvise with unfailing grace, dexterity, and imagination, was the musical organization of Benjamin David Goodman.

The decade from 1935 to 1945 has become known as the swing era, and no single musician did more to crystallize the style, establish the technical standards, and popularize the music than Benny Goodman. Practically all by himself, he revolutionized the dance-band business. As a result, he was loved, admired, and respected by millions, including the jazz musicians themselves. When BG became "King of Swing," he made this music the most vital and exciting kind of social-dance music ever created in America.

Goodman was born in Chicago in 1909 and received his early training in music there. He has earned himself the reputation of being a perpetual student of music and instrumental virtuosity. As a boy, he studied with classical clarinetist Franz Schoepp, a gentleman who also tutored Jimmy Noone and Buster Bailey; and as late as 1949, BG was studying with Reginald Kell, a leading British classical clarinet soloist. In addition to listening to the early Chicago masters—Oliver, Armstrong, Keppard, Johnny and Baby Dodds, Hardin, Noone, Mares, Rapollo, and Brunies—his early experiences in jazz included playing with the Austin High Gang of Jimmy McPartland, Frank Teschmacher, Bud Freeman, and Dave Tough, as well as with Muggsy Spanier. In August of 1923, at the age of fifteen, he played with Bix Beiderbecke on a riverboat gig. He began to job regularly that year and made his first recording with Ben Pollack and his Californians in September of 1926. He was then eighteen years old.

Benny Goodman's first commercial recording as leader of a group was made for Vocalion Records in 1927,[2] and in 1928 Benny Goodman's Boys recorded with Jimmy McPartland and Glenn Miller.[3] By 1935, Goodman was leading his own big band, owned a few dozen Fletcher Henderson arrangements, had picked up the backing of jazz impresario John Hammond, was playing a segment of the National Biscuit Company's Saturday night three-hour dance program on NBC, "Let's Dance," and had an exciting experience with his band on tour at the gigantic Palomar Ballroom in Los Angeles in August of that same year. On that occasion, his best swing arrangements stopped the crowd's dancing and pulled the people around the bandstand like ants at the honeyjar. As Goodman put it:

[2] Vocalion 15705, *That's A Plenty* and *Clarinetitis.*
[3] Vocalion 15656, *A Jazz Holiday* and *Wolverine Blues.*

Benny Goodman and his band: (reading in a circle from left to right) Ted Vesley, trombone; Ziggy Elman, trumpet; Nick Fatool, drums; trombone section: Vesley, Red Ballard, Vernon Brown; Toots Mondello, alto sax; Helen Forrest, vocal; Benny Goodman, clarinet. Sextet: Johnny Guarnieri, piano; Artie Bernstein, bass; Nick Fatool, drums; Charlie Christian, guitar; Lionel Hampton, vibraharp, Benny Goodman, clarinet. The entire band, c. 1939.

After traveling three thousand miles, we finally found people who were up on what we were trying to do, prepared to take our music the way we wanted to play it. The first big roar from the crowd was one of the sweetest sounds I've ever heard in my life—and from that time on, the night kept getting bigger and bigger, as we played about every good number in our book.[4]

Musical Characteristics

What differentiated swing from the music that preceded it? First, the size of the bands; second, the arrangements; third, the characteristics of the solos; and, fourth, the change in the habits of the rhythm section. The first two factors have already been discussed in some detail in Chapter 8; now let us look into the last two; swing solos and swing rhythm-section work.

The influx of schooled musicians into the swing bands quickly raised the level of technical competence of the swing soloists to a higher norm than had been previously operative in jazz. At the same time, however, the melodic patterns tended to become fixed on standard arpeggios and scales that obviously were derived from the hours spent practicing classical etudes. Tone quality and pitch became more refined, especially among the reedmen, and the bawdy and boisterous sounds of classic jazz slowly began to disappear. Trumpet solos differed little from those of Dixieland trumpeters, in the sense that it was common practice to stick close to a melody and rag it by injecting a little rhythmic variety.

But reed solos were beginning to acquire a new sound. Swing was creating a breed of virtuosos who could improvise brilliantly at ever-faster tempos. As they did, they tended to arpeggiate the simple chord patterns of the swing repertoire and group notes into more or less evenly balanced units. When the brassmen took their solos, it was not uncommon to hear a simple melodic riff group notes into patterns that reinforced the normal accents of a 4/4 measure rather than obscure the beat with complex syncopations and unusual rhythmic groupings. The clarinet playing of Benny Goodman is usually considered the epitome of swing clarinet-solo work, so much so that many, if not most, of the other swing reedmen who wished to play clarinet had to copy his sound, his patterns, his speed, and his flawless execution in order just to survive in this competitive world of professional music. We can see in Goodman's solos just how these concepts were transformed into real music.

[4] *Benny Goodman: The Golden Age of Swing,* liner notes to Victor LPT 6703.

In 1939, Benny Goodman recorded *Soft Winds*[5] with his sextet consisting of Lionel Hampton on vibes, Fletcher Henderson at the piano, Art Bernstein on bass, Nick Fatool on drums, and a new electric guitarist who quickly became a headliner, Charlie Christian. In 1945, a new sextet recorded *Slipped Disc*[6] with Red Norvo on vibes, Teddy Wilson on piano, Mike Bryan on guitar, Slam Stewart on bass, and Morey Feld on drums. Notice in the excerpt below that passages are either scalar or arpeggiated, and serve to outline the underlying chord structure.

Excerpts from the Goodman Solo on *Soft Winds*

Excerpts from the Goodman Solo on *Slipped Disc*

In the next excerpt, you can observe passages that reemphasize the normal accents of 4/4 meter, stress on beats one and three.

Soft Winds

Swing-style solos characteristically adhere closely to the well-known melodies of popular songs, and one sees this especially in Goodman's solo work on ballads. Good examples include his closing theme song, *Goodbye*, or his trio recording to *Body and Soul* (*SCCJ*, IV/3). This clarinet-solo style is very closely allied to the structural notes of the original melody. It is not, in fact, improvisatory in nature, but ornamental. The compulsion to stylize the tune or provide

[5] Columbia 35320.
[6] Columbia 36817.

MUSICAL CHARACTERISTICS

the listener with a melody he can "hang his hat on" is one of the important musical elements of the swing style. Teddy Wilson's piano solo on the second chorus deviates somewhat from the melody, as he plays a swing solo with rapid arpeggios and regular groupings.

The swing drummers remodeled the beat of Dixieland. They still played 4/4 on the bass drum, and it was a very insistent and pervasive pulse, but they began to "ride" the sock cymbal, or high hat, with a 2/4 pattern that set up a minor conflict of rhythmic interest.

With both feet going, four beats on the right and two beats on the left, the swing drummer used his hands for decorations and accents: one to "ride" the sock cymbal, as shown above, and the other to lead off on whatever other equipment he had at his disposal. Chick Webb, one of the first drummers to codify the swing conventions, used a set comprised of bass drum, snare drum, high hat, hanging cymbal, and four temple blocks, in about 1935.[7] The com-

---

[7] George T. Simon, *Simon Says: The Sights and Sounds of the Swing Era, 1935–1955*, p. 52.

William "Chick" Webb (1902–39).

plete drum set that became more or less standard from 1937 on consisted of the bass drum, snare drum, tom-tom, floor tom, high hat, and two to four suspended cymbals. In this regard, drummers Gene Krupa and Dave Tough played dominant roles in the stabilization of the jazz drummer's set of traps.

The Dixieland brass bass, in converting to the plucked double bass of the swing ensembles, still tended to play two-beat in the ragtime-Dixieland tradition during the early '30s. Sometimes the bassmen switched back and forth in their playing patterns, and occasionally they played consistent walking four-beat bass. However, the different sound envelope gave the new timbre its most distinctive feature. The string bass, with its noise factor resulting from the plucking attack and its rapid decay of volume, characteristics which differ considerably from the even, sustained pitch of the blown bass tuba, gave a new lightness and liveliness of sound to the rhythm section.

The guitarmen of swing chorded in 4/4, and their relentless strumming actually had much less effect on the big-band drive than the music of the banjo had on the rhythm of the Dixieland combo. Until the development of the electric guitar, toward the middle of the swing era, the acoustic guitar could only be heard when most of the band was not playing. Its effect in the swing combos, of course, was significantly greater, and the sustaining ability of its longer and less taut strings, in contrast to the rapid decay of the banjo sound, helped establish a new characteristic sound for swing ensembles.

The swing pianists, when they were not playing solo, were gradually giving up the notion that they were obliged to simulate the sound of an entire orchestra. We observed the transition taking place as early as 1928 and 1929, when Louis Armstrong and Earl Hines teamed up for *West End Blues (SCCJ*, II/9) and the extraordinary *Weather Bird (SCCJ*, III/1). We noted that the left hand in Dixieland had played both the bass and percussion parts, and the right hand played the harmonies as well as snatches of melody. In swing, the left hand still tended to jump back and forth, as in the old stride tradition, but the right hand played fewer chords and more single-line melodies.

Art Tatum

The absolute master of swing keyboard virtuosity was a blind pianist named Art Tatum, whose total control of his instrument allowed him to execute any musical idea he conceived flawlessly. His technique was so astounding that classical giants like Horowitz and Rubenstein are said to have made a point of visiting clubs where they might hear him play. His style was eclectic,

The incredible Art Tatum in January, 1944, together with Tiny Grimes, guitar, and Slam Stewart, bass.

and his rhythm was not always rock-steady, but his performances never failed to dazzle with pyrotechnic displays. *Willow Weep for Me (SCCJ,* V/1) opens with Gershwinesque passages in free rhythm, measures filled with chromatic chords which luxuriously expand the original harmonies. Then a typical swing-stride bridge is inserted, which, aesthetically, may be out of keeping with the beginning, but is not really unusual for a virtuoso displaying his wares. Finally, with flawless grace and an ease that is simplicity itself, he slips in the incredibly fast arpeggios and scalar passages which leave the listener breathless.

Although Tatum's recording of *Too Marvelous for Words (SCCJ,* V/2) lacks studio-quality sound (the recording was made at a private party), it exhibits the characteristic finesse, speed, dexterity, and sound that made him the model swing pianist. It should be noted that both *Willow* and *Words* were made after swing began to decline as the predominant jazz style, 1949 and 1956 respectively, and this is but another example of the jazz phenomenon in which the latest styles coexist, comfortably or otherwise, with those already developed in an earlier period.

Art Tatum, born in Toledo in 1910, began his career in the 1920s and moved into club engagements and recordings in New York in 1932. His reputation grew so rapidly that he was an international figure by the mid-1930s, and set London on its ear in 1938. Leonard Feather, a jazz pianist and astute critic of the art, describes Tatum's playing accurately in these words:

> Tatum's original appearance on the jazz scene in the early '30s upset all previous standards for pianists. His fantastic technique and original harmonic variations placed him far ahead of all earlier artists, eliciting the praise of Leopold Godowsky and making him the favorite jazz pianist of virtually all his contemporaries. His unequaled technique has never been abused to the point of removing him from his original jazz roots.[8]

Gene Krupa

Around 1935, a drummer with an enormous sense of showmanship, an abundant measure of jazz "time," and a phenomenally quick technique burst on the jazz scene as part of the Benny Goodman band. Gene Krupa did more than almost anyone else to make the drums a popular solo instrument and bring the drummers of the swing era into the limelight. His recording of *Sing, Sing, Sing,*[9] performed with the Goodman band that year, stands as the prime example of the extended drum solo in swing. *Drum Boogie,*[10] the theme song for Krupa's own big band, formed after he left Benny Goodman in 1938, was another significant contribution to the history of jazz drumming. The most obvious characteristics of Krupa's drumming style, in addition to his facial contortions and other theatrics, were his incessant, heavy bass drum on every beat; his driving, 2/4, high hat rhythm; and his accented, syncopated tom-toms.

Although up-tempo (or fast), virtuosic tunes were an important part of the swing style, it should be remembered that ballads accounted for a large part of the swing repertoire. In this domain, the swing drummers developed another important four-beat rhythmic sound: the smart sizzle of wire brushes patting and "stirring soup" on the snare drum. The recording of the Gene Krupa band of 1941 featuring trumpeter Roy Eldridge as soloist on *Rockin' Chair* (SCCJ, V/4) illustrates how the swing drummer switches from the stick technique to

---

[8] Leonard Feather, "Arthur 'Art' Tatum," *The Encyclopedia of Jazz* (New York: Horizon Press, 1955), p. 294.

[9] Verve V-8594.

[10] Ibid.

that of the brushes for the performance of sentimental ballads. The trumpet solo of Roy Eldridge is notable for several reasons. First, the entire piece is trumpet solo; the orchestration consists merely of a few background sounds. Second, it is obvious that the swing trumpet-solo style is not far different from that of the Dixieland solo-trumpet style. As Martin Williams points out:

> Eldridge once said that he thought he was a good trumpet soloist before he had really heard Louis Armstrong, but that when he did, he realized he hadn't been "telling a story."[11]

Satchmo was still the model and most influential trumpet player of this era as well as the last. His sense of melodic continuity, full-bodied sound, and powerful climactic endings carried into the solo styles of all the great swing-era trumpeters.

The successes of 1934 and 1935 marked the beginning of Benny Goodman's flourishing musical career. He and his big band, with featured stars like Gene Krupa and vocalist Helen Ward, continued to be a peak musical attraction in America until mid-1944, when he disbanded the larger organization. At the same time that he fronted a big band, BG led many small combos. The trio of

[11]*SCCJ* liner notes, p. 27.

Gene Krupa in a typically exuberant mood at his drums.

1935 included Krupa and pianist Teddy Wilson. By taking Wilson with him on the road as part of the trio and as an adjunct to the band, Goodman began to break the racial taboos that separated white from black even among jazz musicians. Earlier, when the Jean Goldkette and the Fletcher Henderson orchestras played the same engagement at the Roseland Ballroom in New York, they were on separate stages and played consecutively. Although white and black musicians played together in private and informal jam sessions, integrated bands did not exist before this time. In 1936, Goodman added black vibraphonist Lionel Hampton to his trio, and the new BG quartet was balanced half white and half black. Occasionally, a black musician would be featured with a white band or vice versa. For example, Louis Armstrong recorded with Jimmy Dorsey in 1936,[12] and Roy Eldridge played with the Gene Krupa orchestra in the early '40s;[13] but Armstrong did not live and travel with the Dorsey band or draw a regular salary on the payroll, and Eldridge, even though a featured star of the Krupa band, suffered much indignation from the racial intolerance still prevalent in America at that time. The Goodman quartet was not a white group featuring a black star or two; it was an integrated organization of musical equals.

Beginning in 1938, Benny Goodman pursued a second, less publicized, career, that of a classical clarinetist. He recorded with the Budapest String Quartet, and, in 1939, commissioned Béla Bartók to write *Contrasts*, which he recorded in 1940 for Columbia with violinist Joseph Szigeti.[14] He later also commissioned clarinet concertos from Aaron Copland and Paul Hindemith. The rapport of jazz and classical music was never more comfortably secure than in the talented hands of this remarkable musician.

Charlie Christian

Goodman's contribution to the history of jazz must also include a role, although perhaps but a minor one at that, in the stylistic transition from swing to bebop. In 1939, he brought the talents of black guitarist Charlie Christian to jazz. Although he died tragically and prematurely in 1942, the few years he spent with Goodman brought him fame as the first modern jazzman to feature single string solos on the electric guitar, something that later became the stock-in-trade of the bebop guitarists. Charlie Christian's solo on *I Found a New Baby* (SCCJ, VI/2) reveals his mastery of melodic invention and harmonic un-

[12] Decca 949.
[13] Columbia C2L-29.
[14] Columbia ML 2213.

derstanding, rhythmic suppleness, and sensitivity to the unusual characteristics of the new instrument. His solo has a smooth legato character resulting from the sustaining possibilities of the electronic instrument in combination with a playing technique modeled upon the solo styles of the saxophone players. During the opening clarinet chorus, one can hear the steady four-beat strumming, which matches the chordal accompaniment of the piano and the steady push of the bass drum. Christian's solo, which follows, is totally different in concept, for he has transformed the instrument from a chordal rhythmic device to a melodic voice capable of sustaining a long and intricate line. Through the effects of the electronic amplifier, Christian mellows the tone of his instrument by cutting out the upper-partial twang of steel-string guitar. His influence on subsequent guitar-playing jazzmen is of major proportions, and this is all the more astounding considering the brief period of professional activity fate allowed him.

Born in Dallas in 1919, Charlie Christian grew up in the Southwest and played bass and guitar in various groups around Oklahoma. John Hammond discovered him in St. Louis and recommended him to Benny Goodman, whom Christian joined in 1939. He later played at Minton's Playhouse in Harlem during the first experimental bebop sessions of the early 1940s. His ear for altered chords, running melodic lines, and electric-guitar timbre made him the ideal exponent of the new music which was to follow and ultimately come in conflict with swing, bebop. The legend of Charlie Christian, which sprang up like a phoenix after his death in 1942, was based on his role as a spiritual father of bebop, but his legacy is the stack of superb swing solos he recorded with Benny Goodman and Lionel Hampton.

The Benny Goodman sextet that cut *I Found a New Baby* (SCCJ, VI/2) in 1941 had no weak links, for all six musicians were superb instrumentalists. However, it was not BG's usual group. Benny's standbys—Krupa, Hampton, and Wilson—were not with him for this date, and instead Count Basie and his drummer, Jo Jones, carried the rhythm. Basie influenced Goodman's music in more ways than simply as the pianist in his rhythm section. Not only did Basie's band set an example for all other swing ensembles, but he provided arrangements for Benny's big band. The merger of Kansas City style with Goodman's mainstream swing can be seen in the Count Basie–Benny Goodman–Buck Clayton composition recorded by the Benny Goodman band in 1946, *Rattle and Roll*.[15] The piece is a twelve-bar blues with eight-measure introduction and ending. The first chorus, which, as might be expected, employs clarinet lead, is followed by a sequence of twelve-measure solos and capped by a series of ensemble-drive choruses which build up energy for the climax at the

[15] Columbia 36988.

Rattle and Roll

end. Each of the last two clarinet-solo choruses is introduced by four measures of band-ensemble playing. In the example above, one can see the contrapuntal merger of two riffs in Basie's Kansas City style: octave trumpets driving upward and octave saxophones turning downward.

How the blues worked their way into bebop and became the most pervasive element in jazz can be seen in the composite recording of the Benny Goodman sextet with Charlie Christian, *Blues Sequence* (from *Breakfast Feud, SCCJ*, VI/3). Here, all the Christian solos display the new order and sense of freedom characteristic of bebop, within the context of a tightly structured and closely supervised swing group. The new accentuation was subtle where the old was striking; the new phrasing was extended and unbalanced, the old was regular; the new sound moved into uncharted waters, where the old exuberantly reaffirmed the faith in the long-proven precepts of swing which had so successfully driven American audiences to a pitch of near frenzy. In *Blues Sequence*, the conflict can be experienced as a cold front moving in before a storm.

Coleman Hawkins

Another pivotal figure in the transition from swing to bebop was tenor saxophonist Coleman "Bean" Hawkins, who, although born and educated in Kansas, first made his name as a New York jazz musician working with Fletcher Henderson in 1923. When he left that group in the mid-'30s, he worked in Europe with Benny Carter, Django Reinhardt, and others, returning to the United States in 1939 to record *Body and Soul* (*SCCJ*, IV/4) with his own newly formed nine-piece band. This recording, his most successful, established him as a national jazz name and served as a model of saxophone-solo playing for future generations of reedmen (see Transcriptions). The standard swing treatment of all popular songs, especially ballads, was to place the melody in prominence during the delivery of a solo, but ornament it slightly with tonal inflections, turning figures, modified rhythms, and other musical devices that stylized (or jazzed) the tune but did not obscure the melody. With great assurance, Hawkins digressed entirely from the well-known tune and leaned upon the harmonic structure to guide him in an unprecedented creative melodic effort. The result is a logical and beautiful melody in the instrumental jazz idiom, one that owes little allegiance to the popular song whence it sprung. André Hodeir sums up his analysis of Bean's solo thus: "On the other hand, in the second chorus of the famous improvisation . . . the only thing the theme and

Coleman "Bean" Hawkins, tenor sax.

the variation have in common is the harmonic foundation."[16] It was customary for solo improvisation in the swing style to paraphrase the melody. The new concept demonstrated here discarded the old melody and extemporized a new one, one more idiomatic to jazz, more intimately connected with the technical capacities of the instrument and with the artistic abilities of the performer.

Body and Soul, Second Chorus, Opening of Second Phrase

A little more than two years after the recording session of *Body and Soul,* America was at war. Suddenly, millions of men were in uniform and traveling around the world. Farmers continued their business as usual, for America needed a steady supply of food, but many family members either put on uniforms or left for the cities to work in war plants.

> World War II was one of the great turning points in the history of the United States. . . . [U]ntil the Second World War it [America] was regarded as an isolated, young, and relatively unimportant country by the major European powers that had shaped the destiny of the world, or at least western Europe. . . . Europeans tended to regard Americans as naive, crude, unsophisticated, and often vaguely comic people with little history and culture. This view was shared by many Americans, particularly musicians and other artists. . . . World War II changed the whole image of the United States. . . . At the end of the war, American troops were in almost every part of the world, having played a major role in the eventual defeat of the Germans and Japanese. . . .[17]

Americans on the move brought their music with them, and, at that time, Coleman Hawkins was a leading soloist and exponent of jazz. Bob Thiele, owner of Signature Records, who was in the military morale department of the Coast Guard, states: "I can testify that anyone who entered a jazz nightclub in 1944 would probably hear 'The Man I Love' performed at this interesting tempo [as played by Coleman Hawkins]. . . . It was just about the hippest thing one could do. . . ."[18] (*SCCJ,* IV/5). The double-time outburst over the slow chordal pattern was no Hawkins innovation, for it was part of the standard

[16] André Hodeir, *Jazz: Its Evolution and Essence,* p. 144.

[17] Charles Hamm, "Changing Patterns in Society and Music: The U.S. Since World War II," in Charles Hamm, Bruno Nettl, and Ronald Byrnside, *Contemporary Music and Music Cultures,* p. 36 f.

[18] Quoted by Martin Williams, liner notes to *SCCJ,* p. 24.

repertoire of jazz-solo ideas developed twenty years earlier by Louis Armstrong. The excellence and excitement of this solo, however, captivated the ears of jazz-loving Americans and carried the name of Coleman Hawkins to the forefront of leading swing soloists. Although some of Hawkins's ideas were transitional, his style of playing was firmly rooted in the tradition popularized by the big bands and small combos of Goodman, Basie, Ellington, and Henderson. This unified style was both dominant and continuous from the early '30s through World War II.

The Basie Band

Harking back to Bennie Moten's *Moten Swing* of 1932 (*SCCJ*, III/8) and comparing it with Count Basie's *Doggin' Around* of 1938 (*SCCJ*, V/7), one can hear the many musical elements they have in common. The later band is more polished, able to maintain an up-tempo beat with great ensemble precision, but it is playing scores that are virtually identical to those played in 1932. The

The Count Basie orchestra with Jimmy Rushing, vocalist, c. 1945.

thickened-line saxophone chorus is answered by chording brass; the rhythm section presses a metronomic four-beat pattern; the arrangement forms a boundary within which soloists may operate.

The continuity of the Basie tradition was unbroken well beyond World War II, and one can hear in his 1947 recording of *House Rent Boogie*[19] the instrumental blues transformed into a big-band arrangement in swing style.

William "Count" Basie, the piano man from Red Bank, New Jersey, opened, with his band, at the Roseland Ballroom in New York in December of 1936 after John Hammond, Columbia Records executive and star talent scout, arranged the engagement. He had worked in a nine-piece band with Buster Smith as coleader and Walter Page on bass the year before at the Reno Club in Kansas City, but it took the "discovery" by Hammond and the date at the Roseland, opposite Woody Herman's first band, to start him on the road to recognition. Eventually, he formed a quality band that came to be called The Big Swing Machine. For his first band recording under his own name in January, 1937, Basie had already engaged the kind of sidemen who would bring his band to the forefront: in addition to Walter Page and himself, he had Buck Clayton on trumpet, Herschel Evans and Lester Young on tenor saxophones, Jo Jones on drums, and "Mr. Five by Five," Jimmy Rushing, for vocals.

In the 1940s, Basie added three key soloists to his roster—Don Byas, Illinois Jacquet, and J. J. Johnson, but the band eventually broke up, for economic reasons, in January, 1950. The disruption was only temporary, however, and Basie fronted a variety of groups after this date in addition to his usual big band: The Count Basie Seven, featuring Clark Terry, Marshall Royal, and Wardell Gray, plus rhythm; the Count Basie Quintet/Sextet/Nonet, featuring Joe Newman, Henry Coker, Marshall Royal, Paul Quinchette, and Charlie Fowlkes, plus rhythm; and other combinations. Employing swing arrangements from some of the best hands available—Ernie Wilkins, Neal Hefti, Thad Jones, Benny Carter, and Quincy Jones, among others—he fearlessly raised the banner of swing in territories occupied by troops of the bebop, cool, progressive, and West Coast schools. His band sound always began with the forward-driving propulsion of the rhythm section. Walter Page, Jo Jones, Freddie Green, and Basie formed a rhythmic unit capable of carrying a band on its back. Page and Jones were eventually replaced, but their tradition continued. The Basie sound was always exciting, and in the words of one observer:

> Blasting ensembles taking over from a light piano solo; big brass explosions behind a moving, murmuring sax solo; a bit of light piano tinkling after a brilliant brass barrage—these dynamic devices have always been part of the excitement that the Basie band has brewed.[20]

[19] Victor 20-2435.
[20] George T. Simon, *The Big Bands* (New York: Macmillan, 1967), p. 87.

House Rent Boogie

In *Doggin' Around*, the new element was provided by a particular saxophone soloist who played in a manner totally unlike that of his fellow musicians. His sound-image was neither that of the big-band sideman nor that of the Dixieland musician, but resembled the smooth solo lines of white cornetist Bix Beiderbecke. The qualities that characterized the playing of Lester "Prez" Young, making him unique among the saxophonists of swing, were his harmonic inflection, straight tone, and restricted timbre alongside a new, smooth-flowing melodic line.

Prez

Lester Young was born in Woodville, Mississippi, in 1909, and moved with his family in his early teens to Minneapolis. He toured with his father, a minstrel-show musician, through Nebraska, Kansas, and the Dakotas during these formative years and adopted Frankie Trumbauer and Bix Beiderbecke for his musical idols. He worked the Midwest during the 1930s and played with Walter Page's Blue Devils, later the Bennie Moten–George Lee band. He left a small Count Basie combo briefly to replace Coleman Hawkins in the Fletcher Henderson orchestra, but he didn't stay with them very long, for he was sharply criticized for lacking Hawkins's loud, resonant, and vibrato-laden tone. He rejoined Basie and remained with him until the end of 1940. He has been deemed the founding father of a new school of jazz (eventually dubbed "cool") and was certainly the most decisive influence on the tenor men of the late '40s and '50s, especially Stan Getz. His solo on *Doggin' Around* was, at that time, interpreted as the ultimate in understatement. The light sound and slightly accented melodic lines extracted the essence of the music, distilling the residue still further into jazz ideas of great intensity. The worship of power and drive, of virile overexuberance, was an important factor in the promulgation of swing, but amidst the most rhythmic swing band of them all, the Count Basie orchestra, Prez stood out as a cool oasis on a blistering desert.

Tragically, he, like several other great black jazz musicians, suffered debilitating wounds from the stabs of racial prejudice. From his days in the army at the end of World War II until his death in New York City in 1959, Young traveled a steadily declining road of alcoholism, nervous breakdowns, and malnutrition. In these relatively enlightened times, it is difficult to remember that during World War II blacks were drafted into the services but were segregated into all-black units, which were never allowed to travel to the European or Pacific theaters because they were considered unfit for combat. Southern cities

**Lester Willis "Prez" Young (tenor sax)
with Vic Dickenson (trombone).**

had separate washrooms, drinking fountains, rest rooms, and even railroad plat-
forms for black Americans, and it mattered not whether you were a soldier in
the service of your country or an internationally known jazz artist. Young's role
in the history of jazz was that of a pioneer, and it is terribly sad that times
changed too slowly to award him, during his lifetime, the recognition he so
justly deserved.

A further demonstration of the solo skill of this improvisatory jazz giant may
be heard in *Taxi War Dance*, recorded by Count Basie in 1939 (*SCCJ*, V/8),
and *Lester Leaps In*, recorded by a small Basie group that same year (*SCCJ*,
VI/1). The characteristics of swing are unmistakable in the ensemble work of
the other musicians, and even Prez's solos (see Transcriptions) retain a tendency toward regular accentuation, arpeggiated and diatonic passages which are
not harmonically adventurous, and occasional swing clichés. However, his melodic lines are constructed with an intuitive logic which invents graceful musical statements out of preceding figures and phrases. The motive is caught,
reworked, and transformed. The new motive statement is once again reworked
in a manner which tends to bridge the regular phrase structure and move, with
even greater dispatch, toward the final cadence of the chorus. The strong inter-
nal logic is thus based on the notes of the solo rather than on the fixed ideas of
the composer or arranger.

Lionel Hampton

Lionel Hampton played a totally different kind of instrument and functioned entirely within the stylistic limits of swing. Yet he, too, had an incredible talent for creative melodic continuity. Born in Kentucky in 1913, he was raised in Chicago, where he played in the *Chicago Defender* Boys' Band. The *Chicago Defender* was a leading black newspaper with national circulation, and it carried news of jazz and dance musicians of the black community far and wide. It was an especially powerful and significant force during the '20s, when so many leading jazzmen were based in Chicago. Still in his teens, Hampton moved to California and began playing the vibraphone, a new instrument, around 1930. From 1936 to 1940, he played with Benny Goodman, Teddy Wilson, and Gene Krupa in what quickly became the most popular small group of the era. He later fronted his own band, but in 1939 recorded, with an all-star pickup band, *When Lights Are Low*, by Benny Carter, the alto saxophonist of the group (*SCCJ*, V/6). A comparison of Hampton's work on vibes with the guitar solo of Charlie Christian discussed earlier reveals Hampton to be a master of

Lionel Hampton, vibes

swing, a musician whose accomplishments are measured not in terms of innovation, but of technical mastery. His execution is flawless, exciting in the clarity his precise rhythmic touch lends to his melodic improvisation. The classical regularity of his phrasing and the lucidity of his musical thought result from his dependence upon standard harmonic progressions already well developed in the swing era. This style of playing established Hampton's reputation as an equal of the other three members of the quartet—Goodman, Wilson, and Krupa—and opened the eyes of jazz percussionists to the musical potential of the vibraphone

Territory Bands

Benny Goodman was indeed the "King of Swing," but there were countless other swing bands operating in the United States during the 1930s and '40s. Although nationwide fame and financial rewards were possible only if a band established a reputation in one of the major cities, preferably New York or Chicago, there were numerous territory bands that achieved a more localized fame. They contributed not only to the dissemination of jazz, but also to the development of the music in many subtle ways. Many of these bands are still remembered with admiration by living musicians who heard them while touring on the road. Unfortunately most of these local musicians never recorded, or if they did, it was for personal use only.

The blues bands of Alphonso Trent, Troy Floyd, Jesse Stone, Lloyd Hunter, and Andy Kirk were all traveling the southwest territory in the 1920s.[21] San Antonio, Texas, was a local base for territory bands, and Troy Floyd worked a band out of a San Antonio home in the late '20s and early '30s. His superb trumpeter, Don Albert, formed his own band in those early depression years and also traveled the territory well into the swing era, recording on Vocalion in 1936. Another name native to the Lone Star State was Clifford "Boots" Douglas, who, between 1935 and 1938, rose to local prominence, recording blues and up-tempo pop songs with surprising frequency.

Of course, the major orchestras, like Ellington's and Cab Calloway's, set the

[21] See Gunther Schuller, *Early Jazz*, p. 290 f., for a remarkable transcription of a chorus of *Starvation Blues* by the Jesse Stone band, the Blues Serenaders, recorded for Okeh in 1927. Two new recordings of territory bands are now available: *Sweet and Low Blues: Big Bands and Territory Bands of the 20s* (New World Records, NW 256), and *Jammin' For the Jackpot: Big Bands and Territory Bands of the 30s* (New World Records, NW 217).

musical pace, but other bands, like Jimmy Gunn's group from North Carolina and the Carolina Cottonpickers from Charleston, South Carolina, toured extensively, recorded occasionally, and brought the public enthusiastic, if somewhat less than polished, live hot jazz. Swing bands in America were a national phenomenon, and both white and black musicians worked at the same jobs. Business had expanded from the dancehall and saloon to include college proms, movie theaters, local radio shows, and private parties. It has been pointed out that:

> These breakthroughs often put considerable pressure on the musicians as they bumped against the color line. Duke Ellington and Kansas City's own Bennie Moten both played to white-only crowds at Kansas City's Elbion Theater. This was not an unusual situation: blacks were often denied admission or limited to Jim Crow balconies for appearances by black bands at nonblack locations. Moreover, black bands in this period often played at hotels where they could not rent a room. On prom dates, black musicians frequently had to stay at private black homes since there were no public accommodations available to them. . . . However, there was little agitation by entertainers against these restrictions. The reasons for this reticence are varied. The musicians frequently felt that their position was precarious and that protests would have a negative effect. Moreover, on the positive side, their appearances before white audiences were viewed as a way of both raising the prestige of blacks and syphoning off some white money into black pockets. [22]

Although name bands made the news during this period, local bands disseminated the style as a national phenomenon. Cities like Cleveland, Detroit, Omaha, and Dallas were important stopovers for national bands on their regional or cross-country tours, but when the luminaries were gone, local leaders—like Red Perkins, Lloyd Hunter, Ted Adams, and Preston Love, all of Omaha—worked the clubs and played the territory on a regular basis.

Within this context, the importance of the Benny Goodman band and combos as models of musical performance and social values takes on an elevated meaning. Goodman established a standard of excellence that required technical virtuosity of professional jazzmen. He applied this standard first to his own playing and then to that of the sidemen he selected and rehearsed to play with him. Allowed a certain amount of freedom because of his national prestige, he was truly the first jazzman, or musician of any genre or style, who was able to recruit musicians purely on the basis of job qualification rather than for reasons of friendship, social environment, racial mores, or other restrictive and extraneous causes. Lionel Hampton and Teddy Wilson played so well that the American public never balked at hiring an integrated quartet and allowing

[22] Thomas Joseph Hennessey, "From Jazz to Swing: Black Jazz Musicians and Their Music, 1917–1935" (unpublished dissertation, Northwestern University, 1973), p. 443 f.

them great freedom of movement. Other musicians equally talented, like Roy Eldridge and Lester Young, were not so fortunate, but the crack in the color barrier that Goodman effectuated was the beginning of a significant breakthrough which has had important ramifications in all aspects of American life.

Duke

All the while, Duke Ellington's band continued to improve. His arrangements became more sophisticated, his compositions acquired greater depth and musical meaning, and his band played with more professionalism than ever before. By 1940, his recordings included four significant pieces which display the scope of his interest and imagination. *Ko-ko (SCCJ,* VII/2) is an uncomplicated and unpretentious big-band blues. The classic formal effect of rounded binary form, **ABA**, is created when the opening baritone-saxophone sound, with heavy vibrato, recurs near the end as a quasi recapitulation. This mid-range tempo is suitable for social dancing, either as a "businessman's bounce" foxtrot or a young jazz fan's slow jitterbug. Variety occurs in the piece not through a series of captivating solo performances, though the format would certainly allow this in the live-performance situation, but rather through the successive display of instrumental tone color principally selected by the arranger: muted and open brass, careful saxophone scoring, the contrast of large ensemble and single instrument, and other timbral ideas.[23]

Harlem Air Shaft (SCCJ, VI/7) is a stunning combination of the New York–style swing arrangement of a piece in pop-song form, **AABA,** combined with the riffs of the Kansas City tradition. The "One O'Clock Jump" riff near the end gives the piece tremendous forward drive, and when the brass open up in ensemble, the band's full power is unleashed.

Mood music began to evolve during the swing era, and *In a Mellotone (SCCJ,* VII/1) epitomizes the then-current American taste for romantic dance music to accompany the dress-up occasions of ballroom dancing. The piano introduction is a standard band cliché inviting the dancers to leave their tables and move to the floor. The saxophones sneak in on a unison melody accompanied by antiphonal trombones, all of which is followed by a gentle trumpet solo with standardized band backing featuring clarinet lead. Meanwhile, the

---

[23] See William W. Austin, *Music in the 20th Century from Debussy through Stravinsky* p. 285 ff., for an excellent analysis of Ellington's scoring of *Ko-ko.*

beat is never obscured by unnecessary complexities, for, in the last analysis, all this big-band music is dance music.

In contrast to the dancelike nature of *In a Mellotone, Concerto for Cootie* (*SCCJ*, VI/8) stands apart as an exceptional work in the jazz repertoire, for it is an example of what must be called absolute music, that is, music which is free from extramusical implications and which derives its aesthetic success or failure solely from the syntactical relationships of its musical elements. In the words of André Hodeir:

> CONCERTO FOR COOTIE is a masterpiece because what the orchestra says is the indispensable complement to what the soloist says; because nothing is out of place or superfluous in it; and because the composition thus attains unity. [24]

Hodeir goes on to point out some of the composition's unusual features: the three sections of the piece are unequal in length (excluding the introduction— 30 measures, 18 measures, and 16 measures); the phrase structure is irregular (6- 8-, and 10-measure phrases); and the composer-improviser relationship is not typical of the classical concerto (the composer's instructions, although specific, allow the soloist great latitude in interpretation). It is very easy to wax eloquent on the "bouquet of sonorities" created by the soloist on his instrument, Thus:

> Few records do more than the CONCERTO to make possible an appreciation how great a role sonority can play in the creation of jazz. The trumpet part is a true bouquet of sonorities. . . . He [Cootie] makes them shine forth in dazzling colors, then plunges them in the shade, plays around with them, makes them glitter or delicately tones them down; and each time what he shows us is something new. . . . It is appropriate that theme A, which we have already described as static, should be handled in subdued colors; that theme B, which is savagely harsh, should invite free use of the muted wa-wa's stridencies, which here have an extra brutality; and the lyricism of theme C can be fully expressed only in the upper register of the trumpet, played open. [25]

If *Concerto for Cootie* is a trumpet soloist's vehicle for timbral expression, then *Blue Serge* (*SCCJ*, VII/3) is a similar example of the jazz composer's exploration in the realm of striking sonorities. The opening phrases played by upper-register woodwinds are answered by brass chords scored to simulate the fullness and richness of an orchestral French horn section. The slippery sound of a glissando-filled trombone solo follows. In this composition, Ellington has left the security of easily remembered tunes. The trombone melody is totally

[24] *Jazz: Its Evolution and Essence,* p. 80.
[25] Ibid., p. 93 f.

instrumental in concept, for it has difficult intervals, a wide range, and unusual changes of harmonic direction. The second phrase, played by a tutti saxophone section, does not restate the once-heard melody, but proceeds with a new phrase that acts as a balance to the former. New sounds constantly follow: muted trombone with wa-wa effect, muted trumpets answered by saxophones, piano solo, open tutti trombones, tenor-sax solo in a full-voiced growl, and more. *Blue Serge* provides a dual function: it is music for listening, and it is eminently danceable. Still, the typical Ellington fan will not go away humming the tune. Although in a totally different context, Martin Williams asks the rhetorical question, " 'Where's the melody?' or, to put it more crudely, 'What are those musicians *doing* up there?' "[26] The discussion that leads to Williams's question concerns itself with improvisation to fixed harmonic patterns and not composed songs without recognizable tunes, but the question is as apt here as in the other situation. The jazzmen are beginning to expect more from their listeners as they began to expect more from themselves. And the same jazz pundit's answer also seems valid for this situation as well:

> And so, we come back again to our question and our answer. Where's the melody? The melody is the one the player is making. Hear it well, for it probably will not exist again. And it may well be extraordinary.[27]

Glenn Miller

Swing is and was many things, and for millions of Americans swing was the magical sound of the Glenn Miller dance band. The six years from the spring of 1939 to the night of December 15, 1944, when Glenn Miller failed to return from a military flight over the English Channel, almost became the Glenn Miller era. Everyone knew "the Miller sound," a penetrating tutti sax-section voice with lead clarinet.

Glenn Miller, born in Clarinda, Iowa, in 1904, served a typical jazz apprenticeship. He played with Boyd Senter, Ben Pollack, Paul Ash, and Red Nichols in the '20s and worked his way into the studios of New York City in the early 1930s. An extremely capable trombonist, he played with the Dorsey brothers and Ray Noble and took up studies in music composition with Joseph Schillinger, a theoretician who applied mathematical principles to musical composition. He tried his own luck at leading a band as early as 1937, and in 1939,

[26] Martin Williams, *Where's the Melody? A Listener's Introduction to Jazz*, p. 4.
[27] Ibid., p. 13.

thanks largely to his sidemen and vocalists Hal McIntyre, Tex Beneke, Al Klink, Marion Hutton, and Ray Eberle, he succeeded in crashing the popular market. The danceable ballads *Moonlight Serenade* and *Sunrise Serenade*[28] and the up-tempo swingers of *Little Brown Jug*,[29] *In the Mood*,[30] and *String of Pearls*[31] became phenomenally popular recordings from 1939 to 1941.

During the three years immediately preceding America's entry into World War II, Glenn Miller and Benny Goodman floated on pinnacles of success and became household words around the world. Still, they were not without competition from several equally fine bands. Charlie Barnet, Bunny Berigan, Les Brown, Cab Calloway, Benny Carter, Jimmy Dorsey, Tommy Dorsey, Woody Herman, Harry James, Andy Kirk, Artie Shaw, Chick Webb, and several others were major dance-band leaders, not to mention those we have already discussed in some detail, all recording impressive sides in 1939. Suddenly, America was coming out of the depression, the market for popular music and jazz was mushrooming, and the younger musicians who had apprenticed in the guild systems of the 1930s were ready to accept the challenge of full employment. The technology of broadcasting and recording improved immeasurably, and the new quality of "canned" sound allowed music, the entertainment industry, and the media to expand at an unbelievable rate. However, the seeds of discontent among the musicians themselves were beginning to thrust shoots through the well-watered soil of jazz at approximately the same time. A taste for the old hot jazz was beginning to manifest itself among those who recalled the sounds of yesteryear with fondness; blues, Dixieland, and ragtime revivals were under way. Suddenly, a compulsion to break free from the restrictive bonds of big-band arrangements and dancehall entertainment attitudes was making the avant-garde jazzmen of the day question both the music they were playing and their status in society. The bebop revolution was about to erupt. In 1939, these phenomena were felt only as slight whispers on the roaring winds of swing, but Alan Lomax, Frederic Ramsey, Jr., Rudi Blesh, and Charlie Parker were all, quite independent of each other, preparing the ground for a major upheaval in what might seem to the casual observer to be an unshakable, unassailable American music. Some young musicians were beginning to pay more attention to the sounds of Lester Young and Charlie Christian than to those of Count Basie and Benny Goodman. Lomax, Ramsey, and Blesh were beginning to search the ghettos and back alleys for authentic old-time blues musicians, ragtime piano players, and Dixieland sidemen, while Bird Parker was learning his horn and the changes.

[28] Bluebird 10214.
[29] Bluebird 10286.
[30] Bluebird 10416.
[31] Bluebird 11382.

World War II

What was the musical effect of World War II? In general, jazz benefited in a most positive way. The Special Services units of the armed forces allowed thousands of young musicians to make music night and day where previously a relative handful of musicians were gainfully employed full-time. Night clubs in major cities were packed with soldiers on leave, and the increase in business provided many new jobs for jazzbands and combos. American fighting men took American popular music and jazz with them wherever they were called to serve via the armed-services radio system. Ironically, even the enemy propaganda agencies served to promulgate a taste for jazz by broadcasting American music in an attempt to lure the "Yanks" from their miserable foxholes, tents, and submarines to an idyllic promised land of pleasure and recreation. Tokyo Rose, infamous voice of the Japanese airwaves, was a favorite disc jockey for the GIs in the Pacific theater. As a result of all these unusual circumstances, American jazzmen not only proliferated and developed skills far above the norm of the prewar years, but the American public, both servicemen and citizens at home, were literally enclosed in an environment of jazz and big-band dance music. Famous musicians became national heroes as Americans took pride in everything that was American, and no town or farm was too isolated to know the names of Dorsey, Miller, Basie, Goodman, and Ellington.

Comedy and quiz shows on the radio, a favorite entertainment form of the time, had backup bands; wherever the comedian Bob Hope traveled, whether to entertain the troops at the front or to braodcast a "toothpaste show" from a studio, one could count on hearing the Les Brown Band of Renown. The music of a subculture had truly become the music of the nation, and that portion of jazz we know as swing was a universally accepted idiom in the United States. Jazz musicians assumed a new pride in their profession, and the effects of the war on this music lasted well after the close of hostilities. In 1946, one critic wrote, "The six years of the World War were years during which jazz advanced more rapidly and more impressively than in any previous period."[32]

Post-War Swing

In the years immediately following World War II, the swing bands were still the most exciting musical organizations of the day. Woody Herman, Duke Ellington, Bennie Goodman, Harry James, Tommy Dorsey, Jimmy Dorsey,

---

[32] Leonard Feather, "A Survey of Jazz Today," *Esquire's 1946 Jazz Book*, ed. Paul Eduard Miller (New York: Barnes, 1946), p. 151.

Lionel Hampton, Gene Krupa, Count Basie, Artie Shaw, Les Brown, Dizzy Gillespie, Charlie Barnet, and Boyd Raeburn were the leaders of the most impressive big bands on the market. Concerts from Carnegie Hall and Town Hall in New York were popular; juke boxes were doing an impressive business; and radio, movies, and dance halls were exuding swing from every loud-speaker.

> To sum up: 1945 was another great year for jazz. You don't have to take any one person's word for this. Just look at the vast selection of musicians for whom votes were cast in this year's New Stars poll—then listen to some of their recorded music. It speaks very eloquently for itself. . . . 1946 will be a great year for jazz, just as the year before it, and the year before that. So much was accomplished, incredibly, during the years of war, that it's hard to conceive what may develop in a world at peace.[33]

The health and vitality of swing during the early postwar years, perhaps generated by the enthusiasm of a successful war effort, gave it an impetus that carried it safely through the '40s and, with diminishing intensity, virtually to the end of the 1950s. Other styles began to develop, and they all coexisted with swing and the revived old-time jazz. Swing remained the most popular of all the jazz styles, even though it was soon supplanted as the greatest influence in the jazz community. The effort may be summarized as follows:

> The free, spontaneous communication between the big bands and their fans was a natural culmination of the music itself. The approach of most outfits was so honest and direct that fans could recognize instinctively whether the bands were really try-ing or merely coasting. When a musician played an especially exciting solo, they'd cheer for it, and when the band as a whole reached especially high musical and emotional heights, it would be rewarded with enthusiastic, honest, heartfelt yelling and cheering—not the kind of hysterics evoked by a rock and roller's shaking his long tresses, but real approval for a musical job well done. . . . By 1940 there must have been close to two hundred dance orchestras, any one of which a know-ing fan could identify after hearing only a few of its stylized musical measures.
> Nothing like it had ever happened before.[34]

In sum, swing was first and foremost a big-band arranged jazz style, and the arrangers were as influential in its development as the performers themselves. Beginning in the New York–jazzband styles of the late '20s, a music with roots in the Dixieland tradition emerged and eventually became a separate and dis-tinct musical idiom. Changes in instrumentation gave arrangers and composers new sonorities with which to work, and the guitar and string bass, which re-

[33] Ibid., pp. 161 and 163.
[34] Simon, *The Big Bands*, pp. 13 and 15.

placed the banjo and tuba, gave jazz rhythm sections an entirely different sound. A steady 4/4 rhythm with a two-beat ride was maintained by the drummers, and the rhythm section provided a more pervasive but less obtrusive rhythmic sound than that of the Dixieland combos. The softer dynamics of guitar and bass helped accelerate the catalysis.

Around 1935, the physical dimensions of swing bands increased to and then standardized at fourteen members: four rhythm instruments, five brass, and five reeds. Frequently, arrangers would fit simple riffs for sections in unison or in a thickened melodic line to the simple chord patterns of the popular songs of the day or the blues, and ballads were as much a part of the repertoire as the up-tempo numbers commonly thought to characterize swing. Performances achieved greater precision as an influx of schooled musicians began to fill the chairs of jazz. Toward the end of the '30s, two new instruments were introduced—the electric guitar and the vibraphone, and the repertoire of possible tonal effects multiplied not only from the variety of newer instruments but also from the imaginative scoring of standard instruments in solo and combination by the arrangers.

Thomas Hennessey summarizes his excellent study with these conclusions:

> Slowly, black jazz moved from being a folk music to being a popular music. The musicians became professionals who earned their living from their music and worked hard at it. For most black jazz musicians by 1935, jazz represented a way of "making it" in American society, an upwardly mobile path to economic success, increased status and public recognition. The bonanzas of the early thirties came as a fitting climax to the efforts of the young, frequently college-trained, musicians with middle-class aspirations who had helped to transform one segment of black music from jazz to swing between 1917 and 1935.[35]

Swing also opened the door of jazz to numerous white musicians who also began to "make it" in American society. But as we shall see, the success of the swing bands and the concomitant necessity to maintain an image eventually led to its downfall as the new bebop movement began to gain momentum in the mid-1940s.

[35] Thomas J. Hennessey, "From Jazz to Swing," p. 492 f.

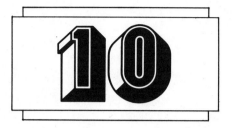

THE JAZZ REVOLUTION—
BEBOP

Origins of a New Style

Toward the end of World War II, it became apparent that a new style of jazz was in the process of being created. A small group of musicians, seeing jazz from a different perspective, felt that big-band swing was in a rut. They felt that arrangers were not leaving enough room in their music for solo improvisation, and the style itself was harmonically empty—chord progressions were limited to triads, seventh chords, and occasional diminished and augmented chords with perhaps an added note; rhythms were too stereotyped and consisted only of formula mixtures of simple syncopations; and melodies were too tradition-bound to the 4- and 8-measure phrase structure of dance music. They heard new harmonic and rhythmic implications in the famous Coleman Hawkins *Body and Soul* improvisation (*SCCJ*, IV/4), realizing that he had constructed his melodic line as if the rhythm section were playing at twice the actual tempo of the original composition. In other words, a second level of harmonic motion and rhythmic activity was superimposed, through the addition of passing chords, upon the original structure.

These same musicians heard new sounds and new ideas in the famous Charlie Christian recordings of 1941: sessions from Monroe's Uptown House and Minton's in New York City with sidemen Thelonious Monk on piano, Kenny Clarke on drums, Don Byas on tenor saxophone, and Dizzy Gillespie on trumpet.[1] As a direct consequence of listening to these pioneer explorations

[1] Society (E) SOC996 and Counterpoint (A) 5548.

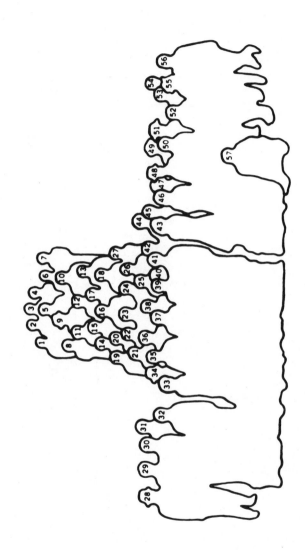

The jazz greats in the historic photograph above are numbered for your ready reference: 1. Hilton Jefferson; 2. Benny Golson; 3. Art Farmer; 4. Wilbur Ware; 5. Art Blakey; 6. Chubby Jackson; 7. Johnny Griffin; 8. Dickie Wells; 9. Buck Clayton; 10. Taft Jordan; 11. Zutty Singleton; 12. Red Allen; 13. Tyree Glenn; 14. Miff Mole; 15. Sonny Greer; 16. Jay C. Higginbotham; 17. Jimmy Jones; 18. Charles Mingus; 19. Jo Jones; 20. Gene Krupa; 21. Max Kaminsky; 22. George Wettling; 23. Bud Freeman; 24. Pee Wee Russell; 25. Ernie Wilkins; 26. Buster Bailey; 27. Osie Johnson; 28. Gigi Gryce; 29. Hank Jones; 30. Eddie Locke; 31. Horace Silver; 32. Luckey Roberts; 33. Maxine Sullivan; 34. Jimmy Rushing; 35. Joe Thomas; 36. Scoville Browne; 37. Stuff Smith; 38. Bill Crump; 39. Coleman Hawkins; 40. Rudy Powell; 41. Oscar Pettiford; 42. Sahib Shihab; 43. Marian McPartland; 44. Sonny Rollins; 45. Lawrence Brown; 46. Mary Lou Williams; 47. Emmett Berry; 48. Thelonious Monk; 49. Vic Dickenson; 50. Milt Hinton; 51. Lester Young; 52. Rex Stewart; 53. J. C. Heard; 54. Gerry Mulligan; 55. Roy Eldridge; 56. Dizzy Gillespie; 57. Count Basie.

of the early 1940s, a group of jazz musicians began playing a new style of music, which came to be called "bebop."[2]

The word "bebop" originated in the jazz musician's practice of vocalizing or singing instrumental melodic lines with nonsense syllables (scat singing). Bebop phrases frequently had abrupt endings with a characteristic long-short pattern on the end: ♩♪⁊ , and this rhythm was often vocalized as "rebop" or "bebop." The name seems to have appeared first in print as the title of a tune recorded by the Dizzy Gillespie Sextet in New York in 1945.[3] A few years later, jazzmen shortened the term to "bop."

> Of all the queer, uncommunicative, secret-society terms that jazz has surrounded itself with, few are lumpier or more misleading than "bebop." Originally a casual onomatopoeic word used to describe the continually shifting accents of the early work of Charlie Parker, Dizzy Gillespie, Kenny Clarke, and Thelonious Monk [c. 1944], it soon became a free-floating, generic one as well, whose tight, rude sound implied something harsh, jerky, and unattractive.[4]

Bebop developed at a period in the history of jazz when some musicians were consciously attempting to create a new elite and to exclude from their number all persons who were not up to predetermined artistic standards. Barriers, real and artificial, were put up, not only between bebop musicians and the public at large, but between themselves and other jazz musicians.[5] It is common knowledge that the jazz musician has usually been held suspect by people unfamiliar with his work, and many factors estranged the jazzman from society at large: the large proportion of black musicians in a predominantly white society; the threat that jazz posed to established art music; the musicians' inverted hours of work, sleep, and recreation; the jazzman's nomadic life. It should be no surprise, then, to discover that in retaliation some jazzmen rejected society as well. An excellent study of the jazz community is concluded with the observation:

> The jazz community . . . is a social grouping drawn together by specific attitudes and behaviors which stress the differences of the musician and his public from people at large, his superiority over the layman, and the advantages to be gained from self segregation and isolation.[6]

[2] Also "rebop" and "bop." The etymology of the word is obscure, even though it is of recent origin. See Marshall Stearns, *The Story of Jazz*, p. 155, and André Hodeir, *Jazz: Its Evolution and Essence*, p. 110.

[3] *Salt Peanuts/Be-Bop* (Manor 5000, Regal 132)

[4] *The New Yorker*, November 7, 1959, p. 158.

[5] Portions of this chapter were taken from the author's "The Silent Theme Tradition in Jazz," *The Musical Quarterly*, 53 (1967), p. 313 ff.

[6] Alan P. Merriam and Raymond W. Mack, "The Jazz Community," p. 222.

The result, both unusual and unexpected, was that the bebop musician be-came disassociated from his own audience, from his own employer, from non-jazz musicians, and even from other jazz musicians as well. One critic writes:

> It was during the Minton's [Play House] era that men like Dizzy [Gillespie], [Ken-ny] Clarke, and Tadd [Dameron], finding that to a great degree they were kindred spirits, started what became in effect a clique of new musicians. It was not difficult to prevent outsiders from crashing this charmed circle. As Kenny Clarke recalls, "We'd play *Epistrophy* or *I've Got My Love To Keep Me Warm* just to keep the other guys off the stand, because we knew they couldn't make those chord changes. We kept the riff-raff out and built our clique on new chords.[7]

The most significant reason why this split occurred was that the bebop musi-cian was trying to raise the quality of jazz from the level of utilitarian dance music to that of a chamber art form. At the same time, he was trying to raise the status of the jazzman from entertainer to artist. His attempts were not im-mediately successful, and when his music was rejected, the bebop musician turned inward. It was not uncommon for the bebop soloist to play with his back turned toward the audience or to walk off the bandstand as soon as he finished with his solo, even though the rest of the group were still playing. The bebop musician's contempt for the public was only equaled by his disdain for musi-cians who called themselves jazzmen but were musically incompetent by his standards. This attitude gave rise to a breed of person who became known as a "hipster." Of this group, Charlie Parker was the leader, the model, and the ul-timate guru. His biographer writes:

> To the hipster, Bird was a living justification of their philosophy. The hipster is an underground man. He is to the second World War what the dadaist was to the first. He is amoral, anarchistic, gentle, and overcivilized to the point of decadence. He is always ten steps ahead of the game because of his awareness, an example of which would be meeting a girl and rejecting her, because he knows they will date, hold hands, kiss, neck, pet, fornicate, perhaps marry, divorce—so why start the whole thing? He knows the hypocrisy of bureaucracy, the hatred implicit in re-ligions—so what values are left for him?—except to go through life avoiding pain, keep his emotions in check, and after that, "be cool," and look for kicks. He is looking for something that transcends all this bullshit and finds it in jazz.[8]

Technical proficiency was a part of the movement, and the bebop musician did his best to belittle anyone who could not maintain the demanding pace. The jam session was the bebop musician's trial by fire. Dizzy Gillespie once

[7] Leonard Feather, *Inside Be-Bop*, p. 8.
[8] Robert George Reisner, *Bird: The Legend of Charlie Parker*, p. 25 f.

told Marshall Stearns, "The modulations we manufactured were the weirdest, especially if some new cat walked in with his horn and tried to sit in with us."[9]

The transition to bebop seemed to happen overnight, but in truth, the foundations of the style were laid over a period of approximately six years, 1939–45. It actually might have taken place more quickly, but a National Federation of Musicians recording ban was imposed from August, 1942, until November, 1944,[10] and a major medium for the transmission of new ideas among the jazz musicians was temporarily denied them.

Musical Characteristics

By 1945, we are certain that bebop had established its stylistic independence from swing, and Richard Wang analyzes a recording session which took place in 1945 that combined musicians from both schools, swing and bebop, for performances of *Congo Blues* and *Slam, Slam Blues*.[11] The musicians at this session were, in addition to Parker, Red Norvo, Teddy Wilson, Slam Stewart, J. C. Heard, Dizzy Gillespie, and Flip Phillips. Wang concludes:

> A comparison of the two styles reveals that: swing phrases are more uniform in length, more symmetrical in shape, and more congruent with the harmonic phrase than those of bebop; swing rhythmic patterns are less varied, more even-flowing, and less disrupted by shifting accents than those of bebop; bebop, on the other hand, is more complex, full of greater contrasts, has more rhythmic subtleties, and makes a greater and more expressive use of dissonance. The arrangement of *Congo Blues* exhibits several characteristics often found in the new style: the exotic rhythm of the introduction, the novel harmony of the interlude, and the unison riff at the end. . . . All the jazzmen discussed . . . attempted to unify their solos. . . . Only Parker, however, was successful in combining long-range unifying techniques with a maximum of expression, thus creating a truly great jazz solo.[12]

The importance of Charlie Parker is further dramatized by the statement of saxophonist Benny Green:

> The advent of Charlie Parker caused more violent irruptions, more bitterness, more sheer apoplectic rage than that of any jazz musician before him. Before he hap-

[9] Stearns, *The Story of Jazz*, p. 157.

[10] Robert D. Leiter, *The Musicians and Petrillo*, pp. 132–40.

[11] Comet T6-B and T7-B.

[12] Richard Wang, "Jazz Circa 1945: A Confluence of Styles," *The Musical Quarterly*, 59 (1973), p. 541 ff.

pened, there was no serious split down the middle of the jazz ranks. After he arrived, it was no longer sufficient to claim you were a jazz fan. . . . [I]t was necessary to qualify the claim, to explain what kind of a jazz fan you were, to commit yourself either to the music that was pre–Charlie Parker or to the music he was playing. [13]

The musical characteristics of bebop are clearly revealed in the Dizzy Gillespie recording of *Shaw 'Nuff* (*SCCJ*, VII/6): the characteristic introduction with "exotic" rhythm; the lightning-fast first chorus with melodic instruments playing a jagged instrumental melody in unison; the choruses of the soloists in the new style of asymmetry and rhythmic complexity; a harmonic framework that changes chords at half-note speed (at whole-note speed in the bridge section); and the unison riff at the end. Although it was Charlie Christian, Coleman Hawkins, and Lester Young, among others, who led the change to bebop, it was Charlie Parker and Dizzy Gillespie who took command and crystallized the style.

The Leaders—Bird and Diz

Charlie Parker was born in Kansas City, Kansas, in 1920, and was raised by his mother in Kansas City, Missouri, where she bought him an alto saxophone when he was 11. He began to work professionally in 1937 and came to play at Clark Monroe's Uptown House in New York City in 1939. After a brief trip back to Kansas City, he returned to New York to record with the Jay McShann band for Decca in 1941. It was at this time that he first met Dizzy Gillespie, and they became partners in establishing the new style. Throughout his life, he was plagued with illnesses resulting from drug addiction and alcoholism, and he died at the age of thirty-five in New York City after a heart attack. In spite of the personal tragedy of his life,

> Charlie Parker is one of the few jazzmen who can be said to have given dignity and meaning to the abused word "genius." It was his desire to devote his life to the translation of everything he saw and heard into terms of musical beauty. Though it was his inspiration, his soul and warmth that earned him an international reputation, and although he had little formal training, he was a man of amazing technical skill, a fast reader and a gifted composer-arranger. His best records were those he made with a small, informal combo, but he was proudest of the series of albums he made, starting in 1950, with a group featuring strings and woodwinds. . . .
>
> In bringing the art of improvisation to a new peak of maturity, Parker had an

[13] Benny Green, *The Reluctant Art: Five Studies in the Growth of Jazz*, p. 159.

Charles Christopher "Bird" or "Yardbird" Parker (1920–55).

John Birks "Dizzy" Gillespie at Duke University, October 19, 1974.

inestimable influence on jazz musicians regardless of what instrument they played. From the mid-'40s on, it was almost impossible for any new jazzman anywhere in the world to escape reflecting to some degree, consciously or unconsciously, a Parker influence; his work set a new standard on every level: harmonic, tonal, rhythmic and melodic. [14]

His friend and musical partner, John Birks "Dizzy" Gillespie, was born in 1917 in Cheraw, South Carolina. He studied harmony and theory, took instruction on several instruments, and began working with Frank Fairfax in Philadelphia in 1935. He replaced Roy Eldridge in the Teddy Hill band in 1937, worked with Mercer Ellington, Cab Calloway, Benny Carter, Charlie Barnet, and others. Fate made an especially wise choice in teaming Gillespie with Parker, for Dizzy was perhaps the only jazz trumpeter in the world who had not only a sophisticated understanding of harmonic theory but also an unprecedented technical virtuosity on that instrument. He was the first trumpet player in jazz capable of performing up-tempo melodies in bebop style. The unison riff and long-line solo lines of *Shaw 'Nuff* prove that Dizzy Gillespie, in 1945, was a virtuoso of almost unlimited technical resources. Still, it should be noted that neither Charlie Parker nor Dizzy Gillespie received universal recognition among jazz musicians and critics at this time for their accomplishments. For the years 1945–47, Johnny Hodges was named the outstanding saxophonist of the year by musicians and critics for the *Esquire* All-American Jazz Band, and the same group of judges selected Cootie Williams twice and Louis Armstrong once as the outstanding jazz trumpter of the year. The big bands were in full swing, the Dixieland revival was at work (*SCCJ*, II/3; recorded in 1944), and the bebop musicians were definitely not part of the musical establishment.

These outcasts developed a number of characteristics, most of which were nonmusical, that set them apart from the rest of the world: language, dress, habitat, behavior. Goatees, berets, wing-collar shirts, and drape-shape suits came into vogue for the hip musician when a tuxedo or a dark-blue suit was standard garb for other musicians. Jazzmen were already on an island; bopsters built a raft and moved offshore. A noted jazz critic explained the function of jazz's special language:

> It is his [the jazz musician's] language that gives him that sense of community for which he fights so hard so much of the time. But his is more than a language; it is a kind of code which gains him admittance to the secure circles of jazz, establishes him as a member of an élite, and makes it possible for him to forbid entrance to his society. [15]

[14] Leonard Feather, *Encyclopedia of Jazz*, p. 376.
[15] Barry Ulanov, A *Handbook of Jazz*, p. 99.

The bebop musicians developed their own language, and although it was similar to the language spoken by other jazz musicians, it varied in enough detail to be useful as the password that immediately distinguished friend from foe. As soon as outsiders picked up and used reserved words, the language changed.

The Music

The music of bebop, as a rule, was performed by a small jazz combo of three to six members. The standard procedure when performing without written music—and this was the norm for bebop musicians rebelling against the written arrangements of swing—was to play the melody in its entirety once (twice if a twelve-measure blues), follow it with several choruses of improvised solos to the accompaniment of the rhythm section (usually piano, bass, and drums), and repeat the melody of the first chorus to end the piece. All the while, the rhythm section maintains the structure of the piece by repeating the harmonic pattern (the changes) of a complete chorus. Even without a complete jazz combo, Don Byas takes the "head chart" understood for *I Got Rhythm* and improvises a full-length jazz number to the accompaniment of Slam Stewart's bass viol (*SCCJ*, VII/4). His one variation from the traditional pattern is the omission of the opening-melody repeat for the last chorus, so he ends with a brief tag. Carlos Wesley "Don" Byas was born in Muskogee, Oklahoma, in 1912 and became one of the best known tenor-sax men of the mid-1940s. He won the *Esquire* Silver Award in 1946 for his outstanding playing. A jobbing musician since the 1930s, he had worked with Don Redman, Andy Kirk, Count Basie, Dizzy Gillespie, and Duke Ellington, and, as can be heard on his performance of *I Got Rhythm*, he plays with the full-voiced sound of the Hawkins school but adds the modern characteristics being explored by the innovators, Gillespie and Parker.

With rare exceptions, the jazz performances of the '40s and '50s were all based on this "melodic improvisation to the changes" technique. The jazz musician, because of his frequent employment at dances, nightclubs, and parties, worked from a repertoire of popular songs, musical-comedy melodies, blues tunes, and a few jazz originals. Also, this style of employment, where the musician was called upon to produce three or four hours of improvised music five to seven days a week, led to the development of a repertoire of melodic patterns, actually a collection of instrumental finger patterns related to keys and chords, which were generally unique to the individual and were called upon as "instant ideas" for the development of long-line, extemporaneous solos.[16] The patterns were not repeated mechanically by the better musicians, and these melodic units were modified, dropped, and incremented through the passage of time so that the state of improvisation for developing jazzmen was that of flux or growth, and not one of impoverished redundancy.

Popular ballads, like *I Can't Get Started*, by Vernon Duke and Ira Gershwin (*SCCJ*, VII/5), were transformed by the precepts of bebop into jazz compositions with characteristics totally different from, and yet related to, those of the original composition. When Dizzy Gillespie recorded this number in 1945 (see Transcriptions), he opened with an 8-measure introduction, played a single 32-measure chorus, and closed with a 4-measure tag. The gradual transformation of the music to a bebop ballad can be seen by studying the opening of each **A** phrase (the form is **AABA**).

I Can't Get Started: Original Tune and Chords

The tune is regular in both its melodic construction and its harmonic framework. The first four measures are divided in half: two melodic statements that are sequential in their intervallic construction and repetitive in their rhythmic construction.

Melodic Rhythm

The harmonic rhythm of the original tune is regular: the first four measures are framed by two whole-note constructions and filled with four half-note motions.

Harmonic Rhythm

The bebop chorus regularizes the harmonic motion to steady half-note changes, the opening whole-note rhythm is changed by inserting a substitute chord, the A-minor seventh in place of the C-major triad, and changes the progression of the last two measures to a substitute chordal pattern, four descending minor-seventh chords, to fill the harmonic gap of a major third.

---

[16] Recently, the first in-depth study of this phenomenon has been completed using the solos of Charlie Parker as the exemplars for study. See Thomas Owens, "Charlie Parker: Techniques of Improvisation."

Altered Harmonic Rhythm

Gillespie's first statement of the ballad melody, except for the long upward flourish, is a straightforward statement of the original theme.

Gillespie's Phrase Opening: First Phrase

His opening for the second phrase totally obscures the melody except for the last few notes,

Second Phrase

and his opening for the fourth, and final, phrase, is elided with the ending of the bridge and rhythmically transformed.

Fourth Phrase

There is no question that Gillespie's choice of notes for these structural passages was made with the original tune in mind and played to allow the listener the comfort of hearing a well-known tune artfully embellished in a jazz style.

A completely different, and more remarkable, transformation took place in Charlie Parker's reworking of the popular song *Cherokee*, by Ray Noble. He totally discarded the old tune and composed his new melody, *KoKo*, over the chord progression of *Cherokee*. He described how he composed *KoKo* in these words:

> I'd been getting bored with the stereotyped changes that were being used all the time at the time, and I kept thinking there's bound to be something else. I could hear it sometimes but I couldn't play it.
>
> Well, that night, I was working over *Cherokee*, and as I did, I found that by using the higher intervals of the chord as a melody line and backing them with appropriately related changes, I could play the things I'd been hearing. I came alive. [17]

[17] Nat Shapiro and Nat Hentoff, *Hear Me Talkin' To Ya*, p. 354.

A comparison of the opening of Parker's *KoKo*

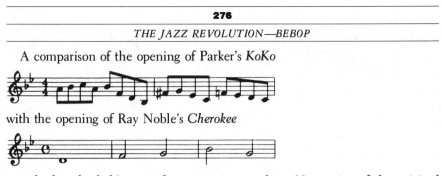

with the opening of Ray Noble's *Cherokee*

reveals that the bebop transformation is complete. No vestige of the original remains visible on the surface of the performance. In a sense, the bebop musician was now composing music exclusively for other jazzmen, and the popular songs, loved by the laymen, were either being transformed or discarded. The music of bebop was complex, music that might be categorized as "art for art's sake," and the best of them certainly did not have an easy appeal. Listeners were expected to be sophisticated, and dancers had no place in the audience.

> Thus with "bop," jazz met the difficulties that had bewildered the critics of new serious music ever since 1910. The best work was so complex in harmony and rhythm that it sounded at first incoherent, not only to laymen but also to professionals very close to it. Good work could no longer be discriminated with any speed or certainty from incompetent work, and incompetent workers, in all good faith, took advantage of this situation to press their claims. Some narrow-minded professionals joined impatient laymen to condemn the whole style as a product of incompetence, if not of charlatanism or madness. At the same time some supporters of the new style preferred to interpret its political or poetical purity as depending on its incomprehensibility. The controversy had a momentary publicity value. But this was soon exhausted while the bewilderment went on. The jazz community had to learn to live with it, just as did people interested in other serious new music.[18]

Significant stylistic changes were also effected by the bop rhythm section. Kenny "Klook" Clarke, who was born in Pittsburgh in 1914, first engaged in serious discussions with Dizzy Gillespie while working with the Teddy Hill band during 1939–40. Clarke worked in Minton's during the early 1940s with a combo extracted from the old Hill band. As a result of his manner of playing at that time, he is credited with being the drummer who modified the swing drum system to a new one suitable for bebop. He stopped playing bass drum on every beat, reserving it for special accentuation and rhythmic effects. He took the ride pattern off the sock cymbal and played it on a suspended cymbal so that beats two and four would not be accented; thus, he was able to use the top cymbal, later renamed the "ride cymbal," for steady rhythm.

[18] William W. Austin, *Music in the 20th Century from Debussy through Stravinsky*, p. 291 f.

Kenny "Klook" Clarke with Elaine Leighton

The Pianists—Tadd, Bud, and Monk

Tadley Ewing "Tadd" Dameron, Thelonious Sphere Monk, and Earl "Bud" Powell were the three bebop pianists who influenced the development of bebop style piano technique most significantly. Although Fatha Hines and Count Basie undoubtedly prepared the way, Powell is usually credited with relieving the left hand of its rhythmic function of maintaining a steady beat, allowing it to "comp" (accompany) in a freely syncopated chordal manner. Thus, the responsibility for laying down a steady pulse was shifted to the ride pattern of the drummer's suspended cymbal and the walking quarter-note pattern of the pizzicato string bass. Just as Gillespie had played melodic solos in a style formerly thought to be reserved for saxophones, that is, rapid running me-

Earl "Bud" Powell.

lodic lines, Powell developed a piano-solo style that adopted the same charac-teristics for the solo melodic work of the right hand. While the right hand improvised long-line scalar solos, the left hand, by contrast, would continue to comp. Tadd Dameron played in a similar manner, but Thelonious Monk de-veloped a personal style that avoided the difficulties of finger dexterity. His playing was, and is, unique. Technical virtuosity, at least in the sense of rapid performance of scales and arpeggios, was not characteristic of his playing. In-stead, he concentrated on harmonic innovation expressed in erratic rhythms and in chords and tonal clusters that were sparse, stark, and economical. Monk's greatest contribution to the bebop style was his influence on other players. He affected all kinds of instrumentalists, not only through his composi-tions, but also through his philosophical approach to listening to music for new effects and procedures and perceiving it from new perspectives. In a sense, his approach to jazz, like Anton Webern's handling of serialism and classical forms, was austere and severely restricted in its material to essential germinal ideas. It was an approach in marked contrast to the overabundant, free-flowing, and often eclectic improvisations of the brilliant virtuosos.

Bud Powell's recording of *Somebody Loves Me* (SCCJ, VIII/5) displays two different aspects of the man's playing personality. The opening chorus is per-formed in a chordal manner, two hands basically operating in parallel motion with the melody pressed out almost entirely with the little finger of the right hand. This style of playing was later popularized by George Shearing. It is not generally thought to be bebop piano playing, but rather a semijazz, semicom-mercial method of performance. However, the improvisation beginning at the second chorus demonstrates why Powell was considered the leading pianist of the bebop era. The rhythmic energy and almost compulsive attack of his play-ing let his fingers sweep across the keyboard mixing accents and blurring phrase structure. His impeccable touch clearly articulates the buoyant phrases, shap-ing them into melodic lines of continuous subtlety. The left hand follows along interjecting occasional chords, signposts to both the player and the listener of the harmonic structure which underlies the improvisation. The steady move-ment of the plucked string bass is quite sufficient to hold the rhythm and change the harmonies. At this medium tempo, the drummer chooses to use wire brushes on the snare rather than ride a cymbal, and the pulsating sizzle of the drum's snare presses a quiet but incessant beat upon the listener. The clar-ity with which all three members of this trio perform underscores the chamber-art nature of this music.

Tadd Dameron's composition *Lady Bird* (SCCJ, IX/2) is interesting for its simplicity, unusual design, and brevity. The composition is only sixteen mea-sures long, and is through-composed and seamless, unlike popular-song form. The harmonic rhythm moves at an erratic speed, and the chord changes, al-though simple, are unusual.

Lady Bird

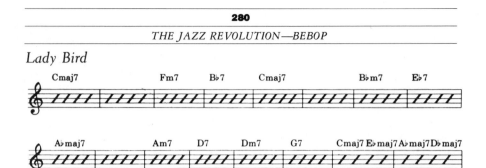

The trumpet solo work of Fats Navarro far outshines that of the pianist and composer on this recording, but Dameron does exhibit here the fully developed bebop style of solo accompaniment. Backing chords are judiciously interspersed in a manner that guarantees harmonic certainty but leaves the air uncluttered for the soloist. The trumpeter Fats Navarro died in 1950 at the age of 26. Drug addiction and tuberculosis robbed the 1940s of its most promising trumpet player, but not before he demonstrated that there were other possibilities for

Tadd Dameron at the piano, Miles Davis on trumpet.

trumpet improvisation within the ranks of bebop than that of Dizzy Gillespie. Unlike other bebop trumpet men, his playing did not totally derive from Dizzy's, and he showed that full-bodied sound, rapid notes in the mid and lower registers, and more jagged lines were also stylistically correct for bop.

Thelonious Monk was cut from a different bolt of cloth; he was eccentric even within the community of bebop eccentrics. As a performer, he seems not to have been influenced by anyone else, and his style of piano playing seems to have attracted no students, even though he influenced the thinking of many others. Still, he was consistently selected by the greatest sidemen of jazz of the '40s and '50s to play in their various groups. He not only recorded with Dizzy Gillespie and Charlie Parker, but with Coleman Hawkins and John Coltrane. These leaders, who all sought sidemen of prodigious technical competence, received a different kind of musical support when they worked with Monk. Many of his compositions have become jazz standards, and *Round Midnight*, *Epistrophy*, *Well You Needn't*, *Straight No Chaser*, and *Blue Monk* are still favorites of modern jazz musicians. Yet even in his piano playing, the astute listener must sense Monk's incredible ability to select just the right notes at just the right time.

> There is, too, a deep interrelationship between Monk's piano style and his composing, the one being parallel and complementary to the other: each shows the same respect for musical logic, the same direct expression of ideas; and decoration that might occur grows out of the musical development rather than from irrelevant instrumental conventions. [19]

In his composition and performance of *Misterioso* (*SCCJ*, IX/4), Monk transforms the blues into a melody comprised of a sequence of sixths:

Earlier in this century, Schoenberg and his two students, Berg and Webern, rejected traditional notions of melody and harmony and developed a new sys-

---

[19] Max Harrison *et al.*, *Modern Jazz: The Essential Records*, p. 26.

Thelonious Sphere Monk.

tem with which to organize their music: the tone row. In a sense, Thelonious Monk was the first jazz musician to discard successfully the traditional concept of melody and the current ideas of melodic rhythm and develop his own system(s) of musical construction. The harmonies of *Misterioso* are those of the traditional blues, and the changes occur regularly. But the rhythm of the melody has little articulation, that is, the note values of the "tune" are undifferentiated and equal. At a time when Dizzy Gillespie and Charlie Parker were exploring the improvisational limits of tonal melodies within the stylistic norms of bebop jazz, it is difficult to explain how Monk, a member of the bebop clique, was able to function in a realm so totally different from that of his cohorts. In a sense, this corroborates the theory that bebop musicians were questioning not only the musical and social values of the establishment, but also the musical and extramusical elements of their own society. This refreshing introspection did much to reshape jazz, and in the gregarious world of nightclub entertainers, Thelonious Monk was the embodiment of solitude and self analysis.

In another 1948 recording, *Evidence* (*SCCJ*, IX/6), Monk experiments with a different system of musical organization by exploring the possibility of working two separate heirarchical levels of music simultaneously. The pointillistic layer of piano sounds is overlaid with the swing-trio sounds of Milt Jackson, John Simmons, and Shadow Wilson. As the music progresses, the two musical ideas become more unified until the piano merges with the trio and sets out on a solo that travels a traditional melodic path. Gradually, the single line of Monk's playing begins to separate into an intervallic construction again, and the vibes return partly to accept the piano's style and partly to reclaim the identity of its original sounds in the piece. Monk is working in the realm of absolute music for instruments, compositions without a tune, pieces maintaining a jazz beat and employing modern harmonic changes.

Big Bands

During the mid-1940s, small-combo bebop was in its heyday. At the same time, however, two important big-band developments were occurring. On the one hand, some big bands were beginning to modify their style to allow greater freedom of improvisation by the sidemen and to incorporate musical developments of the bebop school into their arrangements. The most prominent band to make this change was Woody Herman's. Herman fronted a succession of bands he fondly called "Herds." With the help of arranger Ralph Burns he remade the sound of his group into something more harmonically aggressive, especially in ballads, and more in keeping with bebop-combo sounds for the up-tempo numbers. In 1947 and 1948, the Herman Herd recorded *Four Brothers*[20] and *Early Autumn*.[21] For both these numbers, the arranger took an instrumental melody and scored it with close-harmony voicing and similar motion of saxophones in the same register. In a sense, this was an adaptation of the bebop unison riff, a modification which spread or thickened the unison melody among the members of a homogenous section. In a more traditional manner, the brass section was required to punctuate the up-tempo number rhythmically and to decorate the extended chords of the ballad harmonically and timbrally. The tenor and baritone solos of Al Cohn, Zoot Sims (originally Herbie Steward), and Serge Chaloff are all in the bebop style, and the superb tenor solos of Stan Getz on both *Four Brothers* and *Early Autumn* were the beginnings of a new school in jazz, the "cool school," which would soon separate itself from the parent bebop.

On the other hand, an intentional movement toward a new style of big-band jazz was taking place on America's West Coast. Stan Kenton, Boyd Raeburn, and Earl Spencer were calling their music "progressive jazz," and of the three, Stan was the most successful in developing the idiom and converting young musicians to his concept of big-band sound. He thought of his band as a concert orchestra and, in 1946, recorded *Concerto to End All Concertos*, a modest undertaking![22] The composition, which exploited the talents of tenor saxophonist Vido Musso, hardly accomplished the stated purpose of the title as might have been expected. However, the expanded orchestration—five trumpets, four trombones, plus standard sax and rhythm sections; the nontraditional harmonic changes—frequent root-movement shifts by half step; and the frequent changes of tempo—which implied concert rather than dance—captured the imagination of a large number of jazz musicians and fans. Although popular songs continued to play a major role in the repertoire of the orchestra—*April in Paris, Sophisticated Lady*, etc.—compositions of a more abstract stripe began to appear with greater frequency. In 1947, Kenton recorded *Chorale for Brass, Piano, and Bongo*[23] (cf. Bartók, *Music for Strings, Percussion and Celesta* [1936]), *Fugue for Rhythm Section*,[24] and *Abstraction*.[25] The bebop concept of the musician as artist had definitely influenced Stan Kenton strongly, and although bebop, progressive jazz, and swing were, in a sense,

[20] Columbia 38304.
[21] Capitol 57-616.
[22] Capitol 382.
[23] Capitol 10183.
[24] Capitol 10127.
[25] Capitol 10184.

professional enemies, Woody Herman, Stan Kenton, and Charlie Parker had a great deal in common. *Down Beat* magazine, a trade journal for jazz musicians, had established a "Music Hall of Fame," honoring those who had "contributed the most to modern American music in the Twentieth Century." In 1954, Stan Kenton was elected by the largest poll recorded to that date. Before him, only two others, Louis Armstrong and Glenn Miller, had been elected.

For a short while, bebop developed its own big-band style. In 1945, Dizzy Gillespie, now a famous musician, decided to organize a big band. There was a certain prestige that automatically accrued to successful big-band leaders, and this, plus financial and musical considerations, seems to have led many successful combo musicians down the risky garden path. His band did not last the year, but it was reorganized in July, 1946, when he recorded *Things To Come* in New York City.[26] The tempo was absolutely frantic, the performance ragged, and obviously the philosophy was not that of a dance orchestra. The blinding flashes of speed that were the characteristic virtuosic display of bebop musicians in a small combo only wreaked havoc upon the sections of the big band. Musically, this group never came near the quality produced by the combos with which Dizzy had previously worked.

Shortly thereafter, the band of Claude Thornhill, with arranger Gil Evans, played conflated solos by Charlie Parker in large ensembles. In 1947, Thornhill recorded *Anthropology*[27] and *Yardbird Suite*.[28] Entire sections played the solos in unison, and unlike the ensemble of the Dizzy Gillespie big band, the musicians of Thornhill's band played with great precision. Still, big-band bebop was a hopeless road to travel, for the large organizations were too unwieldy for the style, unsuitable for the economics of small-club engagements, and unwilling to cater to the tastes of the dancing public. As a vehicle for playing to a listening audience via recordings or public concerts, the bebop big bands were filled with unrealized potential. However, the turnover in personnel, the tendency for name musicians to want to play in smaller combos, and the lack of arrangements truly distinct from those of the already-established swing bands eliminated the big bebop bands quickly while the big-band business, in general, deteriorated more slowly. During the 1960s, it almost disappeared.

[26] Musicraft 447.
[27] Columbia 38224.
[28] Columbia 39122.

More about Bird

Toward the end of the 1940s, Bird Parker flew miles above the other musicians of jazz on wings of artistic creation unequaled in his day. He had almost destroyed his career with narcotics in 1946 and spent seven months at Camarillo State Hospital in California before his return to New York in the summer of 1947. At that time, he was in complete control of himself and his music, and produced some of his most mature, polished, and inspired work. According to Thomas Owens:

> He [Charlie Parker] was the most influential player in jazz during the last ten years of his life; the musicians who imitated aspects of his syncopations, articulations, tone quality, and repertory of motives are legion. Many are themselves major jazz figures who have developed distinctive styles of their own, but who nonetheless perpetuate parts of Parker's approach to music in their own performances. . . . In addition, few other jazzmen could improvise as fluently at such rapid tempos; few others could create such ornate, well balanced, and moving solos at slow tempos; few others could play equally fine solos regardless of the environment or of the styles and abilities of the accompanying players.[29]

Parker's ability to grace the melodic line of a ballad with an airy filigree that floats above the chords like a bird coasting on a summer breeze is nowhere better demonstrated than in his recording of *Embraceable You* (see Transcriptions), the first take of October 28, 1947 (*SCCJ*, VII/8). During the first five measures of the solo, Bird develops the initial figure[30] through sequential repetition. As the solo progresses, it becomes both more florid and rhythmically supple. All the while, snatches of the opening motive appear amidst the context of long-flowing melodic lines, but the Gershwin melody is avoided almost entirely. As Martin Williams points out, the second version is slightly less distinguished than the first, but is of great interest because it "not only presents a completely different improvisation, it offers a different kind of overall design."[31]

Charlie Parker, the composer, is indistinguishable from Charlie Parker, the improvising performer. Even in compositions that bear his name, such as *Klacktoveedsedstene*, we see that the formal patterns are generally simple, the harmonic changes derive largely from standard circle-of-fifths progressions, the meter is invariably duple, and the melody is always a tonally organized tune

[29] "Charlie Parker: Techniques of Improvisation," p. 270.
[30] Transcription of the opening motive in *SCCJ* liner notes, p. 33.
[31] Ibid.

which stretches, at most, across a 12- to 32-measure form plus introduction and coda. Some of these "composed" melodies are remarkable, and all are well-constructed riffs, which are used to frame the development section of the piece—the improvisations. *Klacktoveedsedstene* (SCCJ, VIII/1) is a good example of a typical Charlie Parker composition. It is a 32-measure composition in **AABA** (pop-song) form with an 8-measure introduction.

Klacktoveedsedstene

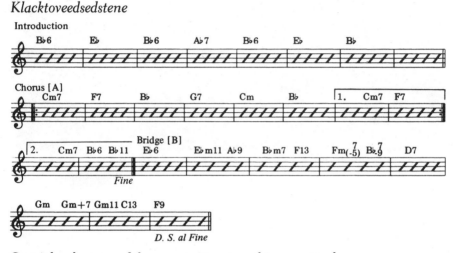

Certainly, the tune of the composition is nothing spectacular.

It is in the improviser's solo choruses that his genius shines forth, and here we see his skill demonstrated in organizing quick-tempo solos into coherent and musically sensitive phrases. The syncopation and discontinuity of the opening of his *Klacktoveedsedstene* chorus has some similarity to the solo ideas of Thelonious Monk, but Charlie Parker was able to organize this disconnected melodic line at an extraordinarily quick tempo. His articulation is always precise, and it serves to heighten the accentuation and syncopation of medial notes within the phrases.

Except for the omnipresent blues harmonies, no other chord progression is used more frequently in jazz throughout the 1930s, '40s, and '50s than those used by George Gershwin for *I Got Rhythm*. Charlie Parker used these same chord progressions in most of the major keys in which he improvised, and *Little Benny* (SCCJ, VIII/2; see Transcriptions), originally released under the

At Bob Reisner's Open Door, Greenwich Village, New York, c. 1953: (left to right) Charles Mingus, Roy Haynes, Thelonious Monk, and Charlie "Bird" Parker.

title *Crazeology,* is one of the many pop-song-form compositions employing this ubiquitous progression.[32]

I Got Rhythm

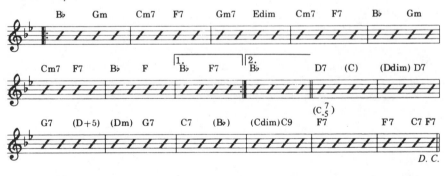

[32] Unfortunately, this recording of *Little Benny* (Roulette RE-105) is technically deficient, for not only was it altered by the record company to add a previous take at the end of the piece—thus destroying the standard formal structure by repeating the final unison riff too many times, but it was also recorded on the disc at too fast a speed—the pitch is raised one half step and the tempo is faster than in the actual performance.

Bird was a master of the blues. In this form alone, under many different titles, he left 175 known recordings,[33] and nowhere was Parker more at ease, less predictable, and musically more interesting than in the middle of a twelve-measure blues chorus. *Parker's Mood* (*SCCJ*, VIII/3), opens and closes with a flourish, and between these markers lay four improvised blues choruses: the first two by Parker (see Transcriptions), the third by John Lewis, and the last by Parker. Typically, the gamut of note values employed by Parker in his solo is large, ranging from a note slightly longer than a half note[34] to thirty-second notes.[35] Many features mark this solo as a melodic improvisation of distinction and importance, but one in particular should be singled out here as the melodic characteristic he controlled better than any other musician in jazz: irregular phrasing that creates a sense of balanced asymmetry as well as an elided phrase structure. The harmonies of *Parker's Mood* move on relentlessly as they would in any other blues composition, but Parker's melodic phrases, separated clearly by rests, resemble the irregular patchwork of a crazy quilt.

No two pieces of the fabric are alike, but all are interwoven. No one statement stands out to dominate the others, but all speak with an eloquent simplicity. A critic who knew the music of Charlie Parker well wrote:

The Durations of Parker's Phrasing

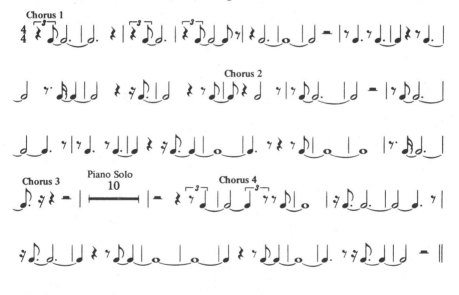

---

[33] Owens, "Charlie Parker: Techniques of Improvisation," p. 9.

[34] Chorus, 4, measure 2.

[35] Groupings of five thirty-second notes to the beat in chorus 2, measure 8.

Charlie Parker's greatness is demonstrated by the body of his recorded art, but what made him great can be heard in even the abbreviated phrase of an individual solo. Listen, for example, only to the end of his first solo on the alternate take, initially unissued, of *Parker's Mood* on the LP *Charlie Parker Memorial* on Savoy. You will hear the soul of a giant.[36]

In his recordings, "Bird Lives!"

[36] Ira Gitler, *Jazz Masters of the Fourties*, p. 57.

THE FIFTIES—A PROLIFERATION OF STYLES

Overview

At the century's halfway mark, the historical strand that linked contemporary jazz to its roots suddenly began to fray. The cohesive thread had been pulled apart in the '40s by the bebop musicians, and now every fiber was bent at a slightly different angle. Classic Dixieland, which had seen a new flowering because of the revival efforts of the '40s, was now competing with its forgery played by youngsters who had never seen New Orleans. The swing bands were scrambling along different musical paths in order to capture a fair portion of a diminishing market. Old-style swing—the Glenn Miller Orchestra fronted by Tex Beneke; progressive swing—the Stan Kenton Orchestra; a modified bebop swing—the Woody Herman Herd; Kansas City–style swing—Count Basie and His Orchestra; the unique swing style of Duke Ellington, and the dozen or so other big bands were feverishly touring the country and hawking their records.

Bebop suffered from the inequities of supply and demand as its imitators proliferated. The "cool school" gave rise to the "West Coast school," which, in turn, generated a competitive "East Coast hard-bop school." An Afro-Cuban element cropped up in jazz, and this gave rise to many short-lived groups that capitalized on this distinctive rhythmic feature. In the struggle to gain secure economic footing, as well as exploit their own musical beliefs, bands and musicians strove to develop unique sounds which would identify them to their public and differentiate them from their competitors. The Billy May band worked out a saxophone-section sound with a distinctive "scoop"; the Pete Rugolo Orchestra amplified an alto flute as a lead instrumental timbre; Jimmy Giuffre developed an amplified clarinet sound that created pitch by minimally vibrating the reed beyond a mere whisper of tonal production; Chico Hamilton introduced a cello into his combo and restricted his own playing, even on up-tempo numbers, to brush-work only; Gerry Mulligan dispensed with the piano as part of the rhythm section in his West Coast quartet; and on and on. No longer was it possible for the historian to look at jazz in the '50s and discern with absolute certainty the mainstream sound, the most influential artists, the most significant developments of the day. In fact, the term "mainstream" gave rise to yet another substyle, "third-stream" music, an attempted merger of classical compositional elements with jazz sounds and performance practices.

But what was happening in jazz was not unique, for the same tearing apart had been taking place throughout the century in literature, the visual arts, and classical music. As the scholar and aesthetician Leonard B. Meyer points out:

> The role and influence of the audience in the ebb and flow of fluctuation [of currently dominant styles] and its relationship to stylistic pluralism are more difficult to assess. One crucial characteristic of the present situation, however, does seem clear and certain: there is not now, and probably will not be, a single cohesive audience for serious art, music, and literature as, broadly speaking, there was until about 1914. Rather, there are and will continue to be a number of different audiences corresponding roughly to broad areas of the spectrum of coexisting styles.[1]

He later continues:

> Particularly in music, the conscious search for new materials, techniques, and principles of organization has led to a significant reduction in the levels of both cultural and compositional redundancy. Or, looked at from the opposite viewpoint: experimentalism has produced a marked increase in the perceptual complexity (information) which listeners are required to comprehend. It is therefore of some importance to consider the arguments for and the consequences of experimentalism in music, especially because both the temptations and the dangers of complexity are greater in music than in the other arts.[2]

Those members of American society who came to jazz for entertainment and relaxation were beginning to turn away from the newer forms because of the increasing levels of musical and intellectual sophistication now being demanded of them. Blithely unaware, or perhaps with premeditated disdain, the younger jazz musicians plunged into the sea of experimental complexity that had already lost the avant-garde of classical music their popular audience. The fruits of these dangerous seeds did not fully ripen until the "new wave" of the 1960s, but the seeds had been planted in the '40s and were beginning to sprout in the '50s.

[1] *Music, the Arts, and Ideas*, p. 175.
[2] Ibid., p. 235.

The first conscious experiments in jazz took place in the mid-1920s, when men like Bix Beiderbecke and Don Redman sought to increase the vocabulary and grammar of jazz materials, but the work of the former affected very few during his lifetime and the work of the latter produced a thoroughly marketable product. The first major step toward increased complexity and lessened redundancy was taken by the first bebop experimenters of the late '30s and early '40s. Their audience was affected, for they no longer had easily remembered tunes, simply understood rhythms, and well-worn harmonic patterns to guide them through the maze of performance; and the musicians were affected first by the philosophy of experimentalism and second by the increasingly complex demands of technical virtuosity. Thus, where classic jazz or swing gave rise to one or two opposing ideas, bebop opened Pandora's box and sent into the world a multiplicty of substyles, each with its own significance and none capable of overpowering all the others.

Cool Jazz

Cool jazz pulled away first. Several musicians in the late '40s can all claim a percentage of the responsibility for this occurrence. Stan Getz, Lennie Tristano, and Miles Davis were the three musicians most instrumental in creating a sound which, in the early 1950s, was quickly labeled "cool." Stan Getz was born in New York City in 1927 and began playing professionally at the age of 15. A year later, he was playing with Jack Teagarden, and during the next four years worked with Stan Kenton, Jimmy Dorsey, and Benny Goodman. In September of 1947, he joined the new Woody Herman band and became part of the "four brothers" saxophone section: Getz, Zoot Sims, Herbie Steward, and Serge Chaloff, three tenor men and a baritone saxophonist who recorded the famous *Four Brothers* that December.[3] The cool sound of Getz's saxophone playing, few overtones and little or no vibrato, on his recording of *Early Autumn* of December, 1948,[4] captured the imagination of many jazz saxophonists and separated them into two camps: the full-voiced, hard-bop style patterned on the sound of Coleman Hawkins and Charlie Parker, and the limpid and airy timbre patterned on Stan Getz. Getz certainly thought of himself as a bebop musician, for his first recording with a group under his own leadership, made in July of 1946, bore the title "Stan Getz and His Be-Bop Boys."[5] Shortly after the *Early Autumn* session,[6] Getz left the Herman band and began

[3] Columbia 38304.
[4] Capitol 57-616.
[5] Savoy MG 12114.
[6] An interesting analysis of the Getz solo may be found in Gunther Schuller, *Early Jazz*, p. 23 f.

Stan Getz, tenor sax

fronting small groups of his own. Nicknamed "The Sound," Getz was internationally recognized as the leading saxophonist of the 1950s, despite a drug problem that almost ended his career. His fully developed artistry, a judicious mixture of cool sound and phrasing with dazzling bebop technical virtuosity, is displayed in his 1952 quartet recording of *Stan Getz Plays.*[7] His melodic lyricism on the ballads *'Tis Autumn* and *Stars Fell on Alabama* and his resplendent technique on the up-tempo numbers, *The Way You Look Tonight* and *Lover, Come Back to Me!,*[8] revealed a technical mastery equal to the best work of any of the bebop saxophonists, and firmly established his leadership.

Leonard Joseph Tristano, born in 1919 and educated in Chicago, was a blind pianist who became the leader of an informal group of progressive jazz musicians including alto saxophonist Lee Konitz, tenor saxophonist Warne Marsh, and guitarist Billy Bauer. He was generally known as a radical thinker and outspoken critic of other contemporary jazzmen, and explored, theoretically and in practice, the possibilities of more complex contrapuntal invention in melodic improvisation. His alto man, Lee Konitz, developed an even lighter tonal conception for his instrument than was being employed by Stan Getz. Konitz's alto sound was virtually free from vibrato, except in carefully controlled situations, and was so devoid of overtones that it closely approximated the timbre of an electronically generated sine-wave tone. In 1949 and 1950, this group, with Arnold Fishkin on bass and various drummers, completed a remarkable series of recording sessions that offered some of the most advanced harmonic and contrapuntal sounds employed in jazz to that date. An example of the complexities these musicians were working with can be heard in their performance of *Tautology*, recorded in June of 1949.[9] The first eight measures of the harmonic progression are not particularly unusual, but the next phrase opens with a striking series of chromatic extended chords:

Tautology

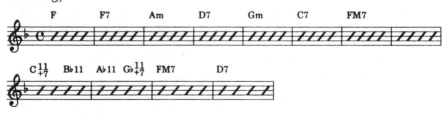

[7] Clef Records MGC-137.

[8] For a detailed analysis of the solo on *Lover, Come Back To Me!* see the author's "Constructive Elements in Jazz Improvisation," *Journal of the American Musicological Society*, 27 (1974), p. 297 ff.

[9] Prestige LP7004.

Leonard Joseph "Lennie" Tristano (piano), with Lee Konitz (alto sax) and Charles Mingus (bass).

The harmonic rhythm of the chord progression is also distinctive, for F chords hold measures 1, 2, 7, and 8 stable; a circle-of-fifths progression moves measures 3–6 at whole-note speed; and then the sudden burst of chromatic chords slips down a whole-tone scale root movement at half-note speed.

Harmonic Rhythm

The contrapuntal opening displays not only careful simultaneous linear writing, but also a melodic style that somewhat approximates serial composition. In the first three measures, the two saxophone lines, considered as a unit, use all twelve of the chromatic half-steps which fill an octave:

The incredible rapidity of their playing and near-perfect unison blend are truly awesome, feats of an unprecedented instrumental virtuosity. The rhythmic ideas and organization were also complex, and the last four measures of the opening riff, which are identical with measures 4–7 of the composition, play duple patterns against syncopated triplets, both within the measure and over the barline.

There is a restless alternation of tension and relaxation in this music which results partly from the extreme tempos, for the listener becomes uncomfortable wondering whether or not the performer will stumble, but for the most part, it is the compositional features which keep one off balance: asymmetry of phrase, avoidance of cliché, constantly shifting accents, and pulsating harmonic rhythm. Tristano's group moved in the direction of decreased redundancy and increased complexity.

Miles Davis at the New York Jazz Festival in 1959, with John Coltrane and Cannonball Adderley in the background.

When the January 21, 1949, recording session of the Miles Davis Orchestra was reissued on a Capitol LP album,[10] the title claimed it was the "Birth of the Cool." In retrospect, however, it seems that the musicians, at that time, were not consciously trying to give birth to anything. Most of the group came from the Claude Thornhill band and were gathered primarily to test some new arrangements by Gil Evans and Gerry Mulligan. The French horn and tuba were unusual additions to a modern jazz ensemble, and the scoring for the reduced orchestration produced a new, light ensemble sonority. Unlike bebop combos, the group had too many melody instruments, and unlike the big bands, it had no homogenous sections. Each instrument in the ensemble was unique: one each of trumpet, trombone, French horn, and tuba for a brass section; one each of alto saxophone and baritone saxophone for reeds; and one each of piano, bass, and drums for rhythm. If a saxophone-section sound was desired, brass would have to fill the mid-range pitches. One of the recordings to emerge from that session was *Boplicity* (*SCCJ*, IX/1), a piece in which Miles Davis carries a mellow and tranquil trumpet lead over the parallel harmonies of the mixed ensemble. This music achieves a casual grace through study and design, and the pleasant, almost unobtrusive, blend marks a clear-cut reform of, if not a sharp break with, the tradition of big-band sounds of the '40s. The rhythm of the opening, with its mixture of quarter-note triplets, eighth notes grouped in three, and duple configurations, shows definite stylistic similarity to the music being created by Lennie Tristano:

Boplicity

and we should note that Tristano's alto man, Lee Konitz, was also the alto saxophonist for the Miles Davis Orchestra.

It would appear that the "crosscurrent" in the title of the piece recorded by Lennie Tristano that same year (*SCCJ*, VIII/8) is the rhythmic tug which takes place between the steady 4/4 of the bass and drums and the irregular groupings of the melodic line played by the alto and tenor saxophones.

[10] Capitol T762.

Lee Konitz, who had played with the Davis and Tristano groups and the Thornhill and Kenton bands, is a central figure in the transformational sounds developing at this time.

Thelonious Monk was another jazz musician fascinated by the rhythmic tug-of-war melodic motives could play with the underlaying pulsation of a jazz rhythm section. In his recording of *Criss-Cross* (*SCCJ*, IX/5), he uses a turning-figure motive to create rhythmic phrases that divide the beat into groups of four and three.

The upward leap after the turn adds interest because of the unpredictable nature of the following interval, and here we see a cliché of bebop being dismembered and reorganized.

Bop was a conscious revolt against swing, but cool jazz was a development of bebop. It went its own way because some musicians found it more interesting and challenging elsewhere, but all of the leaders—Davis, Getz, Konitz, Tristano—were first thoroughly schooled in the bop tradition.

Third Stream

When Miles's orchestra first recorded, at the April 1949 session, Sandy Siegelstein played French horn; at a second recording session in March of 1950, Gunther Schuller came over from the Metropolitan Opera to play French horn with the group. His dual interest in classical music and jazz eventually led to another kind of American music, a substyle labeled "third stream." Classical composition and American jazz were considered the first two streams, and the merger or blending of elements from both was taken to be the third stream. Schuller coined the term, but Charlie Mingus and Teo Macero were successfully experimenting with the incorporation of avant-garde classical ideas into the ensemble work of jazz combos. The Mingus recording of December, 1954, *Minor Intrusion*,[11] has a simple statement of theme by the bass viol, which in turn is followed by a quasi-contrapuntal development. Other independent lines are added to the texture, and at one point Teo Macero uses quarter tones. Once again, the figure of Lee Konitz stands out as a link between the experiments of Charlie Mingus and the other experimental en-

[11] Period SPL1107, also Bethlehem BCP65.

deavors of the early 1950s. In April of 1952, Konitz recorded *Precognition* and *Extrasensory Perception*[12] with the Charlie Mingus ensemble. The instrumentation of this ensemble—alto sax, two cellos, piano, bass, and drums—and the instrumentation for the 1954 session—trumpet, clarinet and alto, tenor and baritone, cello, piano and bass, and drums—shows how the standard jazz sextet combination was being tampered with.

In 1955, Teo Macero brought the most startling sounds to jazz by introducing studio-created electronic effects into the recording of his own composition, *Sounds of May*. [13] He altered the sounds produced by a variety of tone generators electronically, and employed multirecording techniques for voice and instruments. Classical organization of form, polymeters, superimposition of various lines, and new electronic sounds are all combined in a fascinating display.

Gunther Schuller's interest in jazz brought the talents of one of the most accomplished avant-garde composers in America to this music. His technical mastery of the latest compositional techniques allowed him to write a piece that truly merged two distinct sounds. In *Transformation*, a rhythm section of piano, bass, drums, and guitar plus jazz instruments of saxophone, trumpet, trombone, and vibes was combined with the classical woodwinds of flute, bassoon, and French horn. Schuller attempted to maintain both the integrity of the separate ensembles and their idioms while blending them into a musical composition that would produce a new, third sound. [14] Since jazz usually depends heavily upon improvisation, the problems facing a composer who wishes to create a marriage of jazz and classical music are enormous. Most jazz rhythms cannot be notated accurately, most classical performers have not been trained in the jazz idiom and vice versa, and the spontaneity inherent in the improvisational situation is doubly difficult to attain with complex instructions, unfamiliar harmonic sounds, and new structural frameworks. Still, the movement had validity and impact, and the third stream, along with the other prevailing jazz styles, moved on through the 1950s.

West Coast Jazz

The distinction between cool jazz and West Coast jazz is ephemeral at best. Most musicians in the early '50s categorized Stan Getz as a cool-jazz musician and Gerry Mulligan as a West Coast–jazz musician, but there was

[12] Debut M101 and 103.
[13] Columbia CL 842.
[14] Columbia C2L 31.

little deliberate intent on the part of the performers to separate their music into distinct styles. In fact, at the time these names came into being, the musicians were simply playing jazz, most of the white musicians having been trained in the swing big bands and most of the younger black musicians having filtered through the bebop ensembles. However, as the label "West Coast jazz" came into currency, it represented a kind of music that followed the patterns of the Davis Capitol recording sessions: arrangements for middle-sized ensembles or smaller groups, which used single instruments to represent a particular timbre; in other words, one trumpet instead of a trumpet section, one trombone instead of a trombone section. The ensemble would be scored, normally, for a collection of mixed instruments playing the vertical sonorities. For example, a five-tone chord might be scored, from top to bottom, for trumpet, alto saxophone, tenor saxophone, trombone, and baritone saxophone. The Dave Pell Octet used this kind of voicing, with four melody instruments (no alto sax) on *Mountain Greenery*[15] and *Mike's Peak*;[16] and Shorty Rogers and His Giants employed the same technique for five lead instruments on *Popo*[17] and six winds on *Pirouette*.[18] There was great variety in the kinds of ensembles playing in the manner of the West Coast school. Gerry Mulligan fronted a quartet of trumpet, baritone saxophone, string bass, and drums. The opening and closing choruses were carefully arranged, and solos were played to the implied harmonies of the walking string bass, the rhythm of bass and drums, and the occasional backing riff of the other solo instrument. Mulligan's recording of *Makin' Whoopee*[19] is an excellent example of this format, and on the flip side of the disc he adds a guest soloist, the ubiquitous Lee Konitz, who plays outstanding solos on both *I Can't Believe that You're in Love with Me* and *Lover Man*.[20] The removal of a piano from the jazz quartet seems to have stirred others into action, and another West Coast experimenter, Jimmy Giuffre, tried to create jazz by exploiting the little-explored timbres of his clarinet played in novel manners and the rhythmic possibilities of a jazz performance without walking bass and riding cymbal. His 1955 recording, *Tangents in Jazz*[21] removes jazz as far from the dancehall as does the third stream music of Gunther Schuller.

West Coast jazz sold records and caught the public's attention, so, as one might expect, the musicians playing bop in New York and elsewhere tried to

---

[15] Trend LP 1501.

[16] Capitol T659.

[17] Capitol 15763.

[18] Victor LPM 3137.

[19] Pacific Jazz PJLP-2.

[20] A splendid transcription of this remarkable jazz solo is available in John Mehegan, *Jazz Improvisation*, vol. 2 (New York: Watson-Guptill, 1962), p. 111 ff.

[21] Capitol T634.

push their music as a competitive but superior product. These events have been viewed with a certain amount of disdain:

> Reactions to cool jazz were inevitable and, when one remembers some of the derivative claptrap and the pretentiousness produced in its name, to be wished. The reactions centered in the east, and they soon acquired the names "hard bop" and "funky." They were inevitably called "contrived" and "regressive."[22]

Hard Bop

The East Coast musicians resented the lack of emotional involvement inherent in cool and West Coast jazz, so they took their stand around the banner of hot-jazz values: full-voiced instrumental sound, loud dynamics, blistering energy in the up-tempo performances, greater accentuation and emotional fervor in the performance of ballads. They disagreed with the West Coast musicians' concept of swing, that quality of jazz performance which embodies rhythmic life and vitality. Their down-to-earth rhythmic sounds were called "funky," while those of the West Coast basically retained the attitude and values of "cool." Although the East Coast musicians were almost all black, two leading white hard-bop saxophonists were Al Cohn and Flip Phillips. The Al Cohn Quintet, which recorded *Jane Street* and *That's What You Think* in 1953,[23] used Horace Silver, Curly Russell, and Max Roach for a rhythm section, leading bebop musicians all. It was Horace Silver's piano style as much as, or more than, anyone else's playing that gave rise to the term "funky." He played a down-home blues style with strong rhythmic accentuations producing a bouncing rhythmic sound that contrasted sharply with the light-handed, classically oriented piano styles of West Coast men like André Previn. Flip Phillip's recording of *Apple Honey* and *Broadway*,[24] recorded in 1951, are obviously a simple continuation of the mainstream bebop tradition being carried on by Charlie Parker and Dizzy Gillespie.

[22] Martin Williams, "Bebop and After: A Report," *Jazz*, eds. Nat Hentoff and Albert J. McCarthy (New York: Rinehart, 1959), p. 297.

[23] Savoy XP 8123.

[24] Clef 8960.

Something Old and Something New

While cool jazz, West Coast jazz, East Coast jazz, and third-stream jazz were being played and promoted, bebop, swing, and Dixieland could be heard live or "canned" on records. An interesting detail in this complex picture was the successful style change a few musicians were able to accomplish, an unusual, if not extraordinary, feat. As has been noted before, most performers in jazz and dance work develop a musical personality which, when it has reached the level of public recognition, remains virtually unchanged throughout the remainder of the artist's career. The men who have wrought stylistic changes have either been young, and hence working without a recognizable aural personality; or exceptional, in the sense that they were willing to risk their reputations for artistic reasons; or they were the victims of circumstance, in that their innovations were not new but suddenly "discovered" by musicians, critics, and the public. A very few musicians were able to move back and forth from one style to another at will. Stan Getz recorded a hard-bop-style saxophone solo when he joined the Dizzy Gillespie Quintet for a "Dizzy Gillespie–Stan Getz Sextet" session in 1953. The viciously up-tempo performance of *It Don't Mean a Thing* [25] displays all the musicians at their bebop best. Dizzy's muted trumpet

[25] Norgran EPN3.

Oscar Emmanuel Peterson, piano.

flies through his repertoire of bebop licks; Oscar Peterson charges full-speed through a solo that shows him to be one of the most facile and swinging pianists in jazz; Max Roach commands a driving beat that runs the course of the work without letup; and Stan Getz wails with the group as though he had been playing with that particular ensemble for years. It is a remarkable recording, for it blends the talents of several musicians who did not work together regularly, yet the stylistic uniformity of this performance belies that fact.

Maxwell "Max" Roach, percussion.

Bebop was teaching trumpeters to play in a new way, and the technical excellence of Dizzy Gillespie led others to follow in his stylistic footsteps. Miles Davis was one of the many sidemen to work with Charlie Parker and to observe Dizzy Gillespie's playing, but he began to travel a path of lighter sound, understatement, and lyrical melodic lines when he worked with and influenced the musicians developing the West Coast tradition. Fats Navarro was a promising successor to the bebop trumpet crown held by Gillespie, but he died too early in his career to establish the necessary repertoire of performances and recordings needed to supplant the reigning monarch. He was gone by 1950. Suddenly, a new name emerged: Clifford Brown. Born in Wilmington, Delaware,

Clifford Brown (1930–56).

in 1930, he worked with men like Miles and Fats in the late 1940s, and, in the early 1950s, he gained further experience with the bebop pros Tadd Dameron and Max Roach. He won the *Down Beat* "new star" award in 1954. Most musicians and critics considered him the most promising youngster in jazz, a man able to inherit the mantle of Dizzy Gillespie and to combine the best attributes of Davis and Navarro. His recording of *Pent-Up House* with Sonny Rollins in 1956 (*SCCJ*, XI/1) shows him to be a thoughtful soloist who controls his instrument totally and is able to transform phrases into graceful curves brilliantly, even at demanding tempos. Just as he was being fully embraced by the jazz world as a new leader of maturity and stature, he was killed in an automobile accident on the way to a job. He died in 1956, not long after this recording.

"Brownie" was able to play meaningful solos at impossible tempos, and his technique even astounded Charlie Parker, according to legend. However, it was not his speed but his rhythmic feel and unerring sense of structure that earned him a master's reputation after so short an apprenticeship. In an astute analysis of Brown's solo work on *I Can Dream, Can't I*, one authority concludes that Clifford Brown

> 1) apparently thinks at different structural levels simultaneously . . . 2) extracts melodic and harmonic patterns from the original piece and uses them as a means of structural development . . . 3) creates his own rhythmic patterns and uses them as a means of structural development . . . 4) creates pattern unity . . . 7) is not thinking just in terms of playing a variation of the original piece but rather exploring and presenting the structure of the piece. [26]

Highly sophisticated accomplishments such as these are not easily achieved, not even by the talented art-music composer who has the opportunity to reflect on his work and gradually reshape the whole. They were, in fact, the routine products of this extraordinary musician's performance.

/ So many different things were happening in the mid-1950s, it is surprising that yet another revival could take place, but it did. Suddenly, Thelonious Sphere Monk was rediscovered. For several years, in the late '40s and early '50s, Monk had suffered neglect by critics, fans, and musicians, for within the context of the forties' musical values, Monk was an oddball, a strange musician who had little technique and couldn't keep a tune. However, the open-mindedness of the 1950s brought an awareness of the novel and experimental sounds this talented man was creating at the piano and in his compositions. What had earlier been passed off as a lack of technical ability was now being

[26] Milton L. Stewart, "Structural Development in the Jazz Improvisational Technique of Clifford Brown," *Jazzforschung*, 6/7 (1974/75), p. 218.

viewed as a new way of creating musical sounds and organizing musical ideas. He, among others, was beginning to show jazz musicians that successful musical statements are not formulated purely in terms of rapidly moving melodic lines. His improvisation to *Bag's Groove* (SCCJ, X/1) develops a motive consisting of a harmonic crush of half steps, plays with an opening and closing harmonic interval that varies unpredictably, and spreads out the distance between successive statements so that the rhythm does not have the compulsive continuity the old-fashioned listener had come to expect in the standard jazz solo. When working with standard repertoire tunes, for example, *Smoke Gets in Your Eyes* (SCCJ, IX/7) or *I Should Care* (SCCJ, IX/8), Monk approaches the music as an anatomist dissecting a cadaver rather than as a tailor or seamstress clothing a body in folds that elaborate, flatter, hide, and otherwise conform to the latest wrinkles of popular taste. He will pick off a fragment of the melody and set it on its end; he will select a small section of harmony and hold it up to the light; and he will occasionally—and one wonders whether he does it with a sense of satire—throw in an arpeggio with fingers that stumble rather than glide. One critic, in reviewing some Monk recordings of 1952 and 1954, wrote:

> Perhaps because he combined advanced harmonic and rhythmic ideas with an outwardly unsensational technique, it took Monk almost two decades to win acceptance from the jazz public at large. These performances date from a period when most jazz players and the mass of listeners still regarded him merely as an eccentric. The music has a bite and aggressiveness not always present in Monk's later work, though it is only fair to point out that the scope of his talent enabled him to weather the storm. . . . and it is an ironic comment . . . that players of Monk's stature should be virtually ignored at one stage of their careers only to be expected some years later to evince superhuman creativity.[27]

Sonny Rollins

During the 1950s, two tenor saxophonists emerged from the jazz milieu to vie for supremacy on that instrument: John Coltrane and Theodore "Sonny" Rollins. Although Coltrane held the limelight in the early years of the next decade, Sonny Rollins clearly captured the position as most influential tenor man of the late 1950s. Born in New York City in 1930, he is generally considered a product of the Coleman Hawkins and Charlie Parker schools of jazz saxophone performance. Raised in the same immediate neighborhood with Coleman

[27] Michael James, in Max Harrison *et. al.*, *Modern Jazz: The Essential Records*, p. 48.

Theodore Walter "Sonny" Rollins, tenor saxophone.

Hawkins, Thelonious Monk, and Bud Powell, Rollins was a devoted observer of these musicians' efforts at the time bebop was gaining ground as the new voice of jazz. At the age of eighteen, he cut his first professional record with Babs Gonzales, and the next year he recorded with Bud Powell and Fats Navarro, powerful company for a nineteen-year-old musician. He traveled to Chicago in 1950 to study with drummer Ike Day, for he felt his rhythmic conception of saxophone performance could profit from instruction from a percussionist. In 1951, he recorded with Miles Davis and also cut his first recording as a group leader. The years 1951 through 1954 were extremely productive, for Rollins not only recorded with the leading jazz musicians of the era—Miles Davis, Charlie Parker (on tenor), Thelonious Monk, Horace Silver, Kenny Clarke, and the newly founded Modern Jazz Quartet, but he composed three of his best known jazz tunes—*Oleo, Doxy,* and *Airegin.*

Rollins's unorthodox life style had a direct effect on his music, for he periodically went into self-imposed "retirement," probably the apparent result of extreme self-criticism, unrealistic goals, and feelings of inadequacy. From November, 1954, to November, 1955, Rollins "disappeared" to Chicago where he worked as a day laborer. A second period of isolation, from August, 1959, to November, 1961, was spent incognito in New York, where, it is reported, he practiced his saxophone regularly at night on a bridge over the East River. Another period during which he refused to record, 1963–65, coincided with Rollins's trips to Japan and India at the beginning of his formal study of yoga. A fourth period of withdrawal, 1967–72, was suddenly terminated by the release of another record album, "Sonny Rollins' Next Album," and immediate professional activity.

Rollins's most significant contributions to jazz were made during the years between his first and second withdrawal. Joining the Max Roach–Clifford Brown Quintet in November, 1955, Rollins was immediately acclaimed for his new technical mastery of his instrument and for his composition *Valse Hot,* the first of a rash of jazz waltzes that led to greater metric exploration by other jazz musicians. After the death of Clifford Brown in 1956, Rollins's playing became somewhat erratic, but his performance on *Pent-Up House (SCCJ,* XI/1) shows him in complete control of both his instrument and musical ideas.

Another milestone improvisation occurred in 1956 on *Blue Seven*[28] (*SCCJ,* X/3), from his "Saxophone Colossus" album. Gunther Schuller identifies this solo as an example of "real variation technique," a concept not consciously espoused by jazzmen of the period.[29] In one of the most astute analyses of jazz improvisation in the literature, Schuller points out that Rollins employs a me-

[28] Prestige LP7079.

[29] Gunther Schuller, "Sonny Rollins and Thematic Improvising," *Jazz Panorama,* ed. Martin Williams (New York: Collier Books, 1964), p. 248.

lodic motive based on the interval of a tritone (augmented fourth). With this germ motive as a melodic and harmonic stimulant, he improvises employing repetition, thematic variation, diminution, motivic elision, and other compositional devices to lend great structural cohesiveness to the improvisation.

An interesting reaction to Schuller's analysis is made by another scholar, who comments:

> Though analysis reveals Rollins' right to be regarded as a serious artist, it ignores (or glosses over or attempts to explain away) many disparate elements in his musical thinking. For I believe Rollins really a Romantic who has a sense of the "glory of the imperfect."
> Many of these disparate elements may be heard [elsewhere] on this LP.[30]

Indeed, this paradox in both the playing and the personality of Sonny Rollins perhaps explains why it was necessary for him to remove himself from society temporarily on several occasions in order to reassess his life and his music. Few jazzmen are introspective by nature. Sonny Rollins was one of a growing number of jazz musicians who constantly assessed and reassessed their own performance and that of others. This kind of thinking was gradually creating a jazz avant-garde, a group seeking to establish a new order, attempting to expand limits, and constantly searching for better sound. Sonny Rollins, Miles Davis, Thelonious Monk, and Lenny Tristano were but four musicians who placed a positive value on musical development and change. Many of the establishment figures, technically perfect though they might be, chose to maintain their tried and true musical identities at all costs. The existence of a Glenn Miller Orchestra years after the death of the leader is an obvious symptom of this characteristic. Two philosophies were at work in the jazz community: the one to preserve and the other to evolve. And in both camps, the need to survive took precedence over other considerations in driving men forward to their appointed tasks.

Something Borrowed

The introduction of Afro-Cuban rhythms to jazz is thought by many to be no more than a tiny ripple upon a mainstream backwater. However, at least a portion of most groups' repertoire contained a fair percentage of Afro-Cuban numbers. Although some of this music had been around for decades—the

[30] Lawrence Gushee, "Sonny Rollins," ibid., p. 254.

tango was a popular dance in the '20s, the rhumba in the '30s, the conga and the samba in the '40s—it was not until the late '40s that Afro-Cuban came into prominence as a jazz idiom. Dizzy Gillespie hired a Cuban drummer, Chano Pozo, for a Town Hall concert in 1947. He impressed everyone so much that others began to think seriously about some of the implications of the music this man played. At the end of the '30s, Machito and His Afro-Cubans were a popular band group who played in this idiom, but they only touched jazz peripherally. Stan Kenton borrowed some of Machito's drummers in 1948 for a recording of *The Peanut Vendor*,[31] and this in turn seemed to influence trumpeter Shorty Rogers, who produced recordings with his orchestra in 1953 that successfully combined both elements. *Tail of an African Lobster* and *Chiquito Loco*[32] had the swing of West Coast jazz, the freedom of excellent improvising jazzmen, and the Afro-Cuban beat. An exciting combination of jazz and Afro-Cuban rhythms was recorded in 1954 by a nonjazz orchestra featuring Shorty Rogers. Perez Prado composed a score for four saxes, six trumpets, three trombones, French horn, bass, and seven drummers, a larger personnel roster than he maintained in his own mambo orchestra. He recruited some leading West Coast jazz musicians to complete the recording, and *Voodoo Suite*,[33] a multisectioned work, swings through its blend of chanting, drumming, and flashy instrumental sonorities and solos.

The mambo and Spanish and African drums became popular, for a while, in the 1950s, and, like everything else in jazz, can still be found alive and well, in greater or lesser degree, somewhere among the clubs and studios of jazz. For a few brief years, it appeared that Afro-Cuban jazz too would be a major influence, but it was just one more musical idea found at the doorstep of jazz.

Kind of Blue—Miles Davis

One remarkable performer has had a professional history unlike that of most other successful musicians in the trade. Miles Davis started his career amidst the bebop musicians of the '40s, was a leading influence in the development of cool and West Coast jazz in the early '50s, explored the possibilities of jazz modality with both his small combo and a nineteen-piece studio recording orchestra in the late '50s, became part of the radical jazz movement during the 1960s, and is today an enigmatic figure who represents the mystical leading

[31] Capitol W569-5.
[32] Victor LPM3138.
[33] Victor EPB-1101.

edge of the jazz avant-garde. Born in the Midwest in 1926, he began to play professionally in St. Louis from 1941 to 1943. He traveled to New York in 1945 to study at the Juilliard School, and was soon working on 52nd Street with Charlie Parker and Coleman Hawkins. Although his early playing was not spectacular, he gradually acquired more professional competence until he burst upon the national scene with the Capitol recording in 1949 of *Boplicity*[34] (*SCCJ*, IX/1). Leonard Feather correctly notes:

> In the 1960s, Davis was considered by many jazz students to be the foremost trumpeter in the field. . . . [but] Davis' major contributions as soloist and as orchestral innovator were made in the 1950s. Though his performances during the '60s often reached magnificent peaks of brilliance, the historically meaningful work he has brought to jazz dates back to the Capitol band, to the later Evans collaborations, and to the combo in which Cannonball Adderley and John Coltrane were sidemen in 1957-9.[35]

The successful collaboration between Gil Evans and Miles Davis in 1949 obviously had its aftereffects, for in 1957 and 1958, Miles went to the studios again with the master arranger. Their first effort, *Porgy and Bess*,[36] quickly became a popular success, and it was soon followed by similar arrangements. The concept of a jazz soloist featured with a lush orchestra background was not

[34] See the discussion of this recording above, p. 297.
[35] Leonard Feather, *The Encyclopedia of Jazz in the Sixties*, p. 105.
[36] Columbia CL 1274.

Miles Davis is featured soloist with a large, full orchestra.

new, for Charlie Parker, Chet Baker, and others recorded to background sounds of strings, full orchestras, and so on; but in this recording, the orchestration was both novel and perfectly suited to the style of the original music being scored. Also, the soloist, Davis, shed his normal style of solo performance and integrated his lyricism into the whole of the composition and arrangement. He played with the orchestra, not in spite of it, and the blend was so perfect, the sound so refreshing, that this particular recording became immensely popular not only with the layman but in the music world as well. *Summertime* (SCCJ, X/2) is miraculously transformed from Gershwin's classical jazz of the past into the latest music of the '50s. Evans is responsible for inventive instrumental voicing, for accompanying riffs scored for the lush sonorities of French horns, for directing the ensemble in a jazz mood; Paul Chambers and Philly Joe Jones are responsible for infusing rhythmic swing into the large group; but Miles Davis brings to the session improvisations with the full richness of mature understanding. The remarkable achievement of this particular recording lies in the fact that Evans gave full license to his own artistic gifts while creating ideal settings for the gem of Davis's lyricism.

Miles Davis's "Kind of Blue" album[37] was the epitome of avant-garde expression for combo jazz in 1958. No longer were the musicians playing compositions based on a harmonic progression. Instead, the structure rested on modal and scalar themes and patterns. *So What* (SCCJ, XI/3) borrows the framework of popular-song form, **AABA,** but substitutes a single modal scale for a harmonic progression in each eight-measure phrase. After the rubato introduction, it is the bass that plays the melody or scale of the opening chorus. The chording by pianist Bill Evans gives the impression of harmonic changes, but this is merely an illusion, for the first chord serves as a grace to the second.[38] The historical significance of this recording is immense, for not only did the other sidemen of the group—Julian "Cannonball" Adderley and John Coltrane—continue to explore the implications of this session for the remainder of their careers, but it influenced most of the younger musicians who were to establish themselves as professional jazzmen in the 1960s. Davis's solo is spare; those of the saxophonists overflowing with a surplus of fast notes. Coltrane is a little more comfortable working in the new format than Adderley, for the latter creates an illusion of reverting to chordal thinking in his solo by articulating triads on the diatonic degrees of the mode.

When Miles Davis first played with Charlie Parker, he was a novice jazzman in over his head. He floundered occasionally, but was always able to touch bottom, albeit on tiptoe. Through the years, he developed and matured, and by the late 1950s was the most influential musician actively working in jazz.

[37] Columbia CL 1355.
[38] See the example on p. 363.

By the end of the decade, a profusion of jazz styles assailed the unwary listener. Writing in 1961, one astute observer remarked:

> In recent years, activities in the field of jazz have increased so rapidly that the critics seem to be uneasy. A new kind of complaint appears in the columns of the commentators: "Too many unknown musicians are being recorded, too many long-playing recordings are being released, too many jazz festivals are being produced, too many jazz concerts are being staged"—and so on.
>
> A critic known for his determination to let nothing escape him finally admitted, "Man, you can't make all the scenes any more."
>
> It is true that no one human being can keep up with the Niagara of jazz recordings, concerts, and festivals, as well as the radio, night-club, and television appearances of jazz musicians. The increase in both good and bad jazz is enormous, which means, of course, that there is a lot more fine jazz than ever before.
>
> It wasn't always so. [39]

Social Cause and Musical Effect

Or was it? Music and society are thought by some to be a hand-in-glove phenomenon, one the object, the other the image. Music has often been called a mirror of life, a concrete vision of the universe. A thorough intellectual grasp of music gives us both insight and understanding of the society which has produced it. The eminent historian Paul Henry Lang has made the observation in the following elegant statement:

> Every civilization is a synthesis of man's conquest of life. Art is the ultimate symbol of this conquest, the utmost unity man can achieve. Yet the spirit of an epoch is reflected not in the arts alone, but in every field of human endeavor, from theology to engineering. [40]

He takes care to point out that no age necessarily produces a unilateral spirit, and that at any one time three elements are usually present: "the dying past, the flourishing present, and the promising future." [41] Other contemporary writers concur:

---

[39] Marshall W. Stearns, "What Is Happening to Jazz," *Music 1961* (New York: Down Beat, 1961), p. 28.

[40] Paul Henry Lang, *Music in Western Civilization* (New York: Norton, 1941), p. xix.

[41] Ibid., p. xx.

[T]he musician's perception of the world will be conditioned by the intellectual and spiritual climate of his day and this in turn will be reflected in his style. The style of a work of art thus enables us to understand the spirit and ideals of the past.[42]

In a recent, insightful essay, "Changing Patterns in Society and Music: The U.S. Since World War II,"[43] we are told that up until the mid-1950s, American life was stable, traditional, and produced a culture with a distinct flavor. In other words, America, from the war years through 1955, had a unified spirit that exuded "obedience, trust, conformity, cooperation, discipline, of working with others for the common good—with as little friction and disagreement as possible."[44] We learn, further, that "national pride in American military and industrial accomplishments, so strong and universal during and after World War II, was gradually replaced by questions, doubts, and eventual hostility and opposition."[45] The result of this circumstance was that Americans in "every aspect of behavior—dress, speech, political and religious belief, artistic expression, personal relationships . . . [followed] their own individual desires, tastes, and needs."[46] The spirit of the age changed in the mid-1950s, and alongside this change occurred a proliferation of musical styles easily documented by examples from inside as well as outside the jazz idiom. The multiplicity of styles that have emerged from every corner of the music industry in America since 1955 was truly impressive, for we have seen that in jazz alone there was no end of experimentation taking place at the end of the decade. But let us look back a moment to examine the situation of the 1940s. Let us study its implications upon our concept of history, for by using jazz music of the 1940s as a case in point, we will be dealing with known quantities in both the society and its music. We shall scrutinize the events of a single year—1947—because it is equidistant between the advent of cool bop and the close of World War II.

For the moment, let us accept the thesis that in the years immediately following World War II, a feeling of unity and self-righteousness prevailed, brought about by pride in the country's achievements in science, industry, education, and, of course, success in the war. Did this unity, harmony, singleness of purpose extend to the kind of jazz being recorded, broadcast, and played in live performances in 1947?

On February 26, 1947, Charlie Parker recorded *Carvin' the Bird*, a bebop

[42] Beekman J. Cannon, Alvin H. Johnson, and William G. Waite, *The Art of Music* (New York: Thomas Y. Crowell, 1960), p. 3.

[43] Charles Hamm, in Charles Hamm, Bruno Nettl, and Ronald Byrnside, *Contemporary Music and Music Cultures*, chap. 2.

[44] Ibid., p. 69.

[45] Ibid., p. 61.

[46] Ibid., p. 63.

jazz performance. On February 28, 1947, the Stan Kenton Orchestra recorded *Collaboration*, in what was then called the progressive-jazz style. On June 10, 1947, Erroll Garner and his trio recorded *Frankie and Johnny* in a swing piano style. On December 27, 1947, the Woody Herman Orchestra recorded *Four Brothers* in a modern bebop-swing style. On September 23, 1947, Bunk Johnson and His Orchestra played Scott Joplin's *The Entertainer*, a double threat from the classic jazz and the ragtime revival.

This diversity, in one genre only, is in reality only a portion of the sample, for Tristano was offering a precursor to cool jazz in his recording of *Coolin' Off with Ulanov* the same year that Sonny Boy Williamson and Muddy Waters were waxing some down-home blues. The Firehouse Five Plus Two were playing a newly invented Dixieland style in Hollywood, and all in all it is obvious that there was no genuine uniformity of jazz style in 1947.

The situation was no different in popular music, for the popular songs of 1947 included the nonsense songs *Chi-Baba Chi-Baba* and *Managua, Nicaragua*; the sentimental ballads *Tenderly* and *Peg O' My Heart*; the splendid, chromatic jazzlike composition by Sonny Burke, *Midnight Sun*, which Ronny Lang introduced on record with the Les Brown Band of Renown. That same year saw three other songs composed which had tremendous popular appeal: *Fifteen Tons*, a quasi-folk song; *Beyond the Sea*, a pseudo-classical song; and the *Too Fat Polka*, a freshly composed ethnic song.

Popular instrumental ensembles varied from the Harmonicats to the Dorsey brothers to the Guy Lombardo Orchestra. The *Down Beat* poll winners that year were the Stan Kenton Orchestra, the King Cole Trio, Buddy DeFranco, Benny Goodman, Johnny Hodges, Vido Musso, Harry Carney, Ziggy Elman, Bill Harris, Mel Powell, Eddie Safranski, Oscar Moore, Shelly Mann, Frank Sinatra, Buddy Stewart, Sarah Vaughan, June Christy, Sy Oliver, and the Pied Pipers. Not as much variety as 1965 or 1975, but enough to make one wonder about the uniformity of American taste in 1947. Were scholars to attempt to reconstruct a cultural history five hundred years from now, on the basis of stylistic analysis of the music mentioned above, would they arrive at a picture of a unified, tradition-bound society so often suggested as characteristic of the American people in the years immediately following World War II?

On the other hand, can this diversity be explained in terms of the division of a time period into three elements: the dying past, a flourishing present, and a promising future? Not necessarily, and certainly not easily. The death agonies of classic jazz never arrived, or, possibly, death and resurrection took place simultaneously, depending on one's point of view, for the tradition that was handed to Louis Armstrong and was revived by Bunk Johnson, Sidney Bechet, and Louis Armstrong lives in today's renewed interest in classic jazz. In fact, classic jazz has outlived the birth and maturity of many other jazz styles, namely swing and cool. Some of these, if not all, continue to the present in one form or another, and none can fit easily into a tradition that represents the dying past. They are all too much alive. Although one may temporarily prosper while another waxes lean, there does not seem to be any real danger that any of these forms will disappear totally. The music of Parker, Kenton, and Herman were all thought to be the new music of their day. In jazz alone, there were at least three different sounds in 1947 which could fit into the category of flourishing present or promising future. In all probability, there were several others, such as nascent cool, preliminary modal, an early Afro-Cuban.

The concept of uniformity in the American spirit seems to hinge upon the phenomenon of war and its aftereffects as well as a traditional interpretation of history that generalizes about peoples and nations. The victorious nation, forcibly pulled together in a common cause, remains united for a period of time after the close of hostilities. Even if this were so—and one might consider whether the ghetto black and the suburban white identified with each other in 1947—we might wonder what this all has to do with music when we consider that:

> For the student of European political history, for instance, the French Revolution is an event of momentous significance, a point of hierarchic articulation; but for the historian of European music, it is a minor ripple in a style period which runs roughly from 1750 to 1827—or perhaps even to 1914. One cannot assume that history moves in a monolithic fashion.[47]

In other words, does society interact with music at all? Does social cause result in musical effect? It has been suggested that we might do well to inquire further into the question of causality:

> But it may yet be that the same obsession with causality that yields such a curiously one-sided history is responsible also for distortions in the narrative for which so much is sacrificed; that our categorical prejudgments affect not only the interpretation and assessment of art works, but even those matters that we take to be open to "objective," "scientific" treatment: the reading of art works and the attributions of authorship, chronology, and provenance.[48]

Indeed, in the writing of this history, the present author has omitted many people and events, emphasized certain phenomena, and made prejudgments in order to achieve some semblance of a continuous narrative. It would seem, on the basis of this one sample drawn from an era which is scientifically available

[47] Leonard B. Meyer, *Music, the Arts and Ideas*, p. 92.
[48] Leo Treitler, "On Historical Criticism," *The Musical Quarterly*, 53 (1967), p. 205.

to us, that the music of any period is heterogenous and follows its own laws. It is only coincidentally related to the society in which it exists. With regard to jazz, historical certainty is impossible, for in five hundred years, jazz may be seen as a twig floating on the stream of Western music; on the other hand, it may be viewed as the stream itself with classical art music relegated to the museum of the past. Our close proximity to the origins and development of this music has definite advantages, for it allows us to observe all the processes and products of jazz firsthand. We have sufficient objectivity, in the '70s, to view the proliferation of styles in the '50s in relation to the whole picture. We can trace events and musical phenomena back to their beginnings and forward to their present incarnations. We are well removed from the personal conflicts which beset the musicians actively involved in day-to-day performance, yet, thanks to modern technology, we can document each high-water mark in the history of this highly volatile art. We would postulate, further, that it might be quite accurate to say that music is divorced from the realities of daily existence, for it is a man-made abstraction guided by its own rules, shaped by its own creators, and understood only by the members of the society whose ears have been trained to hear it. In this sense, jazz provides us with a greater understanding of current history and the history of music, for it is one of the few recent phenomena which we may study in its entirety. Considered in this way, jazz may be the key to new criteria in musical and historical perception.

LOOSE ENDS AND
PERIPHERAL EVENTS

Loose Ends

In the attempt to construct a coherent narrative which describes and interprets events in a logically unfolding series, it was necessary to omit mention of people, forms, and circumstances that seemed to belong to a tributary or backwater rather than to the mainstream of jazz history. As Donald Tovey explained the problem:

> The source of a river is usually supposed to be that spring which lies farthest from the mouth; but many tributaries must have been united before the waters were worth calling a main stream, and the title is not earned until, as a pious teleologist once preached, it has pleased Providence to bring large rivers into contact with important towns.[1]

Still, it is regrettable that many important musicians should have to suffer neglect because they do not fit neatly into preconceived categories; further, it is lamentable that other noteworthy observations, which could help explain why jazz is as it is, should find no place in these pages. In fact, some of these omissions might be considered distortions of history, for when considered from other valid points of view, their significance may appear heightened and more deserving of mention than some people and events already included. There-

---

[1] Donald Francis Tovey, *The Main Stream of Music and Other Essays* (New York: Meridian Books, 1959), p. 330.

fore, the purpose of this chapter is to pause, temporarily, from the historical narrative and attempt to redress the imbalance.

Vocalists

Singers have been a fundamental part of jazz since its inception, and the fine line of demarcation which separates jazz vocalists from rock, blues, or folk singers is often difficult to draw with certainty. The early classic-jazz singers have already been mentioned in this discussion, but there are others who gained prominence in the '30s as jazz and its boundaries grew. Bing Crosby joined the Paul Whiteman band in 1927 and worked with it for many years. During that time he associated with many jazzmen, including Bix Beiderbecke, Frankie Trumbauer, the Dorsey brothers, Duke Ellington, and Don Redman. Crosby was the first vocalist to take advantage of the advances in electronics, and he developed the modern method of popular singing. He stopped shouting

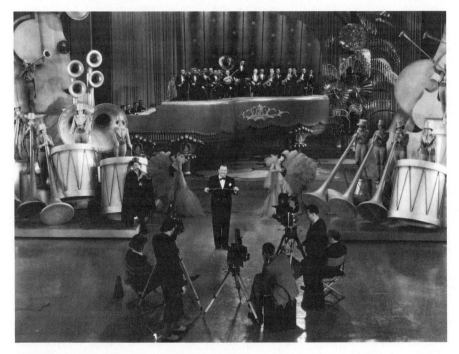

Paul Whiteman, his orchestra, and assorted personnel.

his solos into a megaphone and moved in close to the microphone to sing softly. Most of his recorded vocal work is definitely in the popular idiom—he was the first "crooner," but in 1932, he recorded *Sweet Sue* with the Paul Whiteman band, in which he does some scat singing with Bix Beiderbecke's licks.

The Rhythm Boys—Bing Crosby, Al Rinker, and Harry Barris—reunited with Paul Whiteman several years after leaving his orchestra.

Mildred Bailey, born in Tekoa, Washington, on February 27, 1907, was the first female to sing with a band, and her success was partly responsible for the subsequent fact that nearly every swing band from the '30s through the '50s had to have a woman vocalist. Her brother, Al Rinker, along with Bing Crosby, was one of Paul Whiteman's original "Rhythm Boys," and she joined that band in 1929. She was incidentally, the first white female singer to be completely accepted in jazz circles. Her long career included recordings with the Dorsey brothers, Teddy Wilson, the Casa Loma Orchestra, Red Norvo (whom she married in 1936), and Benny Goodman. Her performance of *Squeeze Me*,[2] featuring Johnny Hodges, Bunny Berigan, and Teddy Wilson, is one of her best performances, for she combined her vocal talents with some of the leading jazz instrumentalists of the day. Although her personal models were the robust voices of the early classic-blues singers, she performed in a light and high-pitched voice that was unusual among female jazz singers.

Billie "Lady Day" Holiday was born in Baltimore, Maryland, in 1915. She began singing in New York clubs in about 1930, when she was just barely a teenager. Her father played banjo and guitar in the Fletcher Henderson band in the early '30s, and she was discovered by John Hammond and Benny Goodman in 1933. The recordings for which she is famous to this day were made between 1935 and 1939. In *He's Funny That Way (SCCJ, IV/6)*, her unique

[2] Columbia 3CL-22.

vocal timbre, her unfailing sense of pitch, and her ability to communicate the emotion of the lyrics as though they were being sung for the first time by the person about whom and for whom they were written are manifest. The warm, intensely personal quality of her singing never obscures her professionalism and talent; her phrasing is always gracious, her dynamics controlled, and her sensitivity to the accompanying instrumental sounds allows for the kind of interplay characteristic of real jazz. Her 1941 performance of *All of Me* (*SCCJ*, IV/7) was so influential that virtually ever female vocalist who sang this number during the following decade tried to imitate Lady Day. The homesick GIs of World War II listened to the young, expressive voice of Billie Holiday offer herself in this romantic ballad, and it became, in its way, a popular classic. The tragedy of Billie Holiday's personal life has been endlessly recounted in print and romanticized on the screen; it would seem that no piece is more closely identified with her own personal tragedy than *Strange Fruit*,[3] recorded in 1949, long after her addiction to narcotics and alcohol had affected her life and her singing.

Another great artist, Ella Fitzgerald brought to jazz singing the kind of virtuosity usually associated with instrumental technique. She was capable of singing melodic lines of a thoroughly instrumental derivation, thereby freeing herself from the strictures of precomposed popular melodies in order to engage in improvised solo singing much as the jazz sidemen were prone to do. Born in Newport News, Virginia, in 1918, she came to New York where she first recorded with Chick Webb in 1935. Throughout her long career, she has performed with virtually every major jazz musician—Louis Armstrong, Count Basie, Duke Ellington, Sy Oliver, Benny Carter, André Previn, and Marty Paich (to mention but a few). In 1946, she began working with Norman Granz, jazz impresario. Her 1964 recording of *You'd Be So Nice to Come Home To* (*SCCJ*, IV/8) is an excellent example of the way she transformed a romantic ballad into a moderately up-tempo, swinging jazz number. Ella considers herself a member of the jazz combo or band, albeit the lead instrument, for in standard format, she states the tune and proceeds with a series of choruses. After the first chorus, the melody of the pop song is discarded, and she improvises a melodic line, occasionally trading phrases with an instrumental soloist, by exploiting intervallic features, range, articulation, rhythmic construction, and so forth. The words of the popular song are entirely incidental to her performance, for they merely provide a vehicle for the articulation of the vocal sounds. Other syllables could be substituted, and indeed, often are. If one compares her solo work with instrumental solos by well-known swing musicians, one cannot fail to see that her vocal lines could be played very successfully by a trumpet or alto saxophone without loss of authority, and that

---

[3] Verve V6-8505. She recorded this song several times from April, 1939, through November, 1956.

most instrumental solo lines could be scat sung by the amazing Miss Fitzgerald. The Roy Eldridge solo on *I Can't Believe that You're in Love with Me (SCCJ,* V/5) is played with the same kind of inflection and articulation that characterizes most of Ella Fitzgerald's vocal solos. In fact, when commenting on the Lionel Hampton performance of *When Lights Are Low (SCCJ,* V/6), Martin Williams compares Hampton's playing to Ella's singing:

> Lionel Hampton was the first jazz vibraharpist. His swing is as impeccable as Ella Fitzgerald's, his harmonic sense is sure (and has grown over the years), and his basic orientation is that of a former drummer.[4]

Frank Sinatra was the first American popular singer to achieve success as a single rather than as a band vocalist. Born in Hoboken, New Jersey, in 1915, he first sang professionally with Harry James in 1939 and Tommy Dorsey from 1940 through 1942. It was at this point in his career that he became a free agent and began to record for Columbia in 1943.[5] Even in his early recordings, such as *The Things We Did Last Summer,*[6] Sinatra sings with a relaxed phrasing and rhythmic sensitivity that have won him the admiration of jazz aficionados for three decades. As his popularity and stature increased, Sinatra seemed to prefer up-tempo numbers for recording with studio bands containing jazz musicians. His 1956 performances of *I Won't Dance*[7] and *The Lady Is a Tramp*[8] were of popular tunes then being played and recorded by jazzmen. His later recordings with Billy May, Neal Hefti, and especially Count Basie and His Orchestra, in October of 1962,[9] are fine examples of Frank Sinatra, jazz singer.

During the early years of the bebop era, Billy Eckstine fronted and sang with a swinging big band of jazz musicians, which included Dizzy Gillespie, Wardell Gray, Oscar Pettiford, Dexter Gordon, Gene Ammons, Leroy Parker, Tommy Potter, Art Blakey, Fats Navarro, Sonny Stitt, and others. His female vocalist was Sarah Vaughan, and both he and Sarah were graduates of the Earl Hines big band. Perhaps the most successful period for the Eckstine musical organization was during the recording ban imposed by the National Federation of Musicians, but a sufficient number of quality recordings was made after April of 1944 to give evidence of the power and swing of this group. In 1949, Sarah recorded *Dedicated to You*[10] with the Billy Eckstine orchestra, and a pop song was transformed into top-flight jazz by both the singer and the rhythmic and

[4] *SCCJ* liner notes, p. 27.
[5] Columbia 36678, *Close to You.*
[6] Columbia CL 1136.
[7] Capitol W803.
[8] Capitol EAP1-912.
[9] Reprise R1008.
[10] MCM 10690.

harmonic devices of the orchestra. In 1954, Sarah recorded *Shulie a Bop*,[11] with her own trio of John Malachi, Joe Benjamin, and Roy Haynes. Her instrumental scat choruses have a precision that puts the subsequent instrumental solos to shame. Even in her nonjazz performances—and she suffered much undeserved criticism from the jazz world as a "sellout"—she was always able to upgrade run-of-the-mill tunes with standard orchestral backgrounds, such as *Dancing in the Dark*, recorded in New York in 1956 (*SCCJ*, VIII/6), by taking command with her pliable and resonant vocal instrument. Her best performances with jazz combos and big bands, such as *Ain't No Use*,[12] show her to be the leading jazz vocalist of the day. One eminent critic is impressed by her voice and musicianship and writes:

[11] EmArcy 16005.
[12] Roulette REP 1026.

Sara Vaughan and Billy Eckstine in rehearsal.

Sarah Vaughan's voice, completely different from that of Billie Holiday, Ella Fitzgerald or any of the other great jazz stylists before her, brought to jazz an unprecedented combination of attractive characteristics: a rich, beautifully controlled tone and vibrato; an ear for the chord structure of songs, enabling her to change or inflect the melody as an instrumentalist might; a coy, sometimes archly naive quality alternating with a sense of great sophistication.[13]

All of these qualities can be heard in her performance of *Ain't No Use*. Sarah Vaughan was the first singer in jazz to exploit the expressive qualities of a vibrato modified in performance from straight tone to wide fluctuation. In this recording, one can hear that rapid notes are attacked dead on pitch, while long cadence notes are frequently begun that way, then slowly widened into a vibrato. The large number of commercial recordings she made during the late '50s and early '60s period caused widespread resentment among jazz musicians, but when she devoted her energies to jazz, she was always welcomed back into the fold, for she sang without peer.

Many other singers could be added to the list of jazz musicians who made contributions to the field: Nat "King" Cole, jazz pianist as well as singer; Joe Williams, blues singer with Count Basie; Mel Tormé, singer, song writer, and drummer; June Christy; Jack Teagarden; and many others have all played their part and had their day. Also, groups like the Four Freshmen and the Hi-Lo's brought refreshing sounds to a market flooded with trite, and often unmusical, popular vocal combinations. One should keep in mind that vocal music and jazz have traveled hand in hand throughout the history of the idiom.

Other Instrumentalists

Quite a few significant instrumental jazz musicians have been omitted from the narrative, either because they seemed not to fit into the categories that were deemed most central to the period under discussion or because they were unique and tended to gather no followers. Without a doubt, however, they more than deserve mention.

Boogie-woogie is a piano style that is characterized by an ostinato figure in the left hand that some people claim derives from an early blues style played in the barrelhouses, honky-tonks, and other places of ill repute. It has, on several occasions, made periodic reappearances in jazz as a popular fad, but very few musicians have used it to the exclusion of other techniques, and it has never

[13] Leonard Feather, *Encyclopedia of Jazz*, p. 449.

Pete Johnson.

enjoyed long-lived success. Clarence "Pinetop" Smith, who died in a brawl in Chicago in 1929 at the age of twenty-four, is reputed to have been the pioneer who developed boogie to its most distinctive form. He recorded only twice, but *Pinetop's Boogie Woogie* was later taken up and replayed as a standard of the repertoire. Many of the influential musicians of jazz played boogie-woogie at one time or another—Count Basie, Mary Lou Williams, Fats Waller, and others, but few musicians achieved any lasting musical success with this rather limited rhythmic form. Meade Lux Lewis, who combined enough musical imagination and technical skill into his performances to overcome boogie's drawbacks, recorded several numbers of merit. His rendition of *Honky Tonk Train* (SCCJ, IV/2) involves an interesting combination of ternary figures with duple. A jagged hemiola results at the quarter-note and eighth-note levels of examples a and b, and the ternary grouping of eighth-notes in the right hand of example c creates a syncopated flutter with the jerky, but regular, pattern of the left hand.

It has been claimed that Jimmy Yancey, a one-time groundskeeper at the Chicago White Sox baseball park, is actually the originator of boogie-woogie, whereas Pinetop Smith, Meade Lux Lewis, Cripple Clarence Lofton, and Albert Ammons later defined the style.[14] Nevertheless, it seems to creep in and

[14] Charles Fox, *Jazz in Perspective* (London: British Broadcasting Corporation, 1969), p. 34.

out of jazz like a panhandler cadging drinks from the doorways. Not too conspicuous, not too important, but always there.

Pianists, because they can work successfully alone, often develop a personal style that is unique, even exciting, but influences no other pianist. When the musician is really good, as was Art Tatum, jazz musicians listened and admired, and what he created was fine. Such was the case with two other well-known pianists closely associated with jazz: Erroll Garner and George Shearing.

Garner is one of the few musicians in jazz, other than the uptown New Orleans musicians of the early days, who had absolutely no formal music education and never learned to read music. Born in Pittsburgh, Pennsylvania, in 1921, he associated with two trained pianists during his youth and learned from them by ear. His early influences were Dodo Marmarosa and Billy Strayhorn, the latter being the talented composer and arranger who collaborated with Duke Ellington during Ellington's peak years. Perhaps as a result of his lack of musical schooling, Garner has never achieved any distinction as a combo or band musician; his fame rests entirely on his solo-piano work, performances most commonly accompanied by string bass and drums. His recording of *Frankie and Johnny* (SCCJ, VIII/4) is typical of his up-tempo piano style, and his unusual rhythmic energy is expressed by spread chords, a strumming left hand, and a right hand that is able to free itself from a lock-step rhythmic conformity with the left-hand work. Among his other distinctions, Garner was the first jazz artist to be booked by the American impresario Sol Hurok, and in 1959 he enjoyed great financial success from his own composition, *Misty*.

George Shearing also has a distinctive style as a featured solo pianist. His standard performance format, piano plus a rhythm section of bass, drums, vibes, and guitar, was distinctive not only because of the instrumentation but also because of his "locked-hands" technique, in which chords are played in both hands moving in similar or parallel motion. In fact, the effect was so startling that it was deceiving, for it disguised both the inventiveness of Shearing's extended harmonies and his interpolation of some pretty sophisticated counterpoint. His 1951 recording of *Over the Rainbow*[15] is typical of his solo style, for it is based on a popular song, employs extended harmonies voiced in his unusual manner, and uses a running flow of counterpoint. The music is scored with the vibraphone and guitar doubling the piano melody in a homophonic texture to which the piano left hand occasionally adds counterpoint lines.

Blind from birth, Shearing was born in London in 1919, one of the few jazz musicians who is not a native American. His keyboard training was thorough, and he was taught to read music from Braille notation. In addition to the vast

[15] MGM 30625.

Erroll Garner

George Shearing and his group in 1949. (Left to right) John Levy, bass; Margie Hyams, vibes; Chuck Wayne, guitar; and Denzil Best, drums.

repository of jazz compositions he has committed to memory, he is capable of recalling all of Bach's *Well-Tempered Clavier* and other similar works note-perfect. In 1952, he wrote a theme song for a New York nightclub, Birdland, and his *Lullaby of Birdland* became one of the best-known jazz tunes of the '50s.

Throughout the history of jazz, few women, vocalists aside, have achieved recognition as performers, arrangers, or leaders. Those who were able to penetrate the inner sanctum of this "man's world" deserve special mention for an accomplishment made doubly difficult by the double standards of sexual discrimination. Lillian Hardin Armstrong, Lovie Austin, Marian McPartland, and Mary Lou Williams are outstanding examples that come to mind, and all four are leaders, composers, and pianists. Of these, Mary Lou Williams has had the most extraordinary career.

Born in Pittsburgh in 1910, Mary Lou Williams was the first woman to achieve recognition as an important figure of the swing era. She began playing professionally at fifteen with the Seymour & Jeanette vaudeville act, and was writing arrangements for the Andy Kirk orchestra, an organization whose success is usually credited to her. Her reputation was established in Kansas City and New York, where she did arrangements for Benny Goodman in the '30s and Duke Ellington in the '40s, and changed her piano style from stride in the '20s, to swing and boogie in the '30s, to bebop in the '40s. She has been closely associated with many other major pianists of jazz—Fats Waller, Earl Hines, Bud Powell, Thelonious Monk, and Cecil Taylor—and is best known today as a soloist, combo leader, and composer of *Zodiac Suite* (1945) and *St. Martin de Porres* (1965).

The Modern Jazz Quartet, well known as the MJQ, was formed in 1951 and capitalized on a growing enthusiasm for jazz among college students. They played concert music that swung gently, and introduced into jazz many elements that were then generally foreign to the style: classical form, greater con-

Mary Lou Williams

The Modern Jazz Quartet: Milt Jackson, vibraharp; Connie Kay (who replaced Kenny Clarke in 1955 and remained with the group ever since), drums; John Lewis, piano; and Percy Heath, bass.

scious attention to counterpoint, and a composed repertoire of longer works. All of its original members were "graduates" of the hard-core bop combos of the forties: John Lewis (piano), Milt Jackson (vibraphone), Percy Heath (bass), and Kenny Clarke (drums). A distinctive feature of this group's sound was the reduced frequency of the mechanical vibrato of the vibraphone. This slowing down of the pulsations of the vibe's vibrato gave the group a sound handle in keeping with the cool and quiet performance, the Brooks Brothers, Ivy League attitude, and the rising popularity of cool jazz in the 1950s. Their recording of *A Cold Wind Is Blowing*[16] was part of a score composed by John Lewis in 1959 for the science-fiction movie *Odds Against Tomorrow*, an anti-war, atom-bomb disaster film. This work takes seven minutes and thirty-one seconds, longer than the standard popular or jazz tune. It depends heavily on the timbral conflict of vibraphone and piano sonorities working against each other, inserts a modified blues format into an extended composition, melts the jazz beat in a plastic effect, and demonstrates the listener-oriented, rather than the dance-oriented, aesthetic in a modern jazz idiom of the 1950s.

Another group that captured the attention of the college market in the 1950s was also led by a pianist, Dave Brubeck. With Paul Desmond on alto saxophone and various players on bass and drums, the Brubeck Quartet recorded at Oberlin College, Ohio University, and the University of Michigan, exploiting the new market for jazz as a concert form where before it had visited the campuses primarily for proms and social dancing. In 1959, the group recorded *Take Five*,[17] a jazz composition in 5/4 time, an unusual meter rarely, if ever, employed in jazz with any success. This recording achieved immediate and universal popularity among the public and jazz musicians, and it led the way for further explorations of metric possibilities in jazz. The Brubeck group quickly followed this recording with a work in 9/8, *Blue Rondo a la Turk*,[18] an up-tempo piece that grouped the nine eighth notes in alternations of ¾ and ⅜.

Classical Musicians

Few classical composers of the twentieth century can claim that jazz had no influence, either positive or negative, on them, for no composer can assert that he has remained totally insulated from this music. Radio, television, mo-

[16] United Artists UAL 4063.
[17] Columbia 41479.
[18] Ibid.

tion pictures, and background music in offices and restaurants have totally permeated our society with jazz and its relatives. Before World War I, however, ragtime was the first American music to catch the ear of European composers. Claude Debussy explored the new idiom as early as 1908, when he composed *Golliwog's Cakewalk* for his daughter.[19] However, John Kirkpatrick has discovered that Charles Ives composed a ragtime dance and thirteen ragtime pieces for theater orchestra between 1902 and 1904.[20]

In 1919, Will Marion Cook took his American Syncopated Orchestra to London and Paris, and the Swiss conductor Ernest Ansermet was so taken by their music, and especially the playing of Sidney Bechet, that he wrote a newspaper article in which he praised them for their "astonishing perfection, superb taste, and fervour of playing."[21] In fact, many serious European musicians were attracted to the new idiom as a source of inspiration. Maurice Ravel composed his *Violin Sonata* between 1923 and 1927, and one of the movements is *Blues*. His *Piano Concerto* for the left hand alone, written in 1930–31, employs jazz timbres, phrases, and rhythms. Neither this nor the *Violin Sonata* could be called a jazz work, but both reveal strong jazz influences. Other Frenchmen incorporated aspects of the idiom into their music: Darius Milhaud in *Le Boeuf sur le toit* (1920) and *La Création du monde* (1923); Erik Satie with *Rag-Time du paquebot* from *Parade* (1917).

Igor Stravinsky wrote a movement called *Ragtime* in *L'Histoire du soldat* (1918); *Ragtime for 11 Instruments* in the same year; and *Piano Rag Music* (1919). In 1945, he composed the *Ebony Concerto* for Woody Herman and his band. Among the other serious and recognized composers who have taken some interest in jazz over the years, one will find Arthur Honegger, Aaron Copland, Paul Hindemith, Ernst Krenek, Kurt Weill, John Alden Carpenter, Louis Gruenberg, Constant Lambert, George Gershwin, Alban Berg, Anton Webern, Pierre Boulez, Roy Harris, William Schuman, Virgil Thomson, Walter Piston, Milton Babbitt, Gunther Schuller, Leonard Bernstein, and many others—an impressive list even if the scope of this study does not extend beyond a mere mention of these men and their music. Jazz not only has its own history, but it is a part of the history of Western music as well. Jazz musicians have listened to their classical counterparts, and, without question, the majority of twentieth-century classical composers have listened to jazz. Many have incorporated jazz elements into their own musical thinking, and, as a historical force, jazz must be taken seriously.

[19] From the *Children's Corner Suite*, 1906–08.
[20] Charles E. Ives, *Memos*, ed. John Kirkpatrick (New York: W. W. Norton, 1972), p. 40n. *et passim*.
[21] Sidney Bechet, *Treat It Gentle* (London: Cassell, 1960), p. 167.

Peripheral Events

A social transformation took place in American society beginning in the mid- and late-1950s, and some aspects of the change affected music directly or indirectly. Youth's disillusionment with American foreign policy and involvement in Asian civil wars as well as their growing awareness of racial injustice at home caused a polarization that later came to be called "the generation gap." A "beat generation" came into existence—drugs, hippies, yippies—and rock 'n' roll, first with Bill Haley and Elvis Presley, later with the Beatles, the Rolling Stones, and the Mothers of Invention, was embraced by teenagers and college students as their music, a sound distinct from the popular music and swing of the older generation. Still later, the young black jazz musicians identified the revolutionary nature and expressionism of the "new thing," free jazz, with the struggles of the militant black nationalists. Music during the '50s and '60s was being more directly affected by extramusical events than it had been in the past. Even religion took a swing at the old order and called for a change in the musical practices of the past. Pope Pius X, in 1903, had called for the return of sacred music for the Roman Catholic Church to the venerable principles of the past; but Pope John XXIII, as a result of the Second Ecumenical Council of the Holy Roman Church, Vatican II, 1963–65, rejected the earlier decree and called for the introduction of vernacular music and languages; this principle of musical reform was accepted by the other Christian churches at about the same time. In America, this was certainly true, for churches suddenly realized that the regular practices of their youth ministry were no longer effective because of the barriers created on both sides of the generation gap. All in all, these socio-political events touched upon jazz as it was being created in those turbulent years.

The Beat Poets

The beat generation and West Coast jazz were children growing up in the same back yard toward the end of the '50s. The simultaneous reading of poetry and the performance of jazz had a brief flurry of popularity, and occasionally (actually rarely) it achieved some artistic distinction. Lawrence Ferlinghetti's poem Dog, written to condemn the Communist "witch hunts" of Senator Joseph McCarthy and his disciples, was satirically heightened by music of the

Bob Dorough quintet. [22] The imagery of an innocent and somewhat personified dog running loose on the streets of San Francisco past meat markets and fire hydrants was in the style of Hollywood cartoons, and the jazz that accompanied the action gave life and interpretation to the words of the poet. The senator was just another fire hydrant to the dog.

On the same recording, Philip Whalen's *Big High Song for Somebody* creates a surrealistic image of the American black in the big-city ghetto—flashy cars, drugs, business, sex, night, all melted together—and achieves great emotional intensity through the sensitive reading of Roy Glenn and the driving musical performance of the Gerry Mulligan quartet. For this particular recording, Mulligan sets aside his baritone saxophone to play a funky, blues piano.

Jazz Educators

The 1950s and college jazz gave birth to yet another phenomenon, the school stage-band movement. A Jazz Educators Association was formed; musicians, some of whom had not apprenticed through the bands and combos of professional jazz, began to publish instruction books on jazz performance;[23] a stage-band instrumentation was standardized (in the image of the Stan Kenton Orchestra); music stores began to push stage-band charts and band paraphernalia;[24] jazz performance was taught in college for credit; and a few institutions began to specialize in this style of instruction. In 1964, four professional jazz schools were operative: the Berklee School of Music in Boston, the Westlake College of Music in Hollywood, the Advanced School of Contemporary Music in Toronto, and the School of Jazz in Lenox.

Some professional jazz musicians have looked with suspicion upon the merits of this undertaking, but over the years many have been won over by the success of the enterprise and quite a few have participated at one time or another in some aspects of the movement. Today, establishment musicians like Dizzy Gillespie, Benny Carter, Maynard Ferguson, Woody Herman, Stan Kenton, and others, as well as younger musicians like Cecil Taylor, Jerry Coker, David Baker, and Christopher White, are all to be found teaching jazz in the classroom. Time is needed to measure the effect of this experience on the music of jazz itself, but undeniably it has been a historical force with some momentum.

[22] World Pacific WP-1244.

[23] A widely used tutor with good results at the high school level is Rev. George Wiskirchen, C.S.C., *Developmental Techniques for the School Dance Band Musician.*

[24] The music being marketed was jazz and quasi-jazz band scores at graded levels of difficulty and arranged for the standard orchestration.

Jazz and the Church

Jazz and organized religion have coexisted, but never integrated, during most of this present century. The immorality of much of its origins made jazz *persona non grata* at the communion table until mid-century. The statement of Pope Pius X in his *Motu Proprio* of 1903 codified a feeling shared by most Christian churches in America:

> The employment of the piano is forbidden in church, as is also that of noisy or frivolous instruments such as drums, cymbals, bells and the like.
> It is strictly forbidden to have bands play in church, and only in special cases . . . will it be permissible to admit wind instruments, limited in number, judiciously used, and . . . [playing music] written in grave and suitable style, and conform[ing] in all respects to that proper to the organ.[25]

As an affirmation of this conviction, Zion City, Illinois, in 1921 condemned and banned jazz music along with smoking and other sinful practices by city ordinance.[26] Still, the intellectual climate changed in the mid-1950s, and an Anglican priest, Rev. Geoffrey Beaumont, composed his *Twentieth Century Folk Mass*, which drew upon the musical materials of the popular-entertainment world in an attempt to bring church music closer to the people of his church through the idiom most familiar to them. The first liturgical jazz compositions were written in 1959, this author's *American Jazz Mass*[27] and Edgar Summerlin's *Liturgical Jazz: A Musical Setting for an Order of Morning Prayer.*[28] The floodgates opened when Pope John XXIII convoked the Second Vatican Council, for among the pronouncements on liturgical reform were instructions concerning sacred music. Article 114 decrees:

> Bishops and other pastors of souls must be at pains to ensure that, whenever the sacred action is to be celebrated with song, the whole body of the faithful may be able to contribute that active participation which is rightly theirs. . . .[29]

Services were translated into the vernacular, instruments were admitted freely into the services, and other musical traditions and idioms were encouraged. In jazz, in 1965 alone, we find Lalo Schifrin composing a *Jazz Suite on Mass*

[25] From the English translation in Nicolas Slonimsky, *Music Since 1900*, 3rd. ed. (New York: Coleman-Ross, 1949), p. 633 f.

[26] Ibid., p. 212.

[27] Evanston, Ill.: Summy-Birchard, 1960.

[28] Unpublished but available, on rental, from the composer (City College, CUNY).

[29] Walter M. Abbott, S. J., ed., *The Documents of Vatican II* (New York: Guild Press, 1966), p. 171 f.

Texts, Mary Lou Williams composing *St. Martin de Porres,* Vince Guaraldi performing at San Francisco's Grace Episcopal Cathedral, and Duke Ellington presenting his first "Concert of Sacred Music" at the same cathedral. Joe Masters wrote a *Jazz Mass* in 1967; Dave Brubeck composed a jazz oratorio in 1968, *The Light in the Wilderness;* and the sight of jazz groups, folk singers, modern dancers, and rock musicians in the churches of America has become commonplace.

Modern-Day Blues

The blues has taken several turns and tumbles, and a recent phase has been labeled the "urban blues."[30] The country-blues singer, the classic-blues singer, and the Southwest territory blues bands eventually turned the corner on a new development.

> The refinements leading to urban blues are best viewed in terms of three phases: the period from 1925 to 1942 chronicled by Driggs—that is, the time when big bands of eight pieces and larger toured the Southwest playing blues in arranged form, an era culminating in the Kansas City florescence; the period from 1942 to 1952 when similar bands toured the same terrain usually featuring a blues singer, electric guitar, saxophone solos, and an even stronger emphasis on rhythm and blues; and what might be called the Memphis synthesis, or the foundation of today's urban blues.[31]

Dominance as a blues center shifted from Kansas City to Memphis and Chicago after World War II, and B. B. King, Junior Parker, and Bobby Bland, with their added accompanimental instruments of brass, electric bass, electric guitar with accessories, and other electronic instruments, created the models for nearly all contemporary modern bluesmen. The following annotated outline of the urban-blues style[32] illustrates various phases and exponents:

> Urban Blues [saxophones added, freer vocal phrasing, arrangements, no harmonicas, etc.]
>
> A. Territories and Kansas City [shouting vocals, big bands, riff accompaniment, 4-beat time flow]

[30] Charles Keil, *Urban Blues.*
[31] Ibid., p. 61.
[32] Ibid., p. 218 f.

(Hot Lips Page, Jimmy Rushing, Joe Turner, Walter Brown, J. Witherspoon, Louis Jordan)

B. Postwar Texas [electric guitar, more relaxed vocals, smaller bands, generally slower tempos, piano still important]
(Charles Brown, Roy Brown, Amos Milburn, T-Bone Walker, Lowell Fulson, Louis Jordan)

C. Memphis synthesis
   1st phase—(Gatemouth Moore, Johnny Ace, Roscoe Gordon, also Jordan and Walker)
   2nd phase—(B. B. King, early Bobby Bland, Jr. Parker)
   3rd phase—(Freddy King, Albert King, Little Milton Campbell, Little Johnny Taylor, James Davis, Buddy Guy, and others who follow the King-Bland-Parker pattern)

D. Industrial [everything electrically amplified, 2 or 3 guitars plus drums, 1 tenor sax optional]
(Otis Rush, Earl Hooker, numerous club bands)

Unquestionably, Jimmy Rushing singing with the Count Basie band represents a phase of blues singing that is jazz oriented, but other developments have followed lines that are only tangential to the subject under study here. However, the influence of urban-blues music on jazz musicians of the '60s is significant, for among the experiments of the avant-garde one will find electronically amplified groups that have emerged from the musical environment of the urban blues.

Rhythm-and-blues was another popular style which had its role in influencing jazz from the 1950s on. The early work of Bo Diddley and Fats Domino laid the groundwork for the extremely popular rhythm-and-blues music of Ray Charles. A merger took place between rhythm-and-blues and popular music on the one hand, resulting in a development labeled "Motown" (a Detroit-based style), and with country-and-western on the other hand, resulting in a folk-rock idiom that was blues-based. The leading exponents of Motown were the Temptations, Little Anthony and the Imperials, and Diana Ross and the Supremes, vocal acts that made dance, dress, and subculture language a part of the style as much as the musical elements themselves. Motown eventually gave birth to another derivative style, soul, in which Aretha Franklin and Isaac Hayes led a musical movement which purported to be the musical voice of the black community. Most of the folk-rock musicians have little, if anything, to do with jazz, but a latter-day white blues singer who died young tragically, Janis Joplin, gained attention not only for herself and her music, but also for a renewed interest in the early classic-blues singers who "belted out" their laments in a manner similar to that which she adopted for her material.

All in all, many events took place in America after World War II that either stemmed directly from jazz or affected jazz in the course of their own developments. A rock 'n' roll historian draws an important conclusion about the imported British groups of the 1960s:

> But the essential significance of the groups in this period, even at their best, is that they generated a wider interest in music that already existed, in the obscurity of Chicago's South Side and Louisiana's bayou country, in the dormant memories of all those who had experienced rock 'n' roll in the mid-fifties, and even in the mass-directed American pop radio stations. To the people who did not know about bar blues and down-home blues, who had relegated rock 'n' roll to a dim memory as a minor experience of their adolescence—or even a major experience but, in any case, irrelevant now—and who had long since ceased listening to the pop radio stations, the Beatles and the Stones were either a revelation or a reincarnation. The British groups reclaimed audiences for popular music who had believed themselves too old and sophisticated for it, who were interested in folk and jazz. And they gave greater confidence to and aroused more interest in some of the singers in the United States who were already interested in the same kind of music. Back across the Atlantic, American record companies . . . began to take a second look at those who presented themselves for audition wearing long hair and scruffy clothes.[33]

Lastly, the record companies themselves were about to become creators of jazz music. With the development of electronic and magnetic tape recording after World War II, refined techniques eventually led to jazz music created in a studio, which could not be reproduced live. Multitrack recordings and electronic creations and distortions produced sounds which were sold to the public as jazz but which could not, as had always been the case before, be reproduced in the flesh by improvising jazzmen. All these developments were, in a sense, a prelude to the 1960s and '70s, a time of change, unrest, experimentation, and general uneasiness. Not only was the music changing at a rate unprecedented in the history of jazz, but the very framework of American society was beginning to show signs of restructuring and renewal. As the 1960s progressed, the turbulence was so great that vision—of artists, laymen, social leaders, politicians, historians—was restricted. Jazz was part of a wild, chaotic stream of assassinations, political chicanery, social confrontations, and multiple ideologies; and jazz musicians, like the rest of society, struggled to keep afloat. These events, which are selective and far from inclusive, were some of the intellectual generators that exerted force on the music and the musicians.

[33] Charlie Gillett, *The Sound of the City: The Rise of Rock 'n' Roll*, p. 292.

FREE JAZZ AND ITS PRICE

A MUSICAL REVOLUTION was brewing in jazz at the same time a social revolution was taking place in America. On November 13, 1956, the Supreme Court ruled that segregation on buses and street cars was unconstitutional. In the fall of 1957, the governor of Arkansas and the people of Little Rock resisted a court order for racial integration of a public high school. Black students were prevented from attending school by armed national guardsmen until the President of the United States ordered U.S. Army paratroopers to Little Rock on September 24, 1957, to guard the students and force the issue. The civil-rights movement in America had momentum.

When a black jazz saxophonist came to New York in 1959 playing an eccentric style of improvised music that rejected traditional musical norms, music that declared itself free of melodic, harmonic, and metric restraints, music that seemed to epitomize an aesthetic of anarchy and nihilism, young musicians of the black community throughout America declared this sound "our thang." Ornette Coleman was as much a spiritual leader as he was a musical innovator, for his music carried with it a message that was interpreted by black Americans to mean freedom, love, and black beauty. Amiri Baraka (LeRoi Jones) writes:

> Ornette Coleman's screams and rants are only musical once one understands the music his emotional attitude seeks to create. This attitude is real, and perhaps the most singularly important aspect of his music. . . . [T]hese attitudes are continuous parts of the historical cultural biography of the Negro as it has existed and developed since there was a Negro in America, and a music that could be associated with him that did not exist anywhere else in the world. The notes *mean something;*

and the something is, regardless of its stylistic considerations, part of the black psyche as it dictates the various forms of Negro culture.[1]

He continues:

> The form of a Coleman solo is usually determined by the total musical shape of what he is playing, i.e., the melody, timbre, pitch and of course, the rhythm—all of these move by Ornette's singularly emotional approach to jazz, in much the same way as the older, "primitive," blues singers produced their music. . . . This *freedom* that Coleman has insisted on in his playing, has opened totally fresh areas of expression. . . . And, of course, Ornette Coleman himself, on his records, or in person, continues to excite intrepid jazz listeners all over the country by the fierceness and originality of his imagination.[2]

Free Jazz—Ornette Coleman

Ornette Coleman was born in Fort Worth, Texas, in 1930, and he is an almost completely self-taught musician. After having made two record albums in Los Angeles in 1958 and 1959,[3] he went to New York City in 1959 to play at The Five Spot. With a white plastic saxophone and a quartet of three other jazzmen who shared his musical sympathies, he packed the house for an extended period but was as much the subject of scorn as of praise. Strong support came from Leonard Bernstein, Gunther Schuller, and John Lewis, men who embraced his music enthusiastically; and violent rejection was almost unanimous from most traditional jazzmen, who saw in his playing a negation of those musical values they had worked so hard to create and fought so long to preserve. Roy Eldridge was quoted as saying, "I listened to him high and I listened to him cold sober. I even played with him. I think he's jiving, baby. He's putting everybody on."[4] Gene Lees has criticized the jazz critics for many unprofessional sins, and he looked to the Ornette Coleman situation as an illustrative example:

> [The critics have a] tendency to be cowed by certain musicians of known erudition because they feel that in taking issue with them they might reveal ignorance or betray inadequacy.

[1] LeRoi Jones, *Black Music* (New York: Morrow, 1968), p. 15.
[2] Ibid., p. 40 f.
[3] Contemporary C3551 and Contemporary M569.
[4] Nat Hentoff, "The Biggest Noise in Jazz," *Esquire* (March 1961), p. 82.

Ornette Coleman.

It seems to me that this problem has found sharp focus in the case of Ornette Coleman. Coleman came to prominence largely on the say-so of John Lewis and Gunther Schuller. Both are exceptionally learned men. Their influence on criticism has been considerable. . . .

Once Lewis and Schuller had put their seal of approval on Coleman, some critics began acclaiming him vociferously: others stood neutralized, afraid of exposing themselves, afraid that Schuller and Lewis, because of their erudition, were able to see things in Coleman's music that they could not. . . .

I would take issue with Coleman's concept of perfect freedom on the grounds that it is anti-music and anti-art. Art is and always has been the ordering of the disparate and chaotic materials of life into a significant shape of expression. Freedom of Coleman's kind is *not* perfect freedom: indeed, in its way, it is perfect slavery.[5]

The strength of the reaction, in retrospect, is somewhat amusing, for Coleman's music, by the standards of the classical avant-garde musicians of the day, was neither new nor shocking. The tone row, atonality, *musique concrète*, electronic music, computer music, random composition, prepared instru-

[5] Gene Lees, "The Compleat Jazz Critic," *Music 1961* (New York: Down Beat, 1961), p. 14.

ments, chance performance, happenings, and even silent music were but a few of the many forays into the possibilities of musical expression being mounted by Western composers before 1959. But the introduction of any of these concepts into jazz had never been accomplished with any security before the thirty-year-old Ornette Coleman took his stand.

Free jazz and aleatoric, or chance, performances have much in common; they are similar in many essential details. Attempts to destroy feelings of structure, direction, and tonality and the introduction of elements of surprise are common to both. The main distinction between the two usually lies in the instrumentation of the ensembles and the nature of the musical training of the performers. The free-jazz instrumentation tends to approximate that of the normal jazz group—melody instruments and rhythm section—but eventually these traditional instruments gave way to sitars, tablas, amplified thumb pianos, police whistles, electronic octave machines, psychedelic lighting, and a host of nonstandard electronic and percussion pieces of equipment. Consequently, some of the free-jazz groups have the appearance of nonjazz avant-garde ensembles.

Both kinds of performers, free jazz and aleatoric avant-garde, operate in aesthetic systems that negate stylistic rules which formerly were valid, rather than in rule-structured systems created for the moment which organize musical sounds toward a definitive style. One tenet of their philosophy is the rejection of style or norms. John Cage claims, "I try to arrange my composing means so that I won't have any knowledge of what might happen. . . . [M]y purpose is to eliminate purpose."[6] In like manner, Ornette Coleman explains:

> I don't tell the members of my group what to do. I want them to play what they hear in the piece for themselves. I let everyone express himself just as he wants to. The musicians have complete freedom, and so, of course, our final results depend entirely on the musicianship, emotional make-up and taste of the individual member.[7]

The random improviser's goal is singular novelty, and this has at least two positive values: it multiplies and expands media, and it makes new and different demands of acuity of perception on the listener. Therein the music begins to demand its price. Noise and silence become relevant. When a style exists, perceptive attention focuses on the permissible; when style is absent, all is allowable, and if the listener is to function sympathetically, he must attempt to accept all stimuli that result from the immediate situation.

[6] Quoted by David Hamilton, "A Synoptic View of New Music," *High Fidelity* 18 (1968), p. 56.
[7] Liner notes by Ornette Coleman, *Ornette Coleman: Change of the Century* (Atlantic 1327), 1959.

It would be a gross exaggeration to say that all the music of Ornette Coleman and his group consists of random improvisation, for this certainly is not the case. His recording of *Bird Food*,[8] a blues-based composition, takes the standard 12-measure format and forces it irregularly into the **AABA** pop-song format. Each **A** is a blues variant, for after a 2-measure introduction, the first **A** uses the first 9 ½ measures of a blues chorus; the second **A** uses 11 measures; and the last uses 10.[9]

Likewise, not all nonjazz avant-garde improvisation is random; in fact, most improvisation occurs within composed pieces with much structural integrity. Pieces which use indeterminate notation within the context of a composer- or leader-dominated score usually expect the improviser to create new music that is contextually fitting and stylistically correct, a seeming contradiction, since style, in the sense of fixed norms, is not actually established. Attention to ensemble, sensitive regard for the efforts of the other performers, is also demanded. What Coleman brought to jazz was new values, not the absence of values. To quote one informed observer:

> The album *Free Jazz*[10] is one of the monuments of his art. Coleman collected eight jazz musicians in a New York recording studio in 1964 [1960], and grouped them in two quartets: himself, Donald Cherry (trumpet), Scott La Faro (bass), and Billy Higgins (drums) in one; Eric Dolphy (bass clarinet), Freddie Hubbard (trumpet), Charlie Haden (bass), and Ed Blackwell (drums) in the other. With no rehearsal, the eight men performed a free improvisation based on no previously known tunes, no planned chord progressions, no planned structure. . . . In listening, one can notice that although the players listen to one another—an idea played by one may be picked up by others, who play it in their own style—each player, even the drummers and bass players, goes his own way rhythmically, harmonically, and structurally. To ears conditioned to traditional jazz, or traditional music of any kind, this music is chaos. To ears that can listen in other ways, it is a fascinating and exciting collage, rich in detail, that changes with each hearing, depending on which instrument or instruments one listens to most closely.[11]

Coleman's drift to free jazz can be seen in the transitional nature of *Lonely Woman* (SCCJ, XII/1) and *Congeniality* (SCCJ, XII/2), for both use a composed tune to introduce and close the piece, a framework for improvised solos. Both use the bebop pattern of unison performance of the riff by lead instruments, and both still rely on an underlying pulse that is less rigid but still

---

[8] Atlantic 1327.

[9] See the author's transcription of *Bird Food* in "Constructive Elements in Jazz Improvisation," *Journal of the American Musicological Society*, 27 (1974), p. 293.

[10] Atlantic SD 1364. An excerpt is included in *SCCJ*, XII/3.

[11] Charles Hamm, "Changing Patterns in Society and Music," p. 68 f.

apparent and continuous. They differ from bebop jazz numbers in the omission of piano, totally unnecessary in an environment without chord progressions; they both stretch phrase lengths into plastic shapes; and they both employ improvisations which lack the goal orientation of harmonically directed solos. But the discarding of traditional values does not imply the casting away of all values, for the solos have motivic integrity, the ensemble adheres cohesively through timbral and rhythmic organization, and the nuances of ensemble balance are carefully maintained by the members of the organization.

The 1947 Dexter Gordon recording of *Bikini* (*SCCJ*, IX/3) was modern for its day and exhibits the fully developed characteristics of bebop, the obvious stylistic parent of Ornette Coleman's music. The 1959 Coleman recording of *Congeniality* was modern for its day, but demonstrated, instead of a fully developed style, a distillation or abstraction of bebop stylistic elements which are reorganized and combined with some of the newer musical thoughts that no longer derive from jazz.

Musical Reactions

Several musicians were immediately taken by the music of Ornette Coleman, but to varying degrees. John Lewis, early defender of free jazz, recorded *Django* in 1960 with his MJQ (*SCCJ*, X/4). Although his words of support indicate an intellectual acceptance of the new music, his recording shows a personal rejection. *Django* follows the well-trod path of his earlier recordings with the quartet, and the listener quickly feels comfortable with the circle-of-fifths progressions, the vibraphone sonorities, and the modified bebop solos.

Charles Mingus, on the other hand, absorbed the new music as a revitalizing influence. His 1963 recording of *Hora Decubitus* (*SCCJ*, X/5) shows an interesting combination of new ideas blended with some of the oldest. The basic structural framework of the piece is the twelve-bar blues, but the sonority is atypical of mainstream jazz groups. The string-bass lead for the introduction is followed by more low-range sonorities played by the baritone saxophone. The blues begin gradually to separate at the seams, and all the while, a second ensemble sound of the remaining instruments, recorded on a separate track, builds in dynamics to effect a textural counterpoint with the first sound. Many jazz musicians were distressed at the seeming absence of beat in free jazz even when they were attracted to other of its features, for it is generally accepted that a solid beat, the jazzman's sense of time, was the key to swing. In *Hora Decubitus*, Charles Mingus attempts to preserve both the beat and the blues within the context of greater freedom of sonority and solo improvisation.

Charles Mingus.

The music of Cecil Taylor shows a preoccupation with complexity. His music boasts well-organized melodies; clever orchestral sonorities; a large repertoire of harmonic materials such as tone clusters, nonfunctional harmonies, and extended chords in multiple voicings; and solid formal structures that are organized on principles other than melodic or harmonic repetition. The free jazz of Ornette Coleman provided external support for the kinds of musical thinking in which Taylor was already engaged, an approach which had already crossed the borderline from jazz to the avant-garde of the university composers. On the most superficial level, the musics of Coleman and Taylor are similar— neither employs traditional melodies and harmonies; beyond that, they are totally different. The former depends heavily on chance; the latter is carefully organized. The former has widely varying performances of the same piece; the latter polishes a singular musical idea.

Taylor's composition and performance of *Enter Evening* (SCCJ, XI/2) brings European compositional thought to jazz as much as it brings the skills and habits of jazz to the workshop of the modern classical composer. He has purposely removed from his jazz its last ties to the world of entertainment and dancing and created a music that can be understood and find acceptance only on a concert stage or on a recording destined for a serious and well-trained listener. At this point, we clearly observe that avant-garde jazz has cost working jazz musicians more than one pound of flesh. It has been intellectualized to a

Cecil Taylor playing at the Newport Jazz Festival, 1957. (Buell Neidlinger, bass, is visible in the background.)

point where a popular market is no longer possible. The listeners for *Enter Evening* must be as musically sophisticated as the performers themselves, a somewhat Utopian dream. Jazzmen of the 1960s found it difficult, almost for the first time, to support themselves by their music. The "new thing" had opened some doors, but it was even more rapidly closing others. Milton Babbitt's outcry, in "Who Cares If You Listen?",[12] was beginning to take its toll on musicians who depended on the public, rather than universities and foundations, for support.

Summarizing the year in jazz in 1963, one critic writes:

> The disparity between the popularity of jazz on records and in person grew apace. There were more jazz records than ever, but there were fewer rooms across the country where the music could be found. In those New York clubs where jazz and only jazz had been the rule, sick comedians and folksingers now provided considerable competition, and the prospect of the hootenanny as a substitute for the jam session became a very real and dismal possibility.[13]

Some of the leading jazzmen rejected the "new thing," and one, Stan Getz, came up with a marketable new sound that caught popular attention for several

[12] Milton Babbitt, "Who Cares If You Listen," *High Fidelity*, (Feb., 1958).
[13] Stanley Dance, "The Year in Jazz," *Music Journal Anthology 1963* (1963), p. 44.

years. In 1963, he and guitarist Charlie Byrd recorded a "Jazz Samba" album,[14] and the totally unexpected popularity of *Desafinado* launched *bossa nova*, the new fad, onto the commercial lanes of American music. Brazilian "experts" were flown to New York for a Carnegie Hall concert, and soon cut-rate records were flooding the display racks in drug stores and grocery stores.

A Central Figure—John Coltrane

John Coltrane was a musician, who, in the parlance of youth, "had it all together." Born in 1926 in Hamlet, North Carolina, he served his musical apprenticeship during the 1940s and '50s working with Dizzy Gillespie, Earl Bostic, Johnny Hodges, Miles Davis, and Thelonious Monk. Coltrane first began playing tenor saxophone with the Miles Davis quintet in late 1955, but his performances at that time received adverse criticism. When the quintet disbanded in 1957, he began working with Thelonious Monk and apparently received enough inspiration from this unique personality to effect a noticeable change in his musical thinking. He began to play more extended solos, thematically organized rather than harmonically derived and directed, and when he rejoined Miles Davis later that year, his solo style had a new distinctive character that critics soon labeled "sheets of sound." A flurry of notes, sometimes over modal scales, an extended range, a new mastery of the upper partials of his instrument, began to draw critical acclaim and attention from fellow jazzmen. It was about this time that Trane began to compete with Sonny Rollins for the distinction of leading tenor saxophonist in jazz. His solo on *So What* (*SCCJ*, XI/3) displays the new improvisational freedom that Coltrane was attempting along modally organized lines. The pianist of the group, Bill Evans, writes in the liner notes of the album:

> Miles conceived these settings only hours before the recording dates and arrived with sketches which indicated to the group what was to be played. Therefore, you will hear something close to pure spontaneity in these performances. The group had never played these pieces prior to the recordings. . . . Although it is not uncommon for a jazz musician to be expected to improvise on new material at a recording session, the character of these pieces represents a particular challenge.[15]

It was the music and thinking of this group that was to give Coltrane his first exposure to the style of playing that would characterize most of his work in the

[14] Verve 8432.
[15] Columbia GCB 60.

John Coltrane.

1960s. It was at this time, too, that he began to take an interest in the music of India, a music which is primarily melodic, devoid of harmony, and organized along principles unrelated to traditional modes of Western musical thought. In the same year, 1959, he recorded the album "Giant Steps";[16] his composition and solo on *Giant Steps* (see Transcriptions) became a new jazz standard, a number imitated by all the young saxophonists apprenticing in the trade.

Coltrane sensed a lack of unifying element in the free jazz of Ornette Coleman, and he found his solution to the problem in the playing of pianist McCoy Tyner and in the modal thinking developed in his earlier days with Miles and Monk. Tyner's use of pedal point in the left hand, which helped organize pitches around a tonal center without resorting to functional harmony, gave the free improvisations of Coltrane a sense of focus absent in the work of his predecessors. This pedal, which resembles the sound of the drone strings of classical Indian instruments in performance, provides a pitch level around which the musical structure can be organized with both increased tension and eventual release.

His recording of *Alabama* in 1963 (*SCCJ*, XII/4) opens with the drone and a simple statement of melodic units or patterns that will be expanded and reorganized in the measures to follow. Even the brief section in regularly measured meter holds to the scalar organization of the modal materials; and the ending, which recapitulates the beginning, employs more activity in the accompaniment, to avoid the monotony of a literal repeat. Even so, *Alabama* is a relatively short number with the air of a jazz ballad and consequently can be viewed as a step along the road to greater freedom and more intense explorations.

"A Love Supreme,"[17] released in early 1965, was the culmination of his thinking in this manner. *Pursuance* is a devastating orgy of furious saxophone and drum interplay. The shrill cries and blur of notes issuing from the saxophone are relentless in the chase, and there is no question that the extramusical ideas stemming from the mysticism that was beginning to pervade the musician's thinking had its effect on the sound produced. At this point in his career, Coltrane achieved his highest public acclaim, for he won simultaneously the Record of the Year award for "A Love Supreme," Jazzman of the Year award, and Tenor Saxophonist of the Year award in the 1965 *Down Beat* reader's poll.

Almost immediately, however, Coltrane formed a new group, augmented with two trumpets, two alto saxophones, two more tenor saxophones, and a second bass player. *Ascension* was recorded in June of 1965, and a seamless fabric of wild and turbulent instrumental and ensemble sounds rips apart.

[16] Atlantic 5003.
[17] Impulse (A) S77.

Sheets of sound rain down in a cloudburst of incredible activity. Total group improvisation created a music that is curiously static, for like a tragedy without comic relief, the principle of unity and variety is violated in favor of one or the other. His last recording session took place in February of 1967, and suddenly, at the age of forty, he was dead. The most intense, effective, and vibrant leader of avant-garde jazz was gone, and the new music floundered, lost its momentum, and began to give way.

But jazz was not dead, and different ideas took hold quickly.

Miles Davis

No jazz musician of the 1960s and early 1970s commanded more respect than trumpeter Miles Davis. Whatever he recorded became the current jazz mode, not because a worshiping fan club idolized his every movement, but because he had the gift for finding and hiring the most promising young jazzmen for sidemen in his groups and giving them a sense of musical direction and awareness which stemmed from his own current thoughts and remarkable talent. When Coleman and Coltrane were making the headlines in the early 1960s, Davis did not jump on the first available bandwagon but, instead, stepped out of the limelight temporarily to listen and ponder. He continued to be professionally active in the early '60s, but his efforts were in the direction of solidifying the ideas of the late '50s—more recording with Gil Evans[18] and further work along the lines of the "Kind of Blue" session. *So What* and a Davis blues, *Walkin'*, were recorded and rerecorded as late as 1964.[19]

In 1966, Davis recorded his "Miles Smiles" album[20] with Wayne Shorter, Herbie Hancock, Ron Carter, and Tony Williams, and as Ronald Atkins explains:

> Often a man will stagnate artistically as a result of plodding constantly through the same material, until he reaches the stage where music no longer offers a challenge.

> To avoid this fate, the wise leader surrounds himself with young musicians of talent and lets their ideas affect the music. Davis has always done this. . . . Once Shorter joined the Quintet, the improvisations became even freer from harmonic ties than before, and Davis's own playing took on new characteristics.[21]

[18] 1961, Columbia CL 1812; and 1962, Columbia CL 2106.
[19] Columbia CL 2453.
[20] Columbia CL 2601.
[21] Max Harrison *et al.*, *Modern Jazz: The Essential Records*, p. 90.

The Miles Davis Quintet playing a dance at the St. Nicholas Arena in November, 1959.

While Coltrane and Coleman, and their younger exponents like Archie Shepp in New York and Roscoe Mitchell and Joseph Jarmen in Chicago, were carrying the implications of free jazz to the extremes of undifferentiated novelty, Miles capitalized on the best ideas of both men and added a framework of musical guideposts within each composition to satisfy the demands of tension and release. A dramatic intensity is added to the fabric of free fluctuation by imposing recognizable shapes of written melodic patterns which recur throughout the progress of extended pieces lending a ritornello or rondo sense of unity to the long improvisations.

Then, while exploring fewer restrictions and looser structures on the one hand, Davis turned about in "Nefertiti"[22] to work with tighter organization and more disciplined ensemble interplay. Suddenly, Miles found the means to blend both these concepts into a unified whole. His recording "Bitches Brew"[23] had a new personnel roster of twelve musicians plus himself and a new instrumentation that included four percussionists and as many as three electric pianos. The sculptured sounds of the electronic instruments provided a structure of floating instrumental timbre underpinning the liquid instrumental solos of Wayne Shorter and Miles Davis. The concept of rondo form, a constantly recurring musical passage or idea, gave vitality and a sense of direction to each of the pieces. The new timbres of the electronic instruments and the new rhythmic flexibility of the young musicians gave Davis one of his best opportunities to explore a variety of soloistic devices. His natural lyricism and ear for color allowed him to create sounds that mesh and contrast with the tonal fabric of the orchestra.

The New Groups

A key figure in jazz thought of the '60s was George Russell, a college-trained musician whose theoretical writing, *The Lydian Chromatic Concept of Tonal Organization for Improvisation*,[24] influenced countless young aspiring jazzmen. Born in Cincinnati in 1923, Russell apprenticed as a drummer and arranger with Benny Carter and later wrote arrangements for Earl Hines and Dizzy Gillespie. Gillespie recorded Russell's Afro-Cuban originals *Cubana be* and *Cubana bop* in 1947,[25] and these Russell charts were some of the most ex-

[22] Columbia CS 9594.

[23] Columbia GP 26.

[24] New York: Concept Publishing Co., 1959.

[25] Victor 20-3145, reissued LPM2398.

ploratory orchestrations the band played during that period. A few years later, the Lee Konitz Sextet with Miles Davis and Max Roach recorded two Russell originals, *Odjenar* and *Ezz-thetic*,[26] in the then-current sound of cool. By this time, Russell had already achieved stature as an arranger for Claude Thornhill, Charlie Ventura, Artie Shaw, and Buddy De Franco, and it was at this point in his career that he completed work on his jazz treatise. In it, he reexamined the traditional tonal resources of jazz and reinterpreted the chromatic implications from a different point of view, one based on Lydian modality. He offered a practical demonstration of these ideas in his 1956 recording, "The Jazz Workshop,"[27] an album demonstrating a good balance between composition and improvisation.

Russell taught at the Lenox School of Jazz, composed for a Brandeis University commission, and, in 1960, formed his own group, which travelled to Europe in 1964 and '65. To a certain extent, the sounds of jazz of the '60s are based on his principles, and for this reason, he is a key figure in the totality of a complex decade.

Many of the Miles Davis sidemen moved on to form significant groups of their own. Josef Zawinul and Wayne Shorter joined forces and formed

[26] Prestige 753 and 853, reissued Prestige 7013.
[27] Victor LPM1372.

George Russell relaxing at a recording session.

Weather Report; John McLaughlin gathered together the Mahavishnu Orchestra; Herbie Hancock, Chick Corea, and Bill Evans went their separate ways to form groups of their own. Modern jazz of the '60s and '70s was exciting and intellectual, and the younger musicians, ones not schooled in the swing bands or postwar bebop combos, were beginning to supplant the older men as artistic leaders.

Mahavishnu John McLaughlin.

The new sounds, however, were not being met with great public acclamation. The combos were hard hit financially, but the big bands, even though they were least responsible for the state of jazz music, suffered most. The large personnel rosters required sizable capital risks by promoters and managers. Still, the genre did not die, and a few innovations in big-band sound enlivened the jazz scene. Maynard Ferguson, who was the first screech trumpet player to play consistently in the ultrahigh range was doing so as early as 1950 with Stan Kenton.[28] He began leading his own band in the early '50s, and its eventual

[28] Capitol 28000-6.

success was due not only to his talent, but also to his sidemen's ability and enthusiasm and, most especially, to the quality of the arrangements being produced by Al Cohn, Ernie Wilkins, Bob Brookmeyer, and Willie Maiden.

Ferguson continued touring with his band until 1965 and reorganized a band again in the early 1970s. His performances contrasted sharply with the feats of the avant-garde musicians who were playing and recording at this time, for he capitalized on his virtuosic skill as a pyrotechnic lead-trumpet player at a time when soloistic virtuosity was being cast aside by others; he depended on the skill of young arrangers to infuse new life into traditional forms while avant-garde musicians were denigrating the concept of form. Willie Maiden was especially talented at adapting West Coast arranging principles of light ensemble sound to the forces of a standard big band. He would weave the counterpoint of saxophone-section work against the lead lines of the trumpet or trombone sections.

Maynard Ferguson kept the possibility of a big-band revival alive, for although the ideas were traditional and not particularly innovative, the sounds were fresh and the players' skills were exciting. Another trumpet player, Don Ellis, formed a studio recording band that did indeed exploit new possibilities

Maynard Ferguson.

for big band: electronic instruments, studio manipulation of sound, and arrangements employing complicated meters. "Electric Bath"[29] is a dazzling exposition of studio musician virtuosity. *New Horizons* has the group playing meters of 17/8 divided into groups of 5 + 5 + 7; *Indian Lady* merely divides 5/4 into groups of 3 + 2, but the lively tempo complicates the problem and multiplies the swing. The leader improvises on a four-valve quarter-tone trumpet, and in one number, *Open Beauty,* improvises in real time to his own improvisations which are being fed back to him through a loop-delay echo chamber. The timbres of sitar, timbales, and standard instruments with their sounds distorted through reverberation amplifiers creates a new kind of avant-garde experiment within the standard framework of jazz composed and arranged for a big band.

Today's jazz is being played by musicians surrounded by stacks of speakers, amplified by solid-state units capable of vibrating the floor of an amphitheater, and generated by electric pianos, keyboard and analog synthesizers, electric guitars and basses, microphoned standard instruments, fuzz boxes, wa-wa pedals, exotic percussion instruments, African and Indian musical devices, and, as always, the voice. The last decade and a half has seen not only the development of portable synthesizers, but also the emergence of young musicians developing a virtuoso technique in the live performance of these devices. Formerly, synthesizers were studio instruments which could only be used for the creation of sound in a piecemeal manner—recorded snippets of tape that would later be joined, laboriously, into complete compositions. Now, Herbie Hancock, Joe Zawinul, and other keyboard players command entire repertoires of synthesized sound which they may call upon freely during their jazz improvisations. The last decade is still too close to allow us to separate the grain from the chaff, but during this period, a number of recorded performances have attracted sufficient attention to merit further comment.

In 1971, Archie Shepp recorded an album, "Things Have Got To Change,"[30] as an expression of his personal political and musical philosophies. He was identified as a black musician with an outspoken awareness of the black man's condition in American society and his newly rediscovered African roots. He combined the lessons of his musical schooling with Coltrane and Cecil Taylor with his impression of African-derived patterns and applied them in a musical commentary on American social problems—*Money Blues, Dr. King, the Peaceful Warrior,* and *Things Have Got To Change.* In a sense, he has used the jazz idiom as the country folksinger used the blues "to tell it like it is" and relieve the pressure of difficult daily life through a catharsis of expression.

Where Archie Shepp's music perhaps will be remembered best for its expres-

[29] Columbia CS 9585.
[30] Impulse AS 9212.

Archie Shepp.

sion of extramusical thoughts, Don Ellis and his musicians continued to explore purely musical ideas. In 1971, they recorded a "Tears of Joy" album,[31] in
which he and his musicians tried again to revitalize the big-band concept. The
instrumentation is one of the most significant features: the leader plays quarter-
tone trumpet and four-valve fluegal horn, the former a strident high-brass instrument with nondiatonic pitch possibilities and the latter similar but producing a mellow high-brass sound; the brass section employs three trumpets,
French horn, and three bass brass instruments (trombones and tuba); the wood-
wind section of four players makes great use of doubling on single reeds, double
reeds, and flutes (all amplified); a string quartet plays amplified instruments;
and a four-member rhythm section of piano, bass, drums, and conga also controls amplified piano, electric piano, ring modulator, pianette, and clavinette.
The composers and orchestrators apparently took a certain amount of inspiration from Near Eastern folk music and arranged scores in meters that grouped
subdivisions of 5, 7, 9, 11, . . . 25, 27, and 33. It is partially the virtuosity of
the orchestra which gives the album its significance, for although these meters
and electronic sounds have been used by others, this jazz group, along with the
Mahavishnu Orchestra,[32] demonstrates their ability to use these devices with
ease and even improvise in a stylistically satisfying manner within complex
contexts.

[31] Columbia G 30927.
[32] *Inner Mounting Flame*, Columbia KC 31067.

The Third World

The search for extraterritorial inspiration by American jazz musicians frequently extended to India. The first importations of these ideas seemed ephemeral, probably done as much for the publicity value as for genuine musical reasons. Eventually, jazz musicians traveled to India to study, not simply to tour, and the increasing popularity of transcendental meditation among college students gave rise to an increased knowledge of Far Eastern ways, both aesthetic and musical. The lasting effect on jazz may be minimal, but in the meantime, some jazz musicians took these matters seriously. In 1967, Paul Horn, a young jazz saxophonist, recorded his "Cosmic Consciousness" album[33] in Kashmir. He is the only jazz musician in the quartet; the other three are native Kashmiri musicians who play sitar, tabla, and dilruba and tamboura. Horn himself restricts his performance to alto flute, and the musical designs created by the quartet are interesting, although they may well not be jazz.

The importance of Africa and its musical traditions on black American jazz-men has taken on new significance in recent years. Africa no longer represents simply the roots, but now it is the source of rhythms, melodic ideas, and extramusical inspiration for much modern jazz. Pianist McCoy Tyner, in 1972, recorded his album "Sahara,"[34] and on the cover we see pictured the modern musician seated amidst the rubble of urban renewal with a koto (a Japanese zither) on his lap. The intended comparison of the distant Saharan sands and the urban trashscape is further qualified by the titles of the five parts of the composition: *Ebony Queen, A Prayer for My Family, Valley of Life, Rebirth, Sahara.* The music of Tyner, on acoustic piano, remains in the style developed earlier by John Coltrane, but added to his playing are rhythmic and tonal effects, by the remainder of the quartet, which occasionally add a layer of impressionistic, neo-African sounds.

Herbie Hancock is one of the most facile and adept improvisers of electronic keyboard sounds, and his 1972 album, "Crossings,"[35] is a remarkable demonstration of sculptured electronic sounds in a jazz context. Although the music is as close to absolute music as jazz can get, the seeming importance of Africa to the musicians becomes obvious when one reads the listing of their names: Mwandishi Herbie Hancock, Mganga Eddie Henderson, Pepo Mtoto Julian Priester, Jabali Billy Hart, Mwile Benny Maupin, and Mchezaji Buster Wil-

[33] World Pacific WP-1445.
[34] Milestone MSP 9039.
[35] Warner Brothers BS 2617.

The cover of McCoy Tyner's album, *Sahara*.

Herbie Hancock listening to a playback during a recording session.

liams. Two additional musicians play Moog synthesizer and congas, and five voices are blended into the total mix.

Postwar jazz piano took a quantum jump in the late 1950s when Red Garland and Bill Evans, both pianists with the Miles Davis combos, revoiced keyboard chords by omitting the root as the lowest sounding pitch and replacing it with the seventh or the third of the chord on the bottom. Garland's 1955 and 1956 recordings with Davis[36] show the transition, and Bill Evan's 1959 work on *So What* (*SCCJ*, XI/3) demonstrates the fully developed modern voicings.

Keyboard Voicing

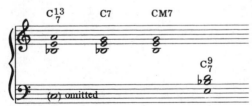

[36] Prestige LP 7007, 7014, and 7116.

In actuality, *So What* is not harmonic in the traditional sense, for it is based on a D Dorian scale, a sound that earlier jazzmen would have accompanied with a minor seventh:

Untransposed Dorian Scale

Evans, however, employs quartal harmony, chords based on fourths rather than thirds, to harmonize the modal scale and uses a sliding progression of parallel chords with roots, or modal tonic, removed from the bass to embellish the harmonic sound.

Bill Evans.

Since that time, Bill Evans, along with Hancock, Tyner, Corea, and other modern keyboard men, has been a prime model for jazz pianists. One of his best albums, "Interplay"[37] is one of the finest examples of combo work, but his later album "Conversations With Myself,"[38] had more impact on the jazz world. Overdubbing, up until that date, had been condemned by most of the jazz musicians as an artificial device incapable of producing quality jazz. In this recording, Evans simply plays music with himself by first recording one track and then adding, successively, others. It is his keyboard technique, best demonstrated here, that has been adopted as the standard practice for all modern keyboard men since.

Progress Report

Rock 'n' roll, technology, developing nations, and American social change have all played their part in the history of jazz during the last two decades. New means and new ideas became available to young improvising musicians, and it is likely that jazz will continue to proliferate, for a time at least, in a somewhat disorderly manner. The determinant remains, as it always has, in the talents of the individual musician, and the variety of exponents who now crowd the field would lead one to expect that jazz will follow no set line of development but will, instead, become separate and distinct parts of a pluralistic world. The jazz-rock bands of the Chicago Transit Authority and Blood, Sweat & Tears will coexist with the Preservation Hall Jazz Band and the piano stylings of Billy Taylor, Josef Zawinul, and Teddy Wilson. The peaceful coexistence of Eastern music and Western jazz may be heard in the sounds of Weather Report and the Mahavishnu Orchestra. Carnegie Hall, the shrine of Western classical music, which has so often offered its stage to jazz musicians, is celebrating a union, at the time of this writing, of traditional with avant-garde jazz in a duo concert by Mary Lou Williams and Cecil Taylor. Jazz is more than a historical style, it is a living music that will continue to change. As one detail in the total picture of world history, it is a new idiom created by obscure American musicians after the Civil War, and it is unlike other Western music in that it relies heavily upon improvisation for its creation, performance, and reconstruction. It is documented chiefly through phonograph recordings, but since most of its past is within living memory, its musicians, critics, and audiences are also able to tell us much about it. As time goes on, the heroes of jazz will be enshrined, the lasting monuments of this art will be preserved in places of honor, and our understanding and appreciation of the past will of necessity be modified by the music yet to come.

[37] Riverside RLP 445.
[38] Verve (A) 68526.

TRANSCRIPTIONS

S.O.L. Blues, Louis Armstrong Solo

Struttin' With Some Barbecue, Louis Armstrong Solo

West End Blues, Louis Armstrong Solo

Lester Leaps In, Head and Lester Young Solo

I Can't Get Started, Dizzy Gillespie Solo

Embraceable You, Charlie Parker Solo

Little Benny, Head and Charlie Parker Solo

Parker's Mood, Introduction and Charlie Parker Solo

Giant Steps, Head and John Coltrane Solo

383

Piano solo

SYNOPTIC TABLE

The following chronology attempts to place the history of jazz in historical context and help the reader view it as a living tradition within the framework of other cultural and sociological events.

JAZZ	ART, LITERATURE, AND CONCERT MUSIC	HISTORY AND SCIENCE
1850	Hawthorne, *The Scarlet Letter*. Jenny Lind sings in New York.	Woman's Suffrage Convention in Salem, Ohio. National population— 23,191,876.
1851	Wagner, *Oper und Drama*. H. B. Stowe's *Uncle Tom's Cabin* appears serially. Melville, *Moby Dick*.	Wabash-Erie Canal completed.
1852	H. B. Stowe's *Uncle Tom's Cabin* appears as book.	Direct rail service, New York to Chicago.
1854	Thoreau, *Walden*.	
1855	Whitman, *Leaves of Grass*.	
1859	Wagner, *Tristan und Isolde*. Gilmore organizes his band.	Darwin, *Origin of Species*. John Brown raids Harper's Ferry.
1860		First pony express. National population— 31,443,321.
1861		Beginning of American Civil War.

JAZZ	ART, LITERATURE, AND CONCERT MUSIC	HISTORY AND SCIENCE
1863		Gettysburg Address and Emancipation Proclamation.
1865		Civil War ends. Lincoln is assassinated.
1866	Dostoevsky, *Crime and Punishment*.	
1867	Marx, *Das Kapital*. First collection of black-American spirituals, *Slave Songs of the United States*.	Alaska purchased. The curve ball invented by William Arthur Cummings.
1868 Buddy Bolden born.		
1869	Jules Verne, *Twenty Thousand Leagues Under the Sea*.	First transcontinental railway completed with a golden spike.
1870		Reconstruction of South completed. National population—38,558,371.
1871	Fisk Jubilee Singers begin first concert tour. Verdi, *Aïda*.	Chicago fire, burns for two days.
1872	In Boston, Gilmore conducts his second Peace Jubilee.	
1873	Degas, *Place de la Concorde*.	
1875	Brahms's *Deutsches Requiem* sung in U.S.	
1876	Twain, *Tom Sawyer*.	United States Centennial. Bell invents the telephone.
1877		Railroad strikes, riots, paralyze the nation. Edison invents the phonograph.
1878	Gilbert and Sullivan's *H.M.S. Pinafore* plays in U.S.	Edison invents an incandescent platinum lamp.
1879	Bland, *Oh! dem Golden Slippers*.	The Richmond and Cleveland baseball clubs play the first no-hit game on record.
1880		Discovery of gold in Alaska. National population 50,155,783.

JAZZ	ART, LITERATURE, AND CONCERT MUSIC	HISTORY AND SCIENCE
1881	Boston Symphony Founded. James, *Portrait of a Lady*.	Panama Canal begun. President Garfield assassinated.
1882		Harvard opens a school of higher education for women (later renamed Radcliffe College). Jesse James shot.
1883	Brahms, *Third Symphony*. Metropolitan Opera House opens.	Maxim invents the machine gun.
1885 Jelly Roll Morton born.	Gilbert and Sullivan, *The Mikado*.	First special delivery postage stamp. Brooklyn Bridge built.
1888	Van Gogh, *The Sunflowers*. Rimsky-Korsakov, *Scheherazade*.	
1889	Rodin, *The Thinker*.	Eiffel Tower completed. Paris World's Fair. The last heavyweight bare-knuckles bout.
1890	R. Strauss, *Death and Transfiguration*.	Oklahoma land rush. National population— 62,979,766.
1891	Tchaikovsky conducts in New York. Nevin, *Narcissus*.	Congress passes International Copyright Act.
1892	Toulouse-Lautrec, *At the Moulin Rouge*.	Direct telephone connection between New York and Chicago.
1893 Scott Joplin plays at Chicago's World's Columbian Exposition.	Verdi, *Falstaff*. Tchaikovsky, *Sixth Symphony*. Dvořák, *New World Symphony*.	Edison builds the first movie studio in America.
1894	*Tom Sawyer Abroad*, by *Huck Finn*, edited by Mark Twain. Debussy, *Prélude à l'après-midi d'un faune*.	
1895	Bates, *America, the Beautiful*.	Congress passes income-tax law; declared unconstitutional. Roentgen discovers X rays.

	JAZZ	ART, LITERATURE, AND CONCERT MUSIC	HISTORY AND SCIENCE
1896		MacDowell, *Indian Suite*. Puccini, *La bohème*. Hogan, *All Coons Look Alike to Me*.	
1897		Sousa, *The Stars and Stripes Forever*.	Klondike gold rush begins. Queen Victoria's Diamond Jubilee.
1898		R. Strauss, *Ein Heldenleben*. Rostand, *Cyrano de Bergerac*.	Spanish-American War. U.S. annexes the Hawaiian Islands. Trans-Mississippi-Omaha Exhibition.
1899	Joplin, *Maple Leaf Rag*. Duke Ellington born. Buddy Bolden playing in New Orleans. Eubie Blake playing in Baltimore.	Schoenberg, *Verklärte Nacht*.	U.S. announces Open Door Policy.
1900	Louis Armstrong born.	Chicago Orchestra plays R. Strauss, *Ein Heldenleben*. Philadelphia Orchestra founded.	Marines help terminate Boxer Rebellion. National population— 76,303,387.
1901		Shaw, *Caesar and Cleopatra*.	Pan-American Exposition in Buffalo. Marconi transmits telegraph signal across Atlantic. Planck develops quantum theory. President McKinley assassinated.
1902	The year in which Jelly Roll Morton claims to have invented jazz.	Mascagni tours the U.S. with his own opera company.	Curies discover radium.
1903		Yeats lectures in the U.S.	Wright brothers' first successful airplane flight.
1904		Puccini, *Madama Butterfly*. Rolland, *Jean Christophe*.	St. Louis Exposition. American occupation of Panama Canal Zone and beginning of American construction of Canal.
1905		Debussy, *La Mer*.	Freud founds psychoanalysis. Ty Cobb joins Detroit Tigers.

JAZZ	ART, LITERATURE, AND CONCERT MUSIC	HISTORY AND SCIENCE
1906	Sinclair, *The Jungle.* Scriabin concertizes in U.S.	San Francisco earthquake and fire.
1907 Buddy Bolden committed to state mental institution. Scott Joplin moves to New York.	R. Strauss's *Salome* opens in New York and creates scandal.	U.S. endures its twentieth depression since 1790.
1908	Bartók, *First String Quartet.*	Automobile manufacture passes 50,000 mark. Peary sails for Arctic.
1909	Schoenberg, *Piano Pieces, Op. 11.* Wright, Robie House in Chicago.	Peary reaches the North Pole.
1910 Papa Celestin Orchestra at the Tuxedo Dance Hall in New Orleans. James Reese Europe organizes the Clef Club in New York.	Ravel, *Daphnis et Chloé.* Stravinsky, *The Firebird.*	Halley's Comet reappears. National population 93,402,151.
1911 Joplin's opera *Treemonisha* performed in New York.	Mahler, *Das Lied von der Erde.*	Amundsen reaches the South Pole.
1912 King Oliver joins Olympia Orchestra under A. J. Piron. Freddie Keppard takes a New Orleans group to Los Angeles. W. C. Handy writes *The Memphis Blues.*	Schoenberg, *Pierrot Lunaire.* Duchamp, *Nude Descending a Staircase.*	The liner *Titanic* sinks after striking an iceberg.
1913 The word "jazz" first appears in print.	D. H. Lawrence, *Sons and Lovers.* Webern, *Six Orchestral Pieces.* Stravinsky, *Le Sacre du printemps.*	60-floor Woolworth Building completed, tallest in the world.
1914 Handy writes *St. Louis Blues.*	Vaughan Williams, *A London Symphony.*	World War I begins in Europe. Panama Canal opens to commercial traffic.

	JAZZ	ART, LITERATURE, AND CONCERT MUSIC	HISTORY AND SCIENCE
1915	King Oliver forms own band in New Orleans. Bechet on clarinet. Morton publishes *The Jelly Roll Blues*. Tom Brown's New Orleans Jazz Band to Chicago.	Ives, *Concord Sonata*.	Einstein, General Theory of Relativity.
1916	Handy, *Beale Street Blues*.	Diaghilev's Ballet Russe to Metropoliton Opera House.	Bolshevik Revolution in Russia. Liner *Sussex* torpedoed.
1917	Storyville area of New Orleans closed. Original Dixieland Jazz Band records for Columbia and Victor in New York. Frisco Jazz Band records on cylinder for Blue Amberol.	Jascha Heifetz, at 16, has Carnegie Hall debut.	U.S. enters World War I.
1918	King Oliver leaves New Orleans for Chicago. The Louisiana Five record in New York for Emerson.	Cather, *My Antonia*. Spengler, *Decline of the West*.	End of World War I.
1919	Original Dixieland Jazz Band plays in London. Will Marion Cook's American Syncopated Orchestra plays in London and Paris. Ansermet praises the artistry of Bechet.	Mencken, *The American Language*.	President Wilson collapses. Race riots in Chicago. First Atlantic airplane crossing.
1920	Charlie Parker born. First blues recording, *Crazy Blues*, by Mamie Smith in New York for Okeh.	Lewis, *Main Street*.	First commercial radio broadcast. The U.S. goes dry—prohibition. National population 105,710,620.
1921	James P. Johnson records *The Harlem Strut* and *Carolina Shout* for Black Swan and Okeh. New Orleans Rhythm Kings working at Chicago's Friar Inn.	Picasso, *Three Musicians*.	First Miss America bathing-beauty contest.

	JAZZ	ART, LITERATURE, AND CONCERT MUSIC	HISTORY AND SCIENCE
1922	Armstrong joins Oliver in Creole Jazz Band in Chicago. Kid Ory records in Los Angeles with Spikes' Seven Pods of Pepper Orchestra (also called Ory's Sunshine Orchestra). Coleman Hawkins records with Mamie Smith and her jazz band for Okeh. Fats Waller records *Birmingham Blues* for Okeh.	Schoenberg, Method of Composing with Twelve Tones. Eliot, *The Waste Land.* Joyce, *Ulysses.*	Carter and Carnarvon open the tomb of King Tutankhamen. Episcopal Bishops eliminate word "obey" from marriage ceremony. Babe Ruth becomes an outfielder.
1923	Jelly Roll Morton's first recording session for Paramount in Chicago. Fletcher Henderson forms his own 10-piece band. Joined by Coleman Hawkins. Ellington returns to New York. Bessie Smith records *Downhearted Blues* for Columbia.	*The Hunchback of Notre Dame,* a silent movie with Lon Chaney.	5,000 "speakeasies" in New York alone.
1924	Louis Armstrong joins Fletcher Henderson in New York. First Wolverine Orchestra recordings with Bix Beiderbecke for Gennett.	Gershwin, *Rhapsody in Blue.* Mann, *The Magic Mountain.* Kafka, *The Trial.*	Stalin becomes dictator of Russia.
1925	Armstrong's first recordings as a leader. Ellington's first recordings as a leader.	Berg, *Wozzeck.* Fitzgerald, *The Great Gatsby.*	Columbia and Victor issue the first electrical recordings.
1926	The first Jelly Roll Morton's Red Hot Peppers recordings in Chicago for Victor.	First talking motion picture. Hemingway, *The Sun Also Rises.* Toscanini guest conductor of New York Philharmonic.	Brigadier General Billy Mitchell court marshalled.
1927	Armstrong Hot Seven recordings. Earl Hines joins Armstrong.	Sandburg, *The American Songbag.*	Charles Lindbergh solos across the Atlantic. First Oscar awarded. Babe Ruth hits 60 home runs.

	JAZZ	ART, LITERATURE, AND CONCERT MUSIC	HISTORY AND SCIENCE
1927 (cont.)	Ellington opens at Cotton Club in New York for a 5-year engagement including national radio broadcasts.		Columbia Broadcasting System inaugurated.
1928	Count Basie joins Walter Page's Blue Devils. Pine Top Smith records *Pine Top's Boogie Woogie* for Vocalion in Chicago. Johnny Hodges joins Duke Ellington. Sidney Bechet joins Noble Sissle in Paris.	Weill, *Threepenny Opera*. First radio broadcast of the New York Philharmonic. Lawrence, *Lady Chatterley's Lover*. Gershwin, *An American in Paris*.	106 radio stations across the U.S.
1929	Fats Waller writes *Black and Blue*.	Faulkner, *The Sound and the Fury*. Hoagy Carmichael, *Stardust*.	Stock market crash: New York Stock Exchange closed for three days. St. Valentine's Day Massacre in Chicago.
1930	Ellington makes first hit recording, *Mood Indigo*.	Stravinsky, *Symphony of Psalms*. Frost, *Collected Poems*.	National population— 122,775,046. Thirty lynchings during year.
1931	Don Redman forms own big band. Duke Ellington records *Creole Rhapsody*.	Stokowski performs Berg's *Wozzeck* in Philadelphia and New York.	Japan invades Manchuria. *The Star Spangled Banner* declared the national anthem. The Empire State Building opened, 102 floors and tallest in the world.
1932	Louis Armstrong visits Europe.	Folger Shakespeare Memorial Library dedicated.	Charles Lindbergh's son kidnapped. Olympic Games in Los Angeles.
1933	Duke Ellington, *Sophisticated Lady*. Billie Holiday records with Benny Goodman and His Orchestra for Columbia. Duke Ellington and Band tour Europe.	Schoenberg comes to America as teacher at Malkin Conservatory.	Franklin D. Roosevelt becomes President of the U.S. Adolph Hitler becomes Chancellor of Germany.

	JAZZ	ART, LITERATURE, AND CONCERT MUSIC	HISTORY AND SCIENCE
1934	Benny Goodman starts the "Let's Dance" series on network radio. Jimmy Lunceford records extensively for Victor and Decca.	Virgil Thomson, *Four Saints in Three Acts,* with all-black cast. Howard Hanson, *Merry Mount.*	Dust storms and drought in Midwest. Adolph Hitler becomes "Der Führer."
1935	Count Basie forms own band. Dizzy Gillespie replaces Roy Eldridge in Teddy Hill Band. Benny Goodman tours to California. The Palomar Ballroom success. Tommy Dorsey starts his own swing band.	George Gershwin, *Porgy and Bess.* Eliot, *Murder in the Cathedral.* Berg, *Violin Concerto.*	Italy invades Ethiopia. W.P.A. established. First night games in baseball.
1936	Woodie Herman forms his own band. First Lester Young dates with the Count Basie combo.	Eugene O'Neill awarded Nobel Prize for literature.	Spanish Civil War. Mussolini completes Ethiopian campaign.
1937	Charlie Parker joins the Jay McShann Band. Gillespie tours France and England with Hill Band. Andy Kirk's Kansas City Band in New York with Mary Lou Williams. Benny Goodman records *Sing, Sing, Sing.*	Orff, *Carmina Burana.* Berg, *Lulu.* Picasso, *Guernica.* Hindemith settles in U.S. Toscanini appointed director of NBC Symphony Orchestra.	Japan invades China. Nylon patented.
1938	The first Benny Goodman Carnegie Hall Concert. The first John Hammond "Spirituals to Swing" concert at Carnegie Hall. Ella Fitzgerald records *A-Tisket a-Tasket* with Chick Webb.	Thomas Mann settles in U.S. Society for the Preservation and Encouragement of Barbershop Quartet Singing in America founded.	Cellulose-acetate-based magnetic tape used for music recording. Bobby Feller strikes out 18 batters in one game.

	JAZZ	ART, LITERATURE, AND CONCERT MUSIC	HISTORY AND SCIENCE
1939	Charlie Parker goes to New York; plays at Monroe's Uptown House. Charlie Christian joins Benny Goodman. Coleman Hawkins records *Body and Soul*. Billie Holiday records *Strange Fruit*.	Bartók, *Sixth String Quartet*. Prokofiev, *Alexander Nevsky*. Roy Harris, *Third Symphony*. Joyce, *Finnegans Wake*. Steinbeck, *The Grapes of Wrath*. Sandburg, *Abraham Lincoln: The War Years*.	World War II breaks out in Europe. International Exposition in San Francisco. New York World's Fair
1940	Charlie Parker's first recordings with Mc-Shann. Ellington records *Concerto for Cootie*. Harry James forms own band; hires Frank Sinatra.	Hemingway, *For Whom the Bell Tolls*. Milhaud settles in America.	Roosevelt elected to third term. National population— 131,669,275.
1941	Stan Kenton's Band opens at the Rendez-vous Ballroom in Balboa, California. Gil Evans joins the Claude Thornhill Orchestra.	National Gallery of Art opens.	Japanese bomb Pearl Harbor; U.S. enters the war. Joe DiMaggio hits safely in 56 straight games.
1942	Max Roach joins Charlie Parker at Monroe's. Bunk Johnson cuts his first New Orleans revival records. Swing bands become service bands. RCA sprays the first gold disc—Glenn Miller's *Chattanooga Choo-Choo*.	All-black performance of *Aïda* at Chicago Lyric Opera.	Recording ban begins. American Federation of Musicians strike against record companies. United Nations Alliance. Congress of Racial Equality founded.
1943	Parker, Gillespie, and Vaughan on Earl Hines Band. Ellington's first Carnegie Hall Concert—*Black, Brown, and Beige*.	Chagall, *Crucifixion*.	Mussolini resigns. Women's Army Corp initiated. 30,000 Sinatra fans riot at Paramount Theater in New York.
1944	Norman Granz presents first "Jazz at	Copland, *Appalachian Spring*.	Roosevelt elected to fourth term.

	JAZZ	ART, LITERATURE, AND CONCERT MUSIC	HISTORY AND SCIENCE
1944 (cont.)	the Philharmonic" concert. Thelonious Monk, 'Round Midnight.		Recording ban ends.
1945	Dizzy Gillespie tours his first big band. Parker and Gillespie record Shaw 'Nuff, Hot House. Woody Herman tours first Herd.	Britten, Peter Grimes.	Surrender of Germany. Atomic bombs dropped on Japan.
1946	Parker records Ornithology and Confirmation. Stravinsky writes Ebony Concerto for Woody Herman and his band.		The Nuremberg war trials begin.
1947	Herman's second Herd records Four Brothers. Ellington, Deep South Suite. Gillespie plays John Lewis's Toccata for Trumpet and Orchestra at Carnegie Hall.	Williams, A Streetcar Named Desire. Charles Ives awarded Pulitzer Prize for Third Symphony (composed 1911!).	Marshall Plan put into operation. Independence of India from British Empire.
1948	Stan Getz records Early Autumn. Stan Kenton begins concert series at the Hollywood Bowl. Louis Armstrong at Nice, France, Jazz Festival.	Cage, Sonatas and Interludes for Prepared Piano.	Columbia introduces first commercial 33⅓-rpm 12" record. First telecast of a major American symphony orchestra.
1949	Lennie Tristano and Lee Konitz record Marshmallow and Subconscious-Lee. Miles Davis records "The Complete Birth of the Cool." George Shearing organizes a quintet. Dave Brubeck records a trio and an octet.	Orwell, 1984. Albert Schweitzer visits U.S.	Communist government in China.

	JAZZ	ART, LITERATURE, AND CONCERT MUSIC	HISTORY AND SCIENCE
1950	Paul Desmond joins Dave Brubeck. Count Basie organizes a septet. Stan Kenton organizes a 40-piece *Innovations in Modern Music Orchestra*. Woody Herman begins his third Herd.	Heyerdahl, *Kon-Tiki; Across the Pacific by Raft*.	Beginning of the Korean War. Hydrogen-bomb development approved. National Population— 150,697,361.
1951	Louis Bellson joins Duke Ellington. Kenton records Graettinger's *City of Glass*. Dave Brubeck forms a quartet with Paul Desmond.	Menotti, *Amahl and the Night Visitors*. Boulez, *Polyphonie X*.	Formation of NATO.
1952	Gerry Mulligan organizes a quartet without a piano. The Modern Jazz Quartet record *Vendome* and *La Ronde*. Granz takes "Jazz at the Philharmonic" to Europe.	Columbia University electronic studio founded. Hemingway, *The Old Man and the Sea*.	Hydrogen bomb exploded in the Marshall Islands.
1953	Miles Davis records *Walkin'*.	Stockhausen, *Kontra-Punkte*. Stravinsky, *The Rake's Progress*. Baldwin, *Go Tell It on the Mountain*.	Eisenhower inaugurated President. End of the Korean War. Sen. Joseph McCarthy reigns as chairman of the Senate Permanent Investigating Committee.
1954	J. J. Johnson and Kai Winding organize a trombone-duo-lead quartet. The first Newport Jazz Festival takes place. Blues singer Joe Williams joins Count Basie. Sonny Rollins records *Airegin* and *Oleo*.	Gershwin's *Porgy and Bess*, with black company, sent on worldwide State Department tour.	Vietnam War begins. Supreme Court rules racial segregation in public schools unconstitutional. First atom-powered submarine.
1955	Death of Charlie Parker. John Coltrane joins Miles Davis quintet.	Boulez, *Le Marteau sans maître*.	Salk perfects polio vaccine. NBC telecasted in "compatible color."

	JAZZ	ART, LITERATURE, AND CONCERT MUSIC	HISTORY AND SCIENCE
1955 (cont.)	Clifford Brown records *Joy Spring*. Teo Macero incorporates electronic music techniques in third-stream work, *Sounds of May*.		
1956	Jazz used as international exchange item: Gillespie tours Middle East; Kenton tours England; Heath tours America; Goodman tours Far East. Horace Silver forms a quartet and records *Opus De Funk*. Clifford Brown dies in an auto accident.	Bernstein, *Candide*. Schuman, *New England Triptych*.	Russian tanks invade Hungary. Grace Kelly marries Prince Rainier III of Monaco. Don Larsen pitches first World Series no-hitter, for the Yankees.
1957	John Coltrane records "Blue Train" album. Brandeis University Festival of the Arts Jazz Concert with commissioned works by Mingus, Giuffre, Schuller, Babbitt, and Shapero.	Bernstein, *West Side Story*.	Gov. Faubus calls out National Guard to prevent desegregation of Little Rock public schools. First Sputnik orbited.
1958	First Ornette Coleman recording. Davis and Gil Evans collaborate for *Porgy and Bess* album.	Barber and Menotti, *Vanessa*. Pasternak, *Dr. Zhivago*.	The first stereo records issued. Nautilus cruises under the North Pole.
1959	Coleman, in New York, records "The Shape of Jazz to Come" and "Change of the Century." Miles Davis records "Kind of Blue" with J. Adderley, Coltrane, and B. Evans. Coltrane records his "Giant Steps" album.	Barzun, *The House of Intellect*. Frank Lloyd Wright, Guggenheim Museum in New York.	Alaska and Hawaii become 49th and 50th states. Castro overthrows Batista government in Cuba.

	JAZZ	ART, LITERATURE, AND CONCERT MUSIC	HISTORY AND SCIENCE
1960	A riot takes place at the Newport Jazz Festival. The Ornette Coleman Double Quartet records "Free Jazz."	Boulez, *Pli selon pli.* Pinter, *The Caretaker.*	Recording studios begin to use multitrack tape recorders. Black students in Greensboro, N.C., stage a sit-down demonstration against segregated lunch counters. National population— 179,323,175.
1961	Eric Dolphy and John Coltrane collaborate.	Carter, *Double Concerto.* Penderecki, *Lament for the Victims of Hiroshima.* "Art of Assemblage" show at Museum of Modern Art.	Berlin Wall erected. First manned space flights. Roger Maris hits 61 home runs, topping Babe Ruth's record.
1962	Archie Shepp leaves Cecil Taylor and forms Shepp-Dixon Quartet.	Britten, *War Requiem.* Albee, *Who's Afraid of Virginia Woolf?* Lincoln Center for the Performing Arts opens in New York.	Cuban missile crisis. Vatican Council II convenes.
1963	Coltrane's *Alabama* a reaction to racial tension in South. Mingus records *Hora Decubitus.* Successful venture in multirecording improvisation: Bill Evans, "Conversations With Myself."	Carson, *Silent Spring.*	President Kennedy assassinated. Increasing U.S. involvement in Vietnam.
1964	Coltrane and Tyner in "A Love Supreme" session.	Bellow, *Herzog.*	U.S. Civil Rights Bill passed. Martin Luther King awarded Nobel peace prize.
1965	John Coltrane, *Ascension.* Ornette Coleman reemerges in New York with a Trio.	*The Autobiography of Malcolm X.* First performance of Ives's *Fourth Symphony.*	Civil Rights March in Alabama. Malcolm X assassinated.
1966	Cecil Taylor records "Looking Ahead" album.	Pinter, *The Homecoming.* Barber, *Antony and Cleopatra.*	First space walk.
1967	Davis, Shorter, Hancock, Carter, and Williams record *Nefertiti.* John Coltrane dies.	The Beatles, *Sergeant Pepper's Lonely Hearts Club Band.*	Israeli-Arab Six Day War. First successful heart transplant.

	JAZZ	ART, LITERATURE, AND CONCERT MUSIC	HISTORY AND SCIENCE
1968	The Jazz Composers' Orchestra, a cooperative, forms and records.	Davies, *Eight Songs for a Mad King*.	Assassination of Dr. Martin Luther King, Jr. Assassination of Robert Kennedy. Massive antiwar protests in U.S. Soviet invasion of Czechoslovakia.
1969	Don Cherry in Paris; records *Mu*. Miles Davis, *Bitches Brew*. The Art Ensemble of Chicago moves to Paris.	Roth, *Portnoy's Complaint*. Puzo, *The Godfather*.	Men walk on the moon. Lottery system established for draft.
1970	Formation of the London Jazz Composers Orchestra. Coleman releases "Ornette Lives at Prince Street: Friends and Neighbors."	Toffler, *Future Shock*. Segal, *Love Story*. Crumb, *Ancient Voices of Children*.	Voting age lowered to 18. U.S. intervention in Cambodia. First complete synthesis of a gene accomplished.
1971	Archie Shepp, *Things Have Got to Change*. Louis Armstrong dies.	Blatty, *The Exorcist*.	The first quadraphonic discs released. Indo-Pakistan War. Independence of Bangladesh.
1972	Weather Report, *I Sing The Body Electric*. The complete works of Scott Joplin published. Miles Davis, *On The Corner*.		Nixon visits Communist China and U.S.S.R. Israeli athletes murdered at Munich Olympics.
1973	Eubie Blake, at 90, releases three new albums. Swing men Goodman, Krupa, Hampton, and Stewart featured at Newport Jazz Festival—New York.	Vonnegut, *Breakfast of Champions*.	"Watergate Affair" begins. Peace agreement signed by U.S., North and South Vietnam, and Vietcong.
1974	Duke Ellington dies. Two jazz repertory companies, the National Jazz Ensemble	Peter Benchley, *Jaws*. Solzhenitsyn, *The Gulag Archipelago*. Britten, *Death in Venice*.	Richard Nixon resigns the Presidency of the U.S. in disgrace.

	JAZZ	ART, LITERATURE, AND CONCERT MUSIC	HISTORY AND SCIENCE
1974 (cont.)	and the New York Jazz Repertory Company, perform in Alice Tully Hall and Carnegie Hall.		
1975	Bill Watrous, *The Manhattan Wildlife Refuge.* Cecil Taylor attracts overflow audiences at New York's "Five Spot."	Bellow, *Humboldt's Gift.* Doctorow, *Ragtime.* Joplin's *Treemonisha* has a Broadway run.	Apollo-Soyuz project, a cooperative space venture between the U.S. and U.S.S.R.

ANNOTATED BIBLIOGRAPHY

The following is a highly selective bibliography, for it contains only a few of the thousands of published items that are now available to help the serious student of jazz learn more about this fascinating subject. More complete bibliographies are available, and they are listed below, but this compilation 1) emphasizes books in English; 2) organizes material by subject; 3) includes items on African music, American music, and related subjects not often found in jazz bibliographies; and 4) omits writings which have not proved particularly useful for the preparation of this study.

General Bibliography

DICTIONARIES AND ENCYCLOPEDIAS

American Society of Composers, Authors and Publishers. *The ASCAP Biographical Dictionary of Composers, Authors and Publishers.* 3rd ed. New York: Lynn Farnol Group, 1966. Brief biographies of ASCAP members.

Bogaert, Karel. *Blues Lexicon.* Antwerp: Standaard Uitgeverij, 1971. Accurate biographies and brief discographies of American bluesmen. In Dutch.

Charters, Samuel B. *Jazz: New Orleans, 1885–1963.* Rev. ed. New York: Oak Publications, 1963. An index to the black musicians of New Orleans, divided by period, with biographies, information on groups, and short textual surveys.

Chilton, John. *Who's Who of Jazz: Storyville to Swing Street.* London: Bloomsbury Book Shop, 1970. Brief biographies of over 1,000 jazzmen.

Ewen, David. *Popular American Composers, from Revolutionary Times to the Present.* New York: H. W. Wilson, 1962. First supplement, 1972. Guide to the most important composers, with an index of songs.

Feather, Leonard. *The Encyclopedia of Jazz in the Sixties.* New York: Horizon Press, 1967. Similar to the following.

————. *The New Edition of the Encyclopedia of Jazz.* New York: Horizon Press, 1960. Chiefly individual biographies, with introductory essays on the history and sociology of jazz.

Fell, Frederick Victor (pseud. Vic Fredericks). *Who's Who in Rock 'n' Roll.* New York: F. Fell, 1958. Brief, useful biographies of popular rock 'n' roll musicians.

Gammond, Peter, and Peter Clayton. *Dictionary of Popular Music.* New York: Philosophical Library, 1961. Listing of works and recordings of principal composers, terms, and song titles, with a British emphasis.

Gentry, Linnell. *A History and Encyclopedia of Country, Western, and Gospel Music.* 2nd ed. Nashville: Claimon, 1969. Anthology of magazine articles, list of country musicals, and biographies.

Gold, Robert S. *A Jazz Lexicon.* New York: Knopf, 1964. A dictionary of jazz-world terms, with sociological emphasis.

Kinkle, Roger D. *The Complete Encyclopedia of Popular Music and Jazz 1900–1950.* New Rochelle, N.Y.: Arlington House, 1974. Detailed study in four volumes: music year by year 1900–50, biographies with lists of compositions and recordings, and exhaustive indices.

Laade, Wolfgang. *Jazz-Lexikon.* Stuttgart: G. Hatze, 1953. A useful jazz dictionary in German.

Ortiz Oderigo, Nestor R. *Diccionario del Jazz.* Buenos Aires: Ricordi Americana, 1959. Terms and phrases associated with jazz and its history. In Spanish.

Panassié, Hugues, and Madeleine Gautier. *Dictionnaire du jazz.* New ed. Paris: Albin Michel, 1971. (Transl. of first edition appeared as *Guide to Jazz.* Boston: Houghton Mifflin, 1956.) Entries for individuals, bands, song titles, and terms.

Rice, Edward Le Roy. *Monarchs of Minstrelsy from "Daddy" Rice to Date.* New York: Kenny, 1911. Chronologically arranged biographies of the leaders of nineteenth-century American minstrelsy.

Rose, Al, and Edmond Souchon. *New Orleans Jazz: A Family Album.* Baton Rouge: Louisiana State University Press, 1967. Copiously illustrated, with brief entries on people, places, and bands in New Orleans.

Roxon, Lillian. *Rock Encyclopedia.* New York: Universal Library, 1971. Short sketches of individuals and groups, with discographies.

Stambler, Irwin. *Encyclopedia of Pop, Rock, and Soul.* New York: St. Martin's Press, 1974. Mostly critical biographies of individuals and groups, with some entries for terms and shows.

————. *Encyclopedia of Popular Music.* New York: St. Martin's Press, 1965. Terms, biographies, and titles in one alphabet.

————, and Grulun Landon. *Encyclopedia of Folk, Country, and Western Music.* New York: St. Martin's Press, 1969. Mainly entries on performers and groups.

Ténot, Frank. *Dictionnaire du jazz.* Les dictionnaires de L'homme du XXe Siècle. Paris: Larousse, 1967. A typical "Larousse" with brief biographies and term entries.

Testoni, Gian Carlo *et al. Enciclopedia del Jazz.* 2nd ed. Milan: Messaggerie Musicali, 1954. Extended textual surveys on the art and history of jazz, brief biographies, and detailed discographies of jazz recordings issued in Italy, 1920–52.

HISTORIES AND CHRONOLOGIES

Austin, William W. *Music in the 20th Century from Debussy through Stravinsky.* New York: W. W. Norton, 1966. Excellent general textual survey, with two chapters devoted to jazz and an extensive annotated bibliography.

Berendt, Joachim Ernest. *The Jazzbook: From New Orleans to Rock and Free Jazz.* New York: Hill and Wang, 1966. Well-considered but brief survey from the European viewpoint.

Blesh, Rudi. *Shining Trumpets, a History of Jazz.* 4th ed. London: Cassel, 1958. Pioneering work of major importance to jazz history.

Boeckman, Charles. *Cool, Hot and Blue: A History of Jazz for Young People.* Washington, D.C.: Luce, 1968. General introductory survey with emphasis on pre-1930s period.

Charters, Samuel Barclay, and Leonard Kundstadt. *Jazz: A History of the New York Scene.* New York: Doubleday, 1962. Detailed treatment of the 1920–62 period, including the big bands.

Dauer, Alfons M. *Der Jazz: seine Ursprünge und seine Entwicklung.* Kassel: E. Röth, 1958. Particularly valuable for the copious transcribed examples of African music and early jazz.

Dexter, Dave. *The Jazz Story, from the '90s to the '60s.* Englewood Cliffs, N.J.: Prentice-Hall, 1964. A superficial treatment.

Feather, Leonard G. *The Book of Jazz: A Guide to the Entire Field.* New York: Horizon Press, 1965. Sections on sources, instruments, sounds, and performers, the nature and the future of jazz.

Finkelstein, Sidney W. *Jazz: A People's Music.* New York: Citadel Press, 1948. Analytical survey up to the beginning of the bop era, with a Marxist political orientation.

Goffin, Robert. *Jazz from the Congo to the Metropolitan.* New York: Doubleday, Doran & Co., 1944. Influential treatment of early jazz.

Hansen, Chadwick Clarke. "The Ages of Jazz: A Study of Jazz in its Cultural Context." Ph.D. dissertation, University of Minnesota, 1956. University Microfilm 59-6054. Some interesting material, but the study lacks focus and the conclusions are inadequately supported.

Harris, Rex. *Jazz.* 5th ed. Harmondsworth, England: Penguin Books, 1957. Particularly good on the origins and traditional styles of jazz.

Hitchcock, H. Wiley. *Music in the United States: A Historical Introduction.* 2nd ed. Englewood Cliffs, N.J.: Prentice-Hall, 1974. Well-documented general survey by the editor of the Prentice-Hall History of Music series.

Hobson, Wilder. *American Jazz Music.* New York: W. W. Norton, 1939. Important, perceptive survey through the swing period.

Hodeir, André. *Jazz: Its Evolution and Essence,* trans. W. David Noakes. New York: Grove, 1956. A major work of analysis and criticism with emphasis on the modern-jazz style.

Keepnews, Orrin, and Bill Grauer, Jr. *A Pictorial History of Jazz: People and Places from New Orleans to Modern Jazz.* New ed. New York: Crown, 1966. Major collection of photographs.

Leonard, Neil. *Jazz and the White Americans: The Acceptance of a New Art Form.* Chicago: University of Chicago Press, 1962. Significant study with strong sociological emphasis.

Longstreet, Stephen. *The Real Jazz, Old and New.* Baton Rouge: Louisiana State University Press, 1956. Highly individualistic survey of traditional styles, with many factual errors.

Murray, Albert. *Stomping the Blues.* New York: McGraw-Hill, 1976. Perceptive treatment, well written. Splendid collection of photographs.

Newton, Francis. *The Jazz Scene.* New York: Monthly Review Press, 1960. Particularly good on the sociological and cultural aspects of jazz.

Ostransky, Leroy. *The Anatomy of Jazz.* Seattle: University of Washington Press, 1960. Analytical study of jazz as a phenomenon within the general history of music, with an extensive bibliography of books and journals.

Polillo, Arrigo. *Jazz: A Guide to its History.* London: P. Hamlyn, 1969. A superficial work whose most interesting portions deal with recent musicians.

Sargeant, Winthrop. *Jazz, Hot and Hybrid.* New York: Arrow Editions, 1938. Penetrating insights into early jazz, with good musical analyses.

Schuller, Gunther. *The History of Jazz.* New York: Oxford University Press, 1968–. Vol. 1, *Early Jazz: Its Roots and Musical Development.* Significant contribution to the history of the pre-1930 period, with an ethnomusicological approach to African elements in jazz.

Southern, Eileen. *The Music of Black Americans: A History.* New York: W. W. Norton, 1971. Excellently documented history of all aspects of black American music from the African heritage to the mid-20th century.

Stearns, Marshall Winslow. *Jazz Dance: The Story of American Vernacular Dance.* New York: Macmillan, 1968. The only book dealing with the subject from a serious historical perspective.

———. *The Story of Jazz.* New York: Oxford University Press, 1970. Scholarly and well-documented comprehensive history. The 1958 New American Library edition contains an expanded bibliography and a syllabus of lectures on the history of jazz.

Tanner, Paul Ora Warren. "A Technical Analysis of the Development of Jazz." Unpublished thesis, University of California at Los Angeles, 1962. Technical analyses of jazz music from various periods.

———, and Maurice Gerow. *A Study of Jazz.* 2nd ed. Dubuque: Wm. C. Brown, 1973. A textbook survey of jazz history with constructed musical examples and little reliance on the work of other writers.

Ulanov, Barry. *A Handbook of Jazz.* New York: Viking Press, 1957. Textual essays on the history and cultural context of jazz, with very brief biographies.

———. *A History of Jazz in America.* New York: Viking Press, 1955. Reliable, well-balanced study.

Williams, Martin. *The Jazz Tradition.* New York: Oxford University Press, 1970. Essays, many revised from earlier publications, on fifteen different jazz musicians and their careers.

BIBLIOGRAPHIES

Carl Gregor, Herzog zu Mecklenburg. *International Jazz Bibliography: Jazz Books from 1919 to 1968*. Sammlung musikwissenschaftlicher Abhandlungen, 49. Strasbourg: Heitz, 1969. Extensive listing, without annotations.

——. 1970 *Supplement to International Jazz Bibliography and International Drum and Percussion Bibliography*. Beiträge zur Jazzforschung, 3. Graz: Universal Edition, 1971. Includes items omitted from the original bibliography and new titles from autumn, 1968, to 1970.

——. *1971/72/73 Supplement to International Jazz Bibliography and Selective Bibliography of Some Jazz Background Literature and Bibliography of Two Subjects Previously Excluded*. Beiträge zur Jazzforschung, 6. Graz: Universal Edition, 1975. The two new subjects are Poetry and fiction, and Cartoons and drawing.

Colvig, Richard. "Black Music," *Choice*, November, 1969, p. 1169 ff. Annotated selection of English-language monographs.

Cooper, David Edwin. *International Bibliography of Discographies*. Littleton, Colorado: Libraries Unlimited, 1975. Aprpoximately one-third of the volume is devoted to jazz and blues, with sections on genres and individual performers.

Dimmick, Mary. *The Rolling Stones: An Annotated Bibliography*. Pittsburgh: University of Pittsburgh, 1972. Superb bibliographic guide with critical and descriptive annotations.

Epstein, Dena J. "Slave Music in the United States before 1860: A Survey of Sources," *Notes*, 20 (1963), pp. 195–212 and 377–390. An extensive description and synoptic "preliminary report" of contemporary accounts.

Gillis, Frank, and Alan P. Merriam. *Ethnomusicology and Folk Music: An International Bibliography of Dissertations and Theses*. Middletown, Conn.: Wesleyan University Press, 1966. Includes both masters and doctoral theses.

Handy, William Christopher. *Negro Authors and Composers of the United States*. New York: Handy Brothers Music Co., c. 1936. A short list of historical interest.

Hippenmeyer, Jean Roland. *Jazz sur films; ou, 55 années de rapports jazz-cinéma vus à travers plus de 800 films tournés entre 1917 et 1972*. Yverdon: Éditions de la Thièle, 1973. Introductory essay on the appearance of jazz in motion pictures, with a detailed 1917–72 filmography and analytical indices.

Kennington, Donald. *The Literature of Jazz: A Critical Guide*. Chicago: American Library Association, 1971. Eight textual surveys, each followed by an annotated bibliography.

Markewich, Reese. *The Definitive Bibliography of Harmonically Sophisticated Tonal Music*. Riverdale, N.Y.: Markewich, 1970. A pompously titled but modest accomplishment.

——. *Jazz Publicity II: Newly Revised and Expanded Bibliography of Names and Addresses of Hundreds of International Jazz Critics and Magazines*. Riverdale, N.Y.: Markewich, 1974.

——. *The New Expanded Bibliography of Jazz Compositions Based on the Chord Progressions of Standard Tunes*. Riverdale, N.Y.: Markewich, 1974. Listing of standard tunes under title, with indications of composer, publisher, significant recordings, and original appearances.

Merriam, Alan P., and Robert J. Brenford. A *Bibliography of Jazz*. Philadelphia: American Folk-lore Society, 1954; repr. New York: Da Capo, 1970. A most comprehensive bibliography of books and journal articles with a separate listing of jazz-oriented magazines.

Nettl, Bruno. *Reference Materials in Ethnomusicology*. 2nd ed. Detroit: Information Coordinators, 1967. Textual survey of major reference works, organized by topic.

Reisner, Robert George. *The Literature of Jazz: A Selective Bibliography*. New York: New York Public Library, 1959. Checklist of books (including fiction) and magazine articles, and a list of jazz journals.

Stanley, Lana. *Folk Rock: A Bibliography on Music of the 'Sixties*. San Jose: San Jose State College Library, 1970. Organized by topic, groups, and individuals.

DISCOGRAPHIES

Bruyninckx, Walter. *50 Years of Recorded Jazz, 1917–1967*. Mechelen, Belgium: Bruyninckx, 1968. An excellent discography, not readily available.

Carey, David A., and Albert J. McCarthy. *The Directory of Recorded Jazz and Swing Music*. London: Cassel, 1950–. Detailed, annotated listing by performer and group, alphabetically through "Longshaw." Continued by Jepsen and by McCarthy (q.v.).

Connor, Donald Russell, and Warren W. Hicks. *BG on the Record: A Bio-discography of Benny Goodman*. New Rochelle, N.Y.: Arlington House, 1969. Exhaustive discography, arranged chronologically, with textual commentary interspersed.

Cullaz, Maurice. *Guide des Disques de Jazz*. Paris: Buchet/Chastel, 1971. Critical and historical commentaries on 1,000 selected recordings of spirituals, gospel songs, blues, and jazz.

Delaunay, Charles. *New Hot Discography: The Standard Dictionary of Recorded Jazz*. New York: Criterion, 1963. A work of the "father of jazz discography," particularly valuable for the earlier decades of jazz recording.

Flower, John. *Moonlight Serenade: A Bio-Discography of the Glenn Miller Civilian Band*. New Rochelle, N.Y.: Arlington House, 1972. Detailed chronological discography with brief background commentaries.

Godrich, J., and R. M. W. Dixon. *Blues and Gospel Records, 1902–1942*. 2nd ed. London: Storyville Publications, 1969. The basic discography in this particular field.

Harris, Rex, and Brian Rust. *Recorded Jazz: A Critical Guide*. Harmondsworth, England: Penguin Books, 1958. Critical discography of pre-1957 recordings of traditional jazz only.

Harrison, Max, *et al. Modern Jazz: The Essential Records*. London: Aquarius Books, 1975. Extensive historical, analytical, and critical discussions of 200 jazz recordings of "permanent worth."

Jasen, David A. *Recorded Ragtime 1897–1958*. Hamden, Conn.: Archon, 1973. International discography, indicating label, number, and date of recording.

Jepsen, Jorgen Grunnet. *A Discography of Charlie Parker*. Copenhagen: Knudsen, 1968. A listing extracted from his larger work, *Jazz Records*.

————. *Jazz Records: A Discography*. Holte, Denmark: Knudsen, 1963–. The standard work in the field, to be continued with future volumes.

Kendoziora, Carl, and Perry Armagnac. "Perfect Dance and Race Catalogue (1922–1930)," *Record Research*, 51/52 (1963). A useful, highly-specialized discography.

Lange, Horst H. *Die deutsche Jazz-Discographie. Eine Geschichte des Jazz auf Schallplatten von 1902 bis 1955*. Berlin: Bote & Bock, 1955. A good jazz discography in German.

Leadbitter, Mike, and Neil Slaven. *Blues Records, 1943–1966*. London: Hanover Books, 1968. A virtually complete listing arranged by artist and group.

Lonstein, Albert I. *The Compleat Sinatra Discography, Filmography, Television Appearances, Motion Picture Appearances, Radio, Concert, Stage Appearances*. Ellenville, N.Y.: Cameron, 1970. "Primarily an authoritative listing of the professional career of Frank Sinatra" (Introd.).

McCarthy, Albert J. *et al. Jazz on Record: A Critical Guide to the First 50 Years, 1917–1967*. London: Hanover Books, 1968. Selective listing with significant biographical and critical matter.

Panassié, Hugues. *Discographie critique des meilleurs disques de jazz*. Paris: Laffont, 1958. A standard jazz discography in French.

Ramsey, Frederic. *A Guide to Longplay Jazz Records*. New York: Long Player Publications, 1954. Analytic guide with title and performer indices.

Rust, Brian. *The American Dance Band Discography 1917–1942*. New Rochelle, N.Y.: Arlington House, 1976. Extensive listing of "all known recorded work of dance bands" for the period with a comprehensive artists' index.

————. *The Complete Entertainment Discography, from the Mid-1890s to 1942*. New Rochelle, N.Y.: Arlington House, 1973. This complementary volume to Rust's other discographies includes people on the peripheries of jazz.

————. *Jazz Records, 1897–1942*. London: Storyville Publications, 1970. The standard work of recordings before 1942 of ragtime, jazz, and swing by American and British performers.

Sanfilippo, Luigi. *General Catalog of Duke Ellington's Recorded Music*. 2nd ed. Palermo: New Jazz Society, 1966. A full documentation of Ellington's recordings up to 1965.

Stagg, Tom, and Charlie Crump. *New Orleans, The Revival: A Tape and Discography of Negro Traditional Jazz Recorded in New Orleans or by New Orleans Bands 1937–1972*. Dublin: Bashall Cabes, 1973. A guide to issued and unissued recordings with a special section on religious recordings.

Wante, Stephen, and Walter De Block. *V-Disc Catalogue*. Antwerp: De Block, 1954. A guide to noncommercial recordings made for use by the armed services.

Whitburn, Joel. *Top Pop Records, 1955–1970: Facts About 9800 Recordings Listed in Billboard's "Hot 100" Charts*. Detroit: Gale Research, 1972. The songs are listed by principal artist with data on chart ratings and record issue number.

————. *Top Rhythm and Blues Records, 1949–1971: Facts About 4000 Recordings Listed in Billboard's "Best Selling Rhythm & Blues (Soul) Singles" Charts*. Menomonee Falls, Wisc.: Record Research, 1973. Useful discographical information. Chronicles a related field during a period of transition in jazz.

Williams, Tony. "Charlie Parker Discography," *Discographical Forum*, 8–20 (1968–70). The most exhaustive and accurate Parker discography to date.

Wilson, John Steuart. *The Collector's Jazz: Modern*. Philadelphia: Lippincott, 1959. Critical discography of LPs arranged by group or individual artist.

―――. *The Collector's Jazz: Traditional and Swing*. Philadelphia: Lippincott, 1958. Similar to the preceding.

INDICES AND BIBLIOGRAPHIES OF MUSIC

Armitage, Andrew D. *Annual Index to Popular Music Record Reviews*. Metuchen, N.J.: Scarecrow Press, 1973–. Locating guide to reviews, grouped by genres with appendices of selected books and significant journal articles in the field.

Burton, Jack. *The Blue Book of Tin Pan Alley*. Watkins Glen, N.Y.: Century House, 1962; expanded new ed., 2 vols., 1962–65. Textual surveys and biographies with detailed song listings of major popular composers, arranged chronologically, 1776–1965.

―――. *The Index of American Popular Music*. Watkins Glen, N.Y.: Century House, 1957. Extensively cross-referenced guide to songs in anthologies.

Chipman, John H. *Index to Top-Hit Tunes, 1900–1950*. Boston: B. Humphries, 1962. Alphabetical title index of America's most popular songs, with composers, authors, publishers, and dates indicated.

Ewen, David. *American Popular Songs: From the Revolutionary War to the Present*. New York: Random House, 1966. Brief, informative entries on over 3,600 songs.

Mattfeld, Julius. *Variety Music Cavalcade, 1620–1961: A Chronology of Vocal and Instrumental Music Popular in the United States*. 3rd ed. Englewood Cliffs, N.J.: Prentice-Hall, 1971. Chronological bibliography, with annual surveys of cultural and historical events.

Shapiro, Nat. *Popular Music: An Annotated Index of American Popular Songs*. New York: Adrian Press, 1964–. Each of the five published volumes is devoted to a decade from the '20s through the '60s, with detailed information on the original appearance of songs in all popular fields.

PERIODICALS

Billboard Magazine. Directed to popular-music industry, with marketing data, news releases, book reviews, personnel notices.

The Black Perspective in Music. Addressed to a general audience interested in black studies. Occasional worthwhile articles about black jazz musicians.

The Black Scholar. Concerns itself with major political and cultural issues affecting black America.

Down Beat. Trade journal for American jazz musicians. News and analysis of the music world, especially jazz, with special review sections for records and live performances.

Ethnomusicology. International, interdisciplinary scholarly journal with current bibliographies, discographies and reviews.

High Fidelity/Musical America. Coverage of live and recorded performances and audio equipment.

Jazz Journal. Leading British jazz periodical with articles and reviews by noted authorities.

Jazz Magazine. French publication (in French) of real merit. Informative articles and reviews.

Jazz-Podium. Principal German jazz periodical with newsstand trade. Interesting news, features, and reviews.

Jazzforschung/Jazz Research. Journal of the International Society for Jazz Research. Authoritative, scholarly, generally well written. Articles and reviews in English as well as German.

Journal of Jazz Studies. Scholarly papers on musical, historical, and social aspects of jazz.

Journal of Popular Culture. Deals with all aspects of contemporary popular culture.

Living Blues. Contemporary and historical coverage of the black American blues tradition.

Mecca: The Magazine of Traditional Jazz. Newsletter for New Orleans traditional-jazz enthusiasts.

Metronome. A trade journal for the entertainment business. An important record for the swing era.

NAJE Journal [National Association of Jazz Educators]. Principally useful to music instructors who direct school jazz-lab bands.

Record Research. Important source for recording information and statistics.

Rolling Stone. Covers contemporary pop music, films, social issues, and lifestyles. Has become a trade journal for rock musicians.

INDICES TO PERIODICAL LITERATURE (especially useful for locating material in nonjazz and nonmusic periodicals)

Music Article Guide. Philadelphia, 1966–. Author-title-subject index to c. 150 American periodicals, including some house organs and trade journals, with brief annotations.

The Music Index. Detroit: Information Coordinators, 1949–. International index of c. 300 journals, scholarly and popular, by author and subject.

New York Times Index. New York, 1913–. Careful subject index to this most important American newspaper, with brief synopses of articles. An earlier index for 1851–58, 1860, 1863–1905 is available on microfilm.

Readers' Guide to Periodical Literature, 1900–. New York, Wilson, 1905–. Full dictionary catalogue index, with entries under author, subject, and title where appropriate, of general and popular U.S. periodicals with a selection of nontechnical magazines from specific subject fields.

RILM Abstracts of Music Literature. New York, International RILM Center, 1967–. Abstracts, indexed by computer, of all significant literature of music (books, articles, essays, reviews, dissertations, etc.) which has appeared since January 1967. Five-year 1967–1971 cummulative index available.

JAZZ ARCHIVES

Arkansas Arts Center, Little Rock, Ark. (John D. Reed Collection of American Jazz).

Detroit Public Library, Music Division, Detroit, Mich.

Emory University, Atlanta, Ga.

Fisk University, Nashville, Tenn. (Scott Joplin).

Free Library of Philadelphia, Philadelphia, Pa. (Harvey Huston Jazz Library).

Indiana University, Bloomington, Ind. (Archives of Traditional Music).

Library of Congress, Music Division, Washington, D.C.

New Orleans Jazz Museum, New Orleans, La.

New York Jazz Museum, New York City.

New York Public Library, Harlem Branch (Schomburg Collection of Negro Literature and History).

New York Public Library, Lincoln Center (Rogers and Hammerstein Archive of Recorded Sound).

North Texas State University, Denton, Tex.

Rutgers University, Newark, N.J. (Institute of Jazz Studies).

The Smithsonian Institution, Division of Performing Arts, Washington, D.C.

Tulane University Library, New Orleans, La. (William Ransom Hogan Jazz Archive).

University of California at Los Angeles, Los Angeles, Ca. (John Edwards Memorial Foundation).

Williams College, Williamstown, Mass. (Paul Whiteman).

Yale University, New Haven, Conn. (James Wilden Johnson Collection).

PEDAGOGY

Aebersold, Jamey. *A New Approach to Jazz Improvisation*. Libertyville, Ill.: National Educational Services, 1967.

Baker, David. *Arranging and Composing for the Small Ensemble: Jazz/R & B/Jazz-Rock*. Chicago: Maher, 1970.

———. *Jazz Styles and Analysis: Trombone; A History of the Jazz Trombone in Recorded Solos Transcribed and Annotated*. Chicago: Downbeat Music Workshop Publications, 1973.

———. *Techniques of Improvisation*. Chicago: Maher, 1971.

Berle, Arnie. *Complete Handbook for Jazz Improvisation*. New York: Amsco, 1972.

Coker, Jerry. *Improvising Jazz*. Englewood Cliffs, N.J.: Prentice-Hall, 1964.

———. *The Jazz Idiom*. Englewood Cliffs, N.J.: Prentice-Hall, 1975.

———, Jimmy Casale, Gary Campbell, and Jerry Greene. *Patterns for Jazz*. Lebanon, Ind.: Studio P/R, 1970.

Dankeworth, Avril. *Jazz: An Introduction to Its Musical Basis*. London: Oxford University Press, 1968.

Ellis, Norman. *Instrumentation and Arranging for the Radio and Dance Orchestra.* New York: Roell, 1936.

Garcia, Russell. *The Professional Arranger Composer.* New York: Criterion, 1954.

Giuffre, Jimmy. *Jazz Phrasing and Interpretation.* New York: Associated Music Publishers, 1969.

Jenkins, John, and Jon Smith. *Electric Music: A Practical Manual.* Bloomington: Indiana University Press, 1975.

Lapham, Claude. *Scoring for the Modern Dance Band.* New York: Pitman, 1937.

Levey, Joseph. *Basic Jazz Improvisation.* Delaware Water Gap, Penn.: Shawnee Press, 1971.

LaPorta, John. *A Guide to Improvisation.* Boston: Berklee Press, 1968.

Lindsay, Martin. *Teach Yourself Jazz.* London: English Universities Press, 1958.

Mancini, Henry. *Sounds and Scores: A Practical Guide to Professional Orchestration.* N.p.: Northridge, 1967.

Markewich, Reese. *Inside Outside: Substitute Harmony in Jazz and Pop Music.* New York: n.p., 1967.

Mehegan, John F. *Contemporary Styles for the Jazz Pianist.* 3 vols. New York: Sam Fox, 1964–70.

———. *Jazz Improvisation.* 4 vols. New York: Watson-Guptill, 1959–1965.

———. *The Jazz Pianist: Studies in the Art and Practice of Jazz Improvisation.* 3 vols. New York: Sam Fox, 1960–61.

———. *Studies in Jazz Harmony.* New York: Sam Fox, 1972.

———. *Styles for the Jazz Pianist.* New York: Sam Fox, 1972.

Murphy, Lyle. *Swing Arranging Method.* New York: Robbins Music Corp., 1937.

Russell, George. *The Lydian Chromatic Concept of Tonal Organization for Improvisation.* New York: Concept, 1959.

Russo, William. *Composing for the Jazz Orchestra.* Chicago: University of Chicago Press, 1961.

———. *Jazz Composition and Orchestration.* Chicago: University of Chicago Press, 1968.

Schillinger, Joseph. *Schillinger System of Musical Composition.* 2 vols. New York: Carl Fischer, 1941–42.

Stuart, Walter. *The Chord Approach to Improvising.* New York: Charles Colin, 1966.

———. *Jazz Improvising.* New York: Charles Colin, 1961.

Wiskirchen, Rev. George, C.S.C. *Developmental Techniques for the School Dance Band Musician.* Boston: Berklee, 1961.

MISCELLANEOUS—LITERATURE, PHILOSOPHY, INTERVIEWS, ETC.

Balliett, Whitney. *Dinosaurs in the Morning.* Philadelphia: Lippincott, 1962.

———. *Ecstasy at the Onion.* Indianaplis: Bobbs-Merrill, 1971.

———. *The Sound of Surprise.* New York: Dutton, 1969.

———. *Such Sweet Thunder.* Indianapolis: Bobbs-Merrill, 1966.

Blesh, Rudi. *Combo U.S.A.: Eight Lives in Jazz.* Philadelphia: Chilton, 1971.

Brown, Rap. *Die Nigger, Die.* New York: Dial Press, 1969.

Denisoff, R. Serge. *Sing a Song of Social Significance*. Bowling Green, Ohio: Bowling Green University Press, 1972.

———, and Richard A. Peterson, comp. *The Sounds of Social Change: Studies in Popular Culture*. Chicago: Rand McNally, 1972.

De Toledano, Ralph, ed. *Frontiers of Jazz*. 2nd ed. New York: F. Ungar, 1962.

Dexter, Dave, Jr. *Jazz Cavalcade*. New York: Criterion, 1946.

Ellison, Ralph. *Shadow and Act*. New York: Random House, 1964.

Erlich, Lillian. *What Jazz Is All About*. New York: J. Messner, 1962.

Ewen, David. *The Life and Death of Tin Pan Alley*. New York: Funk and Wagnalls, 1964.

Gammond, Peter. *Fourteen Miles on a Clear Night: An Irreverent Book About Jazz Records*. London: Owen, 1966.

Gant, Roland. *World In A Jug*. New York: Vanguard, 1960.

Gleason, Ralph J., ed. *Jam Session: An Anthology of Jazz*. New York: Putnam, 1958.

Gold, Robert S. *Jazz Talk*. Indianapolis: Bobbs-Merrill, 1975.

Guthrie, Woodie. *Bound for Glory*. New York: Dutton, 1970.

Haas, Robert Bartlett, comp. *William Grant Still and the Fusion of Cultures in American Music*. Los Angeles: Black Sparrow Press, 1972.

Hamm, Charles, Bruno Nettl, and Ronald Byrnside. *Contemporary Music and Music Cultures*. Englewood Cliffs, N.J.: Prentice-Hall, 1975.

Hentoff, Nat. *Jazz Country*. New York: Harper and Row, 1965.

———. *The Jazz Life*. New York: Dial Press, 1961.

———. *Journey Into Jazz*. New York: Coward-McCann, 1968.

———, ed. *Jazz: New Perspectives on the History of Jazz*. New York: Rinehart, 1959.

Hippenmeyer, Jean Roland. *Le jazz en Suisse, 1930–1970*. Yverdon: Éditions de la Thièle, 1971.

Hodeir, André. *Toward Jazz*. New York: Grove Press, 1962.

———. *The Worlds of Jazz*. New York: Grove Press, 1972.

Jablonski, Edward. *From Sweet and Swing to Rock 'n' Roll*. New York: F. Ungar, 1961.

Jones, LeRoi. *Black Music*. New York: W. Morrow, 1967.

———. *Blues People: Negro Music in White America*. New York: W. Morrow, 1963.

———. *Home: Social Essays*. New York: Morrow, 1966.

Kofsky, Frank. *Black Nationalism and the Revolution in Music*. New York: Pathfinder Press, 1970.

Lange, Horst Heinz. *Jazz in Deutschland*. Berlin: Colloquium Verlag, 1966.

Mingus, Charles. *Beneath the Underdog*. New York: Knopf, 1971.

Nanry, Charles, comp. *American Music: From Storyville to Woodstock*. New Brunswick, N.J.: Transaction Books, 1972.

Pleasants, Henry. *Death of a Music? The Decline of the European Tradition and the Rise of Jazz*. London: Gollancz, 1961.

———. *Serious Music and All That Jazz*. New York: Simon and Schuster, 1969.

Roach, Max, *et al.* "On Black Music," *The Black Scholar*, 3 (1972).

Rockmore, Noel. *Preservation Hall Portraits*. Baton Rouge: Louisiana State University Press, 1968.

Shapiro, Nat, and Nat Hentoff. *The Jazz Makers*. New York: Rinehart, 1957.

————, eds. *Hear Me Talkin' To Ya.* New York: Rinehart, 1955.

Shaw, Artie. *I Love You, I Hate You, Drop Dead.* New York: Fleet, 1965.

————. *The Trouble With Cinderella.* New York: Farrar, Straus & Young, 1952.

Sidran, Ben. *Black Talk.* New York: Holt, Rinehart & Winston, 1971.

Simmons, Herbert. *Man Walking on Eggshells.* Boston: Houghton Mifflin, 1962.

Simon, George T. *The Feeling of Jazz.* New York: Simon and Schuster, 1961.

Sinclair, John, and Robert Levin. *Music & Politics.* New York: World Publishing Co., 1971.

Terkel, Louis "Studs." *Giants of Jazz.* New York: Crowell, 1957.

Tormé, Mel. *The Other Side of the Rainbow.* London: Allen, 1971.

Traill, Sinclair. *Concerning Jazz.* London: Faber and Faber, 1957.

Vallée, Rudy. *Vagabond Dreams Come True.* New York: Dutton, 1930.

Whiteman, Paul. *How To Be a Bandleader.* New York: R. M. McBride, 1948.

Wilder, Alec. *American Popular Song: The Great Innovators, 1900–1950.* New York: Oxford University Press, 1972.

Williams, Martin T. *The Art of Jazz: Essays on the Nature and Development of Jazz.* New York: Oxford University Press, 1959.

————. *Where's the Melody? A Listener's Introduction to Jazz.* New York: Funk & Wagnalls, 1967.

Williams, Peter. *Bluff Your Way in Folk and Jazz.* London: Wolfe, 1969.

Wilmer, Valerie. *Jazz People.* Indianapolis: Bobbs-Merrill, 1970.

Yorke, Ritchie. *Axes, Chops and Hot Licks: The Canadian Rock Music Scene.* Edmonton: M. G. Hurtig, 1971.

Chapter Bibliographies

CHAPTER I—THE STATE OF MUSIC IN THE U.S. IN THE LATE
NINETEENTH CENTURY

Austin, William W. *"Susanna," "Jeanie," and "The Old Folks at Home": The Songs of Stephen C. Foster from His Time to Ours.* New York: Macmillan, 1975.

Blum, Daniel. *A Pictorial Treasury of Opera in America.* New York: Greenberg, 1954.

Chase, Gilbert. *America's Music from the Pilgrims to the Present.* Rev. 2nd ed. New York: McGraw-Hill, 1966.

Cron, Theodore O., and Burt Goldblatt. *Portrait of Carnegie Hall.* New York: Macmillan, 1966.

Elson, Louis Charles. *The History of American Music.* New York: B. Franklin, 1971.

Erskine, John. *The Philharmonic-Symphony Society of New York: Its First Hundred Years.* New York: Macmillan, 1943.

Ewen, David. *History of Popular Music.* New York: Barnes & Noble, 1961.

————. *Panorama of American Popular Music.* Englewood Cliffs, N.J.: Prentice-Hall, 1957.

Filby, P. William. *Star-Spangled Books: Books, Sheet Music, Newspapers, Manuscripts, and Persons Associated with the Star-Spangled Banner.* Baltimore: Maryland Historical Society, 1972.

Goldman, Richard Franko. *The Wind Band.* Boston: Allyn & Bacon, 1961.

Hitchcock, H. Wiley. *Music in the United States: A Historical Introduction.* Englewood Cliffs, N.J.: Prentice-Hall, 1969.

Howard, J. T. *Stephen Foster, America's Troubador.* Rev. ed. New York: Crowell, 1962.

Howe, M. A. DeWolfe. *The Boston Symphony Orchestra 1881–1931.* Boston: Houghton Mifflin, 1931.

Isaacs, Edith. *The Negro in the American Theatre.* New York: Theatre Arts, 1947.

Jackson, George Pullen. *White Spirituals in the Southern Uplands.* Chapel Hill: University of North Carolina Press, 1933.

Kmen, Henry A. *Music in New Orleans: The Formative Years 1791–1841.* Baton Rouge: Louisiana State University Press, 1966.

Lang, Paul Henry. *One Hundred Years of Music in America.* New York: G. Schirmer, 1961.

Lengyel, Cornel. *A San Francisco Songster 1849–1939.* San Francisco: W.P.A. History of Music Project, 1939.

Mattfeld, Julius. *A Hundred Years of Grand Opera in New York.* New York: New York Public Library, 1927.

Morris, Berenice Robinson. *American Popular Music: The Growing Years, 1800–1900.* New York: F. Watts, 1972.

Mueller, John. *The American Symphony Orchestra.* Bloomington: Indiana University Press, 1951.

Niles, John J. "Shout, Coon, Shout!" *The Musical Quarterly,* 16 (1930), pp. 516–30.

Pearsall, Ronald. *Victorian Sheet Music Covers.* Detroit: Gale Research, 1972.

Revett, Marion S. *A Minstrel Town.* New York: Pageant Press, 1955.

Rich, Arthur. *Lowell Mason.* Chapel Hill: University of North Carolina Press, 1946.

Sablosky, Irving L. *American Music.* Chicago: University of Chicago Press, 1969.

Schwartz, H. W. *Bands of America.* Garden City, N.Y.: Doubleday, 1957.

Southern, Eileen. *The Music of Black Americans: A History.* New York: W. W. Norton, 1971.

Spaeth, Sigmund Gottfried. *A History of Popular Music in America.* New York: Random House, 1948.

Stevenson, Robert. *Protestant Church Music in America.* New York: W. W. Norton, 1966.

Stoutamire, Albert. *Music of the Old South: Colony to Confederacy.* Rutherford, N.J.: Fairleigh Dickinson University Press, 1972.

Swoboda, Henry. *The American Symphony Orchestra.* New York: Basic Books, 1967.

Upton, W. T. *Art-Song in America.* Boston: Oliver Ditson, 1930; Supplement, 1938.

CHAPTER II—AFRICAN MUSIC

Allen, William Francis, *et al. Slave Songs of the United States.* Westport, Conn.: Oak Publications, 1965.

CHAPTER II

Bebey, Francis. *African Music: A People's Art*. New York: Lawrence Hill, 1975.

Blacking, John. "Some Notes on a Theory of African Rhythm Advanced by Erich von Hornbostel," *Journal of the African Music Society*, 1 (1955), pp. 12–20.

Blassingame, John W. *Black New Orleans 1860–1880*. Chicago: University of Chicago Press, 1973.

——. *The Slave Community: Plantation Life in the Antebellum South*. New York: Oxford University Press, 1972.

Borneman, Ernest. "Black Light and White Shadow," *Jazzforschung*, 2 (1970), pp. 24–93.

Brandel, Rose. *The Music of Central Africa*. The Hague: Martinus Nijhoff, 1961.

Charters, Samuel B. *The Country Blues*. New York: Rinehart, 1959.

Chase, Gilbert. *America's Music, from the Pilgrims to the Present*. 2nd ed. New York: McGraw-Hill, 1966.

Courlander, Harold. *Negro Folk Music, U.S.A.* New York: Columbia University Press, 1963.

DeLerma, Dominique-René. *Reflections on Afro-American Music*. Kent, Ohio: Kent State University Press, 1973.

Epstein, Dena J. "African Music in British and French America," *The Musical Quarterly*, 59 (1973), pp. 61–91.

——. "Slave Music in the United States Before 1860: A Survey of Sources" *Notes*, 20 (1963), pp. 195–212, 377–90.

Herskovits, M. J. *The Myth of the Negro Past*. Boston: Beacon Press, 1958.

Howard, Joseph H. *Drums in the Americas*. New York: Oak, 1967.

Johnson, James Peter. *Bibliographic Guide to the Study of Afro-American Music*. Washington, D.C.: Howard University Libraries, 1973.

Jones, A. M. *Africa and Indonesia: The Evidence of the Xylophone and Other Cultural Factors*. Leiden: Brill, 1971.

——. *Studies in African Music*. London: Oxford University Press, 1959.

King, Anthony. *Yoruba Sacred Music from Ekiti*. Ibadan, Nigeria: Ibadan University Press, 1961.

Krehbiel, Henry Edward. *Afro-American Folksongs*. New York: Frederick Ungar, 1962.

List, George, and Juan Orrego Salas. *Music in the Americas*. Bloomington: Indiana University Research Center in Anthropology, Folklore, and Linguistics, 1967.

Locke, Alain LeRoy. *The Negro and His Music*. New York: Arno Press, 1969.

Lovell, John. *Black Song: The Forge and the Flame*. New York: Macmillan, 1972.

Lucas, John. "Rhythms of Negro Music and Negro Poetry." Unpublished thesis, University of Minnesota, 1945.

Mason, Bernard Sterling. *Drums, Tomtoms and Rattles: Primitive Percussion Instruments for Modern Use*. New York: Dover, 1974.

Music in the Americas. Bloomington: Indiana University Research Center in Anthropology, Folklore, and Linguistics, 1967.

Nathan, Hans. *Dan Emmett and the Rise of Early Negro Minstrelsy*. Norman: University of Oklahoma Press, 1962.

Nettl, Bruno. *Folk and Traditional Music of the Western Continents*. Englewood Cliffs, N.J.: Prentice-Hall, 1973.

——. *Music in Primitive Culture*. Cambridge: Harvard University Press, 1956.

Nikiprowetzky, Tolia. *Trois Aspects de la musique Africaine: Mauritanie, Senegal, Niger.* Paris: Office de Cooperation Radiophonique, 1967.

Nketia, J. H. Kwabena. *African Gods and Music.* Legon: University of Ghana, 1970.

———. *African Music in Ghana.* Evanston: Northwestern University Press, 1963.

———. *The Music of Africa.* New York: W. W. Norton, 1974.

Patterson, Lindsay. *The Negro in Music and Art.* New York: United Publishers Co., 1970.

Roberts, John Storm. *Black Music of Two Worlds.* New York: Praeger, 1972.

Rublowsky, John. *Black Music in America.* New York: Basic Books, 1971.

Southern, Eileen. *The Music of Black Americans: A History.* New York: W. W. Norton, 1971.

Standifer, James A., and Barbara Reeder. *Source Book of African and Afro-American Materials for Music Educators.* Washington, D.C.: Contemporary Music Project, 1972.

Tallmadge, William H. *Afro-American Music.* Rev. ed. Buffalo: State University College, 1969.

Tracey, Hugh, *et al. Codification of African Music and Textbook Project: A Primer of Practical Suggestions for Field Research.* Roodepoort, South Africa: International Library of African Music, 1969.

Trotter, James M. *Music and Some Highly Musical People.* Boston: Lee and Shepard, 1881; repr. New York: Johnson Reprint, 1968 (The Basic Afro-American Reprint Library).

Varley, Douglas H. *African Native Music, An Annotated Bibliography.* London: Dawsons of Pall Mall, 1970.

Wachsmann, Klaus P., ed. *Essays on Music and History in Africa.* Evanston: Northwestern University Press, 1971.

Walton, Ortiz M. *Music: Black, White and Blue.* New York: Morrow, 1972.

Warren, Fred, with Lee Warren. *The Music of Africa: An Introduction.* Englewood Cliffs, N.J.: Prentice-Hall, 1970.

Waterman, Richard A. " 'Hot' Rhythm in Negro Music," *Journal of the American Musicological Society,* 1 (1948), pp. 24–37.

———. "African Influence on the Music of the Americas," in *Acculturation in the Americas,* ed. Sol Tax. Chicago: University of Chicago Press, 1952.

Williams, Raymond. *The African Drum.* Highland Park, Mich.: Highland Park College Press, 1973.

Wittke, Carl. *Tambo and Bones.* Durham, N.C.: Duke University Press, 1930.

CHAPTER III—JAZZ BEFORE THE NAME "JAZZ" EMERGED

In addition to the writings of Borneman, Courlander, Goldman, Hitchcock, Lengyel, Locke, Lovell, Nathan, Revett, Roberts, Schwartz, Southern, Walton, Waterman, and Wittke, cited in the bibliographies for Chapters I and II, see:

Armstrong, Louis. *Satchmo: My Life in New Orleans.* New York: Prentice-Hall, 1954.

Bechet, Sidney. *Treat it Gentle: An Autobiography.* New York: Hill and Wang, 1960.

Blesh, Rudi. *Shining Trumpets: A History of Jazz.* 2nd ed., New York: Knopf, 1958.

Buerkle, Jack Vincent, and Danny Barker. *Bourbon Street Black: The New Orleans Black Jazzman*. New York: Oxford University Press, 1973.

Charters, Samuel, and Leonard Kunstadt. *Jazz: A History of the New York Scene*. Garden City, N.Y.: Doubleday, 1962.

Dauer, Alfons M. *Der Jazz: Seine Ursprünge und seine Entwicklung*. Kassel: E. Röth Verlag, 1958.

Foster, George Murphy. *Pops Foster: The Autobiography of a New Orleans Jazzman, as Told to Tom Stoddard*. Berkeley: University of California Press, 1971.

Goffin, Robert. *Jazz from the Congo to the Metropolitan*. Garden City, N.Y.: Doubleday, 1944.

———. *La Nouvelle-Orléans*. New York: Éditions de la Maison française, 1946.

Handy, William Christopher. *Father of the Blues: An Autobiography*. New York: Macmillan, 1955.

Jackson, Bruce. *Wake Up Dead Man: Afro-American Worksongs from Texas Prisons*. Cambridge: Harvard University Press, 1972.

Jones, Max, and John Chilton. *Louis: The Louis Armstrong Story 1900–1971*. Boston: Little, Brown, 1971.

Lomax, Alan. *Mister Jelly Roll: The Fortunes of Jelly Roll Morton, New Orleans Creole and "Inventor of Jazz."* New York: Grove Press, 1950.

Longstreet, Stephen. *Sportin' House: A History of the New Orleans Sinners and the Birth of Jazz*. Los Angeles: Sherbourne Press, 1965.

McComb, David G. *Houston: The Bayou City*. Austin: University of Texas, 1969.

Merriam, Alan P., and Fradley H. Garner. "Jazz—The Word," *Ethnomusicology*, 12 (1968) pp. 373–96.

Oliver, Paul. *Savannah Syncopators: African Retentions in the Blues*. New York: Stein and Day, 1970.

Olsson, Bengt. *Memphis Blues and Jug Bands*. London: Studio Vista, 1970.

Schafer, William J. "Thoughts on Jazz Historiography: 'Buddy Bolden's Blues' versus 'Buddy Bottley's Balloon,' " *Journal of Jazz Studies*, 2 (1974) pp. 3–14.

Schuller, Gunther. *Early Jazz: Its Roots and Musical Development*. New York: Oxford University Press, 1968.

Smith, Willie. *Music on My Mind: The Memoirs of an American Pianist*. Garden City, N.Y.: Doubleday, 1964.

Souchon, Edmond. "King Oliver: A Very Personal Memoir," in *Jazz Panorama*, ed. Martin Williams, pp. 21–30. New York: Collier, 1964.

Stearns, Marshall W. *The Story of Jazz*. New York: Oxford University Press, 1957.

Williams, Martin. *Jazz Masters of New Orleans*. New York: Macmillan, 1967.

———. *King Oliver*. New York: Barnes, 1961.

CHAPTER IV—RAGTIME

Blesh, Rudi, ed. *Classic Piano Rags*. New York: Dover, 1973.

Blesh, Rudi, and Harriet Janis. *They All Played Ragtime*. 4th ed. New York: Oak Publications, 1971.

CHAPTER BIBLIOGRAPHIES

Joplin, Scott. *The Collected Works of Scott Joplin*. Ed. Vera Brodsky Lawrence. 2 vols. New York: New York Public Library, 1971.

———. *Scott Joplin, King of Ragtime*. Comp. Albert Gamse. Carlstadt, N.J.: Lewis Music, 1972.

Lomax, Alan. *Mister Jelly Roll: The Fortunes of Jelly Roll Morton, New Orleans Creole and "Inventor of Jazz."* New York: Grove, 1956.

Morath, Max, comp. *100 Ragtime Classics*. Denver: Donn Print Co., 1963.

Schafer, William J., and Johannes Riedel. *The Art of Ragtime*. Baton Rouge: Louisiana State University Press, 1973.

Williams, Martin. *Jelly Roll Morton*. New York: Barnes, 1962.

CHAPTER V—THE BLUES

Many, if not most, of the entries for all the chapters listed, save the last, have information about the blues. Borneman, Locke, Schuller, and Stearns are particularly informative. These should be added:

Albertson, Chris. *Bessie*. New York: Stein and Day, 1972.

Bradford, Perry. *Born with the Blues: Perry Bradford's Own Story*. Westport, Conn.: Hyperion Press, 1973.

Broonzy, William "Big Bill." *Big Bill Blues: Big Bill Broonzy's Story as Told to Yannick Bruynoghe*. Rev. ed. New York: Oak, 1964.

Charters, Samuel Barclay. *The Bluesmen: The Story and the Music of the Men Who Made the Blues*. New York: Oak, 1967.

———. *The Country Blues*. New York: Rinehart, 1959.

———. *The Life, the Times, the Songs of Country Joe and the Fish*. New York: Ryerson Music, 1971.

———. *The Poetry of the Blues*. New York: Oak, 1965.

Cone, James H. *The Spirituals and the Blues: An Interpretation*. New York: Seabury Press, 1972.

Fahey, John. *Charley Patton*. London: Studio Vista, 1970.

Ferris, William, Jr. *Blues from the Delta*. London: Studio Vista, 1970.

Grossman, Stefan, *et al. Country Blues Songbook*. New York: Oak, 1973.

Handy, William Christopher, ed. *Blues: An Anthology*. New York: A. and C. Boni, 1926.

———. *Father of the Blues: An Autobiography*. New York: Macmillan, 1941.

Leadbitter, Mike. *Delta Country Blues*. Bexhill-on-Sea, Sussex, England: Blues Unlimited, 1968.

———. *Nothing But the Blues*. Westport, Conn.: Hyperion, 1973.

Lehmann, Theo. *Blues and Trouble*. Berlin: Henschelverlag, 1966.

Malone, Bill C. *Country Music U.S.A.: A Fifty-Year History*. Austin: University of Texas Press, 1968.

Mann, Woody. *Six Black Blues Guitarists*. New York: Oak, 1973.

Moore, Carman. *Somebody's Angel Child: The Story of Bessie Smith*. New York: Crowell, 1969.

Napier, Simon A. *Back Woods Blues*. Bexhill-on-Sea, Sussex, England: Blues Unlimited, 1968.

CHAPTER VII

Oliver, Paul. *Aspects of the Blues Tradition.* Westport, Conn.: Hyperion Press, 1973.

———. *Bessie Smith.* London: Cassell, 1959.

———. *Blues Fell This Morning: The Meaning of the Blues.* London: Cassell, 1960.

———. *Conversation with the Blues.* New York: Horizon, 1965.

———. *The Story of the Blues.* New York: Barrie, 1969.

Oster, Harry. *Living Country Blues.* Detroit: Folklore Assoc., 1969.

Russell, Tony. *Blacks, Whites and Blues: Negro and White Folk Traditions.* New York: Stein and Day, 1970.

Sackheim, Eric. *The Blues Line: A Collection of Blues Lyrics.* New York: Grossman, 1969.

Stewart-Baxter, Derrick. *Ma Rainey and the Classic Blues Singers.* New York: Stein and Day, 1970.

Waters, Ethel. *His Eye Is on the Sparrow: An Autobiography.* Garden City, N.Y.: Doubleday, 1951.

CHAPTER VI—THE EARLY YEARS OF JAZZ, 1900 TO 1917

See the bibliography for Chapter III.

CHAPTER VII—WORLD WAR I AND AFTER—THE TWENTIES

Many of the studies cited earlier provide copious information about this era. In particular, Austin, Blesh (*Shining Trumpets*), Hodeir, and Schuller are especially useful. To these should be added:

Allen, Walter C. *King Joe Oliver.* London: Sidgwick and Jackson, 1958.

Armstrong, Louis. *Louis Armstrong—A Self-Portrait: The Interview by Richard Maryman.* New York: Eakins Press, 1971.

———. *Swing That Music.* New York: Longmans, Green and Co., 1936.

Becker, Howard Saul. "The Professional Dance Musician in Chicago." Unpublished thesis, University of Chicago, 1949.

Berton, Ralph. *Remembering Bix: A Memoir of the Jazz Age.* New York: Harper and Row, 1974.

Brunn, Harry O. *The Story of the Original Dixieland Jazz Band.* Baton Rouge: Louisiana State University Press, 1960.

Chilton, John, and Max Jones. *Louis: The Louis Armstrong Story 1900–1971.* Boston: Little, Brown, 1971.

Condon, Eddie. *Condon's Treasury of Jazz.* New York: Dial Press, 1956.

———. *We Called It Music.* New York: H. Holt, 1947.

Engel, Carl. "Jazz: A Musical Discussion," in *Backgrounds of Book Reviewing*, ed. H. S. Mallory, pp. 343–51. Ann Arbor: G. Wahr, 1923.

Fountain, Pete. *A Closer Walk: The Pete Fountain Story.* Chicago: Regnery, 1972.

Gara, Larry. *The Baby Dodds Story.* Los Angeles: Contemporary, 1959.

Goffin, Robert. *Aux Frontières du jazz.* Paris: Éditions du Sagittaire, 1932.

———. *Horn of Plenty: The Story of Louis Armstrong.* New York: Allen, Towne and Heath, 1947.

Hadlock, Richard. *Jazz Masters of the Twenties.* New York: Macmillan, 1965.

Hennessey, Thomas Joseph. "From Jazz to Swing: Jazz Musicians and Their Music, 1917–1935." Unpublished dissertation, Northwestern University, 1973. University Microfilm No. 74-7757.

James, Burnett. *Bix Beiderbecke*. New York: Barnes, c. 1959.

Johnson, Grady. *The Five Pennies: The Biography of Jazz Band Leader Red Nichols*. New York: Dell, 1959.

Kaminsky, Max. *My Life in Jazz*. New York: Harper and Row, 1963.

Lambert, George Edmund. *Johnny Dodds*. New York: Barnes, c. 1961.

McCarthy, Albert. *Louis Armstrong*. New York: Barnes, 1959.

Manone, Wingy, and Paul Vandervoort II. *Trumpet on the Wing*. New York: Doubleday, 1948.

Mezzrow, Milton. *Really the Blues*. New York: Random House, 1946.

Osgood, Henry Osborne. *So This Is Jazz*. Boston: Little, Brown, 1926.

Panassié, Hugues. *Hot Jazz: The Guide to Swing Music*. New York: M. Witmark, 1936.

———. *Louis Armstrong*. New York: C. Scribner's Sons, 1971.

Pyke, Launcelot Allen. "Jazz, 1920–1927." Unpublished dissertation, University of Iowa, 1962. University Microfilm No. 62-4988.

Ramsey, Frederic. *Been Here and Gone*. New Brunswick: Rutgers University Press, 1960.

———. *Jazzmen*. New York: Harcourt, Brace, 1939.

Smith, Jay D., and Len Guttridge. *Jack Teagarden: The Story of a Jazz Maverick*. London: Cassell, 1960.

Sudhalter, Richard M. *Bix: Man and Legend*. New Rochelle, N.Y.: Arlington House, 1974.

Wareing, Charles H., and George Garlick. *Bugles for Beiderbecke*. London: Sidgwick and Jackson, 1958.

CHAPTER VIII—THE BIG-BAND CONCEPT: PRELUDE TO SWING
CHAPTER IX—THE SWING ERA

Carmichael, Hoagy. *The Stardust Road*. New York: Rinehart, 1946; repr. New York: Greenwood, 1969.

Connor, D. Russell, and Warren W. Hicks. *BG on the Record: A Bio-Discography of Benny Goodman*. New Rochelle, N.Y.: Arlington House, 1969.

Dance, Stanley. *The World of Duke Ellington*. New York: C. Scribner's Sons, 1970.

Driggs, Franklin S. "Kansas City and the Southwest," in *Jazz*, ed. Nat Henthoff and Albert J. McCarthy, pp. 189–230. New York: Rinehart, 1959.

Ellington, Edward Kennedy "Duke." *Music Is My Mistress*. Garden City, N.Y.: Doubleday, 1973.

Fernett, Gene. *Swing Out: Great Negro Dance Bands*. Midland, Mich.: Pendell, 1970.

———. *A Thousand Golden Horns: The Exciting Age of America's Greatest Dance Bands*. Midland, Mich.: Pendell, 1966.

Flower, John. *Moonlight Serenade: A Bio-Discography of the Glenn Miller Civilian Band*. New Rochelle, N.Y.: Arlington House, 1972.

Fox, Charles. *Fats Waller*. New York: Barnes, 1961.

Frankenstein, Alfred V. *Syncopating Saxophones*. Chicago: R. O. Ballon, 1925.

Gammond, Peter, ed. *Duke Ellington: His Life and Music*. New York: Roy Publishers, 1958.

Goodman, Benny. *The Kingdom of Swing*. New York: Stackpole Sons, 1939.

Horricks, Raymond. *Count Basie and His Orchestra, Its Music and Its Musicians*. New York: Citadel Press, 1957.

―――. *These Jazzmen of Our Time*. London: Gollancz, 1959.

Kirkeby, Ed. *Ain't Misbehavin': The Story of Fats Waller*. New York: Dodd, Mead, 1966.

Lambert, George Edmund. *Duke Ellington*. New York: Barnes, c. 1959.

McCarthy, Albert J. *Big Band Jazz*. New York: Putnam, 1974.

―――. *The Dance Band Era: The Dancing Decades from Ragtime to Swing; 1910–1950*. Philadelphia: Chilton Book Co., 1971.

Montgomery, Elizabeth Rider. *Duke Ellington: King of Jazz*. Champaign, Ill.: Garrard Publishing Co., 1972.

Panassié, Hugues. *Douze années de jazz (1927–1938). Souvenirs*. Paris: Corréa, 1946.

Rosenkrantz, Timme. *Swing Photo Album 1939*. London: Scorpion, 1964.

Russell, Ross. *Jazz Style in Kansas City and the Southwest*. Berkeley: University of California Press, 1971.

Rust, Brian. *The Dance Bands*. London: Ian Allan, 1972.

Sanford, Herb. *Tommy and Jimmy: The Dorsey Years*. New Rochelle, N.Y.: Arlington House, 1972.

Simon, George Thomas. *The Big Bands*. Rev. enl. ed. New York: Macmillan, 1971.

―――. *Simon Says: The Sights and Sounds of the Swing Era, 1935–1955*. New Rochelle, N.Y.: Arlington House, 1971.

Stewart, Rex William. *Jazz Masters of the Thirties*. New York: Macmillan Co., 1972.

Ulanov, Barry. *Duke Ellington*. New York: Creative Age, 1946.

Walker, Leo. *The Wonderful Era of the Great Dance Bands*. Berkeley: Howell-North, 1964.

Wells, Dicky, and Stanley Dance. *The Night People: Reminiscences of a Jazzman*. Boston: Crescendo Publishing Co., 1971.

CHAPTER X—THE JAZZ REVOLUTION—BEBOP

Dance, Stanley F., ed. *Jazz Era: The Forties*. London: Jazz Book Club, 1962.

Feather, Leonard. *Inside Be-Bop*. New York: J. J. Robbins, 1949.

―――. *Jazz: An Exciting Story of Jazz Today*. Los Angeles: Trend Books, 1958.

Gitler, Ira. *Jazz Masters of the Forties*. New York: Macmillan, 1966.

Goldberg, Joe. *Jazz Masters of the Fifties*. New York: Macmillan, 1965.

Green, Benny. *The Reluctant Art: Five Studies in the Growth of Jazz*. New York: DaCapo, 1976.

Harrison, Max. *Charlie Parker*. London: Cassell, 1960.

James, Michael. *Dizzy Gillespie*. New York: Barnes, c. 1959.

Leiter, Robert D. *The Musicians and Petrillo*. New York: Bookman Assoc., 1953.

McRae, Barry. *The Jazz Cataclysm*. South Brunswick, N.Y.: Barnes, 1967.

Merriam, Alan P., and Raymond W. Mack. "The Jazz Community," *Social Forces*, 38 (1960), pp. 211–22.

Morgan, Alun. *Modern Jazz: A Survey of Developments Since 1939*. London: Gollancz, 1957.

Owens, Thomas. "Charlie Parker: Techniques of Improvisation." Unpublished dissertation, University of California at Los Angeles, 1974. University Microfilm No. 75-1992.

Reisner, Robert George. *Bird: The Legend of Charlie Parker*. New York: Citadel Press, 1962.

——. *The Jazz Titans* [including "The Parlance of Hip"]. Garden City, N.Y.: Doubleday, 1960.

Russell, Ross. *Bird Lives: The High Life and Hard Times of Charlie Parker*. New York: Charterhouse, 1973.

Shaw, Arnold. *The Street That Never Slept*. New York: Coward, McCann, and Geoghegan, 1971.

Wilson, John Steuart. *Jazz: The Transition Years, 1940–1960*. New York: Appleton-Century-Crofts, 1966.

CHAPTER XI—THE FIFTIES—A PROLIFERATION OF STYLES
CHAPTER XII—LOOSE ENDS AND PERIPHERAL EVENTS
CHAPTER XIII—FREE JAZZ AND ITS PRICE

Bart, Teddy. *Inside Music City, U.S.A.* Nashville: Aurora, 1970.

Batten, Joe. *Joe Batten's Book: The Story of Sound Recording*. London: Rockliff, 1956.

Beltz, Carl. *The Story of Rock*. New York: Oxford University Press, 1969.

Broadcast Music, Inc. *Five Decades of Rhythm and Blues*. New York: Broadcast Music Inc., 1969.

Byrnside, Ronald. "The Formation of a Musical Style: Early Rock," in Charles Hamm, Bruno Nettl, and Ronald Byrnside, *Contemporary Music and Music Cultures*, pp. 159–92. Englewood Cliffs, N.J.: Prentice-Hall, 1975.

Cane, Giampiero. *Canto nero. Il free jazz degli anni Sessanta*. Rimini: Guaraldi, 1973.

Chew, V. K. *Talking Machines, 1877–1914: Some Aspects of the Early History of the Gramophone*. London: Her Majesty's Stationery Office, 1967.

Cohn, Nik. *Rock from the Beginning*. New York: Stein and Day, 1969.

Cole, Bill. *John Coltrane*. New York: Schirmer, 1976.

Dalton, David. *Janis*. New York: Simon & Schuster, 1971.

——, ed. *Rolling Stones*. New York: Amsco, 1972.

Daufouy, Philippe, and Jean-Pierre Sarton. *Pop Music/Rock*. Paris: Éditions Champ Libre, 1972.

Eisen, Jonathan, comp. *The Age of Rock, Sounds of the American Cultural Revolution; A Reader*. New York: Random House, c. 1969.

Gabree, John. *The World of Rock*. Greenwich, Conn.: Fawcett, 1968.

Garland, Phyl. *The Sound of Soul*. Chicago: Regnery, 1969.

Gelatt, Roland. *The Fabulous Phonograph: From Edison to Stereo*. Rev. ed. New York: Appleton-Century-Crofts, 1965.

Gillett, Charlie. *The Sound of the City: The Rise of Rock 'n' Roll.* New York: Dell, 1972.

Goldberg, Isaac. *Tin Pan Alley: A Chronicle of the American Popular Music Racket.* New York: John Day, 1930.

Guralnick, Peter. *Feel Like Going Home: Portraits in Blues & Rock 'n' Roll.* New York: Outerbridge & Dienstfrey, 1971.

Hamm, Charles. "Changing Patterns in Society and Music: The U.S. Since World War II," in Charles Hamm, Bruno Nettl, and Ronald Byrnside, *Contemporary Music and Music Cultures,* pp. 35–70. Englewood Cliffs, N.J. Prentice-Hall, 1975.

Hirsch, Paul. *The Structure of the Popular Music Industry.* Ann Arbor: Institute for Social Research, University of Michigan, 1969.

Jost, Ekkehard. *Free Jazz.* Graz: Universal Edition, 1974.

Keil, Charles. *Urban Blues.* Chicago: University of Chicago Press, 1966.

Larkin, Philip. *All What Jazz: A Record Diary 1961–68.* New York: St. Martin's Press, 1970.

Lydon, Michael. *Rock Folk: Portraits from the Rock 'n' Roll Pantheon.* New York: Dial Press, 1971.

McCable, Peter, and Robert D. Schonfeld. *Apple to the Core: The Unmaking of the Beatles.* New York: Pocket Books, 1972.

McGregor, Craig, comp. *Bob Dylan.* New York: Morrow, 1972.

Marcus, Greil, comp. *Rock and Roll Will Stand.* Boston: Beacon Press, 1969.

Mellers, Wilfrid Howard. *The Twilight of the Gods: The Beatles in Retrospect.* London: Faber, 1974.

Meyer, Leonard B. *Music, the Arts, and Ideas.* Chicago: University of Chicago Press, 1967.

Millar, Bill. *The Drifters: The Rise and Fall of the Black Vocal Group.* New York: Macmillan, 1972.

Morse, David. *Motown and the Arrival of Black Music.* London: Studio Vista, 1971.

Orloff, Katherine. *Rock 'n' Roll Woman.* Los Angeles: Nash, 1974.

Price, Steven. *Old as the Hills: The Story of Bluegrass Music.* New York: Viking, 1975.

Read, Oliver, and Walter L. Welch. *From Tin Foil to Stereo.* 2nd ed. Indianapolis: Sams, 1975.

Redd, Lawrence N. *Rock Is Rhythm and Blues (The Impact of the Mass Media).* East Lansing: Michigan State University Press, 1974.

Rivelli, Pauline, comp. *The Rock Giants.* New York: World Publishing Co., 1970.

Scaduto, Anthony. *Bob Dylan.* New York: Grosset & Dunlap, 1972.

Shaw, Arnold. *The Rock Revolution.* New York: Crowell-Collier, c. 1969.

Somma, Robert, ed. *No One Waved Good-Bye: A Casualty Report on Rock and Roll.* New York: Outerbridge & Dienstfrey, 1971.

Spellman, A. B. *Black Music: Four Lives in the Bebop Business.* New York: Schocken Books, 1970.

Stambler, Irwin, and Grelun Landon. *Golden Guitars: The Story of Country Music.* New York: Four Winds Press, 1971.

Sumner, John Daniel. *Gospel Music Is My Life.* Nashville: Impact Books, 1971.

Thomas, J. C. *Chasin' the Trane: The Music and Mystique of John Coltrane.* New York: Doubleday, 1975.

Walley, David. *No Commercial Potential: The Saga of Frank Zappa and the Mothers of Invention.* New York: Outerbridge & Lazard, 1972.

Williams, Martin T. *Jazz Masters in Transition, 1957–69.* New York: Macmillan, 1970.

Wise, Herbert H., ed. *Professional Rock and Roll.* New York: Collier Books, 1967.

SELECTED
DISCOGRAPHY

The following list was compiled as an aid to the jazz novice wishing to invest in a few treasures in order to bring the subject matter of this book to life. The veteran jazzophile may ignore these pages, for he or she will already own a collection of recordings and will have heard far more performances than these few sides can carry. Members of the jazz community who are interested in expanding their present collections will find useful information in the extensive discographies by other authors listed in the bibliography (see p. 410).

The newcomer, however, needs to start somewhere, and I recommend the following titles as a minimal sampling of major artists and significant performances. These recommendations follow, insofar as possible, the chapter discussions of the book, and every item was selected with current availability in mind. The total number of albums—one hundred—was quite arbitrary, and even though it can hardly do the subject justice, it represents, at today's prices, quite a sizable investment. Note well that some albums contain more than one record.

100 Record Albums which Illustrate the History of Jazz

I. BEFORE WORLD WAR I

No jazz, and precious little else, was recorded in this period, but modern recordings of early traditions are better than nothing in piecing together a picture of music in America at the turn of the century.

1. *Nineteenth Century American Ballroom Music*   (Nonesuch 71313)
2. *Songs by Stephen Foster*   (Nonesuch 71268)
3. *Marches of John Philip Sousa*   (Philips 9500151)

4. *Anthology of Music of Black Africa* (Everest 3254/3)
5. *Roots of the Blues* (Atlantic 1348)
6. *Best of Scott Joplin and Others* (Vanguard VSD-39/40)
7. *Country Brass Bands* (Folkways FA 2650)
8. *Jazz I: The South* (Folkways FP 53)

II. AN ANTHOLOGY FROM WORLD WAR I TO THE PRESENT

9. The Smithsonian Collection of Classic Jazz [Keyed to this book] (Available only through two sources: The Smithsonian Associates, Washington, D.C. 20560; and W. W. Norton & Company, Inc., 500 Fifth Avenue, New York, N.Y. 10036—6 records, $27.50.)

III. FROM WORLD WAR I TO WORLD WAR II

10. *Jazz III: New Orleans* (Folkways FP 57)
11. *The Louis Armstrong Story*, Vol. 1 (Columbia CL-851)
12. *A Rare Batch of Satch* (RCA LPM-2322)
13. *Blue Bechet* (RCA LPV-535)
14. *King of New Orleans Jazz* [Morton] (RCA LPM-1649)
15. *The Empress* [Bessie Smith] (Columbia G-31093)
16. *Jazz II: The Blues* (Folkways FP 55)
17. *The Bix Beiderbecke Story*, Vol. 2 (Columbia CL-845)
18. *Fletcher Henderson*, Vol. 2 (Decca 79228)
19. *Father of the Stride Piano* [J. P. Johnson] (Columbia CL-1780)
20. *Quintessential Recording Session* [Hines] (Chiaroscuro 101)
21. *Valentine Stomp* [Waller] (RCA LPV-525)
22. *The Original Sound of "The Twenties"* (Columbia C3L 35)
23. *Jazz VIII: Big Bands (1924–1934)* (Folkways FP 69)
24. *The Big Bands/1933* (Prestige 7645)
25. *Duke Ellington at His Very Best* (RCA PLV-1715)
26. *This Is Duke Ellington* (RCA VPM-6042)
27. *The Best of Count Basie* (Decca DXS-7170)
28. *Benny Goodman Carnegie Hall Concert* (Columbia OSL-160)
29. *Jimmie Lunceford—Harlem Shout* (Decca 79238)
30. *Body and Soul* [Hawkins] (RCA LPV-501)
31. *Young Lester Young* (Columbia J-24)
32. *Giants of the Tenor Saxophone* (Columbia KG-32774)
33. *Things Ain't What They Used To Be* [Hodges] (RCA LPV-533)
34. *Solo Flight* [Charlie Christian] (Columbia G-30779)
35. *Piano Starts Here* [Art Tatum] (Columbia CS-9655)
36. *Jazz X: Boogie Woogie—Jump—Kansas City* (Folkways FP 73)
37. *Lady Day* [Billie Holiday] (Columbia CL-637)
38. *Strange Fruit* [Holiday] (Atlantic 1614)
39. *Jazz IV: Jazz Singers* (Folkways FP 59)

IV. FROM WORLD WAR II TO 1960

40. *In the Beginning* [Gillespie and Parker]	(Prestige 24030)
41. *Strictly Bebop* [Dameron and Gillespie]	(Capitol M-11059)
42. *Our Man in Paris* [Dexter Gordon]	(Blue Note 84146)
43. *Nostalgia* [Fats Navarro]	(Savoy 12133)
44. *The Amazing Bud Powell*, Vol. 1	(Blue Note 81503)
45. *The Charlie Parker Story*	(Savoy 12079)
46. *Echoes of an Era* [Parker and Gillespie]	(Roulette RE-105)
47. *Bird and Diz*	(Verve 68006)
48. *April in Paris* [Parker]	(Verve 68004)
49. *Early Autumn* [Woody Herman]	(Capitol M-11034)
50. *Stan Kenton Hits in Concert*	(Creative World 1074)
51. *Greatest Jazz Concert Ever*	(Prestige 24024)
52. *Sarah Vaughan*	(Archive of Folk and Jazz 250)
53. *Ella Fitzgerald Sings Gershwin*	(Decca 74451)
54. *Crosscurrents* [Tristano and Konitz]	(Capitol M-11060)
55. *Complete Birth of the Cool*	(Capitol M-11026)
56. *The Genius of Gerry Mulligan*	(Pacific Jazz PJ-8)
57. *Stan Getz—History*	(Verve 6S-8815)
58. *Best of Max Roach and Clifford Brown*	(GNP Crescendo 18)
59. *Saxophone Colossus* [Rollins]	(Prestige 7326)
60. *Blue Train* [Coltrane]	(Blue Note 81577)
61. *Giant Steps* [Coltrane]	(Atlantic 1311)
62. *Walkin'* [Miles Davis]	(Prestige 7608)
63. *Round About Midnight* [Davis]	(Columbia CS-8649)
64. *Plenty, Plenty Soul* [Jackson and Silver]	(Atlantic 1269)
65. *Modern Jazz Quartet*	(Prestige 24005)
66. *Time Out* [Brubeck and Desmond]	(Columbia CS-8192)
67. *Thelonious Monk and John Coltrane*	(Milestone 47011)
68. *Horace Silver and the Jazz Messengers*	(Blue Note 81518)
69. *Ezz-thetic* [Konitz and Davis]	(Prestige 7827)
70. *Outstanding Jazz Compositions of the 20th Century*	(Columbia C2S 831)
71. *Kind of Blue* [Davis and Coltrane]	(Columbia CS-8163)
72. *Porgy and Bess* [Davis]	(Columbia CS-8085)

V. FROM 1960 TO THE PRESENT

73. *Shape of Jazz to Come* [Ornette Coleman]	(Atlantic 1317)
74. *Free Jazz* [Coleman and Dolphy]	(Atlantic 1364)
75. *A Love Supreme* [Coltrane]	(Impulse 77)
76. *Ascension* [Coltrane]	(Impulse 95)
77. *Filles de Kilimanjaro* [Davis]	(Columbia CS-9750)
78. *In a Silent Way* [Davis]	(Columbia CS-9875)

79. *Into the Hot* [Cecil Taylor]   (Impulse 9)
80. *Fire Music* [Archie Shepp]   (Impulse 86)
81. *New York, N.Y.* [George Russell]   (MCA 4017)
82. *Better Get It in Your Soul* [Mingus]   (Columbia G-30628)
83. *Village Vanguard Sessions* [Bill Evans]   (Milestone 47002)
84. *Jazz Composers Orchestra*   (JCOA 1001/2)
85. *Electric Bath* [Don Ellis]   (Columbia CS-9585)
86. *M. F. Horn* [Maynard Ferguson]   (Columbia C-30466)
87. *I Sing the Body Electric* [Weather Report]   (Columbia KC-31352)
88. *Inner Mounting Flame* [Mahavishnu Orchestra]   (Columbia KC-31067)
89. *Phase One* [Art Ensemble of Chicago]   (Prestige 10064)
90. *Light as a Feather* [Chick Corea]   (Polydor 5525)
91. *Bitches Brew* [Davis]   (Columbia GP-26)
92. *Sahara* [McCoy Tyner]   (Milestone 9039)
93. *Living Time* [Bill Evans & George Russell]   (Columbia KC-31490)
94. *On the Corner* [Davis]   (Columbia PC-31906)
95. *Goodbye* [Gene Ammons]   (Prestige 10093)
96. *Now Please Don't You Cry, Beautiful Edith*
    [Roland Kirk]   (Verve 68709)
97. *Tom Cat* [Tom Scott]   (Ode 77021)
98. *Thembi* [Pharoah Sanders]   (Impulse AS-9206)
99. *Chuck Mangione and Friends*   (Mercury 800)
100. *Manhattan Wildlife Refuge* [Bill Watrous]   (Columbia KC-33090)

GLOSSARY

back line: the rhythm section in a jazz ensemble, usually consisting of drums, bass (string or brass), and a chordal instrument such as piano, banjo, or guitar.

bebop (bop, rebop): a style which evolved in the early 1940s characterized by asymmetrical phrases, ornate melodic lines with much solo improvisation, complex rhythmic patterns, and more novel and dissonant harmonies than those used in the swing style of the preceding decade.

blue notes: the lowered third, fifth, and seventh degrees of the major scale, which, in blues and jazz performances, vary in intonation and fall somewhere between the normal major and minor tempered scale intervals.

blues: a type of vocal or instrumental music, usually patterned in 12-measure stanzas of three 4-measure phrases over simple tonic, dominant, and subdominant harmonies, incorporating flexible rhythmic patterns over a steady 4/4 pulse, and, in its vocal form, lyrics dealing with social protest or sexual themes.

boogie-woogie: a piano blues style of the 1920s and '30s characterized by a left-hand ostinato figure underlying a rhythmically freer right hand.

bop: *see* bebop.

bottleneck guitar: when an ordinary guitar is retuned so that the open strings sound a chord (e.g., E–G–C–G–C–E) instead of the regular tuning in fourths plus a third (E–A–D–G–B–E), then it may be played for simple blues accompaniment by stopping all the strings at the same fret position with a straight edge, rather than by using complex fingering. A closed pocket knife, clasped between two fingers, is often used to play the instrument in this manner, but a bottleneck, broken off an ordinary soda bottle and worn over the middle finger of the left hand, will also work. Hence, the term "bottleneck guitar" was applied to this combination of tuning and method of performance.

break: a short instrumental bridge between phrases in a vocal line, probably deriving from African call-and-response performance patterns.

cakewalk: a dance characterized by syncopated rhythms, popular in American minstrel shows.

chorus: in jazz performance, the refrain of a popular song (or its harmonic outline), usually repeated over and over by different members of the ensemble.

classic blues (city blues): a type of blues usually performed by female singers accompanied by jazz band or piano, with lyrics relating to sexual or social and racial problems.

classic jazz: the music that originated in the southern part of the United States in the late nineteenth century, which came to be characterized by: 1) group and solo improvisation; 2) rhythm sections in ensembles; 3) steady, underlying pulse to which syncopated melodies and rhythmic patterns are added; 4) reliance on popular-song form and blues form; 5) tonal harmonic organization often using blue notes; 6) vocal and instrumental timbral features such as vibratos, glissandi, etc.; 7) a performer or performer-composer aesthetic rather than a composer-centered orientation.

classic ragtime: the ragtime school represented chiefly by Scott Joplin, James Scott, and Joseph Lamb.

comp: to accompany.

concert pitch: for a transposing instrument, the pitch sounded, rather than the pitch notated. Thus for a B♭ clarinet, for example, written C is concert B♭.

cool jazz: an early 1950s development of the bebop style, combining the technical virtuosity of bebop with a new timbral quality—usually heard in the sax—using few overtones and little or no vibrato.

coon song: a type of song, popular in the 1880s, in syncopated ragtime style, often with lyrics that reflected the white American stereotypes of black Americans.

country blues (rural blues, Southern blues): a type of blues usually performed by a male singer accompanying himself with a simple instrument such as banjo or guitar, and dealing with topics affecting the lives of country blacks, often with implicit sexual references.

Dixieland jazz (New Orleans–style jazz): a style developed in the early 1900s, characterized by group improvisation over a steady two-beat ragtime rhythm. The rhythm section usually consisted of piano (or banjo or guitar), bass (often trombone, which occasionally played melodic figures as well), and trap drums; the melodic instruments were generally clarinet, adding a fast, high-pitched obbligato, and trumpet or cornet, playing the melody in syncopated ragtime style.

East Coast hard-bop school: a 1950s style formed as a reaction to cool and West Coast jazz, incorporating full-voiced instrumental sound, loud dynamics, and emotional, energetic performances.

ensemble "out": the last full chorus in a jazz piece, usually played by the entire ensemble.

free jazz: performances that negate stylistic rules which were formerly valid, by attempting to destroy feelings of structure, direction, and tonality while introducing random improvisation and nontraditional instruments such as sitars, amplified thumb pianos, police whistles, etc.

front line: the melodic instruments of a traditional jazz ensemble, usually consisting of clarinet, cornet, and trombone.

funky: a term used to describe the rhythmic style of East Coast hard-bop jazz, with strong accentuations and a bouncing rhythmic style.

head arrangement: a piece of music which is not written down but is worked out in rehearsals and duplicated as exactly as possible in subsequent performances.

high hat (sock cymbal): a pedal-operated pair of cymbals in which the bottom part is stationary and the top part is moved up and down by the pedal.

jig: an early Midwestern term for ragtime, as in jig band, jig piano.

lick: a riff, a musical idea, a break.

Mickey ending: a term that jazz musicians use to refer disparagingly to a rhythmic cliché often used by commercial bands, such as Guy Lombardo and His Royal Canadians, to signal the end of a dance number. The rhythm is identical to that used in Mickey Mouse cartoon music; hence the term.

minstrel show: a type of American entertainment popular in the nineteenth century, in which whites dressed as blacks and performed songs in black-American dialect, written mostly by white composers.

New Orleans–style jazz: *see* Dixieland jazz.

patting juba: clapping hands, stamping feet, and slapping thighs in syncopated, polyrhythmic patterns, a practice performed by American slaves to produce dance accompaniment.

progressive jazz: a mid-1940s development of the big-band style using expanded orchestration, nontraditional harmonic changes, and frequent changes of tempo, which implied concert rather than dance music.

ragtime: a style popular in the first two decades of the twentieth century characterized by a nonsyncopated bass in duple meter underlying a syncopated treble melody; functional, diatonic harmonies stressing tonic, dominant, subdominant, and applied dominants in major keys; and compounded song-form structures with 16- or 32-measure periods and shorter introductions, vamps, and codas.

rebop: *see* bebop.

ride: to concentrate on playing with virtuosity; to improvise.

ride cymbal: a single cymbal, usually mounted on the rim of the bass drum and hit with a stick.

riff: a repeated musical phrase, usually short, used as a background for a soloist or as a theme for a final chorus. Also, an instrumental blues melody.

rip: upward glissando.

rural blues: *see* country blues.

scat singing: an instrumental solo performed by the voice to vocables, or nonsense syllables.

sideman: a member of a jazz band or swing orchestra.

skiffle band: a novelty orchestra that depends largely on showmanship, slapstick, and extramusical effects for audience appeal.

sock cymbal: *see* high hat.

song form: a design consisting of a section (usually eight measures long) which is repeated and then returns after a contrasting section (usually the same length as the initial section): **AABA.**

Southern blues: *see* country blues.

stomp: the process of repeating a rhythmic figure in the melodic line in a riff pattern, leading to polyphonic accentuation that produces a strong rhythmic momentum within the improvising polyphony.

stoptime: the process of playing a regular, but discontinuous, rhythm, most often a staccato chord played on the first beat of every measure or every other measure. It is usually employed as a background effect for an instrumental solo, and derives from a common accompaniment pattern used to support tap dancing.

stride: a piano style characterized by using the left hand in a downbeat-upbeat pattern (oom-pah, oom-pah rhythm), in which beats one and three (in 4/4) are heavily accented single notes, octaves, or tenths, and beats two and four are unaccented triads.

swing: a style popular from around 1930 to 1945, characterized by arrangements for large ensembles (big bands), with written passages that separate the ensembles by sections in antiphonal writing and solo improvisations at designated points in the score, a lightened rhythm section led by the string bass keeping a regular accentuation on the beat, melodic patterns based on scales and arpeggios, and a generally refined dance-band sound.

tailgate trombone: a New Orleans style of trombone playing, so called from the customary location of the trombonist on a horse-drawn parade cart. Because of the freedom of movement necessary to operate a trombone slide, the open tailgate was the preferred seat of most trombonists.

third-stream music: a term coined by Gunther Schuller to denote the merger of jazz and classical styles.

trap drums: the entire set of drums, including bass drum, snare drum, cowbell, woodblock, etc.

up-tempo: fast.

urban blues: a blues style in which the vocalist is accompanied by a swing-style band—and later, with electric guitar and amplified sax—and sings of love, sex, and society's impact on and meaning for black Americans.

vamp: a short connecting passage, usually four or eight measures long, joining two sections of music which lie at different harmonic levels by modulating. Sometimes no modulation occurs and a simple chord pattern is repeated as a "filler" between sections.

West-Coast jazz: a 1950s style characterized by performance in middle-sized or smaller ensembles using single instruments rather than groups (e.g., one trumpet rather than a trumpet section) playing in a style virtually indistinguishable from cool jazz.

woodshed: to practice or rehearse in private in order to gain technical mastery of one's instrument before going into a jam session.

COPYRIGHT ACKNOWLEDGMENTS

COPYRIGHT ACKNOWLEDGMENTS

INDEX

Boldface numerals (**123**) indicate significant biographical information or musical examples. Italic numerals (*123*) signify photographic illustrations. An "n" is appended to the number of a page on which the reference appears only in the footnotes.

INDEX

INDEX

INDEX

INDEX

Index prepared by J. Samuel Hammond, Music Librarian, Duke University